KB039408

KOREAN YEARBOOK OF INTERNATIONAL LAW

KOREAN YEARBOOK OF INTERNATIONAL LAW

Edited by CHOI Seung-Hwan

Volume 6
2018

PARKYOUNGSA

THE KOREAN BRANCH OF THE INTERNATIONAL LAW ASSOCIATION

KOREAN YEARBOOK OF
INTERNATIONAL LAW

Published by PARKYOUNGSA

PARKYOUNG Publishing&Company
36, Saemunan-ro 3-gil, Jongno-gu, Seoul, 03173, Korea
Tel 82-2-733-6771
Fax 82-2-736-4818

First published 2019
Printed in Seoul, Korea
ISSN 2635-8484 86

For subscriptions to this Yearbook, please contact the sole distributor, PARKYOUNG Publishing&Company
36, Saemunan-ro 3-gil, Jongno-gu, Seoul, 03173, Korea
Tel 82-2-733-6771 Fax 82-2-736-4818 E-mail: pys@pybook.co.kr

THE KOREAN BRANCH OF THE INTERNATIONAL LAW ASSOCIATION

PRESIDENT

SUNG Jae-Ho

HONORARY PRESIDENT

LIMB Thok-Kyu

VICE-PRESIDENTS

LEE Chang-Wee

LEE Keun-Gwan

LEE Hwan-Gyu

YANG Hee-Cheol

SECRETARY-GENERAL & TREASURER

LEE Kil-Won

MEMBERS OF EXECUTIVE COUNCIL

SUPPORTING MEMBERS

Northeast Asian History Foundation

Korea Maritime Institute

Korea Institute of Ocean Science & Technology

SHIN & KIM

Law Firm J & C

YOON & YANG LLC

KH Research Center for International Security and Trade

SKKU BK21+ Research Group
on Educational Reform for Cultivating Law Professional
in ICT Global Legal Standards

All correspondences concerning the Yearbook should be sent to:
Secretary-General, Korean Branch, ILA
#422, Jamsil REZION Officetel, 87, Ogeum-ro, Songpa-gu, Seoul, Korea
E-mail: ilakoreanbranch@gmail.com / Homepage: http://www.ilakorea.or.kr

EDITORIAL ADVISORY BOARD

CONTENTS

EDITOR-IN-CHIEF'S ACKNOWLEDGEMENT

The year 2019 is a meaningful year in the sense that this year is the 100th anniversary since the establishment of the Korean Provisionary Government, and the 74th anniversary since the independence of the Korean peninsula from the Japanese occupation of Korea. Commemorating the 100th anniversary of the Independence Movement on May 1st 1919, MOON Jae-In, the president of the Republic of Korea(ROK), characterized the new order for the coming 100 years, as the New Korean Peninsula Regime, and officially committed to promote the Peace-Cooperation Community and the Economy-Cooperation Community together with North Korea.

With a view to establishing sustainable peace and prosperity in the Korean peninsula, it is very important for political leaders to make a definite decision to settle peacefully international disputes and problems that have occurred in East Asia in accordance with international law and justice. Judging from current international circumstances surrounding the Korean peninsula, there is, unfortunately, an increasing tendency of prioritizing the expansion of national interests by the use or threat or the use of power and economic coercion, rather than pursuing dispute settlement under international law and mutual cooperation.

For the successful launching of the Peace and Prosperity Community in East Asia, it is indispensable for the East Asian countries to restore and maintain political credibility, especially among Japan, the ROK, and China. However, the recent increase of tension caused by the development of nuclear weapons by North

Korea, together with territorial disputes, and the energy and security crisis prevalent in North-East Asia, have cast a cloud over the prospect of the development of the Peace and Prosperity Community in East Asia. It should be noted that France and Germany established the EEC and developed the EU, the peace and prosperity community, with the help of other European countries, by establishing reconciliation and credibility, despite the deep-rooted antagonistic relationship that had accumulated through the two World Wars. Is it impossible for East Asian countries to build this kind of peace and prosperity community in East Asia?

With a view to establishing sustainable peace and prosperity in East Asia filled with deep-rooted historical discord, wise and definite decisions are called upon to utilize various pending issues and problems as a catalyzer for reconciliation and cooperation, not for discord and antagonism. If we do not first empty the dish full of discord and antagonism, reconciliation and cooperation cannot be poured into it. If we do not unfold our hands that are filled with distrust and hegemony, we will not be able to catch peace and prosperity.

In this context, the role of experts on international law is much more significant than ever before for the maintenance of sustainable peace and prosperity in East Asia. I hope that the articles and essays having been contributed to KYIL contribute to the development of sustainable peace and prosperity in East Asia by providing effective and useful solutions based on rule of law and oriental wisdom.

I would like to express my sincere gratitude to all the authors who contributed valuable articles and special reports including useful remarks and documents regarding recent developments and the ROK's practices on the interpretation and application of international law, as well as my colleagues on the editorial board, especially Professor LEE Seryon, the Executive Editor, for her dedicated work on editing Volume 6, KYIL. I also appreciate Professor LEE Jang-

Hie, the former Editor-in-Chief who contributed his sincere efforts to the compilation of five volumes of KYIL (from V. 1 to V. 5). Finally, I would like to thank staff editors and Dr. SEO Jin-Woong, the Secretary of the Korean Branch, ILA, for their heartful assistance in publishing this volume.

CHOI Seung-Hwan
KYIL Editor-in-Chief

He, the former Editor-in-chief, who conducted his [illegible] efforts to the [illegible] of [illegible] KTH [illegible]. Finally, I would like to thank staff [illegible] and the Secretary of the [illegible] for their [illegible] assistance in preparing this volume.

[illegible]

EDITORIAL NOTE

Volume 6 of the *Korean Yearbook of International Law* features 4 main articles, which are complemented by special reports covering a variety of issues and updates on recent development and Korean court cases relevant to international law.

First, Professor Seung-Hwan Choi of Kyung Hee University explores legal issues related to China's economic retaliatory measures against the decision by the Korean government in 2016 to deploy the Terminal High Altitude Area Defense ("THAAD") anti-missile system. He examines illegitimacy of China's economic retaliation under general international law and suggests the feasible ways to ease the tensions between Korea and China by proposing policy-oriented solutions to maintain friendly relations between the two countries.

Second, Professor Jae-Ho Sung of Sungkyunkwan University analyzes some key cases of the International Court of Justice, which dealt with questions of sovereignty over islands. He, then, outlines the implications of the ICJ cases to the issues relevant to the claims of sovereignty over Dokdo by Korea and Japan. Based on various historical sources, Prof. Sung examines how Dokdo had been recognized by Korea and Japan respectively as to its name and location. He further explores the claim of effective control over Dokdo by particularly looking at the measures taken after World War II.

Third, Dr. See-Hwan Doh of Northeast Asian History Foundation examines the so-called comfort women issues in the context of international human rights law. He first traces the postwar-related lawsuits filed by the Korean victims in Japanese courts and introduces the lawsuit filed in Korean court against the Japanese government by a group of victims and surviving family members of wartime sexual slavery in December 2016. Dr. Doh proposes a victim-centered and international human rights-oriented approach to solve the comfort women issue.

Fourth, Professor Gyoo-Ho Lee of Chung-Ang University outlines the international investment agreements signed by Korea and provides a comprehensive overview of Korea's Foreign Investment Promotion Act. Prof. Lee explores the recent investor-state disputes (ISD) involving Korea both as the respondent state and the home state of investor. He advises that the drastic policy change can be subject to the potential ISD and proposes to adopt the precautionary mechanism to warn the risk of potential investor disputes.

The main articles are followed by special contribution by Professor Carlos Esplugues at the University of Valencia in Spain. Prof.Esplugues discusses the possibility of establishing the mechanism to control foreign direct investment on national security grounds and presents the Korean practice with relevant laws and policies.

In the Special Reports section, we have 5 contributions as follows: Emeritus Professor Jang-Hie Lee of Hankuk University of Foreign Studies brings our attention to Japan's review of its high school history textbooks, which included its claim of sovereignty over Dokdo. Prof. Lee rebuts Japan's claim by offering thorough review of historical references and international law to support Korea's position; Emeritus Professor Seok-Yong Lee of Hannam University explores the history of the regime of Island under international law of the sea with a particular focus on the South China Sea arbitration; Visiting Professor Whie-Jin Lee of the University of Seoul examines the interpretation of human rights treaties in Korean courts with a particular focus on the issue of conscientious objection to military service; Judge Young-Seok Kim of Seoul Bankruptcy Court fully outlines the details of the Guidelines for Communication and Cooperation between Courts in Cross-Border Insolvency adopted in 2016 and the subsequent practice of the guideline in Korean court; Dr. Min-Jung Chung of National Assembly Research Service discusses the Korean National Assembly's role with respect to the agreements signed between South and North Korea over the years.

In the Recent Development section, Professor Sun-Young Oh at Soongsil University gives a full chronology of the deployment of THAAD in Korea and Dr. Sung-Jin Kang at Kim & Chang updates the recent WTO disputes involving Korea.

In the Contemporary Practice and Judicial Decisions section, Professor Keun-Gwan Lee of Seoul National University introduces major Korean court's decisions related to public international law, including the Supreme Court's decision in October 2018 on wartime forced labor. Judge Ji-Yong Jang highlights some key court cases related to private international law including the Supreme Court's decision on clause paramount in March 2018. As part of legislative practice, Dr. Min-Jung Chung of National Assembly Research Service presents international law-related resolutions adopted by the National Assembly of Korea during the third quarter of the 20th session.

We sincerely acknowledge the valuable insights provided by all the authors for Vol. 6 of the *Korean Yearbook of International Law* and hope that this Volume can be a vital digest to understand the Korean practice in international law.

LEE Seryon
KYIL, Executive Editor

ARTICLES

Revisiting the Regime of Maritime Features in International Law of the Sea and Its Implications for Korea

LEE Seok-Yong
Professor Emeritus, Hannam University, Daejeon, Korea

Abstract

Article 121 of the UNCLOS Convention has three paragraphs regarding the regime of islands. Paragraph 1 of the Article, following the traditional position codified in 1958 Territorial Sea Convention, defines an island as a naturally formed area of land, surrounded by water, which is above water at high tide. Paragraph 2 is a provision on maritime zones which an island can generate. Paragraph 3 is a provision on rocks which cannot sustain human habitation or economic life of their own.

The definition of an island in Article 121(1) succeeded the traditional one which had been developed since 1930 Hague Codification Conference. Considering the advanced science and technology, this paper examines the conditions for an island such as area of land, natural formation, and emergence at high tide.

Paragraph 2 of the Article 121 of the UNCLOS Convention is a provision regarding maritime zones which an island can generate. As an exception to the provision, Paragraph 3 stipulates that rocks which cannot sustain human habitation or economic life of its own are not eligible for EEZ and continental shelf. But this provision invites heated controversies and discussions. The standards human habitation and economic life of its own which divide fully entitled islands and rocks aggravated the confusion.

Fortunately, in the 2016 South China Sea Arbitration, the Tribunal rendered a creative and ground-breaking award on regime of islands. In this case, the Tribunal classified maritime features into fully entitled islands, rocks, and low-tide elevations to address the conditions and maritime jurisdiction of the features. As the impact of the award on the Regime of Islands are huge, it was carefully analyzed.

This paper explains the history of Regime of Islands under international law of the sea. After that, this paper examine the definition and maritime zones of islands, low-tide elevations, and rocks. In the meantime, decisions by international courts and trobunals including the Award on the South China Sea Arbitration aree analyzed to confirm international judicial organs. The implications on Korea are reviewed where appropriate.

Key Words

Regime of Islands, Low-tide Elevation, Rock, South China Sea Arbitration, Effect of Islands, Dokdo

1. INTRODUCTION

Regarding the regime of islands, Article 121 of the United Nations Convention on the Law of the Sea (hereinafter, UNCLOS Convention) adopted at the Third United Nations Conference on the Law of the Sea (UNCLOS III) consists of three paragraphs. Paragraph 1 of the Article, following the traditional rule codified in 1958 Territorial Sea Convention, defines an island as a naturally formed area of land, surrounded by water, which is above water at high tide. Paragraph 2 is a provision on maritime zones which an island can generate. An island can create the territorial sea, contiguous zone, exclusive economic zone (EEZ) and continental shelf which will be determined in accordance with the provisions applicable to other land territory. Paragraph 3 is a provision on Rocks which cannot sustain human habitation or economic life of their own. According to the provision, rocks shall have no EEZ or continental shelf.

While territorial sea was the sole maritime zone of the coastal states, the definition of islands eligible for the zone was the most important issue in international law of the sea. The definition of an island in Article 121(1) succeeded the traditional one which was adopted at the 1930 Hague Codification Conference. The conditions for an island such as area of land, natural formation, and emergence at high tide needs more review considering the advanced science and technology.

Since the mid 20th century, states, taking advantage of the advanced science and technology, sought to expand their sovereignty or jurisdiction over the ocean space beyond territorial sea. As Professor Oxman put it, while territorial temptation shifted from territory to the ocean, states gradually pay more attention to the vast maritime jurisdiction beyond territorial sea.[1] The utility of maritime features were revalued by states as stepping stones for more maritime jurisdiction. Given the recent tendency of coastal states to expand and strengthen national maritime jurisdiction, it will be certain that maritime features are getting the spotlight.

Paragraphs 2 and 3 of the Article 121 of the UNCLOS Convention are provisions regarding maritime zones which maritime features can generate. At UNCLOS III, there were heated discussions and controversies between countries insisting that every island has entitlement to maritime zones similar to that of main land and those asserting the need to classify maritime features to limit maritime zones of tiny features. Provisions of the Paragraphs 2 and 3 were the product of compromise between the two group of states. In particular, Paragraph 3 stipulates that rocks which cannot sustain human habitation or economic life of its own are not eligible for EEZ and continental shelf, but this provision sparked heated controversy over the exact meaning of the clause. Especially, the ambiguous standards dividing fully entitled islands and rocks aggravated the situation. Coastal states, utilizing the vagueness and confusion raised by the provision, established excessive EEZs or continental shelves around tiny islets. Furthermore, international courts and tribunals were hesitant to render clear decisions on this matter.

However, in the 2016 South China Sea Arbitration between the Philippines and China, the Tribunal constituted under Annex 7 to the UNCLOS Convention (the Tribunal) rendered an epochal award. The Tribunal classified maritime features into fully entitled islands, rocks, and low-tide elevations and indicated criteria differentiating the categories of maritime features.[2] As the impact of the award on the regime of islands are huge, this paper will analyze the points of the decision.

This paper will start reviewing the history of the regime of Islands under international law of the sea. After that, this paper will examine the definition and maritime zones of low-tide elevations, rocks, and fully entitled islands. In particular, conditions for islands such as natural formation and being above water at high tide, and standards differentiating rocks from fully entitled islands will be scrutinized. In the meantime, the award on South China Sea Arbitration will be analyzed to confirm recent practices of international courts and tribunals. The implications for Korea will be reviewed where appropriate.

2. HISTORY OF REGIME OF ISLANDS

While territorial sea was the sole maritime zone attributable to coastal states, the definition of islands was the most important issue in international law of the sea. There were opposing opinions regarding the condition of an island in international law. When the second sub-committee of the 1930 Hague Codification Conference adopted a draft,[3] scholars like Gidel criticized the draft on the ground that an island is an area of land above water at high tide. In fact, the definition of an island has changed over time. Some states and scholars have claimed that a naturally formed area of land projected above sea level at low-tide (low-tide elevation) should be also accorded with the status of an island. There were assertions that artificial islands should be treated as islands as well. After a lengthy process of discussion and compromise, the First United Nations Conference on the Law of the Sea (UNCLOS I) finally reached an agreement on the definition of an island. Article 10 of the 1958 Convention on the Territorial Sea provides, "An island is a naturally-formed area of land, surrounded by water, which is above water at high-tide."[4] Islands are deemed to have entitlement to the continental shelf.

As the expansion of coastal state maritime jurisdiction through newly emerged EEZ and extended continental shelf was expected at UNCLOS III, it became necessary to review the definition of islands. The point of concern was the inequitable results which may be created by EEZ or continental shelf around tiny maritime features. At the Conference, states such as Romania, Turkey, and 14 African states proposed that small features like islets and rocks are not eligible to EEZs and continental shelves,[5] whereas most island states and states possessing outlying islands insisted that all features are entitled to maritime zones. Greece, New Zealand and Fiji proposed that all islands can create territorial sea, EEZ, and continental shelf regardless of their size.[6]

Article 121 of the UNCLOS Convention followed the definition of an island specified in 1958 Territorial Sea Convention and introduced new provision prohibiting tiny islets from creating EEZs and continental shelves. Paragraph 1 of the Article provides that an island is an area of land, naturally formed, which is above water at high tide. Paragraph 2 stipulates that an island can generate maritime zones like territorial sea, EEZ and continental shelf in accordance with the method applicable to other land territory. However, as paragraph 3 provides an exception by stipulating that "Rocks which cannot sustain human habitation or economic life of their own shall have no EEZ or continental shelf," the standards dividing islands eligible to EEZ and continental shelf from rocks eligible only to territorial sea are not clear. States parties to the Convention, taking advantage of ambiguities of the provision, interpreted it for their interests in order to enlarge their maritime jurisdiction. International courts and tribunals avoided taking the burden to interpret and apply the provisions directly.

However, in the South China Sea Arbitration, the Tribunal assessed the status of certain maritime features and the entitlements to maritime zones. For that purpose, the Tribunal classified maritime features into four categories and examined the conditions carefully. According to the Tribunal, features that are fully submerged, even at low tide, are 'submerged features.' A feature that is exposed at low-tide but covered with water at high tide is a 'low-tide elevation.' Features that are above water at high tide are generally called 'islands' or 'high tide features.' Islands or high tide features that cannot sustain human habitation or economic life of their own and thus disqualified from generating an EEZ or continental shelf are 'rocks.' Islands or high tide features which enjoy the same entitlements as other land territory are 'fully entitled islands.' Fully entitled islands and rocks are subsets of the broader category of islands or high-tide features.[7] International lawyers are carefully watching subsequent decisions and state practices to check the influence of the award on regime of islands.

3. ISLANDS AND LOW-TIDE ELEVATIONS

3-1. Islands : Definition and the Conditions Revisited

UNCLOS Convention established a new Regime of Islands through Article 121. There were three basic reasons to introduce new provisions; to overcome the vagueness and generality of the definition contained in Article 10 of the 1958 Territorial Sea Convention; to establish a new mechanism based on fairness and equity to resolve the disproportionate and distorted result, considering the diversity of islands in size, position, population, and economic importance; to prevent an encroachment on the Seabed or common heritage of mankind by establishing excessive maritime zones around small insular features.[8]

Paragraphs 1 and 2 of Article 121 of the UNCLOS Convention provide that islands can generate vast maritime jurisdiction like territorial sea, contiguous zone, EEZ and continental shelf. However, the definition of the term 'island' has changed considerably over time. Generally speaking, up to the 1950s, several states and scholars were of the opinion that an island is a naturally formed area of land above sea level at low tide, thus including low-tide elevations.[9] Not a few states and scholars insisted that artificial islands and installations are islands as well. International society, after decades of vicissitudes, finally reached an agreement on the definition of an island. The definition of an island in Article 121(1) of the UNCLOS Convention succeeded the Article of the 1958 Territorial Sea Convention. It provides that "an island is a naturally-formed area of land, surrounded by water, which is above water at high tide." This paper examines three conditions; 'an area of land,' 'natural formation,' and 'above water at high tide.'[10]

First, an island must be an area of land. The similarity of insular formations to the territory was the reason why international law has treated some insular formations as if they were part of mainland. Thus, to be an island, an insular formation must fulfill two requirements; geographical feature attached to the seabed and the nature of *terra firma.* In other words, islands must be composed of solid material attached to the substrate.[11] Floating natural formations such as reed islands and ice islands, drifting with the wind and water currents, cannot be considered as *terra firma.* Though naturally formed and have soil and rock on them, they are not attached to the substrate and float by the wind and currents.[12] However, in Nicaragua/Columbia case, the ICJ rejected Nicaragua's argument that a feature called QS 32 at Quitasueno cannot be an island, as it is composed of coral debris. The court ruled that international law defines an island by reference to whether it is naturally formed and whether it is above water at high tide, not by its geological composition. The court added that the feature is composed of solid material, attached to the substrate, and not of loose debris.[13]

Ice Islands formed by ice-shelves or ice flows can be treated as floating pieces of territory? Pharand said that it is not reasonable to treat parts of ice shelves floating on the high sea as islands since they do not have the attributes of land such as permanency and stability.[14] Dinkum Sands situated in Beaufort Sea was an object of dispute between the U.S. Federal Government and State of Alaska. Seated eight miles apart from the mainland Alaska, Dinkum Sands was measured about 60x800m in size and the top of the shoal is mostly a mixture of sand and gravel with scattered slabs of ice. According to the U.S. Federal Government, as the 'land' of Article 121(1) of the UNCLOS Convention requires 'land' or similar 'permanency,' sea-ice can not have the status of an island.[15] Often, opinions are divided with regards to the nature of *terra firma* of insular features. For example, in Qatar/Bahrain case, some judges viewed that Qit'at Jarada cannot be an island since it was not *terra firma,* whereas the majority of the judges considered it an island.[16]

Second, an island must be formed naturally. Up to the mid-20th century, few states and international publicists contended that artificial islands and installations should be recognized as islands. However, most scholars including Gidel, Jessup, and Colombos had the views that islands are identified as naturally formed maritime features. Practices of governments and the 1929 Harvard Research Draft on Territorial Waters followed this position. At the 1930 Hague Codification Conference, Germany and the Netherlands insisted that artificial installations should be treated as islands, while the Sub-commission in charge of defining islands made a draft provision which could be interpreted to recognize artificial islands and installations as islands to the contrary of the position of the Expert Commission.[17] During the deliberations at the International Law Commission (ILC), Hersch Lauterpacht's effort to exclude artificial islands from having a territorial sea ended up in a failure. Afterwards, the U.S. proposal to insert 'naturally formed' found its way into Article 10(1) of the 1958 Territorial Sea Convention.[18] As the UNCLOS Convention upheld this provision, natural formation remains a requisite condition for islands.

Artificial islands and installations such as a light house, beacon, and oil platform are not islands in terms of international law. Lighthouses and other installations built on low-tide elevations or submerged rocks do not acquire the juridical status of islands. Furthermore, islands constructed by man from natural materials or dredged or otherwise imported to form an area of land do not qualify as islands in terms of UNCLOS Convention, even if they were areas of land above water at high tide. As Article 13(1) of the Convention provides, natural formation is a necessary condition for low-tide elevation as well. In the South China Sea Arbitration, the Tribunal emphasized that human modification cannot change the seabed into a low-tide elevation or a low-tide elevation into an island. Several features in the South China Sea have been substantially modified as large artificial islands with installations and airstrips constructed on top of the coral reefs. In such circumstances, the Tribunal emphasized that the status of a feature should be ascertained on the basis of its earlier and natural condition, prior to the significant human modification. The Tribunal reached its conclusion on the basis of the best available evidence of the previous status of the area of the sea.[19]

States have tried to preserve or protect islands from erosion or abrasion by building sea defences or breakwaters. These actions to maintain the existing naturally formed islands do not deprive these islands of their status as islands. Nor does the extension of an existing island by artificial means affect its legal status as an island. Islands which are completely washed away by tsunami or hurricane may be rebuilt by artificial means maintaining their status as islands.[20] However, a tiny maritime feature saved with a massive external help may be challenged of its status as an island. For example, Okinotori is formed of two islets situated within a coral reef, most of which is under water even at low-tide. The Japanese government spent $280 million to create an artificial island (a rock) by encasing it with thick concrete and later spent additional $50 million to cover the rock with titanium net.[21] If the fiscal input into a small feature is so excessive, the construction or engineering activities could be interpreted as creating a new island rather than protecting or preserving it.

Third, an island must be above water at high tide. The emergence at high-tide is a requisite to be an island. It means that low-tide elevations which are above water at low tide and under the water at high tide cannot generate territorial sea. Furthermore, in Nicaragua/Columbia case, the ICJ ruled that only islands that are not low-tide elevations are capable of appropriation.[22] However, the Committee of Experts at the 1930 Hague Codification Conference were of the opinion that any land not continuously submerged is an island. In response to a questionnaire prepared for the Conference, more than a few countries like the United States, Denmark, Finland, Germany, Japan, Norway, the Netherlands, Romania, and Sweden took the position that low-tide elevations could be recognized as islands. Meanwhile, Great Britain, South Africa, Australia, India, and New Zealand took the opposite position. According to the compromise made at the Conference, while only legal islands which are above water at high tide may have territorial waters, low-tide elevations within territorial water of mainland may be taken into account for determining the outer limit of territorial sea.[23]

Once recognized as an island by Article 121(1) of the Convention, even the smallest of islands is entitled to a 12 nautical mile territorial sea. An island of the size of a few centimeters can generate 1.551km^2 territorial sea around itself. Nevertheless, the meaning of 'above water at high tide' is not uniform in state practice. There are various methods to measure a tide level; highest astronomical tide, mean high-water spring tide, mean high water neap tide, mean sea level, and etc. Considering that sea level may vary depending on season and location, there may be large differences by which method is used to measure the level. In any case, UNCLOS Convention does not have any provision on which tide is suitable to determine the emergence at high tide. Nor there is an international customary rule requiring mandatory application of a specific sea level. Thus, in the South China Sea Arbitration, the Tribunal ruled that States are free under the Convention to claim a high-tide feature or an island on the basis of any high water datum that reasonably corresponds to the ordinary meaning of the term 'high tide.'[24] As tidal patterns and ranges vary both spatially and temporarily, a tidal model or method is required to convert bathymetric measurements into a standard level. In Nicaragua/Colombia case, Columbia, relying on two surveys conducted by Columbian Navy and an American expert, Dr. Robert Smith, argued that there are 34 features within

Quitasueno which qualify as islands as they are above water at high tide. Nicaragua contested the findings that there are many features which are permanently above water and objected to the method used by Dr. Smith. It considered that the Grenoble Tide Model used by him is not appropriate for determining whether features at Quitasueno are above water at Highest Astronomical Tide (HAT). Columbia contended that Nicaragua's criticism of the Grenoble Model is groundless and the model should not be rejected for several reasons. The court noted that even using Nicaragua's preferred model, QS 32 is above water at high tide by some 0.7 meters. Citing its judgment in Qatar/Bahrain case where Qit'at Jarada was determined as an island, notwithstanding that it was only 0.4 meters above water at high tide, the ICJ ruled that the feature QS 32 is an island and capable of appropriation.[25]

In regards to the emergence at high tide, it needs to be considered how frequent a feature must be above water at high tide. ILC Draft Articles on the Law of the Sea (1956) originally deemed an island as "an area of land which in normal circumstances is permanently above high-water mark." However, by the suggestion of the United States, the expression 'in normal circumstances' was deleted. In any case, a feature must be above water at high tide except in abnormal circumstances.[26] In 1977, Anglo-French Continental Shelf case, a dispute was raised with regard to the use of Eddystone Rocks as a basepoint in maritime delimitation. United Kingdom argued that the Eddystone Rocks should be regarded as islands since they are completely covered only at the time of high-water equinoctial springs and are usually above water at high-water springs. On the other hand, according to France, a feature which does not remain uncovered continuously throughout the year should be ranked as a low-tide elevation, not as an island.[27] The Arbitration Court did not make clear whether Eddystone Rocks are islands in international law or not, but the Court supported the UK's position on the emergence at high tide.[28]

Article 121(2) provides that territorial sea, contiguous zone, EEZ, and continental shelf of an island are determined in accordance with the provisions of this Convention applicable to other land territory. An island could generate maritime zones such as internal waters, territorial sea, contiguous zone, EEZ and continental shelf in accordance with general international law of the sea. Although not expressly mentioned in Article 121(2) of the Convention, islands can have internal waters and give rise to continental shelf entitlements beyond 200 nautical miles.[29] On the other hand, outer limits of any maritime zones are usually measured by the distance from the baselines which are established applying the normal or straight baselines method. Thus, an island for the purpose of generating maritime zone such as territorial sea, contiguous zone, EEZ, and continental shelf becomes an island for the purpose of drawing baselines from which maritime jurisdiction starts in the same manner for any mainland coast.[30]

In the Northeast Asia, China established 49 basepoints on its continental coast and 28 basepoints around Paracel Islands by the 1992 Territorial Sea and Contiguous Zone Act, and some of the straight baselines connect the basepoints situated on tiny features. The basepoints on Macaiheng, Waikejiao, Haijiao, and Dongnanjiao are believed to be set on features which are too tiny and situated far away from the mainland coast. They could affect maritime boundaries between Korea and China, should the equidistant or median line rule is employed for maritime delimitation.[31] On the other hand, when Japan ratified the UNCLOS Convention in 1996, it introduced the straight baseline system over the whole coast. It established 194 basepoints and 165 straight baselines, but some of them were applied on coasts that are not deeply indented or have no fringe of islands in the vicinity.[32] Korea established a baseline system as it enacted the Territorial Sea Act in 1977 and promulgated an enforcement ordinance in 1978. It has drawn normal baselines in the east coast while drawing straight baselines in the west and the south coast of the peninsula. Given the indented and complicated geography of the coasts, straight baselines around the Korean Peninsula are justified.[33]

3-2. Low-tide Elevations

Article 13(1) of the UNCLOS Convention provides that "a low-tide elevation is a naturally formed area of land which is surrounded and above water at low-tide but emerged at high-tide." Occasionally called as 'drying rocks' or 'banks' in the past, low-tide elevations are not islands in international law, and they are not eligible to any maritime jurisdiction.[34]

The legal status of low-tide elevations is a result of compromise reached at the 1930 Hague Codification Conference between the states asserting that only features above water at high-tide are islands and other states arguing that features above water at low-tide are also islands. According to the compromise, a geographic feature which is above water at high-tide is recognized as islands, whereas a low-tide elevation is not an island, which can be used as a base point for the purpose of establishing territorial sea if it is situated within territorial sea of a coastal state. Thus, Article 13(2) of the UNCLOS Convention stipulates that "where a low-tide elevation is situated wholly or partly at a distance not exceeding the breadth of the territorial sea from the mainland or an island, the low-water line on that elevation may be used as the baseline for measuring the breadth of the territorial sea." Thus, a low-tide elevation can be used as a base point if it is within the breadth of territorial sea from the coast, but using another low-tide elevation situated within the breadth of territorial sea from a low-tide elevation (leapfrogging) it is not allowed.[35]

As explained above, there are a variety of tide levels and methods to measure them. Unfortunately, UNCLOS Convention does not have any provision on these matters. International society has no customary rule requiring mandatory application of a specific method, so the Tribunal in the South China Sea Arbitration ruled that States can freely claim a feature an island or a low-tide elevation on the basis of any high water datum that reasonably corresponds to the ordinary meaning of the term 'high tide.'[36]

In fact, a low tide elevation can be transformed into an insular formations due to natural accretion. If a coral boulder is pushed onto reef and above high water or a sand cay or sand bar is formed by storm, an island (or a rock) can be formed. On the other hand, a feature raised by reclamation cannot be an island. UNCLOS Convention requires that not only an island but also a rock must be 'naturally formed.'[37] In the same vein, the South China Sea Tribunal emphasized that human modification cannot change the seabed into a low-tide elevation or a low-tide elevation into an island. Even though many tiny features in the South China Sea underwent substantial modification to be artificial islands, the Tribunal decided that the status of a feature should be ascertained on the basis of its earlier and natural condition prior to the human modification.[38]

As low-tide elevation is not an island, the question was raised whether a low-tide elevation is susceptible to appropriation or not. In the Qatar/Bahrain case, the ICJ observed that a coastal state has sovereignty over low-tide elevations which are situated within its territorial sea, but the really important question was whether a state can acquire sovereignty over a low-tide elevation when it lies within the territorial sea of another state. Qatar and Bahrain agreed that Fasht ad Dibal is a low-tide elevation. The former asserted that a low-tide elevation is not suitable for appropriation, but the latter preferred decision based on the effectiveness of the states. According to the Court, international treaty law is silent on the question of whether low-tide elevations can be considered to be 'territory.' Nor is the Court aware of a uniform and widespread state practice which might have given rise to a customary rule which unequivocally permits or excludes appropriation of low-tide elevations. The Court said the few existing rules do not justify a general assumption that low-tide elevations are territory in the same sense as islands. It is thus not established that low-tide elevations can be fully assimilated with islands or other land territory.[39] In the Pedra Branca case, the same Court concludes that sovereignty over South Ledge, a low-tide elevation, belongs to the State in the territorial waters of which it is located.[40]

Ieodo is a submerged rock located 82 nautical miles south to the Marado island, the southernmost Korean territory.[41] Ieodo has been considered special to Korean people, as the rock had been spoken and written as utopia to fishermen wrecked in a storm. The existence of Ieodo really exists was ascertained in 1900 when a British ship called Socotra found the rock. It is unquestionable that Ieodo is not an island eligible to generate territorial sea, EEZ, and continental shelf. According to the UNCLOS Convention, Ieodo is neither a rock nor a tide elevation. It is only a submerged rock of which any country could not claim sovereignty and establish maritime zones. What is certain is that this underwater rock is believed to situate on Korean side of the hypothetical median line between Korea and China. Often, Chinese people and Chinese NGOs claim over Ieodo, but the Chinese government has never officially raised the sovereignty issue over the submerged rock. In view of the principle of international law of the sea and the geography of the feature, the issues surrounding Ieodo would be solved, when maritime delimitation between Korea and China is concluded.

4. ROCKS : CRITERIA AND SOUTH CHINA SEA ARBITRATION

4-1. What is a Rock?

As the coastal state maritime jurisdiction was expected to expand through extended continental shelf and newly introduced EEZ and Archipelagic Waters, UNCLOS III reviewed the regime of islands contained in the Territorial Sea Convention adopted at UNCLOS I in 1958. More than a few states anticipated a mechanism to prevent inequitable results that could take place from allowing excessively large maritime zones to tiny features. Suggestions to classify features into several categories for different treatment were proposed. For example, according to the 'Draft Articles on the Regime of Islands' proposed by 14 African States, maritime features are classified into island, islet, and rock. Meanwhile, island states and states with outlying islands (Greece and Rumania) insisted that every island should be entitled to the maritime jurisdiction regardless of its size and importance.

After heated discussion and compromise, UNCLOS III decided to keep the traditional definition of islands, but introduced a new provision on rocks. As examined earlier, Article 121(1) of the UNCLOS Convention defines an island as a naturally formed area of land above water at high tide, and paragraph 2 provides that an island can generate territorial sea, contiguous zone, EEZ, and continental shelf. Paragraph 3 of the Article can be seen as an exceptional clause excluding application of paragraph 2 to 'rocks.' It stipulates that "Rocks which cannot sustain human habitation or economic life of their own shall have no exclusive economic zone or continental shelf." It is clear that the purpose of the Article 121(3) lies in preventing excessive claims over the EEZ and continental shelf by limiting the capacity of tiny features. However, the interpretation and application of the provision may vary because of the vagueness embedded in the provision and the desire of coastal states to extend their maritime jurisdiction. Although scholars like Hodgson and Ely and an international organ, International Hydrographic Bureau, classified maritime features into several categories for appropriate treatment, the definitions of a rock mostly based on the area of features were not accepted.[42] After all, the UNCLOS Convention adopted 'human habitation' and 'economic life of its own' as standards classifying islands into fully entitled islands and rocks.

In retrospect, conditions such as 'human habitation' and 'economic life of its own' are not completely new conditions for islands. Gidel, in his book published in 1934, noted island's capacity for effective occupation and habitation as one criterion for an island. For Gidel, habitability was to be proven to avoid the argument about the island's capacity. Furthermore, for him, habitation means stable residence by human groups. Thus, occasional habitation by seasonal fishermen or visiting survey teams are not sufficient.[43] In 1923, the British Imperial Conference decided that coastline of mainland and island forms the starting point for 3 mile territorial sea, and the Common Policy adopted at the Conference made clear that an island should be above water at high tide in normal circumstances and be suitable for use or habitation as well.[44]

The criteria 'human habitation' and 'economic life of its own' are criticized because of their ambiguity and subjectivity. Furthermore, if the term 'human habitation' is interpreted to include actual habitation and the possibility of habitation and the 'economic life of its own' includes economic activities on installations like lighthouses built on a feature and resource extraction activities in neighboring seas, lot of insular formations will become eligible to EEZ and continental shelf. According to Smith, the UNLOS Convention does not refer to uninhabited rocks, but rather to uninhabitable rocks. Also, since the meaning of the phrase "economic life of its own" is not clear, it was disputable whether that condition can be met when a light house or a laboratory is established on a tiny feature.[45] Professor Charney argued that socioeconomic consideration is necessary in interpreting provisions in respect of islands and rocks. According to him, the shift in price of resources, technical developments, and newly emerged human activities could result in reappraisal on insular formations.[46]

Coastal states took advantage of this ambiguity to declare vast maritime zones like EEZ and continental shelf around tiny features. Japan, for example, established 200 mile EEZ around a tiny feature Okinotori which is located 1,800km south of Tokyo, but this islet is considered to be a rock by any standards.[47] Japan tendered its Submission to the UN Commission on the Limit of Continental Shelf (CLCS) for review to establish entitlements to EEZs and continental shelves around small rocks such as Okinotori and Minamitori. As an international lawyer put it, almost all states which have tiny features off their coasts have claimed EEZ and continental shelf around them. United Kingdom and Mexico are rare exceptions. UK withdrew its policy and domestic ordinances which proclaimed EEZ and continental shelf around Rockall. Rockall is situated 162 nautical miles northwest of scotland and the area is $624m^2$ or 0.000241 square miles.[48] Mexico did not claim EEZ and continental shelf around Alijos Rocks either.[49] Given the decentralized state of international community, if a state takes an action against international law without any protests from other countries, it could be developed into a fait accompli.

Furthermore, the international courts and tribunals have been hesitant to dicide clearly the status of disputed maritime features providing standards to differentiatee fully entitled islands from rocks. In Volga case, judge Vukas of the ITLOS deplored in his declaration that international courts and tribunals had disregarded the application of the rules regarding the limited entitlement of tiny islands to maritime zones.[50] In the Black Sea case between Romania and

Ukraine, the ICJ allowed Serpents' Island to be used as a basepoint for territorial sea delimitation, but did not decide whether this feature is an island specified in the Article 121(2) of the UNCLOS Convention or a rock provided in paragraph 3 of the Article. A publicist commented that the ICJ missed a good opportunity to define a rock in international law of the sea more accurately.[51]

4-2. Award on South China Sea Arbitration and Its Implication

In the South China Sea Arbitration between the Philippines and China, the Philippines' Submissions No. 3, 5, and 7 are related to conflicts about the status of maritime features in the South China Sea under the Article 121 of the Convention. The Philippines required the Tribunal to declare that Scarborough Shoal generates no entitlement to an EEZ or continental shelf in Submission No. 3, to rule that Mischief Reef and Second Thomas Shoal are part of the EEZ and continental shelf of the Philippines in Submission No. 5, to declare that Johnson Reef, Cuarteron Reef and Fiery Cross Reef generate no entitlement to an EEZ or continental shelf in Submission No. 7.[52] The Tribunal classified the maritime features into islands, rocks, and low-tide elevations and examined the maritime zones of the features. In particular, the Tribunal indicated criteria differentiating islands and low-tide elevations, but concentrated more on relationship between fully entitled islands and rocks.

As paragraph 3 of the Article stipulates that rocks which cannot sustain human habitation or economic life of their own shall have no EEZ zone or continental shelf, the Tribunal noted that Article 121 contains a distinction between two categories of naturally formed high-tide features, 'fully entitled islands' and 'rocks.' A matter of great concern was the Tribunal's position on the meaning and relationship of the terms 'human habitation' and 'economic life of its own' which are enumerated as criteria drawing a line between 'fully entitled islands' and 'rocks.'

After in depth examination on the text, context, object and purpose, and drafting history of the UNCLOS Convention, the Tribunal revealed the following conclusions with respect to the interpretation of the provision: i) The term 'rock' does not limit the application of the provision to features composed of solid rock; ii) The text of Article 121(3) is disjunctive. So, the ability to sustain either human habitation or an economic life of its own would suffice to entitle a high-tide feature to an EEZ and continental shelf; iii) With respect to "human habitation," the critical factor is the non-transient character of the inhabitation. The term "human habitation" should be understood to involve the inhabitation of the feature by a stable community of people. Such a community need not necessarily be large; iv) The term 'economic life of their own' is closely linked to the requirement of human habitation, and the two will in most instances go hand in hand. Article 121(3) does not refer to a feature having economic value, but a feature sustaining 'economic life.' The economic life will ordinarily be the life and livelihoods of the human population inhabiting and making its home on a maritime feature. As the provision makes clear that the economic life in question must pertain to the feature as 'of its own,' economic life must be oriented around the feature itself and not focused mainly on the waters or seabed of the surrounding territorial sea. Thus, economic activity that is entirely dependent on external resources or devoted to using a feature as an object for extractive activities would not fulfill this condition. Extractive economic activity to harvest the natural resources of a feature for the benefit of a population elsewhere can not be considered to constitute the economic life of an island as its own; v) The status of a feature is to be determined on the basis of its natural capacity, without external additions or modifications intended to increase its capacity to sustain human habitation or an economic life of its own; vi) Article 121(3) is concerned with the capacity of a maritime feature to sustain human habitation or an economic life of its own, not with whether the feature is presently, or has been, inhabited or home to economic life; vii) The capacity of a feature to sustain human habitation or an economic life of its own must be assessed on a case-by-case basis. The principal factors that contribute to the natural capacity of a feature can be the presence of water, food, and shelter in sufficient quantities to enable a group of persons to live on the feature for an indeterminate period of time.[53]

Based on this interpretation, the Tribunal found that Scarborough Shoal is a rock for the purpose of Article 121(3). This islet consists of five to seven rocks that are exposed at high tide, but the protrusions above high tide are minuscule. They obviously could not sustain human habitation in their naturally formed state. They have no fresh water, vegetation, and living space. This Shoal has been used as a fishing ground by fishermen from different States, but there is no evidence that the fishermen working on the reef made use of the high-tide rocks at Scarborough Shoal. There is no evidence that this feature could independently sustain an economic life of its own. The Tribunal ruled that the Scarborough Shoal is a rock.[54] In the Tribunal's view, Johnson Reef, Cuerton Reef, Fiery Cross Reef, Gaven Reef (North) and Mckennan Reef are also rocks.

Although the Philippines did not require in its submission, the Tribunal examined the geography and history of larger features in the South China Sea such as Itu Aba ($0.43km^2$), Thitu ($0.41km^2$), West York ($0.21km^2$), Spratly Island ($0.17km^2$), South-West Cay ($0.15km^2$), North-East Cay ($0.15km^2$) to consider whether they belong to fully entitled islands or rocks. The Tribunal considered that if these features were to be classified as rocks, the same conclusion would hold true for all other high-tide features in the Spratly Islands.[55] All of the significant high-tide features in the Spratly Islands are presently under the control of one of the littoral States due to the construction of installations, but this presence is predominantly for military or governmental purposes and involves significant outside supply. Moreover, many of them have been significantly modified from their natural condition. The tribunal, accordingly, considers historical evidence of conditions on the features to represent a more reliable guide to the capacity of the features to sustain human habitation or economic life.[56]

However, there are consistent reports and historical records of small wells on a number of features in the Spratly Islands. According to those records, the water on Itu Aba was good, and the water on Thitu and South-West Cay was drinkable. The Tribunal noted that the freshwater resources of these features have supported small numbers of people.[57] The Tribunal also considered that Itu Aba and Thitu were heavily forested features in natural condition, and the cultivation of papayas and bananas took place in Itu Aba in the early 20th century by Japanese.[58] As various records indicate, a consistent presence of small numbers of fishermen, most of them being Chinese, Filipinos or Malays, on the main features in the Spratly Islands was confirmed. Thus, the Tribunal found that the islands were historically used by small groups of fishermen, and some of the fishermen were present in the Spratlys for comparatively long periods, but the overall number of individuals engaged in this livelihood appears to have been significantly constrained.[59]

The Tribunal recognized that the principal high-tide features in the Spratly Islands are not too small in area and have small wells, and are capable of enabling the survival of small groups of people. Itu Aba and Thitu used to be fishery sites for Chinese fishermen while Itu Aba and South-West Cay were used by Japanese in 1920s and 1930s as sites for mining and fishing. However, as the Tribunal considers human habitation to be non-transient inhabitation by a stable community of people, the standard was not fulfilled by the presence of fishermen in the past. The same conclusion applies to the commercial activities by Japanese in Itu Aba and South-West Cay.

The presence by laborers from Taiwan was transient in nature, and the objective of the economic activities was to extract the resources of the features for the benefit of the people of Formosa and Japan. The Tribunal does not consider the presence of military or other governmental personnel on the Spratly features as 'human habitation' or 'economic life of its own' for the purpose of Article 121(3) of the UNCLOS Convention. Thus, the Tribunal concludes that Itu Aba, Thitu, West York, Spratly Island, South-West Cay, and North-East Cay are not capable of sustaining human habitation or ecnomic life of their own.[60]

In the South China Sea Arbitration, the Tribunal addressed the issue on the standards dividing a rock and a fully entitled island. Analyzing the Article 121(3) of the UNCLOS Convention, the Tribunal strictly interpreted the meaning of criteria 'human habitation' and 'economic life of its own.' According to the Tribunal's award, 'human habitation' basically should be understood to involve the inhabitation of the feature by a stable community of people. And 'economic life of its own' means that the economic life in question must pertain to the feature as 'of its own,' and economic life must be oriented around the feature itself and not focused mainly on the waters or seabed of the surrounding territorial sea. Thus, if the points of the award, especially the interpretations on human habitation and economic life of its own, are applied directly to the insular formations at issue, most of the maritime features which are deemed to be on the border line between fully entitled islands and rocks will be relocated to rocks.

Dokdo (Takeshima in Japanese) is an island located in the central part of the East Sea (Sea of Japan in Japanese). This is 87.4km southwest to Ulleungdo and 157.5km northeast to Japanese island Oki. Dokdo is composed of two islets and the total area is 0.186km^2. Dokdo is far bigger than Japan's Okinotori or Minamitori, Rockall of the UK, and various islets in the South China Sea claimed by coastal states including China. According to the Tribunal, factors showing the ability of a feature to sustain human habitation can be presence of water, food, and shelter to enable a group of persons to live on the feature for an indeterminate period of time. Unfortunately, there is no sufficient water and vegetation in Dokdo. The Tribunal also suggested that 'human habitation' involves the inhabitation of the feature by a stable community of people, but for Dokdo and other similar insular formations this criterion is hard to be met. In addition, according to the Tribunal, the presence of military or other governmental personnel on the features are not considered to be 'human habitation' or 'economic life of its own' for the purpose of the provision. The economic life in question must be oriented around the feature and not focused on main land or maritime zones of another islands. If the criteria suggested by the Tribunal should be applied to maritime features at crossroad such as Dokdo, Senkaku, Rockall, and islands in the South China Sea, all of the features would be relocated to a rock which can not generate EEZ and continental shelf. What is important is whether the key interpretations and standards suggested by the Tribunal can be sustained and developed to be legal rules. If these strict interpretations on a rock, especially on the criteria such as human habitation and economic life of its own, can be supported by the subsequent decisions of international courts and tribunals and the practices of states, the emergence of new international customary law can be declared. Given the decentralized situation of the international community, it will be a long process to confirm the establishment of practices and presence of *opinio juris.* Meanwhile, many states including important countries in international society maintain their traditional positions actually not to differentiate the fully entitled islands from rocks. United States, China, and Japan are not expected to revoke their measures establishing maritime zones around tiny features in the near future.[61] Korea and Japan have considered Dokdo a fully entitled island eligible to maritime zones like territorial sea, EEZ, and continental shelf. However, as the impact of the Tribunal in the South China Sea Arbitration on the regime of islands in international law of the sea is unpredictable, it will be necessary to pay attention to the subsequent developments of state practices and international judicial organs.

5. EFFECT OF ISLANDS ON MARITIME DELIMITATION

Maritime Delimitation, the process of establishing lines separating the space of coastal states' jurisdiction over maritime space where the legal title overlaps,[62] is one of the most important and complex issues facing the contemporary international law of the sea. Traditionally, maritime delimitation between coastal states had been established according to equidistant or median line method which was technically developed by Boggs in the early 20th century. Article 6 of the 1958 Convention on the Continental Shelf provides that if another boundary line is not justified by special circumstances, the boundary line is set to be the median line (between opposite states) or equidistant line (between adjacent states). The ICJ, however, in its historical judgment on the North Sea Continental Shelf cases in 1969, refused to apply the equidistance (or median) line method to declare equity and equitable solution as the principle and purpose of maritime delimitation. According to the World Court, maritime delimitation is to be effected by agreement in accordance with equitable principles taking account of the relevant circumstances, in such a way as to leave as much as possible to each Party all those parts of the continental shelf that constitute a natural prolongation of its land territory.[63] Subsequent decisions on the continental shelf delimitation cases by international courts and tribunals followed points of the judgment, the principle of equity or equitable solution were referred to as an international customary law rule. In Tunisia/Libya case, the Court emphasized the equity principle to an extreme,[64] but, in Libya/Malta case, the ICJ followed the equitable principles established by the previous judgments in theory, while keeping the balance between the two principles in practice. Then the international courts and tribunals had been under criticism, as their decisions swung between the two principles on maritime delimitation.[65] Recently there are attempts to unify the equidistance principle and the principle of equity into one,[66] but coastal states adhere to a principle which is expected to be helpful to their national interests.

The UNCLOS Convention has articles dealing with maritime delimitation of territorial sea (Art. 15), EEZ (Art. 74), and Continental Shelf (Art. 83). Article 15 was adopted readily at the UNCLOS III and is very similar to Article 12(1) of the 1958 Territorial Sea Convention. Generally, equidistance or median line method is applied to maritime delimitation of territorial sea. Article 74 and Article 81 were the results of a lengthy discussion and compromise between the Equidistance Group and Equitable Principle Group at UNCLOS III. Tommy Koh, the president of the Conference, submitted a compromised proposal in August 1981, which was finally accepted by the Conference. Article 74(1) and Article 81(1) of the Convention provide that "the delimitation of the EEZ (continental shelf) between States with opposite or adjacent coasts shall be effected by agreement on the basis of international law, as referred to in Article 38 of the Statute of the ICJ, in order to achieve an equitable solution." The Equitable Principle Group welcomed the provision since they referred to an equitable solution as the purpose of maritime delimitation whereas the Equidistance Group entertained this provision as well due to the reference to 'international law' which they wanted to insert in delimitation provision. However, since the clauses of the Convention on delimitation of EEZ and continental shelf are not clear, international courts and tribunals take the role once again to interpret the relevant provisions and to establish international practice. Anyway, presence of islands are deemed as a classical case of special circumstances justifying breakaway from the delimitation lines drawn by equidistance or median line method, and a typical factor of relevant circumstances to be considered for equitable maritime delimitation of EEZ and continental shelf.

Recently, maritime delimitation normally proceeds step by step following the three stage method, which was introduced by the ICJ in Libya/Malta case.[67] In the Black Sea case, the ICJ reviewed the method in depth. At the first stage, provisional delimitation lines are drawn using equidistance or median lines, unless there are compelling reasons that make this unfeasible.[68] At the second stage, the relevant factors calling for adjustment of the provisional lines are considered. Those factors are islands, baselines, previous agreements, geology and geomorphology. In particular, disproportionate coastal length, geographic context such as concavity of coasts, and outlying islands of little significance are to be closely considered.[69] At the third stage, equitableness of the boundary lines is examined. Considering balance between the ratio of the respective coastal lengths and that of the relevant maritime areas of the coastal states, the Court verifies whether the delimitation lines produce equitable results or not.[70] Insular formations have been considered as relevant factors at the second stage, but recently these features are taken into account at the first stage establishing provisional lines.

The effect of an island on a delimitation line, generally speaking, varies depending on the size of the island, the number of population, distance from the mainland, and economic importance. However, the need to achieve equitable result has influenced on maritime delimitation. Consequently, according to the circumstances of a specific boundary limitation, islands can be accorded full effect, or partial effect, or no effect.[71]

In general, as the practice of states shows, full weight is given to islands, when they are big enough to sustain large population and economically important. Jeju Island and Hawaii Islands will have full effect on delimitation lines. Also the practice of states shows that full weight is given to islands when it is delimitation between islands. Agreement between Sao tome and Principe and Equatorial Guinea (1999), Agreement between Denmark (Faroe Islands) and Norway (1979), and the Agreement between Cuba and USA (1977) are the examples.[72]

Partial or reduced effect is given to an island, when it is inequitable not only to give full effect to the island but also to give no effect to it, considering the area, location, population, and economy of the island. International judiciary organs have not generally granted full effects on small islands. In the Black Sea case, the ICJ granted the Serpents' Island a limited role as a basepoint for twelve-mile territorial sea.[73] In the Bay of Bengal case, ITLOS said the effect to be granted to islands depends on the geographic realities and the circumstances of a specific case. St. Martins' Island, owned by Bangladesh, is a relatively important feature with a significant size and population, but, because of its location, giving effect to this island would result in a line blocking the seaward projection from Myanmar's coast, and cause an unwarranted distortion of the delimitation line. Thus, the Tribunal did not accorded this island any effect on the delimitation line of EEZ and continental shelf.[74]

Partial effect is given to Kharg Island in Agreement between Iran and Saudi Arabia (1965) and to Scilly Isles in Anglo-French Arbitration (1977) by shifting the delimitation lines, considering the value of the islands. Occasionally, reduced effect was accorded to islands by way of adjusting the azimuth of delimitation line. In Tunisia/Libya case, the ICJ gave Island Kerkenna off Tunisian coast half effect using this method.[75] Enclave, as a method to give reduced effect, is established around an island when it is on the other side of the median line.

No effect has been granted to an island, when it is too small to sustain community of people or it gives rise to inequitable results if any effect is given. Meanwhile, some international lawyers have told that no or reduced effect has been given to an island when its sovereignty is disputed. If a delimitation agreement attributed sovereignty over a disputed island to one of the parties, the other party would expect the price of not giving the island any effect.[76] However, it depends on the situation of the island and sincerity of the states parties to the dispute. The Nicaragua/Honduras case shows how a reduced effect could take place on the boundary line when maritime delimitation is established at the same time with the sovereignty issue. In the case, the issue of sovereignty over Bobel Cay, South Cay, Savanna Cay, and Port Royal Cay was included later in the process of deliberation while the parties had already agreed that the islands have only territorial seas. Honduras insisted twelve mile territorial seas, while Nicaragua argued three mile territorial seas. The Court ruled that the cays along the 15th Parallel can generate twelve mile territorial seas around them.[77]

Regarding the maritime delimitation in the Yellow Sea and the East China Sea, the positions of the Northeast Asian countries are different. China has maintained that continental shelf and EEZ delimitation should be done in accordance with equitable principle taking into account the natural prolongation of the land territory. It has noted that the Okinawa Trough just west of Ryukyu Islands of Japan should be considered as maritime delimitation line in the East China Sea. China is also of the opinion that maritime delimitation between Korea and China in the Yellow sea and the East China Sea should be determined by applying natural prolongation method for an equitable results. Whereas, in the South China Sea, Japan has insisted maritime delimitation based on the equidistance or median line principle. Japan has argued that Okinawa Trough is only an incidental sinking. Furthermore, for Japan, geomorphology is not a factor to be considered for maritime delimitation in the East China Sea, since the distance between the coasts of Japan and Korea or China is less than 400 miles. Korea insists that maritime delimitation between itself and China in the Yellow Sea and the East China Sea should be effected in accordance with median line method. Korea suggests that continental shelf between them is connected as one without discontinuity. Meanwhile, Korea has insisted that maritime delimitation with Japan in the East China Sea should consider the geological rupture by the Okinawa Trough.

The Japanese islands that should be considered in maritime delimitation between Korea and Japan in the East China Sea are Torishima and Danjo-gunto. Torishima, which is located west to Kyushu, is only 50m^2 in area, which has been regarded as a rock. Danjo-gunto is located in the southeast of Torishima Island and the area is 4.75km^2. Lighthouse guards used to live there in the past, but now there are no inhabitants. Japan has claimed that Danjo-gunto hold effect in its negotiation with Korea on maritime delimitation. The debate on the effect of Torishima and Danjo-gunto on delimitation line was removed from the table following the conclusion of the 1974 Joint Development Zone (JDZ) Agreement between Korea and Japan. However, this issue will be revived when a new negotiation for maritime delimitation in the East China Sea begins after the expiration of the Agreement. What is not in doubt is that the two islets are rocks eligible only to territorial sea.

Dokdo is located in the central part of the East Sea and has an area of 0.186km^2. The distance from the island to the South Korea mainland is 217km, and it is 87km away from Ulleungdo. On the other hand, it is 158km from Oki Island of Japan. The sovereignty issue over Dokdo is not clearly solved yet, thus full-fledged negotiation between Korea and Japan on maritime delimitation in the Sea cannot be launched yet. Although the sovereignty issue over Dokdo cannot be properly considered here and disputes over territory has proved to be the most intractable, this paper examine the status of this island from the perspective of international law of the sea based on the premise that Dokdo belongs to Korea.

In spite of the Tribunal's Award on the South China Sea Arbitration, Korea and Japan will not change their position in the near future that Dokdo is a fully entitled island eligible to territorial sea, EEZ, and continental shelf. Although there used to be controversies over the ability of Dokdo to generate EEZ and continental shelf in Korea, Japan has taken the position that all islands and islets, no matter how small, should be entitled to maritime zones, without regard to their size and habitability.[78] Korea insists that the delimitation line should be the median line between Dokdo and Oki of Japan, whereas Japan asserts that the median line between Ulleungdo and Dokdo should be the delimitation line.

The effect of Dokdo on maritime delimitation line, in principle, will be determined considering its area, location, and economic importance. If the sovereignty issue over Dokdo is clearly resolved, Korea and Japan will easily reach an agreement on maritime delimitation in the East Sea. That's because the geography and geomorphology of the area where Dokdo is located is relatively simple and both countries have favored the application of the median line method for the maritime delimitation in the East Sea. If Korea and Japan agree to begin negotiation for maritime delimitation in the East Sea, they can apply the three stage method which is proved to be useful and usually brings an equitable result. In Nicaragua/Colombia case, in spite of the high complexities of the relevant area and strong objection from Nicaragua, the ICJ decided to apply this method. Once Korea and Japan agreed to apply this method, provisional delimitation lines will be established using median line, and relevant circumstances will be considered one by one. Dokdo is a typical relevant circumstance to be considered for equitable maritime delimitation in the East Sea. For more equitable result, the provisional median delimitation lines, considering relevant circumstances such as overall geography and disproportion in lengths of relevant coasts, can be moved or adjusted. In Nicaragua/Colombia case, the ICJ accorded different weights on the base points located on the Nicaraguan and Colombian islands. In the case, the Court is of the opinion that an equitable result could be achieved by giving a weighting of one to Colombian base points and weighting of three to each of the Nicaragua base points. After that, the Court proceeded to a further adjustment by reducing the turning points and connecting them by lines, and finally reached the simplified weighted line.[79] Once Korea and Japan agree on provisional delimitation line, deciding weighting which will be given to Dokdo of Korea and Oki of Japan will be next step for final delimitation.

6. OBSERVATIONS

Regarding the regime of islands, the Article 121 of the UNCLOS Convention has three paragraphs. Paragraph 1 of the Article defines an island as a naturally formed area of land, surrounded by water, which is above water at high tide. Paragraph 2 is a provision on maritime zones which an island can generate. Paragraph 3 is a provision on rocks which cannot sustain human habitation or economic life of their own. According to the provision, a rock cannot generate EEZ or continental shelf. Considering the provisions of the Convention, this paper classified maritime features into low-tide elevations, rocks, and fully entitled islands and examine the conditions for the status and maritime zones of the features.

This paper, analyzing the history of Regime of Islands in international law of the sea, examined the conditions for an island such as area of land, natural formation, and emergence at high tide. Given the advanced science and technology, these conditions are closely analyzed. While the legal status of low-tide elevations is reviewed, the status of Ieodo which is actually a submerged rock is examined.

This paper closely examined the issue of a rock in international law of the sea. According to the Article 121(3) of the Convention, rocks which cannot sustain human habitation or economic life of its own are not eligible for EEZ and continental shelf. But this provision sparked heated controversy over the exact meaning of the clause. Especially, the standards differentiating fully entitled islands and rocks, human habitation or economic life of its own, aggravated the confusion.

However, the Tribunal, In the 2016 South China Sea Arbitration, rendered a ground-breaking award. In this case, the Tribunal classified maritime features into fully entitled islands, rocks, and low-tide elevations to address the conditions and maritime jurisdiction of the features. As the impact of the award on the Regime of Islands is huge, this paper carefully analyzed the points of the decision and examined the influence on the status of Dokdo.

This paper reviewed the effect of islands on maritime delimitation line. The effect of an island on a delimitation line varies depending on the size of the island, the number of population, distance from the mainland, and its economic importance. However, maritime delimitation should bring equitable results. Consequently, according to the circumstances of a specific boundary delimitation, an island can be accorded full effect, or partial effect, or no effect.

If the sovereignty issue over Dokdo is clearly resolved, Korea and Japan will easily reach an agreement on maritime delimitation in the East Sea. The geography and geomorphology of the area where Dokdo is located is relatively simple and both countries have favored the median line method for the maritime delimitation in the East Sea. Korea and Japan can agree to apply the three stage method which is proved to be useful and usually brings an equitable result. Once

Korea and Japan agree on provisional delimitation line, deciding weighting which will be given to Dokdo island of Korea and Oki island of Japan will be the next step for final delimitation.

Notes

1. Bernard H. Oxman, "The Territorial Temptation : A Siren Song at Sea," *American Journal of International Law*, vol. 100, 2006, pp. 830-851.
2. The Philippines' Submissions No. 3, 5 and 7 are related to conflicts about the status of maritime features in the South China Sea under the Article 121 of the Convention. *The South China Sea Arbitration(The Republic of Philippines v. The People's Republic of China), Award*, PCA, 2016, paras. 281-282.
3. D. W. Bowett, *The Legal Regime of Islands in International Law*, Oceana Publications Inc., 1979, pp. 8-9.
4. *Ibid.*, pp. 1-2; Alexander Proelss, *United Nations Convention on the Law of the Sea : A Commentary*, C. H. Beck, Hart, Nomos, 2017, p. 860. As American proposal suggested, 'naturally formed' was added to the definition and the terms 'permanently' and 'in normal circumstances' were deleted from the draft.
5. Scholars Hodgson and Ely also asserted that an island should be given appropriate status taking into consideration its area, population, and distance from the mainland. R. D. Hodgson, "Islands : Normal and Special Circumstances," in J. K. Gamble and G. Pontecorvo (eds), *The Law of the Sea : The Emerging Regime of the Oceans*, Ballinger Publishing Co., 1973, pp. 150-151; N. Ely, "Seabed Boundaries between Coastal States : The Effect to be Given Islets as Special circumstances," in *International Law*, vol. 6, 1972, pp. 232-235.
6. U.N. Doc. A/Conf. 62/C. 2/L. 50 (1974); U.N. Doc. A/Conf. 62/C. 2/L. 30 (1974).
7. *South China Sea case, op. cit., Arbitration (The Republic of Philippines v. The People's Republic of China), Award*, PCA, 2016, paras. 279-280.
8. Clive Ralph Symmons, *The Maritime Zones of Islands in International Law*, Martinus Nijhoff, 1979, p. 16.
9. Proells, *op. cit.*, p. 860.
10. *Ibid.*, pp. 862-863. International law does not prescribe a minimum size of land area to qualify as an island. Thus, even a tiniest land above water or pin-point rock can be a legal island in international law.
11. *Ibid.*
12. Symmons, *op. cit.*, p. 22.
13. *Territorial and Maritime Dispute (Nicaragua v. Columbia), Judgment, ICJ Reports*, 2012, para. 37.
14. Donat Pharand, *The Law the Sea of the Arctic: With Special Reference to Canada*, University of Ottawa Press, 1973, p. 196.
15. Clive Symmons, "When is an Island not an Island in Interantional Law? The Riddle of Dinkum Sands in the Case of US v. Alaska," *Maritime Briefing*, vol. 2, No. 6, International Boundaries Research Unit, 1999, pp. 1-2; No. 84 (Original) Supreme Court of the United States (March 1996), *Report of the Special Master*, p. 3 : Erk Reimnitz, "Dinkum Sands-A Recently Foundered Arctic Island," *Journal of Coastal Research*, vol. 21, No. 2, 2005, p. 276.
16. *Maritime Delimitation and Territorial Questions between Qatar and Bahrain (Qatar v. Bahrain),*

Judgement, ICJ Reports, 2001, para. 195.

17. Bowett, *op. cit.*, p. 2; Clive Ralph Symmons, *The Maritime Zones of Islands in International Law*, Martinus Nijhoff, 1979, pp. 29-30. According to the Subcommittee's accompanying observations, the term island does not exclude artificial islands. *Report Adopted the Second Committee on April 10th, 1930, Appendix II.*
18. Proells, *op. cit.*, pp. 863-864; Bowett, *op. cit.*, p. 4.
19. *South China Sea case, op. cit.*, paras. 305-306.
20. Proells, *op. cit.*, p. 864.
21. Leticia Diaz, Barry Hart Dubner, and Jason Parent, "When is a rock an Island? Another Unilateral Declaration defies Norms of International Law," *Michigan State Journal of International Law*, vol. 15, 2007, note. 2.
22. *Nicaragua/Columbia case*, paras. 25-26.
23. Proells, *op. cit.*, pp. 865-866; Bowett, *op. cit.*, p. 6.
24 *Ibid*, p. 866; *South China Sea case, op. cit.*, para. 311.
25. *Nicaragua/Colombia case, op. cit.*, paras. 28-37.
26. Proells, *op. cit.*, p. 867.
27. *Anglo French Continental Shelf Case, Award*, 1977, paras. 125, 138.
28. Symmons, *op. cit.*, pp. 44-45.
29. Ever since the Truman Declaration initiated the concept of the continental shelf, it appears to have been taken for granted in international practice that the doctrine applied not only to the continental shelves of mainland but also of the islands. *Ibid.*, p. 130.
30. Bowett, *op. cit.*, p. 9.
31. United States Department of State, "Straight Baselines and Territorial Sea Claims : China," *Limits in the Seas*, No. 117, 1996, pp. 2-5.
32. United States Department of State, "Straight Baselines and Territorial Sea Claims : Japan," *Limits in the Seas*, No. 120, 1998, pp. 5-6.
33. United States Department of State, "Straight Baselines and Territorial Sea Claims : South Korea," *Limits in the Seas*, No. 121, 1998, pp. 3-5.
34. R. R. Churchill and A. V. Lowe, *The Law of the Sea*, Manchester University Press, 1999, p. 48.
35. *Ibid.*, p. 35.
36. Proells, *op. cit.*, p. 866; *South China Sea case, op. cit.*, para. 311.
37. *Ibid* (Proells), p. 867.
38. *South China Sea case, op. cit.*, paras. 305-306.
39. *Qatar/Bahrain case, op. cit.*, paras. 205-206.
40. *Sovereignty over Pedra Branca/Pulau Batu Puteh, Middle Rocks and South Ledge (Malaysia/Singapore), Judgment, ICJ Reports*, 2008, paras. 298-299.
41. As 'do' means an island, the name 'Ieodo' can invite misunderstanding. In spite of the name of the feature, Ieodo is not an island. Furthermore, in spite of the English name of the feature 'Socotra Rocks,' the feature is not a rock for the

purpose of classification of maritime features.

42. Former United States Department of State Geographer R. D. Hodgson proposed to classify maritime geographic features on the basis of area to rock (under 0.001 square mile), islet (up to 1 square mile), isle (up to 1,000 square mile), and island (over 1,000 square mile). Hodgson, *op, cit.*, pp. 150-151; Ely, *op. cit.*, pp. 232-235.
43. Gidel, *Le Droit International Public de la Mer*, vol. 3, 1934, p. 681; Bowett, *op. cit.*, pp. 7-8.
44. Imperial Conference 1923, *Report of Inter-Departmental Committee on the Limits of Territorial Waters (Document T.118/118/380(1924))*, Public Record Office GeoRef. F. O. 372/2108 at 5.
45. Robert W. Smith, "Maritime Delimitation in the South China Sea: Potentiality and Challenges," *Ocean Development & International Law*, vol. 41, 2010, p. 221.
46. Jonathan Charney, "Rocks that Cannot Sustain Human Habitation," *American Journal of International Law*, vol. 93, 1999, pp. 866-871.
47. Diaz, Dubner, and Parent, *op. cit.*, pp. 519-521.
48. Smith, *op. cit.*, p. 222.
49. Ashley Roach, "Maritime Boundary Delimitation : United States Practice," *Ocean Development and International Law*, vol. 44, 2013, pp. 6-7.
50. In the 2002 Volga case, ITLOS vice president Vukas said that he voted in favour of the Tribunal's findings since he agreed with the findings with regard to their main objective, the release of the Volga. Besides, he expressed regrets as to the establishment of the EEZ off the shores of those 'uninhabitable and uninhabited' islands such as Heard and Mcdonald. *The Volga Case, Judgement, ITLOS*, 2002, Declaration of Judge Vukas.
51. *Black Sea case*, *op. cit.*, para. 187; Jon M. Van Dyke, "The Romania v. Ukraine Decision and Its Effect on East Asian Maritime Delimitations," *Ocean and Coastal Law Journal*, vol. 15, 2010, p. 261. Serpents' Island is $0.17km^2$ in area and the distance from the Danube triangle is about 20 miles.
52. *South China Sea case*, *op. cit.*, paras. 281-282.
53. *Ibid.*, paras. 534-548. The Tribunal found that the capacity of a feature should be assessed with due regard to the potential for a group of small island features to collectively sustain human habitation and economic life. A feature that is only capable of sustaining habitation through the continued delivery of supplies from outside does not meet the requirements of Article 121(3). Nor does economic activity that remains entirely dependent on external resources or that is devoted to using a feature as an object for extractive activities, without the involvement of a local population, constitute a feature's 'own' economic life.
54. *Ibid.*, paras. 554-556.
55. *Ibid.*, para. 407.
56. *Ibid.*, para. 578.
57. *Ibid.*, paras. 582-584.
58. *Ibid.*, paras. 585-593.

59. *Ibid.*, paras. 597-601.
60. *Ibid.*, paras. 615-622.
61. China protested Japan's use of Okinotori as a basepoint in a note dated 9 February 2009. However, China claimed all the insular formations in the Spratly Islands in order to establish EEZs and continental shelves around them. Smith, *op. cit.*, pp. 222-223.
62. Yoshifumi Tanaka, *The International Law of the Sea*, Cambridge, 2nd Edition, 2015, p. 197.
63. *North Sea Continental Shelf cases, Judgement, ICJ Reports*, 1969, para. 101.
64. L. D. M. Nelson, "The Roles of Equity in the Delimitation of Maritime Boundaries," *American Journal of International Law*, vol. 84, 1990, pp. 837-838.
65. According to Prosper Weil, since the judgment on North Sea cases in 1969, the applicability of the equidistance rule was gradually diminished and the equity doctrine gained strength the most at the Tunisia/Libya and Gulf of Maine cases. Equidistance rule, however, returned to the middle ground at the Libya/Malta case partially due to the emergence of EEZ. Prosper Weil, *The Law of Maritime Delimitation-Reflections*, Grotius Publications, 1989, pp. 169-177.
66. ICJ noted that equidistance/special circumstances rule and equitable principles/relevant circumstances rule are closely related. Qatar/Bahrain case, *op. cit.*, paras. 230-231.
67. *Continental Shelf (Libyan Arab Jamahiriya/Malta), Judgment, ICJ Reports*, 1985, para. 60.
68. *Dispute Concerning Delimitation of the Maritime Boundary between Bangladesh and Myanmar in the Bay of Bengal (Bay of Bengal), Judgment, ITLOS*, 2012, para. 116.
69. *Ibid.*, para. 120; Roach pointed out that population, socioeconomic factors, conduct of parties in other negotiations, size of landmass, and lack of natural resources are not generally considered relevant.
70. *Black Sea case, op. cit.*, para. 122.
71. United Nations, Division for Ocean Affairs and the Law of the Sea, *Handbook on the Delimitation of Maritime Boundaries*, 2000, p. 33.
72. *Ibid.*
73. David H. Anderson, "Maritime Delimitation in the Black Sea Case (Romania v. Ukraine)," *The Law and Practice of International Courts and Tribunals*, vol. 8, 2009, p. 323.
74. Bay of Bengal, *op. cit.*, paras. 318-319.
75. *Ibid; Continental Shelf (Tunisia/Libyan Arab Jamahiriya), Judgment, ICJ Reports*, 1982, pp. 74-75.
76. United Nations, *op. cit.*, p. 34.
77. *Territorial and Maritime Dispute between Nicaragua and Honduras in the Caribbean Sea (Nicaragua v. Honduras), Judgment, ICJ Reports*, 2007. para. 300.
78. Jon M. Van Dyke, "Legal Issues Related to Sovereignty over Dokdo Its Maritime Boundary," *Ocean Development and International Law*, vol. 38, 2007, pp. 196-198.
79. *Nicaragua/Colombia case, op. cit.*, paras. 228-236.

The Illegality of China's Economic Retaliation for the Republic of Korea's Deployment of the THAAD System under General International Law*

CHOI Seung-Hwan
Professor, Kyung Hee University Law School, Seoul, Korea

Abstract

The decision made by the government of the Republic of Korea ("ROK" or "Korea") on July 8, 2016 to deploy the Terminal High Altitude Area Defense ("THAAD") anti-missile system in Korean territory resulted in China's fierce condemnation and unilateral economic retaliation against a variety of Korean products and services. China's fierce opposition to the deployment of the THAAD system has brought tensions in the Northeast Asian region to an all-time high, and it has been predicted that North Korea's development of nuclear weapons and missiles will lead to further proliferation, despite economic sanctions imposed on North Korea by the international community according to the Resolutions for non-proliferation against North Korea, which had been adopted by the UN Security Council eleven times as of December 30, 2018.

This article reviews major legal issues related to China's THAAD economic retaliations and appraises its legality under international law, taking into account the realities of China's retaliatory measures taken since the decision of the deployment of

* This article is a modified and extracted version of my paper ("Legal Issues and Appraisals of China's Economic Retaliations for South Korea's THAAD Deployment under International Law") which was published at 62 *Korean Journal of International Law* 169, September 2017. The author may be contacted at: tomichoi@khu.ac.kr.

the THAAD system in July, 2016. Based on relevant cases and materials, the author argues that China's economic retaliation for the deployment of THAAD is not justified as a lawful retortion or reprisal, nor consistent with the duty of non-intervention in the internal affairs of other States under general international law, and violates the duty of peaceful settlement of disputes under the United Nations (UN) Charter (Article 2.3).

This article also proposed a reasonable policy solution for the peaceful settlement of ROK-China THAAD disputes pursuant to general international law. Considering China's uncompromising position that the deployment of the THAAD system in Korea must be withdrawn because it impairs one of China's key values and interests, the Korean government should properly reflect China's concerns over the deployment of the THAAD system, and may suggest a compromise: First of all, the ROK may make official commitments to limiting the detecting range of THAAD to the North Korean territory rather than Chinese territory, and then to revoking the THAAD system immediately when the North Korean nuclear dispute is fully solved.

The ROK and China should be particularly aware that actively promoting 'win-win cooperation' to maintain power for economic development to ensure the continuous reciprocal growth of trade and investment is indispensable for securing sustainable peace and prosperity in the Northeast Asian region, certainly including job creation and the stabilization of livelihoods.

Key Words

Terminal High Altitude Area Defense (THAAD), economic retaliation, economic coercion, economic sanctions, national security, nuclear weapons, non-proliferation, World Trade Organization (WTO)

1. INTRODUCTION

On the background of four nuclear tests carried out and 76 ballistic missiles launched by North Korea between October 14, 2006 and March 2, 2016, the decision made by the government of the

Republic of Korea ("Korea" or "ROK") on July 8, 2016 to deploy the 'Terminal High Altitude Area Defense' ("THAAD") missile system within its territory led to a dramatic deterioration in what had been amicable relations between the ROK and China.[1] As a key part of the arsenal of the U.S. missile defense system, the THAAD system is capable of destroying short distance and intermediate ballistic missiles with less than 3000km-level range, by directly colliding with them at a high altitude of 40km~150km with intercept missiles, based on information received from radar and satellites, etc.[2]

As soon as the Korean government deployed the THAAD system, the Chinese government extended and reinforced the coverage and level of THAAD economic retaliation, through a so-called Chinese Restriction Order on the Korean Wave[3] ("CRO") covering home shopping, electronic commerce, fire safety facilities and tax investigation into places of business of Lotte Mart (Korean company) in China, a variety of cultural cooperation, travel and tourism services, activities of Korean Wave stars in China, customs clearance and import of commodities made in Korea and so on, not to mention a range of trade regulations.

China and Russia's fierce opposition to the deployment of the THAAD system has brought tensions in the Northeast Asian region to an all-time high, and it has been predicted that North Korea's development of nuclear weapons and missiles will lead to further proliferation. This is despite the economic sanctions imposed on North Korea by the international community according to the Resolutions for non-proliferation against North Korea, which had been adopted by the UN Security Council eleven times as of January 1, 2019.[4]

China's economic retaliation against the deployment of the THAAD system, the subject of analysis in this article, has been used as an economic [non-military] means to force the Korean government to reverse its decision on the deployment of the THAAD system. Generally, economic retaliation functions as a tool to achieve a particular political purpose by registering a complaint about a policy enforcement by another country, or compelling it to change its policy on a specific pending issue.

Powerful states such as the United States and China in particular have frequently taken advantage of economic retaliation as an effective means of dispute resolution, in relation to intervention in the internal affairs of other States and the peaceful settlement of international disputes, under the system of modern international law that completely prohibits the use or threat of force.[5]

Since 1978 China in particular has consistently used foreign policy as a means of promoting its own economic interests; however, since 2002 it has tended to prefer economic retaliation as an efficient medium to attain political and diplomatic goals related to 'China's strategic core interests.'[6] It may be presumed that this change of policy by China, which had traditionally condemned unilateral sanctions as illegal, began with the foreign policy of the new Hu Jintao administration (2002~2008), which intended to reflect China's growing economic and political influence in the international community in its international relations, following China's accession to the World Trade Organization (WTO) in December 2001.

For example, China's ban on the export of rare earth minerals to Japan, imposed in response to an incident in which the Japanese government arrested the Chinese captain of a vessel that trespassed the territorial sea of Senkaku Archipelago (Diaoyudao in Chinese) on September 8, 2010, ultimately led to the release of the Chinese captain on September 24, 2010.[7]

In this article, economic retaliation will be clearly distinguished as a concept from economic sanctions. In general, while economic sanctions under international law are economic and coercive measures taken by State(s) individually or collectively according to international law or resolutions of international organizations which are endowed with competency over sanctions, economic retaliation is a forceful economic measure taken by State(s) unilaterally that is not based on international law or resolutions of international organizations.[8]

Generally, powerful states in particular tend to prefer the terminology 'economic sanctions' as a means of ensuring friendly public opinion internationally and securing public support domestically, as economic sanctions are legitimate countermeasures against violations of international law, and thus the use of this term suggests the legitimacy of a national policy domestically and internationally. In this article, the author will use the terminology 'economic retaliation' because China's countermeasures against the deployment of the THAAD system failed to meet the requirement of legitimacy under general international law and the WTO Agreements.[9]

The main purpose of this article is to examine major issues in relation to China's THAAD economic retaliation against the ROK, and to appraise whether such retaliation may be considered legal and legitimate under general international law. For this purpose, part II of this article will introduce the realities of China's retaliatory measures against the ROK taken since the decision of the deployment of the THAAD system on July 8, 2016. In part III, this article will examine and assess primary issues in relation to China's economic retaliation measures under general international law. Finally, the article will propose a policy solution for the peaceful settlement of ROK-China THAAD disputes pursuant to general international law in part IV.

2. TYPES OF THAAD ECONOMIC RETALIATION MEASURES

According to the Industrial Policy Report published by the Korea Institute for Industrial Economics and Trade in May 2017, the number of Chinese tourists in Korea (7 million people in total as of 2017) was reduced by approximately 60% for a month after the sales ban on Korea tour products triggered by THAAD retaliation on

March 15, 2017, compared to the same month in the previous year.[10] An analysis that takes the shopping cost per person (about 1,600 US dollars) into account estimates that the damage of revenue loss in the field of domestic distribution will range from 4.9 billion dollars to 5.5 billion dollars, if the 'CRO' lasts 6 months and the number of Chinese tourists drops in arange from 30% to 70% in comparison to the same period in the previous year.[11]

According to research data on international balance of payments issued by the Bank of Korea on August 3, 2017, the deficit of travel account balance for the first half of 2017 amounted to 7.74 billion dollars, a dramatic increase of more than two times compared to the deficit (3.5 billion US dollars) of the same term in the previous year. In the meantime, the number of Chinese tourists was reduced by 66%, and it was said that the deficit in the travel account balance was the largest ever.

The THAAD controversy has had negative effects on the sales performance of Korean automobiles in the Chinese market.[12] As of June 1, 2017, sales of Hyundai and Kia automobiles in China had declined by about 65% in comparison to the same period in the previous year. The decline in sales of Hyundai and Kia automobiles in China has had an adverse effect on even medium- and small-sized subcontractors which export automotive components.

It is estimated that Lotte Group, a Korean conglomerate which agreed to allow the Korean government to use some of its property in Korea for the THAAD system and has invested in China through companies including Lotte Mart, suffered a loss of about 1 billion 55.5 million dollars due to China's THAAD economic retaliation.[13] Another study also evaluated that total amount of damage to Korean companies caused by China's economic retaliation amounted to 14 billion 74 million dollars.[14]

China's economic retaliation measures related to the deployment of the THAAD system have been pursued through diverse means, including buyers' boycotts of commodities (cars, cell phones, and home appliances and so forth) made in Korea, adjustment of regulations on customs clearance and import and sanitary and phytosanitary measures of products (cosmetics, bidet, and food and so on) made in Korea, tax investigations into Lotte Mart and safety regulations, business suspension of 23 branches of Lotte Mart, anti-dumping investigations into polyacetylene and polysilicon made in Korea, exclusion or cancellation of a subsidy for battery-equipped vehicles made in Korea, disapproval of navigating non-periodic flights (chartered flights) to Korea, cancelation and indefinite postponement of concerts for famous Korean musicians (Kunwoo Paik, Sumi Jo, EXO, etc.), musicals (Jekyll and Hyde) and art exhibitions (Shanghai Municipal Yuzu Museum) in China, rejection and suspension within China of broadcasting distribution for movies, teleplays, and entertainment programs made in Korea, and a sales ban on tourism service products heading for Korea.

3. MAJOR ISSUES AND APPRAISAL OF THAAD ECONOMIC RETALIATION MEASURES UNDER GENERAL INTERNATIONAL LAW

3-1. Illegitimacy of Retortion

Under general international law, the concept of retortion is clearly distinguished from reprisal which is exempted from its illegality, as the latter is taken as a countermeasure against an act by another state having violated international law. Retortion does not constitute an illegal act because it is merely an unfriendly act taken as a countermeasure against an unfriendly or unfair act by another state.

For instance, retortion includes measures revoking economic aid conferred without an obligation under international law, or withdrawing privileges provided for nationals of other States. But to secure its legitimacy, a retortion must not breach international law. Countermeasures taken as retortion do not have any constraints, unless they are illegal under international law.

For this reason, for its countermeasures to be justified as retortion under international law, China's economic retortion measures against the deployment of the THAAD system must not violate international law or its other obligations under international treaties such as the United Nations Charter, WTO Agreements, and the ROK-China FTA. Although China does not have to abide by the rule of proportionality in order to justify retortion measures under international law, it must withdraw immediately once the act that provoked the retortion ceases to exist.[15]

3-2. Illegitimacy of Reprisal

Since reprisal is defined as countermeasures taken against measures of other States that violate international law, it is not considered as illegal under international law. Reprisal has a coercive and punitive nature, because it compels target States to change their policy, or is used to punish their acts violating international law. The legality of economic reprisal under international law was confirmed in the Indonesian tobacco nationalization case in the Bremen Appellate Court of Germany.[16] Economic reprisal, i.e., the suspension of compensation and concession, has also been recognized as having legitimacy, within the range that is compatible with the GATT 1994 (Article XXIII) and the Dispute Settlement Understanding (DSU; Article 22, Article 23) in the WTO system.

In order for China's economic retaliation against the deployment of the THAAD system to be considered a legitimate reprisal under international law, the ROK must have acted in violation of international law as a precondition for such reprisal. Since the deployment of the THAAD system within the Korean territory is a legitimate measure based on the right of self-defense under international law to protect its territorial integrity and political independence from North Korea's nuclear attacks, it is likely impossible for the Chinese government to justify its economic retaliation against the deployment of the THAAD system as a reprisal that is allowed under international law.

In general, for a reprisal to be legitimate under international law, the following four conditions must be met: i) there must exist acts or measures in breach of international law, which triggered countermeasures for reprisal, ii) redress by other means must be completed or impossible, iii) reprisal must be made only to the extent necessary and iv) the reprisal must be immediately revoked as soon as the illegal acts are rectified - i.e., when the State in question takes proper measures to rescind its state responsibility under international law.[17]

3-3. Violation of the Duty of Peaceful Settlement of Disputes

Does China's economic retaliation against the deployment of the THAAD system violate the duty of peaceful settlement of disputes under international law? All other means of dispute settlement which do not involve the use of force and threat may be considered as peaceful means in the sense that any coercive measure violates the UN Charter (Article 2.3, Article 33) which provides the duty of peaceful settlement of disputes, and that under Article 2.4 of the UN Charter (principle of non-use of force), "force" does not include economic sanctions or retaliation.[18]

However, it should be noted that Article 2.3 of the UN Charter imposes the duty of dispute settlement by peaceful means on Members in a manner that ensures international peace and security, and justice are not endangered, while Article 33.1 demands that

Members engaged in any dispute, the continuance of which is likely to put the maintenance of international peace and security at risk, first of all must settle the dispute by negotiation, enquiry, mediation, conciliation, arbitration, judicial settlement, resort to regional agencies or arrangements or other peaceful means of their own choice.

Economic retaliation, which can be considered as economic coercion, may also be classified as a type of compulsive and enforced means of dispute settlement because non-military sanctions under Chapter VII (Action with respect to threats to the peace, breaches of the peace and acts of aggression) of the UN Charter on coercive settlement of disputes includes economic sanctions or retaliation, contrary to chapter VI on pacific settlement of disputes. Therefore, China's economic retaliation against the deployment of the THAAD system violates the duty of pacific settlement of disputes provided by the UN Charter, unless such economic retaliation is permitted under international law such as the UN Charter, the WTO Agreements and the ROK-China FTA.

3-4. Violation of the Duty of Non-Intervention in Internal Affairs

Article 2.7 of the UN Charter prescribes the duty of non-intervention by UN in the domestic affairs of its Members. Conversely, the principle of the duty of non-intervention in the internal affairs of other States is a legal principle which corresponds to the principle of sovereign equality as a fundamental right and duty of a State established under general international law. In other words, States cannot exercise their national jurisdiction to endanger the political independence or territorial integrity of other States, or to intervene in their domestic affairs under general principles of international law: "A state cannot exercise jurisdiction over another state." (*par in parem non habet imperium*).[19]

The duty of non-intervention in the internal affairs of other

States established under customary international law is elaborated on more specifically and extensively in other UN Resolutions. 'The Declaration on the Inadmissibility of Intervention into Domestic Affairs of States in accordance with the Charter of the United Nations'[20] adopted at the UN General Assembly in 1965 provides that no State has the right to any form of interference, including armed intervention, against any other State, and further that no State may use or encourage all other forms of coercive interference to obtain from another State the subordination of the exercise of its sovereign rights, or to secure from its advantages of any kind.

The duty of non-intervention in internal affairs was also confirmed in the 'Declaration on Principles of International Law concerning Friendly Relations and Co-operation among States'[21] (Resolution 26/25(XXV) by the UN General Assembly in 1970), the 'Resolution on Permanent Sovereignty over Natural Resources in 1973,'[22] and the 'Charter of Economic Rights and Duties of States' (Resolution 3281(XXIX) by the UN General Assembly in 1974) and so on. In particular, the 'Charter of Economic Rights and Duties of States'[23] of 1974 prescribed that no state may use or encourage the use of economic, political or any other type of measures to coerce (emphasis added) another state to obtain from it the subordination of the exercise of its sovereign rights (Article 32).

Some commentators criticize that if interpreted literally, the prohibition on intervening in the internal affairs of other States is merely a *de facto* meaningless and nominal agreement, because the duty of non-intervention in internal affairs confirmed in Resolutions by the UN General Assembly mentioned above is too general.[24]

However, although some Resolutions adopted by the UN General Assembly lack normative nature as treaties and the texts of the Resolutions mentioned above are very general and comprehensive, the Resolutions may play an important role in concretely confirming and proving the content of the duty of non-intervention in internal affairs established under customary international law, in the sense that the Resolutions reflect the legal conviction of international community. Consequently, the Resolutions by the UN General Assembly which prohibit coercive interference may be recognized as evidence of customary international law, and numerous scholars of international law hold the same view that modern international law does not allow arbitrary and discriminatory economic coercion or retaliation, based on the evidence.[25]

It should be noted that the 'Declaration on Principles of International Law concerning Friendly Relations and Co-operation among States' in 1970 and the 'Charter of Economic Rights and Duties of States' in 1974 provide that government authorities are prohibited from directly utilizing economic coercion to subordinate the exercise of sovereign rights by other States, and also cannot even encourage individuals or private entities to use economic coercion to other States.

Therefore, not only the Chinese government authorities' economic retaliation to coerce the withdrawal of ROK's deployment of the THAAD system but also their acts encouraging individuals or private entities to use economic retaliation are in violation of the duty of non-intervention in the internal affairs of other States, which has been established under customary international law.

4. CONCLUSION: IN SEARCH OF A CREATIVE AND REASONABLE SOLUTION

Although the magnitude of the economic retaliation taken by China should not be overestimated, it is irresponsible for the Korean government to allow serious damage to the affected companies and industries to continue by underestimating or neglecting the severity of its effects. China's economic retaliation against Korean companies may have negative effects on the Korean economy and on national security, in that efforts to enhance Korea's security given North Korea's nuclear threats require enormous financial resources, which are dependent on continuous economic development through the expansion of export and investment.

If the THAAD system can technically protect the national territory from North Korea's nuclear attacks, the system, which is not a weapon to attack, but simply a response system for defense, must be deployed as an effective and legitimate means based on the right of self-defense under international law. However, if the THAAD system is not technically capable of effectively defending Korea's national territory from North Korea's nuclear attacks, the ROK's policy in relation to the deployment of the THAAD system must be reexamined from the perspective of improvement of efficiency for national security and pragmatic settlement of trade disputes. It should be noted that the THAAD system in Korea will put international peace and security in the Northeast Asian region at risk by requiring an astronomical maintenance expense to operate the system, and by accelerating the arms race and weakening the international coordinating system among relevant States (the United States, Japan, China, and Russia in particular) surrounding the Korean Peninsula that aims to block the nuclear proliferation efforts of North Korea.[26]

The most ideal method to make China withdraw its economic retaliation against ROK is to rescind the THAAD system after achieving the denuclearization of the Korean Peninsula by peacefully solving the North Korea's nuclear threat, with the cooperation of the United States, China, Russia and North Korea. It may, however, be very difficult to realize the peaceful settlement of North Korea's nuclear threat in the near future, taking into account North Korea's determination to pursue nuclear development, given that it has carried out nuclear tests as many as six times despite eleven nonproliferation Resolutions against North Korea being adopted by the UN Security

Council.

What is a realistically feasible way of inducing China to withdraw its economic retaliation in order to prevent an irrevocable collapse of the ROK-China's friendly relations? Considering China's uncompromising position that the deployment of the THAAD system in Korea must be withdrawn because it impairs one of China's key values and interests, the Korean government should properly reflect China's concerns over the deployment of the THAAD system, and may suggest a compromise: First of all, the ROK may make official commitments to limiting the detecting range of THAAD to the North Korean territory rather than Chinese territory,[27] and then to revoking the THAAD system immediately when the North Korean nuclear dispute is fully solved.

When China fulfills its responsible political determination as a G2 State for the effective settlement of the North Korean nuclear threat, China's concerns about the deployment of the THAAD system in Korea can be also properly reflected by the ROK for the satisfactory implementation of its operation and policy. The ROK and China should be particularly aware that actively promoting "win-win cooperation" to maintain power for economic development to ensure the continuous reciprocal growth of trade and investment is essential for securing sustainable peace and prosperity in the Northeast Asian region, certainly including job creation and the stabilization of livelihoods.

As one of the optional countermeasures under international trade law to make China withdraw its unilateral economic retaliation, the ROK may bring this case to the Dispute Settlement Body of the WTO, arguing that China's retaliatory measures violate WTO Agreements including the General Agreement on Trade in Services. The option of dispute settlement through the WTO may clarify the basis of ROK's trade policy, separating political and diplomatic matters from trade issues domestically and internationally, while making international public opinion more favorable to the ROK's position, by informing the international community of the Chinese government's illegitimate economic retaliation, and clarifying the Korean government's will to peacefully settle trade disputes related to the THAAD economic retaliation in accordance with the WTO dispute settlement procedures.

As an example, the Chinese government banned the export of rare earth resources to Japan as retaliation, when the Japanese government took the captain of a Chinese vessel which invaded the territorial sea of the Senkaku Islands (Diaoyudao in Chinese) into custody in September 2010. As a response to these export controls by China, the Japanese government brought the case to the Dispute Settlement Body of the WTO, arguing that China's export restrictions on rare earth resources to Japan violated GATT and WTO Agreements, and succeeded in revoking the Chinese government's export control on rare earth resources.[28]

Considering the empirical research by experts on cases of unilateral economic retaliation and the Chinese government's recent tendency to ensure China's essential interests of international law and to use unilateral economic retaliation as an efficient means to attain its foreign policy goals, it is highly likely that the Chinese government will continue to resume its unilateral economic retaliation, whenever its core strategic state interests conflict with those of other states.

Consequently, the Korean government authorities should reinforce the structure of industry to minimize the damage caused by any economic retaliation similar to the consequences of the deployment of the THAAD system, and take the opportunity to diversify exports and investments and to consolidate the diplomatic capacity and status of the ROK.

Notes

1. On April 27, 2017, the Korean government installed 2 launching pads for the THAAD system at Seongju, North Gyeongsang Province, and on September 7, 2017, it completed its additional deployment of 4 launching pads for the THAAD system as a response to North Korea's 6th nuclear test on September 3, 2017. According to the Korean government, this deployment of the THAAD system is temporary, taking into account the severity and urgency of national security, and it expressed its position that it would make a decision on the final deployment of the THAAD system after checking the health and environmental risks posed by the launchers and associated equipment, including a powerful AN/TPY-2 radar, in accordance with the process of general environmental impact assessment. *The Korea Times*, Sept. 10, 2017. <http://www.koreatimes.co.kr/www/nation/2017/09/113_236218.html> [Last visit on July 8, 2018].
2. Whie Jung Kim, "Chinese Restriction Order on the Korean Wave and Challenges for Korean Cultural Content Industry," *Issues and Perspectives* (National Assembly Research Service, 2017. 2. 21), pp. 1-3.
3. The Korean Wave means a phenomenon that those related to Korea including Korean public culture are getting all the more popular and sensational with the people in countries outside of Korean territory.
4. As of January 1, 2019, the Security Council of UN adopted eleven Resolutions for Non-Proliferation against North Korea: Res. 1695(2006.7.15), Res. 1718 (2006.10.14), Res. 1874(2009.6.12), Res. 2087(2013.1.22), Res. 2094(2013.3.7), Res. 2270(2016.3.2), Res. 2321(2016.11.30), Res. 2356(2017.6.2), Res. 2371 (2017.9.11), Res. 2397(2017.12.22).
5. G. Hufbauer and J. Schott, *Economic Sanctions Reconsidered: History and Current Policy* (Institute for International Economics, 1985), p. 7.
6. James Reilly, "China's Unilateral Sanctions," 35 *The Washington Quarterly* 21 (Fall 2012), p. 121. Generally, the Chinese government considers territorial integrity, sovereignty (including one China Policy related to Taiwan), security and human policy (including human right control on dissidents) as its strategic core interests or values.
7. B. S. Glaser, "China's Coercive Economic Diplomacy," *The Diplomat*, July 25, 2012 <http://thediplomat.com/2012/07/chinas-coercive-economic-diplomacy> [Last visited on July 8, 2018].
8. Seung Hwan Choi, "The Legality of Export Control as Economic Coercion," *Korean Journal of International Law*, Vol. 37, No. 2 (1992. 12), pp. 232-233.
9. With respect to the characterization of trade restrictions of China against the deployment of the THAAD system, Korean and western commentators prefer economic retaliation, while Chinese scholars and press prefer economic sanctions. Bruce Harrison, "China's Response over Thaad in S. Korea," 32 *Chinese American Forum* 10 (June 2017); B. S. Glaser, D. G. Sofio, and D. A. Parker, "The Good, the THAAD, and the Ugly: China's Campaign Against Deployment, and What

to Do About It," *Foreign Affairs* (Feb. 15, 2017). <https://www.foreignaffairs.com/articles/united-states/2017-02-15/good-thaad-and-ugly> [Last visit on July 8, 2017].

10. Imja Rhee and Youngwon Cho, "The Chinese Government's Restrictions on Travel to Korea and its Influences on Korean Consumer Goods Industry," *i-KIET Issues & Analysis*, No. 19 (KIET, 2017. 5. 22), pp. 6-7.

11. Bank of Korea, Statistics: International Balance of Payment of the Republic of Korea, 2017. 8. 3. <http://www.bok.or.kr/contents/total/ko/boardView.action?boardBean.brdid=138117&boardBean.menuid=559&boardBean.rnum=2&menuNaviId=559&boardBean.cPage=1&boardBean.categorycd=0> [Last visit on August 4, 2017].

12. "Chinese retaliation on THAAD puts squeeze on Hyundai Motor," *The Economist*, August 30, 2017. <http://country.eiu.com/article.aspx?articleid=1325843716&Country=South%20Korea&topic=Politics&subtopic=Forecast&subsubtopic=International+relations &u=1&pid=1715924755&oid=1715924755&uid=1> [Last visit on July 8, 2018].

13. Maeil Business News Korea, October 22, 2018.

14. Dong-A Daily News, March 18, 2017.

15. A. Beirlaen, "Economic Coercion and Justifying Circumstances," 18 *Revue de Droit International* 56 (1984-1985), pp. 63-64.

16. Indonesian Tobacco Case, 28 *International Law Report* 16 (Court of Appeal, Bremen, 1959): "Reprisals are, however, ---, a legal institution recognized in international law and in private law." *Ibid.*, p. 38.

17. D.W. Bowett, "Economic Coercion and Reprisals by States," 13 *Virginia Journal of International Law* 1 (1972), pp. 9-10; A. Beirlaen, *supra* note 15, p. 66; B. A. Weston, R. A. Falk, A. A. D'Amato, *International Law and World Law* (West Publishing Co., 1980), pp. 738-739.

18. Y. Z. Blum, "Economic Boycotts in International Law," in R. M. Mersky (ed.), Conference on Transnational Economic Boycotts and Coercion, Vol.I (Oceana Publications, 1978), p. 6; D. A. Baldwin, *Economic Statecraft* (Princeton University Press, 1985), pp. 346-347.

19. M. Schröder, "Non-Intervention, Principles of," in R. Bernhardt(ed.), *Encyclopedia of Public International Law*, V. 7 (Elsevier Science Publishers, 1984), p. 358.

20. Declaration on the Admissibility of Intervention into Domestic Affairs of States, G.A. Res.2131(xx) 20 U.N.GAOR, Supp.14, at 11, U.N.Doc.A/6014 (1965).

21. Declaration on Principles of International Law concerning Friendly Relations and Co-operation among States in accordance with the Charter of the United Nations, G.A. Res.2625(xxv) 259 U.N.GAOR, Supp.28, at 121, U.N.Doc.A/8028 (1970).

22. Resolution on Permanent Sovereignty over Natural Resources, G.A.Res.3171 (xxVIII) 28 U.N.GAOR, Supp.30, at 52, U.N.Doc.A/9030 (1973).

23. Charter of Economic Rights and Duties of States, G.A.Res.3281(xxix), 29 U.N. GAOR, Supp.31, at 50, 55, U.N.Doc.A/9631 (1974).

24. R. B. Lillich, "Economic Coercion and the New International Economic Law: A Second Look at Some First Thoughts," 16 *Virginia Journal of International Law* 223 (1976), p. 238.

25. D. W. Bowett, "International Law and Economic Coercion," 16 *Virginia Journal of International Law* 245 (1976), pp. 248-249; I. Seidl-Hohenveldern, "The United Nations and Economic Coercion," 18 *Revue Belge de Droit International* 9 (1984-85), p. 12; R. A. Falk, "On the Quasi-Legislative Competence of the General Assembly," 60 *American Journal of International Law* 782 (1966); R. Higgins, *The Development of International Law through the Political Organs of the United Nations* (Oxford University Press, 1963), p. 5.
26. Brianni Lee, "THAAD Deployment in South Korea," 38 *Harvard International Review* 34 (Special Issue, Winter 2017), p. 37(arguing that the THAAD deployment in the Republic of Korea will result in a destructive armament race).
27. The Chinese authorities have strongly protested that the THAAD's radar system could be used to spy on its territory. "A geopolitical row with China damages South Korean business further," *The Economist*, Oct. 19, 2017. <https://www.economist.com/business/2017/10/19/a-geopolitical-row-with-china-damages-south-korean-business-further> [Last visit on July 8, 2018].
28. *China-Measures Related to the Exportation of Rare Earths, Tungsten and Molybdenum*, WT/DS 431, 423, 433/AB/R, Aug. 7, 2014.

A Supplementary Consideration of Professor Schrijver's Study on the ICJ's Precedents Related to Sovereignty over Disputed Islands and the Study of Dokdo

SUNG Jae-Ho
Professor, Sungkyunkwan University Law School, Seoul, Korea

YOO Jun-Koo
Research Professor, Korea National Dipomatic Academy, Ministry of Foreign Affairs, Seoul, Korea

Abstract

The ICJ has made some decisions on small islands and terra nullius which can be analogically extended to the dispute over Dokdo Island. Professor Schrijver made an analysis of the trend in the recent ICJ's rulings in the five cases of territorial dispute focusing three key issues of the cases: original title, treaty-based title and title by effective control.

Since the disputing parties' claims to the islands are respectively grounded on original title and title by the occupation of terra nullius, historical or original title is an important issue in the territorial dispute over islands. Professor Schrijver pointed out, regarding the dispute over Dokdo between Korea and Japan, that in the case of the absence of crucial historical sources on original title to Dokdo, weight is put on acts à titre de souverain on the island and the effective control of it in the determination of sovereignty over it, noting that Korea is seemingly in a strong position in this respect. The ICJ referred to the Eastern Greenland Case to establish criteria for the degrees of effective control of the disputed islands. One country's claim to sovereignty over a territory based on its continuous exercise of the sovereignty needs to be grounded on the facts about such exercise of the territorial rights and the intention to exert them. The effective control of Dokdo seems appropriate when considered from one side. However, Japan asserts, regarding its sovereignty over Dokdo, both treaty-based title and historic title to it, which are logically incompatible in some cases. For this reason, Japan has also changed its positions from time to time.

One may agree with Professor Schrijver's view that the ICJ place treaty-based title above other title. However, as seen in the five cases he discussed, it is rash to say that the ICJ has consistently put emphasis on treaty-based title handling disputes over territorial sovereignty. However, it is reasonable to consider that the Court has made rulings depending on the relative certainty and validity of the three kinds of title. From this viewpoint, the dispute over Dokdo between Korea and Japan seems to be centered on differences in the two countries' assertions regarding their historic title to and effective control of the island. The historical sources show that Korea's recognition of Dokdo and management of it as an act of state had existed long before the dispute arose and the two countries' recognitions represented in the above sources suggest that Korea's sovereignty over Dokdo had been established during the earlier times.

Key Words

Dokdo, historic title, treaty-based title, effective control, acts à titre de souverain, SCAPIN No. 677, 1951 Treaty of San Francisco

1. TRENDS AND FEATURES OF RECENT ICJ PRECEDENTS ON SOVEREIGNTY OVER ISLANDS

1-1. ICJ Precedents on Disputes over Small Islands and Terra Nullius, and Implications for the Dokdo Issue

As pointed out by Professor Schrijver, over the last 15 years the International Court of Justice has made significant decisions about small islands and *terra nullius* that can be analogically extended to the dispute over Dokdo Island. The issues raised in those ICJ cases provide several implications for the Dokdo issue. The precedents represent the ICJ's attitudes and positions towards historical facts and evidentiary issues, and Professor Schrijver analyzed five of these rulings. First, the *Case Concerning Maritime Delimitation and Territorial Questions between Qatar and Bahrain* (Qatar v. Bahrain) (2001) is a good precedent that suggests on which principles of international law judgments are made when a dispute arises between states regarding territorial or maritime boundaries[1] As the ICJ ruled on the sovereignty over the Hawar Islands and Janan Island and the delimitation of maritime boundaries in this case, it provides many implications for Korea.

Next, the *Case Concerning Sovereignty over Pulau Ligitan and Pulau Sipadan* (Indonesia v. Malaysia) (2002) is a case on the territorial dispute over Ligitan and Sipadan Islands, and provides insights into the recent trend in theories on the general principles of international law in relation to the acquisition and loss of territories and relevant precedents. As such, it is a significant case that can also be analogically extended to the dispute over Dokdo.[2] Based on the facts and legal issues regarding the case, Ligitan and Sipadan can be substituted by Dokdo, Malaysia by Korea and Indonesia by Japan, respectively. Among the key issues raised in the case were the cession and succession of the title to the two islands, the effective exercise of state functions, and the title to and the effective control of the islands in accordance with Article 4 of the Convention between Great Britain and the Netherlands Defining Boundaries in Borneo, which was concluded on June 20, 1891.

The third important case analyzed by Professor Schrijver is the *Case Concerning Territorial and Maritime Dispute between Nicaragua and Honduras in the Caribbean Sea* (Nicaragua v. Honduras) (2007). In this case, the ICJ first made a ruling on the delimitation of boundaries in the Caribbean maritime territories between the two countries and then ruled on the sovereignty over Bobal, Savanna, Port Royal, and South

Cays in the disputed waters.[3] This case provides significant implications for the major issues related to Dokdo on which Japan and Korea have different positions, such as original title, *uti possidetis* and effective control.

Fourth, the *Case Concerning Sovereignty over Pedra Branca/Pulau Batu Puteh, Middle Rocks, and South Ledge* (Malaysia v. Singapore) (2008) is a case in which the ICJ ruled on the sovereignty on the three maritime features, that is Pedra Branca Island (former Portuguese dependency), Middle Rocks and South Ledge, all allocated between Malaysia and Singapore.[4] Making the ruling, the ICJ put weight on the legal implications of one state's acts à titre de souverain and the opponent's acquiescence in the situation where the maritime boundaries between the disputing parties were not delimited. In this respect, significant implications with regard to the Dokdo issue can be drawn from this case.

The fifth ICJ ruling discussed by Professor Schrijver was made on the Territorial and Maritime Dispute between Nicaragua and Colombia (2007/2012). The Court, dealing with the dispute over the Caribbean maritime territories between Nicaragua and Colombia, made decisions on the sovereignty over three islands-San Andrés Archipelago, Providencia and Santa Catalina-and seven reefs-Alburquerque Cays, East-Southeast Cays, Roncador Atoll, Serrana, Serranilla, Bajo Nuevo, and Quita Sueño Banks.[5] For the dispute over Dokdo, the case is deemed to have important implications, particularly in relation to treaty-based title and decisions on effective control.

1-2. Original Title as Grounds for Sovereignty over an Island

Historical or original title[6] is an important issue in the territorial dispute over Dokdo, and for the settlement of the dispute over Ligitan and Sipadan as well, a review of the title to the islands and their succession was carried out. The commonalities between the dispute and that over Dokdo can be summarized as follows. First, all of the three islands have been uninhabited for a long time, but there have been economic interests related to fishing activities around the islands. Second, like Japan and Korea, Indonesia and Malaysia both claim the historic title to the disputed islands, asserting that they have effectively controlled them since the times of their predecessors, and thus stress that the title currently belongs to them through concession or succession.[7] Third, Indonesia and Japan share commonalities in that both insist on the title to the disputed islands based on treaties signed in the past by imperialist or Western powers. Fourth, Malaysia and Korea both claim sovereignty over the islands in dispute mainly based on the historic title belonging to their predecessors and the cession and succession of it,[8] along with their present effective control of the islands.[9] Lastly, the two cases are similar in that the disputing countries are in a sharp conflict of interests over the determination of a critical date and its functions in the litigation.

The case concerning sovereignty over Pedra Branca/Pulau Batu Puteh, Middle Rocks, and South Ledge also set an important precedent regarding original title. It was the second East Asian territorial dispute to be brought before and ruled on by the ICJ, following the above-discussed case concerning sovereignty over Ligitan and Sipadan. In the case, Malaysia insisted that the maritime features belonged to its territory, claiming its original title to them. In other words, Malaysia asserted that Pedra Branca had been under the sovereignty of the Sultanate of Johor from time immemorial, and there was no evidence that Johor had ceded the island or abandoned its sovereignty over it; thus, Johor's title to the island had never been lost. Singapore, for its part, argued that Pedra Branca had been occupied by the United Kingdom, its predecessor. Since international law allows occupation only for *terra nullius*, Singapore denied Malaysia's original title to the island on the grounds that it had not belonged to the territory of Johor at the time of occupation.[10] The differences in the positions of Malaysia and Singapore is similar to that between Korea and Japan over Dokdo, particularly in that the disputing parties' claims to the islands are respectively grounded on original title and title by the occupation of *terra nullius*.

1-3. Treaty-Based Title and Title by an Arbitration Award

In most cases, to resolve territorial disputes, attempts are made to prove the title of the territory in question with a large volume of evidentiary documents. As noted by Professor Schrijver, the ICJ has recently placed particular emphasis on treaty-based title and title by an arbitration award in its handling of such disputes. Since treaty-based title and title by an arbitration award have been issues dealt with in the Qatar v. Bahrain and Nicaragua v. Colombia cases, they can provide a few implications for the Dokdo issue, particularly given that the judgments of the ICJ on the cases can analogically apply to Dokdo.

In the Qatar v. Bahrain Case, the ICJ reviewed the dispute over the sovereignty over the Zubarah region, the Hawar Islands and Janan Island and the delimitation of maritime boundaries between the two countries by analyzing the treaty-based title and title by an arbitration award to the region and islands in depth. The ICJ's ruling on the Zubarah region implies that a treaty serves as a considerably important basis for the determination of territorial sovereignty, and that even a treaty that has not entered into force can be given substantial significance in cases concerning territorial dispute. In other words, it seems that the ICJ does not regard the effectivity of a treaty as a decisive criterion for resolving such disputes. The ICJ also gave significance to the content "delivered" to the monarch of Bahrain in 1875, regardless of his consent. In other words, due to the fact that no strong resistance or objection had been expressed by the Bahraini monarch at that time, it was considered that he had "acquiesced." This implies the need to wisely respond to any problems raised through formal diplomatic channels in a territorial dispute between two countries, as a meaningless non-response runs a risk of being considered acquiescence.

Making a ruling on the title to the Hawar Islands, the ICJ reviewed the nature of an arbitration award and whether it could serve as a basis for determining territorial sovereignty.[11] Stating the procedure leading up to the decision of 1939 in detail, the ICJ expressed a negative view towards Bahrain's position that the decision of 1939 should be considered an arbitration award operating as a res judicata. Bahrain's claims implied that the ICJ had no jurisdiction to re-examine the arbitration award already in force.[12] Regarding this, the ICJ also reviewed the meanings of arbitration in international law: according to the Hague Convention for the Pacific Settlement of International Disputes of 1899, arbitration is defined as "settlement of any dispute between states concerned by arbitrators that they have chosen on the basis of respect for law." Regarding the decision made in 1939, the ICJ concluded that Qatar and Bahrain had only agreed that they let the UK, the "Protectorate" settle the case, and thus it held that the decision of 1939 did not qualify as an arbitration award.

This view of the ICJ suggests that consent to any procedure has great significance. In other words, the ICJ gives great significance to the conclusions drawn through any agreed upon procedure between two states. Therefore, the ICJ held that throughout the procedure leading up to the decision of 1939, Qatar should have been continuously raising complaints and objections if it were dissatisfied with the procedure or the direction of the settlement of the dispute through the procedure. From the ICJ's perspective, a country that faithfully participates in the procedure without such expression of complaints or objections may be deemed to have consented to the conclusions to be brought by it, as well as the procedure itself. Consent to any procedure or the direction of dispute settlement through the procedure is ultimately interpreted as consent to the results. Therefore, this case suggests that Korea should not make light of consent to any procedure. This is what Korea needs to keep in mind if the Dokdo dispute is brought to the ICJ.

1-4. Acts à Titre de Souverain and Effective Control

Regarding the dispute between Korea and Japan over Dokdo, Professor Schrijver pointed out that in the absence of crucial historical sources on original title to Dokdo, weight is put on acts à titre de souverain on the island and the effective control of it in the determination of sovereignty over it, noting that Korea is seemingly in a strong position in this respect. However, as Japan has continuously raised objections to Korea's acts à titre de souverain on Dokdo and effective control of it, he noted that those performed by the Korean government before 1952, when the dispute over the island had not yet been brought to the surface, can be important in settling the dispute. In the case of Indonesia v. Malaysia, Indonesia asserted that it had long maintained effective control of the islands in dispute, submitting evidence to confirm the activities of the Indonesian Navy and fishermen around the islands and the Royal Navy of the Netherlands' anchoring of their ships on the islands for a rest during their patrols.[13] On the other hand, Malaysia claimed to have effective control of the disputed islands on the grounds of the following three acts. First. the British colonial authorities, the predecessor of Malaysia, had established measures to control the hunting of turtles and the taking of turtle eggs and to settle related conflicts since the early 1900s.[14] Second, Malaysia argued that the British colonial authorities had designated Sipadan Island as a bird sanctuary, and made this fact public in official gazettes in 1933.[15] Third, after the independence of Indonesia, the authorities had installed lighthouses on Sipadan and Ligitan Islands in 1962 and 1963, respectively. The lighthouses still remain on the islands, maintained and managed by Malaysia.[16]

In light of Professor Schrijver's argument, Indonesia, claiming its sovereignty over the disputed islands, finds its title in the treaty concluded between two European imperialist countries of the time - that is, the UK and the Netherlands. In this respect, it can be evaluated that Indonesia is providing a stronger international legal basis for its sovereignty. In other words, the probative power of the treaty-based title claimed by Indonesia seems to be superior to that of the evidence submitted by Malaysia regarding its historic title and its effective control. However, the ICJ ruled that the two disputed islands are territories of Malaysia, contrary to this evaluation.[17]

The dispute over Dokdo between Japan and Korea and that over Ligitan and Sipadan between Indonesia and Malaysia share commonalities in several aspects. First, there have been economic interests from fishing activities around the islands since old times, and they are uninhabited. Second, like Indonesia and Malaysia, Japan and Korea both claim the historic title to the disputed islands, asserting that they have effectively controlled them since the times of their predecessors, and thus argue that the title currently belongs to them through concession or succession. Third, Indonesia and Japan insist on the title to the disputed islands based on the treaties signed by imperialist or Western powers in the past. Fourth, Malaysia and Korea claim sovereignty over the islands in dispute mainly based on the historic title belonging to their predecessors and the cession and succession of it, along with their present effective control of the islands. The ICJ made effective control before the critical date the basis upon which it judged the sovereignty of a country.[18] In other words, it rejected the succession of the title asserted by Malaysia and the title based on the Treaty of 1891 insisted on by Indonesia. The

Court, apart from the above two issues, compared the probative power of various evidence of the two countries' acts à titre de souverain - that is, their effective control - and ruled on whether they had sovereignty over the disputed islands or not.[19]

As pointed out by Professor Schrijver, it is noteworthy that the ICJ referred to the Eastern Greenland Case[20] to establish criteria for the degrees of effective control of the disputed islands and evaluate the acts of Indonesia and Malaysia. In the Eastern Greenland Case, the Permanent Court of International Justice ruled that one country's claim to sovereignty over a territory based on its continuous exercise of such sovereignty needs to be grounded in the objective facts about such exercise of the territorial rights and the intention to exert them. And in the case of a territory where people do not or cannot live, the Court ruled that a country's claim to sovereignty over it can be accepted though the degree of its exercise of such sovereignty is slightly weak, if the opponent has failed to provide evidence with superior probative power.[21] These conditions are similar to those of Indonesia and Malaysia in the case concerning their dispute over Ligitan and Sipadan in some aspects.[22]

2. KOREAN AND JAPANESE RECOGNITION OF DOKDO IN RELEVANT HISTORICAL SOURCES

2-1. Historical Sources on Dokdo

Professor Schrijver, regarding Korean historical sources on Dokdo and the country's historic title to it, noted that in many of them Dokdo is clearly mentioned, including *Samguk Sagi* (*History of the Three Kingdoms*, 1145), *Sejong Sillok Jiriji* (*Gazetteer in the Annals of King Sejong*, 1454), *Goryeosa Jiriji* (*Gazetteer of the History of Goryeo*, 1452), *Sinjeung Dongukyeojiseungram* (*Augmented Survey of the Geography of Korea*, 1531),

Dongguk Munheon Bigo (*Reference Compilation of Korean Documents*, 1770), and *Mangi Yoram* (*Book of Ten Thousand Techniques of Governance*, 1808).[23] In particular, *Dongguk Munheon Bigo* (1770) and *Mangi Yoram* (1808) clearly state that "Ulleungdo and Usando Islands are all belonging to Usanguk, and Usando is the island that the Japanese call Matsushima (松島, 'Songdo' in Korean)." In other words, these sources demonstrate that Usando and Dokdo were the same island, and Matsushima was the name by which the Japanese called Dokdo.[24] In addition, the activities of Korean fisherman Ahn Yong-bok are very important in the validation of Korea's claim to its sovereignty over Dokdo, and the historic records of his activities include *Sukjong Sillok* (*Annals of King Sukjong*, 1696) Volume 30, Entry September and *Jeungbo Munheon Bigo* (*Revised and Enlarged Edition of the Comparative Review of Records and Documents*) Volume 31, Entries Uljin, Usando, and Ulleungdo.[25]

Among the major Japanese sources that include records on Dokdo are *Onshu Shicho Goki* (*Records on Observations on Oki*), *Sangoku Tsuran Zusetsu* (J*apanese Rare Book Collection*, 1786) authored by Hayashi Shihei, *Chosenkoku Kosaishimatsu Naitansho* (*Confidential Inquiry into the Particulars of Korea's Relations with Japan*, 1870), the cadastral survey conducted in October 1876 by the Japanese Home Ministry, and *Chosen Engan Suiroshi* (*Sealanes along the Korean Coasts*) published by the Japanese Ministry of the Navy in 1933. According to some Japanese documents recognizing Korean sovereignty over Dokdo, in 1876 (Meiji 9), the Japanese Home Ministry, after reviewing the documents on the country's relations with Korea in the late 17th century, concluded that the Japanese government had already confirmed that Takeshima (Ulleungdo) and Matsushima (Dokdo) were territories of Korea in 1699 (Genroku 12) and thus that Japan had nothing to with the two islands, deciding to exclude them from the subjects of their cadastral survey.[26] The Japanese Home Ministry consulted the Dajokan Order (the Great Council of State), then the highest organ of the Japanese government, on this matter, thinking that it was necessary to do so. The Council also recognized that Takeshima (Ulleungdo) and "another island" - that is, Matsushima (Dokdo) - were the territories of Korea, and made the following directive in March 1877: "Note that our country has nothing to do with Takeshima (Ulleungdo) and another island (Dokdo) inquired about."[27]

As regards the activities of Ahn Yong-bok, some significant historical sources were found in Shimane Prefecture in May 2005. "Genroku Kyu Heishinen Chosen Bune Chakugan Ikkan no Oboegaki" (Sovereignty over Dokdo-Focus to the 9th year of Genroku Investigation Record), which is the report submitted to the bakufu on the results of the interrogation of Ahn who arrived at Oki District through the Oki Islands in May, 1696, contains the following record: "In Gangwon Province, there are Takeshima (Ulleungdo) and Matsushima (Dokdo) Islands." With this, the document invalidates the Japanese government's claim that the historical facts about Ahn Yong-bok were fabricated.[28] In other words, the report, which mentions the names of the eight provinces of Korea by referring to the map that Ahn was carrying with him, articulates that Ulleungdo and Dokdo belonged to Gangwon Province. Thus, the report clearly verifies Ahn's statement that Dokdo was the territory of Korea at the time of the interrogation.[29]

These historical sources show that Korea's recognition of Dokdo and management of it as an act of state had existed long before the dispute arose, and the two countries' recognitions represented in the above sources suggest that Korea's sovereignty over Dokdo had been established in earlier times. At present, for Korea to supplement its research on Dokdo from a historical point of view, it is deemed necessary to collect sources articulating that Dokdo and Usando are the same island and other relevant sources from countries other than Korea and Japan, particularly China. It is still questionable whether the above historical sources, as Professor Schrijver pointed out, so strongly support one country's claim to historic title that it overwhelms the other's arguments. Therefore, Korea needs to secure evidence for its historic title to Dokdo, as well as prepare itself to validate its effective control of the island and its treaty-based title to it.

2-2. The Names of Dokdo

There have been confusion over differences in how Dokdo had been historically referred to by Korea and Japan, respectively. Koreans have called Dokdo by the names "Usando," "Jasando," "Sambongdo" and others. In Japan, the island has been referred to as "Matsushima" or "Takeshima." Contrary to Korea's assertion that Usando is Dokdo, Japan has insisted that the two are different islands, citing Korean sources. An entry in *Taejong Sillok* (*Annals of King Taejong*) states that when a man named Kim In-u returned from Usando to the capital in 1417, he brought sorghum, cowhide, cotton seeds and other goods and offered them to the king, while mentioning that the island is inhabited by 86 people from 15 households.[30] In the record included in Taejong Sillok, "Usando" seems to refer to Ulleundo. This great confusion over the names of Dokdo implies limitations in the validation of title to the island based on historical sources. In addition, though it is a different issue, its is contradictory that the Japanese government has designated Okinotorishima, a reef as small as a bed, as an EEZ, while it regarded Dokdo as an uninhabitable reef due to its small size.

Meanwhile, sources supporting Korea's claim that Usando and Dokdo are the same island were found in 2007. *Seogye Jamnok* authored by Park Se-dang (1629-1703), a statesman of the late Joseon Dynasty, contains the entry "Ulleungdo" where he wrote: "The two islands (Ulleungdo and Usando) are not far apart from each other, so that you can sail from one to another in a short while if a strong wind blows. As Usando has a low terrain, you cannot see it (from Ulleungdo) unless the weather is very clear or you climb to the top of Ulleungdo." (不因海氣極清朗, 不登最高頂, 則不可見)[31] The significance of this source lies in the fact that it verifies that Usando and Ulleungdo are different islands, and that the former is not an island adjacent to Ulleungdo like Jukdo or Gwaneumdo, as had been asserted by Japaon. Jukdo and Gwaneumdo can be seen with the naked eye from Ulleungdo even on cloudy days, without the need to go up to higher places; therefore, the Usando in the source cannot be any other island but Dokdo. Meanwhile, *Ulleungdo Sajeok* authored by Jang Han-sang, who was a contemporary of Park Se-dang's and a special army officer dispatched to Samcheok, states "On the sea to the east (of Seonginbong Peak), you can vaguely see an island in the southeast from here; the island is only one-third the size of Ulleungdo and only about 300 ri (118 km) away from it."[32] Based on these sources, it can be logically concluded that the residents of Ulleungdo owned and managed Dokdo, an island found within a visible distance from it.

2-3. The Location of Dokdo

Another difference in the interpretation of historical sources between Korea and Japan is related to the location of Dokdo. The confusion over the island's location has also been mentioned by the Japanese Ministry of Foreign Affairs.[33] Japan has argued that Usando, which Korea has asserted to be Dokdo, is a different island, as Usando is closer to the coast than Ulleungdo on "Paldo Chongdo" (Map of the Eight Provinces) published in the 16th century. However, Usando is accurately located to the right of Ulleungdo on the maps published later, namely "Gangwon-do Do" (Map of Gangwon Province) and "Dongguk Jido" (Map of Korea). Dokdo is closer to the coast on "Paldo Chongdo" and regarding this, the possibility has been raised that Dokdo was perceived as being closer to the land than Ulleungdo due to the currents around the latter. The possibility of boats being drifted eastwards and moving fast towards Dokdo due to the warm currents has been verified through the "Balhae 1300" project (a study on the ship route of the Balhae Kingdom across the East Sea from a reproduction of the trip using 'Balhae 1300,' a man-powered raft).[34] This confusion over the location of Dokdo might have been inevitable at that time due to a lack of scientific or geographical information. Even today, when scientific knowledge is highly advanced, the distance between Ulleungdo and Dokdo sometimes varies depending on the source. For instance, the distance is specified as 92 km by the Japanese Ministry of Foreign Affairs and as 87 km by the Korea Hydrographic and Oceanographic Agency, a difference of about 5 km.[35] If Koreans' recognition of Dokdo should be denied, as Japan insists, on the basis of the location of the island on "Paldo Chongdo," the evaluation of legal facts with the assumption of the accuracy of old maps, some of which describe Daemado (Tsushima) as a Korean territory, needs to be reconsidered.[36]

3. CLAIMS TO THE EFFECTIVE CONTROL OF DOKDO

3-1. The Assertions of the Two Countries

Among the bases for the establishment of sovereignty over an island mentioned by Professor Schrijver - namely, original title, treaty-based title, and effective control - what Korea can relatively more convincingly verify based on historical evidence is its effective control of Dokdo. As it is true, on the part of Korea, that Korea has effectively been controlling Dokdo from old times to the present, it is important in the dispute with Japan to validate its effective control of the island with various historical evidence.

Some such evidence includes the following: The implementation of the island vacancy policy in Ulleungdo and Dokdo by the Joseon Dynasty as a way to exercise its territorial sovereignty over the islands; Imperial Decree No. 41 of 1900 (Gwangmu 4) stipulating that Dokdo is administratively under the jurisdiction of Uldo County (Ulleungdo); the governor of Ulleungo Shim Heung-taek's internal reports made about Dokdo in 1906. After World War II, Korea's sovereignty over Dokdo was recovered through the Cairo Declaration, the Potsdam Declaration and the Supreme Commander for Allied Powers Instruction (SCAPIN) No. 677 and 1033, and the Treaty of San Francisco. Since then, Korea has effectively controlled the island through various acts of state such as the installation of a lighthouse, the registration of residents, the dispatch of security guards, and the completion of berth facilities.[37] In response to Korea's claim to sovereignty over Dokdo based on these historical facts, the Japanese government asserts that it occupied the island first, from which territorial title arises under international law, in the following process. In 1618, the bakufu allowed the Oya and Murakawa families in Yonago, Tottori Prefecture to rule Dokdo, granting permission to voyages to Ulleungdo and its management for over 80 years. Afterwards, Dokdo, which Japan claims as its territory, was officially incorporated into Shimane Prefecture. Japan insists that it exercised effective control of the island, and performed an on-site survey on the island and issued licenses for fishing activities there after the incorporation of Dokdo, and that Korea did not make any objection to these acts at that time. In addition Japan argues that Dokdo should belong to Japan, as it regained its pre-war territories in 1951 under the Treaty of San Francisco.[38]

The two countries' respective claims to effective control of Dokdo through the exercise of the acts seems reasonable when considered from one side. However, regarding its sovereignty over Dokdo, Japan asserts both treaty-based title and historic title to it, which are logically incompatible in some cases. For this reason, Japan has also changed its positions from time to time. In particular, since modern times, Japan has engaged in an imperialist territorial invasion, taking advantage of international law through its response to the dispute over Dokdo, and this has made it difficult to resolve the Dokdo issue in a short period of time.

3-2. Imperial Decree No. 41 of 1900 (Gwangmu 4)

Imperial Decree No. 41 of 1900 (Gwangmu 4) is deemed the most important source on Korea's acts of state on Dokdo. The decree stipulates, "Ulleungdo shall be renamed Uldo and included in Gangwon Province as a county. The post of dogam (administrator) shall be promoted to gunsu (magistrate), and the county shall have an administrative level of five."[39] It also provides, "The office of the county shall be located in Taeha-dong and it will have jurisdiction over the entirety of Ulleungdo, Jukdo and Seokdo."[40] As in these articles, the name "Dokdo" is not found in this decree. It refers to Dokdo as Seokdo, instead of Sando, one of the common old names of Dokdo, as in Article 2. Contrary to Korea's claim that this Seokdo is the same island as Dokdo, Japan asserts that Seokdo is Juksedo, another island found near Ulleungdo. Here, the two countries show differences in their interpretation of these articles of the decree.[41]

Japan's assertion is based on an article in the Hwangseong Shinmun Newspaper dated July 13, 1906. The article writes that, "Uldo County has jurisdiction over Ulleungdo, Jukdo (now Jukseodo) and Seokdo Islands. This is a total of 200 ri (78 km), including 60 ri (23 km) to the east and the west and 40 ri (15 km) to the south and the north." Japan argues that these figures represent the scope of jurisdiction of the county, and as the current Takeshima (Jukdo) - that is, Dokdo - is 92 km southeast of Ulleungdo, it is outside the jurisdiction of Korea. Apart from the question of how the scope of jurisdiction that was not provided in the Imperial Decree was mentioned in this article, Korea sees that these figures do not indicate the scope of jurisdiction of the county but its total area.[42] Regardless of how the figures would be interpreted, however, the newspaper functions only as a reference for any facts, and cannot be a source of any rights or obligations. Therefore, rather than concentrating on the interpretation of the figures not provided in the Imperial Decree, Korea needs to focus on research to discover new sources that will confirm Seokdo as Dokdo. If the Seokdo mentioned in Imperial Decree No. 41 is clearly identified as Dokdo, the Shimane Prefecture Notice No. 40 under which Dokdo. an owned island, was regarded as terra nullius, and occupied by Japan, will be nullified, making Korea's sovereignty over Dokdo indisputable.

3-3. Shimane Prefecture Notice No. 40

Some of Japan's major assertions about its effective control of Dokdo have factual errors. One such assertion centers on Shimane Prefecture Notice No. 40, under which Japan claims that its sovereignty over Dokdo is perfectly established under modern international law. The Notice is about the official incorporation of Dokdo into Shimane Prefecture on February 22, 1905, after the cabinet decision on it on January 28 of the same year. Japan highly evaluates its significance in international law mainly for the following four reasons. First, the Notice is based on the relevant cabinet decision and home secretary instruction. Second, under the Notice, Takeshima (Dokdo) was officially named Takeshima. Third, Dokdo was incorporated into the Oki Islands. Fourth, all these were publicized in newspapers and widely known to the general public at the time.[43] Some of the major points refuting this Notice currently known in Korea can be summarized as follows. First, though a cabinet decision can be an expression of a state's intention, it is inadequate to serve as a ground for the acquisition of an area unless it is made public by a government agency.[44] Second, although Japan asserts that it met the requirements under international law for the incorporation of Dokdo into its territory through the issuance of Shimane Prefecture Notice No. 40, a notice issued by a local government cannot be regarded as the proclamation of a state's intention to take a certain external area as its territory. The areas subject to occupation are confined to terra nullius, but Dokdo was not terra nullius at the time of the issuance of the Notice. In addition, while any intention to occupy an area should be made public under international law, as the Japanese government failed to do so, the Korean government remained uninformed of it at that time. Even if Korea had known it, it would not have been able to protest against Japan, as it had already been deprived of its diplomatic rights.[45]

Sources raising questions about the existing Japanese sources on Shimane Prefecture Notice No. 40 were presented by the late Lee Jong-hak, who at the time was director of the Dokdo Museum of Korea. Lee found something strange about the Notice during his on-site investigation in Shimane Prefecture: an original copy of the Notification was stamped "for circulation." Until then, Korean scholars analyzing the document had considered it an official local government-level notice, though it was not issued by the central government. However, Lee insisted that the document was formulated only for circulation among local government officials.[46]

Two assumptions can be made regarding the meaning of the stamp "for circulation." First, it may imply that the document is very important and needs to be read by everyone so that they will become well-acquainted with it. Or, it may suggest that the document is intended to be internally circulated within the organization as it should not be exposed to the outside world, namely the Korean Empire. If the first assumption were true, its issuance should have been made public through newspapers. But, for some reason, no Japanese newspaper source mentioning it has been found so far. As the Notice was drafted only to be circulated among a few officials of the Shimane Prefecture Office, this kind of measure taken to incorporate Dokdo as a Japanese territory was neither known to local newspapers nor made public through them. This explains why the 104 local newspapers as well as the official gazettes of the time remained unaware of the Notice.[47] The online leaflet "Ten Points to Understand the Takeshima Dispute" posted on the web site of the Ministry of Foreign Affairs of Japan insists that the Japanese government had reaffirmed its sovereignty over Takeshima (Dokdo) through the incorporation of it into Shimane Prefecture. However, it bases the assertion not on this important notice but on a 1905 cabinet decision.[48] As such, it is necessary to look into this further. Also, it is most urgently needed to identify the reason why the original copy of the Notice is stamped "for circulation."

3-4. Measures Taken inside Japan After World War II

3-4-1. *Japan's Domestic Ordinances Excluding Dokdo from Its Territories*

Some of Japan's domestic regulations that are significant in relation to the country's acts à titre de souverain on Dokdo and effective control of it have been found and analyzed so far. They include Ministry of the Treasury Order No. 4 (1951), Prime Minister's Ordinance No. 24 (1951) and Ministry of the Treasury Notice No. 654 (1946). More specifically, Ministry of the Treasury Order No. 4 intended to identify islands belonging to the Japanese territory based on Article 4 (3) of the Act on Special Measures for Those Receiving Pension from Mutual Aid Societies and Others in Accordance with the Existing Orders, while Prime Minister's Ordinance No. 24 was promulgated in relation to the enforcement of the cabinet order[49] on the liquidation of the property of the Japanese Government-General of Korea Ministry of Transport Mutual Aid Society within Korea. Ministry of the Treasury Order No. 4,[50] which was promulgated on February 13, 1951, provided that islands belonging to Japan based on the abovementioned article of the act were islands other than the

Chishima Islands, the Habomai Islands, Shikotan Island, Ulleungdo, Dokdo and Jejudo Islands,[51] excluding Dokdo from the islands belonging to the country. Prime Minister's Ordinance No. 24 was promulgated on June 6, 1951 for the liquidation of the property of the Japanese Government-General of Korea's Ministry of Transport Mutual Aid Society, which had been owned by the Japanese government during its colonial rule of Korea. The Ordinance specifies the following islands as excluded from those belonging to Japan: the Chishima Islands, the Habomai Islands, and Shikotan Island; the Ogasawara Islands and Iwo Island; Ulleungdo, Dokdo and Jejudo Islands; the Nansei Islands (except for the Ryuku Islands) below 30 degrees north latitude; the Daito Islands, Okinotorishima, Minami Torishima and Nakano Torishima; and others.[52]

Ministry of the Treasury Notice No. 654, issued on August 15, 1946, confirmed the areas that had been occupied by Japan during the war but newly classified as "foreign territories" by the enforcement ordinances of the Act on Emergency Measures for Company Accounting[53] that was enacted for the settlement of Japanese companies' debts after the war.[54] The above three ordinances were enacted in the post-war restoration process, and Korea and Japan have completely different interpretations of these laws. For Korea's part, these ordinances are significant sources, as Japan officially admitted that Dokdo did not belong to its territory. Also, these ordinances demonstrate that Japan, at least before the signing of the Treaty of San Francisco in 1952, did not perceive Dokdo as its territory. These ordinances, being enacted by the Japanese government itself, can be used as basic sources to prove its claim to Dokdo as being false.[55] Professor Schrijver, while noting that these ordinances seem to be the first sources ever found to clearly show that the Japanese government excluded Dokdo from its territory in the past and that they can be very helpful for Korea's attempts to validate its claim to Dokdo as its territory, remains careful when it comes to affirming that they will serve as crucial sources to stop Japan from asserting its sovereignty over Dokdo.[56] In fact, the Japanese government, regarding the promulgation of the ordinances excluding Dokdo from islands belonging to it in 1951, insisted that the ordinances only excluded the island from the areas subject to Japanese law - that is, areas under its administrative control - and did not define the scope of its territory.[57]

3-4-2. *Collection of Taxes on Mining Activities on Dokdo*

Japan took a number of measures to create sources to later serve as evidence of its effective control of Dokdo under international law. One of them is the collection of mining lot tax, which is considered to have been an elaborate tactic to prepare for future international trials. On February 26, 1954, Shimane Prefecture granted Tsuji Tomizo (Tsuji Tomizo) in Tokyo permission to carry out phosphorite mining on Dokdo, after which it collected a mining lot tax from him. However, later, Tsuji sued the Japanese government and Shimane Prefecture for damages in 1959, claiming that it was unreasonable to collect mining lot tax as he was not able to perform mining activities on Dokdo due to Korea's "illegal occupation" of the island. In November 1961, the Tokyo District Court dismissed the case, finding no problems in the taxation, setting a precedent related to the Japanese government's control of Dokdo.[58] Japan will likely to try to use the ruling of the domestic court as a basis for its effective control of Dokdo. However, according to the Japanese government's assertions about the above-discussed three ordinances, Dokdo is an area where the administrative authority of Japan is not applied. Therefore, it is rather contradictory to rule that it is reasonable to collect tax on mining activities on the island as an exercise of administrative authority there. Thus, the imposition and collection of such a tax may have been intended to "create" evidence to justify Japan's acts à titre de souverain on the island, and its effective control of it.

4. CONCLUSIONS

The study by Professor Schrijver analyzes some of the ICJ's previous cases on disputes over islands with a focus on major issues of the conflicts, and then provides implications of these precedents for the dispute over Dokdo, with the assumption that it will be brought before the ICJ. He carried out an analysis of the trend in recent ICJ rulings in five cases of territorial disputes with a focus on the three key issues of the cases: original title, treaty-based title and title by effective control. It seems to be meaningful to focus on these issues when reviewing the assertions made by Korea and Japan. First, in terms of treaty-based title, no bilateral or mutilateral treaty directly mentions Dokdo. But the 1943 Cairo Declaration, the 1945 Potsdam Declaration,[59] the SCAPIN No. 677 (Governmental and Administrative Separation of Certain Outlying Areas from Japan) issued on January 29, 1946,[60] and the 1951 Treaty of San Francisco, all of which were signed in the post-war settlement process after World War II, mention Dokdo in a subsidiary manner or contain provisions that can analogically apply to the Dokdo issue. As is generally known, Japan has denied the validity of these documents, arguing that these agreements cannot function as treaties and that Japan did not participate in the agreement process. In particular, as Article 2 of the Treaty of San Francisco only mentions Jejudo, Geomundo and Ulleungdo Islands ("the islands of Quelpart, Port Hamilton and Dagelet"), omitting Dokdo, Japan has continuously asserted its sovereignty over the island.[61] Jejudo, Geomundo and Ulleundgo, which are mentioned in Article 2 of the Treaty of San Francisco, are all located at the edges of Korea's territorial waters. For this reason, Japan has claimed that Dokdo, being located further out from these islands, belongs to Japan. However, this assertion is logically groundless as the provision does not mention Marado, located south of Jejudo or other islands in the Yellow Sea. The inconsistency when it comes to the inclusion of Dokdo in the drafting process of this treaty makes the determination of title over Dokdo based on this treaty more complicated.

On initial consideration, one may agree with Professor Schrijver's view that the ICJ places treaty-based title above other title. Yet as seen in the five cases that the author has discussed, it is rash to say that the ICJ has consistently put a greater emphasis on treaty-based title in handling disputes over territorial sovereignty. However, it is fair to consider that the Court has made rulings depending on the relative certainty and validity of the three kinds of title. From this viewpoint, the dispute between Korea and Japan over Dokdo seems to be centered on differences in the two countries' assertions regarding their historic title to and effective control of the island. There are Korean sources demonstrating the country's sovereignty over Dokdo, including *Samguk Sagi* (History of the Three Kingdoms, 1145), *Sejong Sillok Jiriji* (Gazetteer in the Annals of King Sejong, 1454), *Sinjeung Dongukyeojiseungram* (Augmented Survey of the Geography of Korea, 1531), *Dongguk Munheon Bigo* (Reference Compilation of Korean Documents, 1770), and *Mangi Yoram* (Book of Ten Thousand Techniques of Governance, 1808), while in Japan, the Great Council of State officially concluded that the country has nothing to do with Dokdo in 1870.

What is most noteworthy about the dispute over historic title to Dokdo is the confusion over the names of Dokdo, especially due to the mixed use of the different names for the island and Ulleungdo in both the countries. It also needs to be considered in future study of Dokdo that both Korea and Japan tend to choose and interpret only the sources favorable to their own countries, making it difficult for the general public to accurately understand historical sources on Dokdo. Meanwhile, Korea needs to find sources to validate the discovery of Seokdo by Jeolla Province residents through their fishing activities, and their continuous use of the island since the discovery as provided in Imperial Order No. 41 of the Korean Empire. There should be further research on why Seokdo mentioned in the Imperial Order can be identified as Dokdo. Regarding this, it is recommended to reproduce the situation of the time with a computer simulation program and verify Korea's arguments in a scientific way. If the Seokdo mentioned in Imperial Order No. 41 is proven to be Dokdo, this will nullify Shimane Prefecture Notice No. 40 that was issued in 1905, bringing the dispute over Dokdo to an end. With regard to Shimane Prefecture Notice No. 40, based on which Japan claims its sovereignty over Dokdo, further research to link the reason why its original copy is stamped "for circulation" and the legal effects of a local government's notice. Although the exclusion of Dokdo from the areas under the Japanese administrative authority in its domestic ordinances cannot be understood as the country's official abandonment of sovereignty over the island, the legislations and ordinances enacted after the Potsdam Declaration also need to be analyzed, as they reflect Japan's ambition of imperialist territorial invasion.

Notes

1. Nico J. Schrijver & Vid Prisian, Cases Concerning Sovereignty over Islands before the International Court of Justice and the Dokdo/Takeshima Issue, *Ocean Development & International Law*, Vol. 46, No.4. pp. 281-314.
2. *Sovereignty over Pulau Ligitan and Pulau Sipadan (Indonesia/Malaysia),* (2002 Indonesia/Malaysia Judgment).
3. *Territorial and Maritime Dispute between Nicaragua and Honduras in the Caribbean Sea (Nicaragua v. Honduras),* (2007 Nicaragua/Honduras Judgment).
4. *Sovereignty over Pedra Branca/Pulau Batu Puteh, Middle Rocks, and South Ledge (Malaysia/ Singapore),* (2008 Malaysia/Singapore Judgment).
5. *Territorial and Maritime Dispute (Nicaragua v. Colombia)* (2007/2012), (2007/2012 Nicaragua/ Columbia Judgment).
6. The territorial title of a country to a territory or a land that it has controlled since it started to be recognized as an entity in international law or since before that can be referred to as "original title" while territory belonging to a country on the grounds of the original title is called "original territory." Original title is sometimes referred to as historic title. Regarding this, *see* Park, Pae-Keun (2005) A Consideration of Japan's Claim to Title to Dokdo: Original Title v. Title by Occupation. *Korean Journal of International Law,* vol. 50, no. 3. pp. 99-100.
7. Indonesia asserted its title to the two disputed islands on the grounds of the cession and succession of the title to the islands, the effective exercise of state functions, and Article 4 of the Convention between Great Britain and the Netherlands Defining the Boundaries in Borneo (June 20, 1891). Specifically, Indonesia focused on claiming and validating its title based on the Convention of 1891. On the other hand, Malaysia denied Indonesia's title to the islands in dispute, insisting that the Convention of 1891 could not serve as evidence that the predecessor of Indonesia (the Netherlands) had sovereignty over the islands. Malaysia concentrated on asserting and proving the cession and succession of the title to it and its effective control over the islands. 2002 Indonesia/Malaysia Judgment, paras. 32-3.
8. With respect to the cession and succession of the title, Indonesia asserted that it owned the title through succession from the Sultanate of Bulungan to the Netherlands, and to Indonesia; while Malaysia insisted that it owned the title through the succession from the Sultanate of Sulu to Spain (1878), the United States (1900), the British Empire (1930), and to Malaysia (1963). *Ibid.*, paras. 92-7.
9. Regarding its effective control of the islands, Indonesia submitted evidence before the Court to prove the activities of the Indonesian Navy and fishermen around the islands and historic sources demonstrating that the Royal Navy of the Netherlands rested on the islands during their patrols. On the other hand, Malaysia insisted on its effective control of the islands on the grounds of the control of natural resources such as turtles and turtle eggs, the designation of bird sanctuaries and the notification of it in official gazettes, and the

establishment of lighthouses by the British colonial authorities since the 1900s. *Ibid.*, paras. 130-44.

10. 2008 Malaysia/Singapore Judgment, paras. 40-48.
11. *Ibid.*, para. 110.
12. *Ibid.*, para. 111.
13. 2002 Indonesia/Malaysia Judgment, para. 130.
14. *Ibid.*, paras. 141-42.
15. *Ibid.*, para. 144.
16. *Ibid.*, paras. 131-32.
17. *Ibid.*, paras. 133-34.
18. *Ibid.*, paras. 126-27.
19. *Ibid.*, para. 127.
20. *Legal Status of Eastern Greenland Case* (Denmark/ Norway), 1933 PCIJ(Ser. A/B) No. 53 (Apr. 5).
21. *Ibid.*, pp.45-6.
22. 2002 Indonesia/Malaysia Judgment, para. 134.
23. LEE Han-gi. (1996). *Korea's Territory.* Seoul: Seoul National University Press. pp. 234-235.
24. Northeast Asian History Foundation. (2008). *A Refutation of Arguments in the Japanese Ministry of Foreign Affairs' Promotional Leaflet on Dokdo.* p. 10. Retrieved from http://www.dokdohistory.com/03_inform/issue_view.asp?i_ident=2881.
25. LEE Han-gi, *op. cit.,* p. 243.
26. 日本海内竹島外一島地籍編纂方伺.
27. However, Japan has argued that "another island" referred to here is not Dokdo. Retrieved from http://www.historyfoundation.or.kr/?sub_num=97.
28. Japanese sources on the activities of Ahn include *Chosen Kozudaigi* (朝鮮交通大記), *Hoki Mintanki* (伯耆民譚記), *Shoryo Zatki* (焦慮雜記), *Korin Koryaku* (交隣高略), *Takeshima Ko* (竹島考), *Inpu Nenpyo* (因府年表). *See* Gyeongsangbuk-do. (2007). A Proper Understanding of Dokdo.
29. Northeast Asian History Foundation. (2008). *A Refutation of Arguments in the Japanese Ministry of Foreign Affairs' Promotional Leaflet on Dokdo.* p. 10.
30. 1956.9.20.字 日側口述書 (No. 102/A1). On the Korean government's opinion on Takeshima (Dokdo) announced on September 25, 1954, the Japanese government reacted as follows: "小岩島たる今日の竹島は, 人の常住に適せず, また海産物以外の生産はないからである"
31. For a detailed analysis of "Ulleungdo" by PARK Se-dang, *see* YOO Mi-rim, Discovery of Historical Records from Joseon Dynasty to prove 'Usando is Dokdo,' *Trends in Maritime Fisheries*, Vol. 1250 (2007.11.), p. 5.
32. For a detailed analysis of *Ulleungdo Sajeok* and other sources on Dokdo related to Jang Han-sang, refer to YOO Mi-rim, *Ibid.,* p. 4.
33. http://www.mofa.go.jp/mofaj/area/takeshima/index.html.

34. http://cafe.naver.com/correctkorea/4578.
35. http://www.mofa.go.jp/region/asia-paci/takeshima/index.html, http://dokdo.nori.go.kr/uri/uri01.asp.
36. Apart from the question on the significance of ancient maps in the determination of sovereignty today, Professor Lee Han-gi has the same viewpoint as the author. LEE Han-gi. *op. cit.,* p. 269.
37. The Korea-Japan Historical Society. (1996). *Dokdo and Tsushima.* Seoul: Spring of Intelligence, pp. 209-15.
38. The Korea-Japan Historical Society. *op. cit.* pp. 209-15.
39. The Imperial Decree No. 41, Article 1.
40. The Imperial Decree No. 41, Article 2.
41. YOO Mi-rim, Seokdo is Dokdo, *Trends in Maritime Fisheries,* Vol. 1256 (2008), pp. 1-9.
42. The article in question does not specify that these figures have something to do with Ulleungdo, but they have been considered as related to the island based on the comparative analyses of different sources. YOO Mi-rim, *Ibid.,* pp. 4-10.
43. http://www.mofa.go.jp/mofaj/area/takeshima/index.html.
44. Indeed, in 1876, before incorporating the Ogasawara Islands into its territory, Japan had a prior consultation with the interested parties, the United Kingdom and the United States, and informed Europe (12 countries) of it to get official recognition from the international community. 安岡昭南,「明治維新と領土問題」(1980), pp. 196-213.
45. Jeong Gap-yong, Van Dyke, Jon M. & JU Mun-bae. (2004). *A Study on International Law Issues on Sovereignty over Dokdo.* Seoul: Korea Maritime Institute. p. 48.
In the case of Minami-Tori-shima (a coral atoll), Japan publicly announced its decision to incorporate it into Tokyo Prefecture and put it under the jurisdiction of Ogasawara Subprefecture through Tokyo Prefecture Notice No. 58 issued on July 24, 1898, and in local newspapers. LEE Jong-hak. "The Korean and Japanese Viewpoints towards the Seas Surrounding Dokdo." A presentation made at the first Dokdo Museum Symposium (May 31, 2000), p. 8.
46. LEE Jong-hak. *op. cit.*
47. Currently, only one original copy of this Notification is preserved in the Shimane Prefecture Office. The Notice is not found in the collections of the prefectural orders or instructions published at that time (February 22, 1905). Some have argued that the Shimane Prefecture Notice No. 40 was made public, yet attracted little attention, based on a relevant news article dated February 24, 1905 in the *San-in Chuo Shimpo*, a local newspaper operating in the region. But, the notification of any matter needs to be completed on the day of the decision on it, and a news article does not function as a notice. LEE Jong-hak, *Ibid.,* pp. 15-16.
48. The Japanese Ministry of Foreign Affairs. (2008). *Ten Points to Understand the Takeshima Dispute.* p. 8. Retrieved from https://www.mofa.go.jp/files/000092147.pdf
49. 朝鮮総督府交通局共済組合の本邦内にある財産の整理に関する政令 was enacted as Cabinet Order No. 40 on March 6, 1951 (Showa 26) and finally amended into

Act No. 116 on April 26 in 1952 (Showa 27). This act was enacted based on Imperial Decree No. 542 following Japan's acceptance of the Potsdam Declaration. For details, refer to http://hourei.hounavi.jp/hourei/S26/S26SE040.php

50. http://hourei.hounavi.jp/hourei/S26/S26F03401000004.php.

51. The original text of the Order, the above islands were referred to as "① 千島列島，歯舞列島(水晶島，勇留島，秋勇留島，志発島及び多楽島を含む.)及び色丹島 ② 鬱陵島，竹の島及び済州島." Dokdo is not indicated as "竹島" (Takeshima) but "竹の島," here, a difference from the Ministry of the Treasury Notice No. 654. As this, the Ministry of the Treasury Order No. 4 and the Prime Minister Ordinance No. 24 excluded Dokdo (Takeshima) from islands belonging to Japan; as regards this, some argue that it was because Dokdo was an uninhabited island and there was no residents to receive pension. http://blog.naver.com/musawe2/110040091490.

52. http://hourei.hounavi.jp/hourei/S26/S26F03101000024.php.

53. It was enacted as Act No. 7 on August 15, 1946 (Showa 21) and then finally amended into Act No. 87 on July 26, 2005 (Heisei 17).

54. According to the Notice, Korea, Taiwan, Sakhalin Island, the Kuril Islands and the South Sea Islands were classified as foreign territories, as well as Takeshima (Dokdo), which was specified as a foreign territory in a separate paragraph. *See* KIM Yeong-sik & LEE Tae-hun. (2009, January 5). Japanese Ordinances Confirming Dokdo as a Korean Territory Found. Dong-A Ilbo. Retrieved from http://news.donga.com/List/3/10/20090105/8679777/1.

55. http://blog.daum.net/angelkissmail/15714058.

56. http://www.hankyung.com/news/app/newsview.php?aid=2009010398588&sid=0106&nid=006.

57. http://issue.chosun.com/site/data/html_dir/2009/01/08/2009010800596.html

58. LEE Jong-hak. (1962). Permission for and Taxation on Mining Right on Dokdo and a Precedent: Why Is it Problematic? *Pallye Sibo,* Vol. 13, No. 280.

59. Dokdo is not directly mentioned in the Cairo and Potsdam Declarations, but the Cairo Declaration states that its purpose is to compel Japan to return the territories that it took from other countries and liberate Korea. In addition, as Article 8 of the Potsdam Declaration stipulates, "The terms of the Cairo Declaration shall be carried out and Japanese sovereignty shall be limited to the islands of Honshu, Hokkaido, Kyushu, Shikoku, and such minor islands as we determine," the declaration is also considered to have the intent to limit the scope of Japan's sovereignty.

60. SCAPIN No. 677 identified Dokdo as a Korean territory and SCAPIN 1033, issued in June 1946, banned Japanese fishermen from accessing Dokdo and territorial waters 12 nautical miles off the island, articulating that Dokdo is a Korean territory.

61. As is well known, Dokdo was included in the Korean territory in the first to fifth drafts (November 2, 1947), the seventh, tenth and eleventh drafts of the Treaty of San Francisco. However, the sixth (December 29, 1949), eighth, ninth,

and twelfth drafts describe Dokdo as a Japanese territory. In the thirteenth draft, the name Dokdo was deleted, based on which the final draft did not include Dokdo among the islands to which Japan was required to give up all rights, ownership and claims.

Lessons from Investor-State Dispute Settlements Related to Korea or Korean Investors*

LEE Gyoo-Ho
Professor of Law, Chung-Ang University School of Law, Seoul, Korea

Abstract

The mechanism for investment dispute settlement is necessary for independent, depoliticized and effective dispute settlement. Its availability to investors and states helps to promote international investment by providing confidence in the dispute resolution process. Sometimes, some popular domestic policies can be subject to ISD. Hence, the Korean government and its officials need to be aware that its drastic policy change may be subject to the risk of ISD. Whenever the Korean government drastically changes its policies, it needs to take into account its impact on foreign investors.

In this regard, this Article explores international investment agreements signed by the Republic of Korea and the Korean foreign investment law. Also, it explains the details of investor-State disputes where the Republic of Korea is the respondent State or the Home State of investor. In Conclusion, the Article proposes the adoption of the mechanism forecasting and warning the potential ISD because, otherwise, politicians and governmental officials in Korea will pursue popularity-driven policies without knowing the ISD risks.

---

* This Article is an updated and revised version of my paper which was previously published in Gyooho Lee, *The Korean Foreign Investment Law and Investor-State Dispute Settlement*, in Carlos Esplugues ed., Foreign Investment and Investment Arbitration in Asia, Intersentia, 2019, pp. 139-178.

Key Words

ISDS, Korea, Foreign Investment Law, Policy Change, BIT, TIP, Investor-State Dispute Settlement

1. INTRODUCTION

In September, 2017, the Korean government announced to implement a selective 25 percent discount for mobile fees for new subscribers as part of its policies to lower the overall burdens of mobile fees for households. As of August, 2017, more than 40% of the shares of the three telecommunication companies, SK Telecom, KT, and LG Uplus, were held by foreign investors.

Even though the artificial mobile fee cut plan of the Korean government gained popularity as political agenda, it might be considered by foreign investors as unfair in light of globally accepted standards. In this regard, foreign investors may seek some legal measures such as investor-state dispute settlement (hereinafter 'ISDS').[1] Hence, domestically popular plans of the Korean government need to be revisited in terms of global standards and possible legal measures including ISDS.

Under the Korea-US Free Trade Agreement, each state has the right to protect investors from one another due to the Investor-State Dispute settlement clause. If an American investor faces losses due to the Korean government's policy measures, the investor can file a claim against the Korean government with the International Center for Settlement of Investment Disputes.[2]

In this context, the three big Korean mobile carriers strongly opposed the Korean government's mobile fee cut plan to protect foreign investors. Instead, they improved their data fee policies on their own initiatives to provide more data capacity without broadband speed limit for their consumers.[3]

Unaffected by investment arbitration for a long time, Korea became the subject of its first investment treaty claim in 2012.[4] Hence, they have emerged cases related to investor-state dispute settlement (hereinafter 'ISDS') involving both Korea as a respondent state and Korea as home state of an investor. ISDS plays an important role in the investment determination of most companies investing abroad. On one hand, if ISDS does not work well, it will discourage investors to invest abroad.[5] On the other hand, the size of ISDS awards may result in the chilling effect of ISDS on public interest regulation such as environmental, public health, and transportation policies.[6] In this context, Korea's international investment agreements need to be discussed.

As of 30 April 2019, Korea has concluded 145 international investment agreements, which consist of 95 (89 in force) bilateral investment treaties (hereinafter 'BIT'),[7] 22 (17 in force) treaties with investment provisions (hereinafter 'TIPs'),[8] and 28 investment-related instruments (hereinafter 'IRIs').[9] Those TIPs include fee trade agreements involving Chile (2014), Singapore (2006), EFTA (2006), ASEAN (2007), India (2010), EU (2011), Peru (2011), USA (2012),[10] Turkey (2013), Australia (2014),[11] Canada (2015), New Zealand (2015),[12] Viet Nam (2015), China (2015), and Republics of Central America (2018).

Also, the foreign investment law of Korea needs to be explored.

2. FOREIGN INVESTMENT LAW OF KOREA

2-1. Objectives

Foreign investment is governed by the Foreign Investment Promotion Act(hereinafter "FIPA"). The purpose of the FIPA is to promote foreign investment in Korea by offering necessary support and benefit and to contribute to the sound developments of the Korea's economy.[13]

2-2. Definitions

Article 2 of the FIPA defines foreign investor, foreign investment, and asset or enterprise. The term "foreigner" means an individual with a foreign nationality, a corporation established in accordance with a foreign law (hereinafter referred to as "foreign corporation") or an international economic cooperative organization prescribed by Presidential Decree.[14] According to Article 2 (1) 4 of the FIPA, the term "foreign investment" means any of the following terms: (a) Where a foreigner holds stocks or shares (hereinafter referred to as "stocks, etc.") of a Korean corporation (including a Korean corporation in the process of establishment; hereafter the same shall apply in (i) below) or a company run by a national of the Republic of Korea, as prescribed by Presidential Decree, by any of the following methods ((i) Acquisition of stocks, etc. newly issued by the Korean corporation or company run by the national of the Republic of Korea; (ii) Acquisition of stocks, etc. previously issued by the Korean corporation or company run by the national of the Republic of Korea (hereinafter referred to as "existing stocks, etc.")), in order to establish a continuous economic relationship with the Korean corporation or company, such as participating in the management of such Korean corporation or company in accordance with the FIPA; (b) A loan with maturity of not less than five years (based on the loan maturity prescribed in the first loan contract), which is provided to a foreign-capital invested company by any of the following entities; (c) Where a foreigner contributes to a nonprofit corporation pursuant to this Act in order to establish a continuous cooperative relationship with the corporation which satisfies the standards prescribed by Presidential Decree in terms of research personnel, facility, etc. and which is a corporation (including a corporation in the process of establishment) of the Republic of Korea in the field of science and technology; or (d) other contributions to a non-profit corporation by a foreigner, which the Foreign Investment Committee established under Article 27 (hereinafter referred to as the "Foreign Investment Committee")[15] recognizes as a foreign investment in accordance with the standards prescribed by Presidential Decree regarding the business contents, etc. of the non-profit corporation. In addition, the term "foreign investor" means a foreigner who holds stocks, etc. or has contributed as prescribed by the FIPA.[16] The word "foreign-capital invested company or foreigner-contributed nonprofit corporation" refers to a company in which a foreign investor has invested, or a nonprofit corporation to which a foreign investor has contributed.[17]

The word "operator of establishments built to improve foreign-investment environment" means any person who operates establishments prescribed by Presidential Decree, including schools and medical institutions, etc. for foreigners in order to improve foreign investment environment.[18] The term "object of investment" means any object in which a foreign investor invests in order to possess stocks, etc. under the FIPA, and which falls under any of the followings:

(i) Foreign means of payment under the Foreign Exchange Transactions Act or domestic means of payment incurred by the exchange of such foreign means of payment;
(ii) Capital goods;
(iii) Proceeds from the stocks, etc. acquired by this Act;
(iv) Industrial property rights, intellectual property rights prescribed by Presidential Decree, other technologies corresponding thereto, and rights pertaining to the use of such rights or technologies;
(v) Where a foreigner closes his/her own branch company or office in Korea and converts the branch company or office into another domestic corporation, or where a domestic corporation

the stocks of which are possessed by a foreigner is dissolved, the remaining property that will be allotted to such foreigner upon the liquidation of such branch company, office, or corporation;
(vi) The amount of redemption of loans with maturity of not less than five years (based on the loan maturity prescribed in the first loan contract), which is provided to a foreign-capital invested company by any of the following entities or of other loans from foreign countries;
(vii) Stocks prescribed by Presidential Decree;
(viii) Real estate located in Korea;
(ix) Other means of domestic payment prescribed by Presidential Decree.[19]

The term "capital goods" means machinery, apparatus, facilities, equipment, parts, accessories as industrial facilities (including vessels, motor vehicles, aircraft, etc.), livestock, breeds or seeds, trees, fish and shellfish which are necessary for the development of agriculture, forestry, and fisheries, raw materials and reserve supply deemed necessary by the competent Minister (referring to the head of the central administrative agency in control of the project concerned; hereinafter the same shall apply) for the initial test (including pilot projects) of the facilities concerned, and the fees for transportation and insurance required for the introduction thereof and other know-how or service necessary therefor.[20]

2-3. Entry Conditions

2-3-1. *Safeguards: national security and public order, environmental protection, and public health*

No foreigner shall be restricted from making any foreign investment prescribed in this Act, except in the following circumstances: (i) where he/she threatens national security and public order; (ii) where he/she has harmful effects on public health and sanitation or environmental preservation or is against Korean morals and customs; or (iii) where he/she violates any Act or subordinate statute of the Republic of Korea.[21] Where the head of a relevant administrative agency restricts foreign investment, such as treating foreigners or foreign-capital invested companies unfavorably compared to Korean nationals or Korean corporations, or charging additional liabilities to foreigners or foreign-capital invested companies, in other Acts and subordinate statutes or public notifications than this Act, the Minister of Trade, Industry and Energy shall combine and publicly announce the details thereof each year, as prescribed by Presidential Decree. If the head of a relevant administrative agency intends to amend or add any restriction, he/she shall seek prior consultation with the Minister of Trade, Industry and Energy.[22] Except as otherwise prescribed by the Acts of the Republic of Korea, a foreigner may engage in, without restraint, various activities of foreign investment in the Republic of Korea.[23]

2-3-2. *Authorization and registration: Foreign Investment*

A foreign investor or foreign-capital invested company (including where any of the following circumstances arise to him/her or it due to capital increase) shall file for registration as a foreign-capital invested company, as prescribed by Presidential Decree, in any of the following circumstances:

(i) where he/she or it has completed the payment for the object of investment; (ii) where he/she or it has completed the acquisition of stocks, etc. (meaning having paid for the stocks, etc.) by the method prescribed in Article 2 (1) 4 (a)[24] of the FIPA; (iii) where he/she or it has completed contribution by the methods prescribed in Article 2 (1) 4 (c) and (d)[25] of the FIPA.[26]

Nonetheless, when a foreign investor or foreign-capital invested company making a foreign investment defined under Article 2 (1) 4

(a) of the FIPA[27] meets requirements prescribed by Presidential Decree, such as the investment amount, he/she or it may file for registration as a foreign-capital invested company even prior to completing payment for the object of the investment or the acquisition of stocks, etc.[28]

A foreign investor or foreign-capital invested company shall file for registration of alteration, as prescribed by Ordinance of the Ministry of Trade, Industry and Energy, in any of the following circumstances:

(i) Where he/she or it has filed a report on foreign investment by any of the methods prescribed in Article 5 (2) 2 through 6 of the FIPA;[29]
(ii) Where he/she or it falls under Article 121-5 (2) 2 of the Restriction of Special Taxation Act;[30]
(iii) Where stocks, etc. owned by the foreign investor are reduced following transfer of the stocks, etc. he/she has acquired under Article 5[31] or Article 6[32] of the FIPA to a third person, or the capital reduction of the relevant foreign-capital invested company; or
(iv) Where any of the matters prescribed by Ordinance of the Ministry of Trade, Industry and Energy, such as the foreign investment ratio, the trade name or name of a foreign-capital invested company, is changed.[33]

Where a foreign investor or foreign-capital invested company falls under any of the following cases, the Minister of Trade, Industry and Energy may revoke permission or cancel the registration thereof: Provided, That in cases falling under the following (ii) or (iii), he/she must revoke permission or cancel the registration thereof:

(i) Where the foreign-capital invested company reports the

closure of its business under Article 8 (6) of the Value-Added Tax Act;[34]
(ii) Where the foreign investor has transferred all of the stocks, etc. owned by himself/herself to a national of the Republic of Korea or a Korean corporation, or has ceased to hold any of the stocks, etc. previously owned by himself/herself due to the capital reduction of the relevant foreign-capital invested company;
(iii) Where he/she or it has filed for registration as a foreign-capital invested company as if payment for the object of investment were completed.[35]

No company registered as a foreign-capital invested company shall engage in any of the following conducts, except in cases meeting the criteria prescribed by Presidential Decree:

(i) Running a business in which foreign investment is restricted under Article 4 (3) of the FIPA,[36] in excess of the allowed limit;
(ii) Acquiring stocks of any third domestic company that runs a business in which foreign investment is restricted under Article 4 (3) of the FIPA,[37] in excess of the allowed limit.[38]

No foreign investor or foreign-capital invested company shall use investment funds for any purpose other than the reported or permitted purpose reported, or transfer or lend the registration certification of the relevant foreign-capital invested company to any third person.[39]

2-4. Investor rights and guarantees

2-4-1. *National Treatment*

According to Article 3 (1) of the FIPA, "Remittance of proceeds accruing from the stocks, etc. acquired by a foreign investor, proceeds from the sale of stocks, etc., and the principal, interests, and service charges paid under the loan contract referred to in Article 2 (1) 4 (b) of the FIPA[40] to a foreign country, shall be guaranteed in accordance with the details of the report or permission of the foreign investment at the time of such remittance."[41] Except as otherwise prescribed by the Acts of the Republic of Korea, foreign investors and foreign-capital invested companies shall be treated in the same way as nationals of the Republic of Korea or Korean corporations in respect of their business operation.[42] Except as otherwise prescribed by other Acts, the provisions concerning tax exemptions and reductions of the tax Acts applied to nationals of the Republic of Korea or Korean corporations shall also apply to foreign investors, foreign-capital invested companies, and persons who grant loans under Article 2 (1) 4 (b)[43] of the FIPA.[44] Matters necessary concerning procedures for remittance foreign countries shall be prescribed by Presidential Decree.[45]

2-4-2. *Access to land or real estate*

Article 13 of the FIPA prescribes access to domestic land or real estate. Under the title 'Lease and sale of state or public property,' the Minister of Strategy and Finance, administrative agencies of State property, heads of local governments, heads of public institutions under the Act on the Management of Public Institutions (hereinafter referred to as "public institution") or the heads of local public enterprises under the Local Public Enterprises Act (excluding local government-directly operated enterprises; hereafter referred to as "local public enterprise" in this Article) may allow foreign-invested companies or the operators of establishments built to improve a foreign-investment environment (hereafter referred to as "foreign invested companies, etc." in this Article and Article 14 of the FIPA[46]) to use or profit from land, factories or other property (hereinafter referred to as "land, etc.") owned by the State, local governments, public institutions or local public enterprises, or may lend (hereinafter referred to as "lease") or sell such land, etc. to foreign invested companies, etc. by a negotiated contract, notwithstanding the relevant provisions of the following Acts:

(i) The State Property Act;
(ii) The Public Property and Commodity Management Act;
(iii) The Act on the Management of Public Institutions;
(iv) The Urban Development Act;
(v) The Act on the Development and Management of Logistics Facilities;
(vi) The Fishing Villages and Fishery Harbors Act; or
(vii) The Act on the Development, Management, etc. of Marinas.[47]

Foreign-capital invested companies that are allowed to legitimately use, profit from, lease or purchase land, etc., shall be limited to companies meeting the minimum foreign investment ratio prescribed by Presidential Decree, and such companies shall maintain the minimum foreign investment ratio for a period prescribed by Presidential Decree (excluding where such companies temporarily fail to maintain the minimum foreign investment ratio for a period prescribed by Ordinance of the Ministry of Trade, Industry and Energy; hereinafter the same shall apply) after concluding a negotiated contract under the same paragraph: Provided, That the foregoing shall not apply to a foreign-capital invested company, which has made great contributions to the national economy in terms of the scale of employment creation, amount of foreign investment, effects of technology transfer, etc.:

(i) If the foreign-capital invested company files a report on foreign investment with details for creating new employment exceeding the number of regular workers prescribed by Presidential Decree within three years;
(ii) If the foreign-capital invested company files a report on

foreign investment with details for making at least an investment amount prescribed by Presidential Decree within five years;
(iii) If the foreign-capital invested company is granted a tax reduction or exemption under Article 121-2 (1) 1 of the Restriction of Special Taxation Act;[48]
(iv) In cases recognized as necessary by the Minister of Trade, Industry and Energy after deliberation by the Foreign Investment Committee from among the foreign-capital invested companies which have made substantial contributions to the expansion of social overhead capital, industrial restructuring, financial independence of local governments, etc.[49]

Where land, etc. owned by the State, local governments, public institutions or local public enterprises are leased, the lease term corresponding to the State Property Act, Public Property and Commodity Management Act, the Act on the Management of Public Institutions, Urban Development Act, and the Act on the Development and Management of Logistics Facilities may be set within a maximum period of 50 years, notwithstanding the following provisions:

(i) Articles 35 (1) and 46 (1) of the State Property Act;[50]
(ii) the duration of use and benefit prescribed under Articles 21 (1) of the Public Property and Commodity Management Act and the duration of lease under Article 31 (1) of the same Act; or
(iii) Article 69 (2)[51] of the Urban Development Act.[52]

Where land owned by the State or a local government is leased pursuant to paragraph (1), building a factory or other permanent facilities on such land may be allowed, notwithstanding Prohibition on Constructing Permanent Facilities under Article 18 of the State Property Act[53] and Article 13 of the Public Property and Commodity Management Act. In such case, such land may be leased on condition that the relevant factory or other facilities be donated to the State or the local government, or returned after such land is reinstated at the end of the lease term, considering the type of relevant facilities, etc.[54] Where land, etc. owned by the State, a local government, public institution or local public enterprise is leased, rental charges corresponding to the State Property Act, Public Property and Commodity Management Act, the Act on the Management of Public Institutions, Urban Development Act, and the Act on the Development and Management of Logistics Facilities shall be, as prescribed by Presidential Decree, notwithstanding the following provisions, and may be indicated in a foreign currency if necessary:

(i) Articles 32 (1) and 47 of the State Property Act;[55]
(ii) Articles 22, 32 and 35 of the Public Property and Commodity Management Act;
(iii) Articles 26[56] and 69[57] of the Urban Development Act; or
(iv) Article 50[58] of the Act on the Development and Management of Logistics Facilities.[59]

Where land, etc. referred to in paragraph (1) is sold to a foreign-invested company, etc. and a purchaser is deemed to have difficulty making a lump-sum payment of the purchase price, payment may be deferred or made in installments, as prescribed by Presidential Decree, notwithstanding Article 50 (1) of the State Property Act,[60] Article 37 of the Public Property and Commodity Management Act and Article 39 (3) of the Act on the Management of Public Institutions.[61][62] Where the Minister of Strategy and Finance or an administrative agency of State property leases any of the following State-owned land, etc. to a foreign-invested company running a business prescribed by Presidential Decree, he/she or it may reduce or exempt rental charges for the relevant land, etc., as prescribed by Presidential Decree, after consulting with the Minister of Trade, Industry and Energy, notwithstanding Article 38 of the Industrial Sites and Development Act:[63]

(i) Land, etc. located within a foreign investment zone designated under Article 18 of the FIPA;
(ii) Land, etc. located within a national industrial complex designated under Article 6 of the Industrial Sites and Development Act (hereinafter referred to as “national industrial complex”); or
(iii) Land, etc. located in a general industrial complex, urban high-tech complex or agro-industrial complex designated under Articles 7, 7-2 and 8 of the Industrial Sites and Development Act.[64]

Where State-owned land, etc. is leased to an operator of establishments built to improve a foreign-investment environment, the Minister of Strategy and Finance or the administrative agency of State property may reduce or exempt rental charges for the relevant land, etc., as prescribed by Presidential Decree, notwithstanding Articles 32 (1) and 47[65] of the State Property Act.[66]

Where the head of a local government leases land, etc. owned by the local government to a foreign- invested company, etc., he/she may reduce or exempt rental charges for the land, etc., as prescribed by Presidential Decree, notwithstanding Articles 22, 24, 32 and 34 of the Public Property and Commodity Management Act.[67] Where land, etc. leased to a foreign-invested company, etc. with rental charges reduced or exempted pursuant to paragraphs (7) through (9) is located within an industrial complex as defined in subparagraph 8 of Article 2 of the Industrial Sites and Development Act, the lease term may be set within a maximum period of 50 years, notwithstanding Article 38 of the same Act.[68] The lease term referred to in paragraphs (3) and (10) may be extended. In such case, the lease term so extended on each occasion shall not exceed the period provided for in paragraphs (3) and (10).[69]

2-5. Investor-State Dispute Settlement

For ISDS, the FIPA states foreign investment ombudsman system. In order to resolve complaints from foreign investors and foreign-capital invested companies, foreign investment ombudsmen shall be commissioned from among persons with abundant knowledge and experience in foreign investment affairs.[70] The foreign investment ombudsmen shall be commissioned by the President, after the recommendation of the Minister of Trade, Industry and Energy and deliberation thereon by the Foreign Investment Committee.[71] Where necessary for resolving complaints from foreign investors and foreign-capital invested companies, any foreign investment ombudsman may request the head of a relevant administrative agency and the head of a foreign-investment related agency (hereinafter referred to as "relevant administrative agency, etc.") to render the following necessary cooperation. In such cases, the head of a relevant administrative agency, etc. in receipt of such request shall comply therewith, except in extenuating circumstances:

(i) Giving explanations to a relevant administrative agency, etc. or submitting data in accordance with the standards prescribed by Presidential Decree;
(ii) Stating opinions of related employees, interested persons, etc.;
(iii) Requesting cooperation for site visits.[72]

Where deemed necessary after resolving complaints of foreign investors and foreign-capital invested companies, any foreign investment ombudsman may recommend the heads of relevant administrative agencies and the heads of public institutions to take corrective measures on related affairs.[73] Upon receipt of the recommendations, the heads of relevant administrative agencies or public institutions shall, in writing, notify foreign investment ombudsmen of handling results within the period prescribed by Presidential Decree.[74] Where the heads of relevant administrative agencies or public institutions fail to implement the recommendations, foreign investment ombudsmen may request them to submit matters concerning such recommendations to the Foreign Investment Committee as an agenda.[75] In order to promote the improvement of regulations on complaints of foreign investors and foreign-invested companies in an organized manner, foreign investment ombudsmen shall prepare an annual report on reorganization activities, such as the current status of regulations and systems obstructing foreign investment, results of improvement thereof, etc., and submit the report to the Foreign Investment Committee, as prescribed by Presidential Decree.[76] No foreign investment ombudsmen shall use data received from the heads of the relevant administrative agencies, etc. or confidential information that they have become aware of in the course of performing duties for any purposes other than those prescribed by the FIPA, or divulge it to any third party.[77] Foreign investment ombudsmen shall be deemed a public official for the purposes of penal provisions under Articles 129 through 132 of the Criminal Act.[78] A grievance committee shall be established within the Korea Trade-Investment Promotion Agency in order to support the duties of foreign investment ombudsmen.[79]

2-6. Institutional set-up: Investment Promotion Agency

A Foreign Investment Support Center (hereinafter referred to as the "Investment Support Center") shall be established in the Korea Trade-Investment Promotion Agency in order to conduct consultations, guidance, advertisement, investigation, research, and treatment of civil petitions either directly or by proxy, the nurturing of business start-up, etc. concerning foreign investment and provide comprehensive support measures for foreign investors and foreign-capital invested companies.[80] Where necessary to properly perform foreign investment-related affairs, the president of the Korea Trade-Investment Promotion Agency may request the relevant administrative agencies, corporations or organizations related to foreign investment (hereinafter referred to as "foreign-investment related agencies") to dispatch their public officials or executives and employees to render service at the Investment Support Center: Provided, That where the service of public officials is required, prior consultation with the competent minister shall be made.[81] Where necessary to efficiently manage foreign investment-related duties by foreign investors or foreign-capital invested companies, the president of the Korea Trade-Investment Promotion Agency may request the head of a relevant administrative agency having jurisdiction over the relevant duty to establish a sub-branch of the agency within the Investment Support Center. In such cases, the head of the agency upon receipt of such request shall comply therewith, unless other specific grounds exist to the contrary.[82] The Investment Support Center shall be run mainly by officers and employees of the Korea Trade-Investment Promotion Agency who have considerable knowledge and experience in foreign investment, and public officials or the officers and employees of foreign-investment related agencies dispatched to the Investment Support Center (hereinafter referred to as "dispatched officers") shall render their support for the business matters of the Investment Support Center.[83]

The head of a relevant administrative agency or a foreign-investment related agency to whom a request for dispatching public officials or officers or employees has been made in accordance with paragraph 15 (2) of the FIPA[84] shall select those who are well-suited for the business matters in question and dispatch them, unless other specific grounds exist to the contrary, and where he/she intends to stop the dispatched service before the period for service expires, he/she shall consult in advance with the president of the Korea

Trade-Investment Promotion Agency.[85] The head of a relevant administrative agency or a foreign-investment related agency who dispatches public officials or officers or employees under his/her jurisdiction may give preferential treatment to the dispatched officers in terms of their promotion, position transfer, rewards, and welfare measures.[86] Where necessary to conduct consultations, guidance, advertisement, investigation, research, and treatment of civil petitions either directly or by proxy, the nurturing of business start-up, etc. concerning foreign investment and provide comprehensive support measures for foreign investors and foreign-capital invested companies, the president of the Korea Trade-Investment Promotion Agency may request the relevant administrative agency or the foreign-investment related agency to request cooperation, and the head of the agency in receipt of such request shall comply therewith, unless other specific grounds exist to the contrary.[87] Matters necessary for the composition and operation of the Investment Support Center shall be prescribed by Presidential Decree.[88]

2-7. Relationship with other Acts and International Treaties

Except as otherwise expressly provided for in the FIPA, matters concerning foreign exchanges and foreign trades shall be governed by the Foreign Exchange Transactions Act.[89] Notwithstanding the proviso to Article 462-2 (1) of the Commercial Act,[90] a foreign-capital invested company may pay dividends with its newly issued stocks up to an amount equivalent to its total dividend amount, where a special resolution has been passed under Article 434[91] of the Commercial Act.[92] Where a foreign investor makes an investment in kind with the capital goods,[93] the certificate of the completion of the investment in kind for which the Commissioner of the Korea Customs Service verified the implementation of the investment in kind and the type, volume, and price of the objects of the investment in kind, shall be deemed a written report of investigation by an investigator under the Article 299 of the Commercial Act,[94] notwithstanding Article 299 of the same Act. The same shall also apply where he/she makes an investment in kind with the capital goods after he/she has established a company.[95]

Where a technology evaluation agency prescribed by Presidential Decree has evaluated the price of an industrial property right, such evaluation shall be deemed appraised by an appraiser publicly certified under Article 299-2[96] of the Commercial Act.[97]

A national of the Republic of Korea or a Korean corporation that intends to operate a business jointly with a foreign investor who has reported to make a foreign investment by the method prescribed in Article 2 (1) 4 (a) (i) of the FIPA[98] may designate the first day of each month as the re-evaluation day and re-evaluate the objects of the relevant investment, as prescribed in the Assets Revaluation Act, notwithstanding Article 4 of the Assets Revaluation Act.[99]

Notwithstanding Article 8-2 (4) of the Monopoly Regulation and Fair Trade Act, a second-tier company of a general holding company may hold stocks of a joint stock corporation with a foreigner, if it meets all of the following requirements:

(i) Such stock holding shall correspond to a foreign investment meeting the standards referred to in Article 18 (1) 2;
The second-tier company of the general holding company shall hold at least 50 percent of the total number of outstanding stocks issued by such joint stock corporation;
(ii) A foreigner shall hold at least 30 percent (the share-holding ratio of the foreigner shall be calculated only for the stocks held at and after the time the joint stock corporation is formed) of total number of outstanding stocks issued by such joint stock corporation;
(iii) The second-tier company of the general holding company

shall hold all the outstanding shares issued by such joint stock corporation, except those held by foreigners.[100]

Each second-tier company of a general holding company that intends to hold stocks of a joint stock corporation, shall obtain approval from the Foreign Investment Committee. In such cases, the Minister of Trade, Industry and Energy shall submit the relevant case to the Fair Trade Commission for the prior deliberation of the requirements prescribed by Presidential Decree, including the joint stock corporation's business relevance with the second-tier company and the second-tier company's qualification to become a stakeholder in the joint stock corporation.[101] "General holding company," "second-tier company," and "joint stock corporation" have the same meanings defined by the Monopoly Regulation and Fair Trade Act.[102] None of the provisions of this Act shall be construed as amending or limiting any terms and conditions of international treaties the Republic of Korea has entered into and promulgated.[103]

3. INVESTOR-STATE DISPUTE SETTLEMENT RELATED TO KOREA OR KOREAN INVESTORS

3-1. ISDS under ITA with Korea

A good illustrative of the ISDSs related to Korea or Korean investors is the KORUS FTA. The KORUS FTA (FTA between Korea and the USA) includes a chapter on investment protection while the EU-Korea FTA only includes rules on investment liberalization and does not provide for an ISDS system.[104] The EU-Korea FTA's absence of investment chapters can be explained that "the competence to negotiate agreements for the protection of investments belonged severally to the member states, rather than to the Union as a whole."

The development in the ISDS provisions of Korea's ITAs including KORUS FTA has 'potentially lasting effects' throughout Asia-Pacific region and beyond.[105] The procedures for ISDS under the KORUS FTA are in fact identical to those in many other Korean FTAs. Under the procedure under the FTA or under an investment agreement, investors may file a claim to arbitration if a State has breached the substantive protection granted by the international agreement. Before filing the claim, the FTA requires the parties to seek consultation and negotiation.[106] If the parties do not reach an agreement within a specified period of time, the claim may be filed under ICSID Convention, the ICSID Additional Facility Rules, or the U.N. Commission on International Trade Law (hereinafter "UNCITRAL") Arbitration Rules.[107] The parties to the dispute may agree on the legal place of arbitration.[108] If the parties fail to do so, a tribunal shall determine the place in a state that is a party to the New York Convention.[109] The tribunal also has the power to determine the meeting places by taking into account proper factors inclusive of the convenience of the parties, the location of the subject matter, and the proximity of evidence.[110] Irrespective of the location, all arbitration proceedings are carried out in English and in Korean unless the parties to the dispute decide otherwise.[111] The tribunal assumes the factual allegations of all claimants are true if they support any claim in the notice of arbitration.[112] The same holds true under the UNCITRAL Arbitration Rules.[113]

If the arbitration rules have not been specified, or otherwise agreed upon, the law of the respondent State (i.e., the law of a domestic court or tribunal of proper jurisdiction) would apply in the same case.[114] If applicable, rules of international law may be used.[115] The Joint Committee declares the construction of provisions and the applicable law of the Agreement.[116] The construction binds on a tribunal and any decision or award issued by a tribunal must be in line with that construction.[117]

3-2. ISDS cases where the Republic of Korea is the Respondent State

The first known ISDS case against Korea emerged in 1984, when Colt Industries, a US-based company, filed a claim against Korea.[118] The claim was registered at and handled by the ICSID. The claim was based not on an investment treaty but on a defense industry contract. The proceedings were stayed following constitution of the tribunal and then closed in 1990 by agreement of the parties. For that reason, the case did not have pivotal effect on "Korea's IIA regime or ISDS policy."[119]

3-2-1. *Elliot Associates L.P. v. Republic of Korea*[120]

The applicable IIA is Korea-US FTA (2007) and its applicable arbitration rules are UNCITRAL Arbitration Rules. The claimant is Elliott Associates L.P. whereas the respondent is the Republic of Korea. The claims arose out the Korean government's conduct that allegedly led to the merger of Samsung C & T Corporation with Cheil Industries and thereby caused financial losses to the claimant. The claimant alleged the breach of the provisions on fair and equitable treatment, minimum standard of treatment, including denial of justice claims, and national treatment under the Korea-US FTA, seeking for the damages of 770 million US dollars. It is pending as of 10 May, 2019.

3-2-2. *Mason Capital L.P. and Mason Management LLC v. Republic of Korea (PCA Case No. 2018-55)*[121]

The applicable IIA is the Korea-US FTA (2007). Its proceedings are governed by UNCITRAL Arbitration Rules. Its administration institution is PCA (Permanent Court of Arbitration).[122] The seat of arbitration is Singapore. The claims arose out of senior government officials' alleged measures to enable a merger of Samsung C&T with a Samsung affiliate, Cheil Industries Incorporated ("Cheil"), on terms favourable to a large domestic Cheil shareholder. This was allegedly done by substantially undervaluing Samsung C&T and caused losses to the claimants' shareholding. The claimant sought for compensation amounting to 200 million US dollars while alleging the violation of the provisions on the Korea-US FTA providing fair and equitable treatment, and minimum standard of treatment, including denial of justice claims, full protection and security, or (iii) national treatment.[123] It commenced on 13 September, 2018. It is pending as of 10 May, 2019.

3-2-3. *Schindler Holding AG v. Republic of Korea*[124]

The applicable IIA is EFTA-Korea Investment Agreement, which was signed on 15 December, 2005 and effective since 1 October, 2006. The respondent State is the Republic of Korea whereas the Home State of investor is Switzerland. The claims arose out of the government authorities' alleged failure to exercise financial oversight related to Hyundai Elevator's share capital increases and other measures taken by the controlling shareholders, including the ultimate use of the corporate funds. Such actions allegedly caused significant impairments to the claimant's participation rights in Hyundai Elevator as the second largest shareholder. Its proceedings are governed by UNCITRAL Arbitration Rules. The claimant are seeking for the compensation amounting to 300 million US dollars by arguing the IIA breaches on basis of the provisions on fair and equitable treatment and minimum standard of treatment, including denial of justice claims.[125] It is pending as of 10 May, 2019.

3-2-4. *Jin Hae Seo v. Republic of Korea*[126]

The applicable IIA is the Korea-US FTA (2007). The respondent State is the Republic of Korea whereas the Home State of investor is the United States of America. The claims arose out of the allegedly insufficient amount of compensation set by the Government for the claimant's real estate property that had been expropriated following the municipal government's designation of the relevant area for redevelopment. Its proceedings are governed by UNCITRAL Arbitration Rules and its administration institution is HKIAC (Hong Kong International Arbitration Centre). The claimant is seeking for 3 million US dollars for the compensation.[127] Is is pending as of 10 May, 2019.

3-2-5. *Mohammad Reza Dayyani and others v. Republic of Korea (PCA Case No. 2015-38)*[128]

The applicable IIA was the Islamic Republic of Iran-Republic of Korea BIT (1998). Here, the respondent state was the Republic of Korea whereas the home state of investor was Islamic Republic of Iran. Its applicable international investment agreement (hereinafter 'IIA') is Islamic Republic of Iran-Republic of Korea BIT (1998). This case is based on the investment agreement for the acquisition of a majority stake in Daewoo Electronics and 10 per cent down payment of the price. The dispute arose out of Korea Asset Management Corporation's termination of an agreement for the sale of a majority stake in Daewoo Electronics to the claimants' company Entekhab and alleged non-return of the claimants' US$50 million deposit. The UNCITRAL Arbitration Rules are applied to this case. The administration institution was PCA (Permanent Court of Arbitration). It decided in favour of investor on 6 June, 2018. The claimant sought for 93500 million Korean Won (86.80 million US dollars) and the PCA awarded 57000 million Korean Won (53.20 million US dollars) for the investor by finding IIA breaches on basis of the provisions on fair and equitable treatment and minimum standard of treatment, including denial of justice claims. The seat of arbitration was London, UK. Arguing the Korean government found the grounds revoking the arbitral award, it sought for judicial review of the award before High Court of Justice in UK. As of 10 May, 2019, its judicial review is pending.[129]

3-2-6. *Hancal Holding B.V. and IPIC International B.V. v. Republic of Korea (ICSID Case No. ARB/15/17)*

3-2-6-1. The Scope and Contents of the BIT between the Republic of Korea and Netherlands of 2013

In this case, BIT between the Republic of Korea and Netherlands of 2013, which replaced the BIT between the Republic of Korea and Netherlands of 1974 was applied. The BIT between Korea and Netherlands of 2013 coexists with EU-Korea FTA. Here, asset-based definition is used as definition of investment. The definition of investment does not exclude portfolio investment, and other specific assets (e.g. sovereign debt, ordinary commercial transactions, etc.). Also, the scope of investment does not contain "in accordance with host State laws" requirement. In addition, the ambit of investment does not set out closed (exhaustive) list of covered assets. Furthermore, the scope of investment does not list the required characteristics of investment. The BIT includes the definition of investor. The BIT does not include permanent residents nor exclude dual nationals in terms of natural persons. It does not include requirement of substantial business activity nor define ownership and control of legal entities.

The BIT does not include denial of benefits (DoB) clause, so that it cannot be applied to:

(i) "Substantive business operations" criterion under the DoB clause;
(ii) Investors from States with no diplomatic relations or under economic/trade restrictions; and
(iii) Discretionary or mandatory DoB.

The BIT does not excludes taxation, subsides, grants, government procurement or other subject matter. The scope of the BIT covers both pre-existing and post-BIT investments. However, disputes in terms of temporal scope of the treaty are not stipulated.

Here, the BIT includes national treatment principle based on post-establishment but does not refer to "like or similar circumstances" in this context. In terms of most-favoured-nation (MFN) treatment, the type of MFN clause under this BIT is post-establishment. Exceptions from MFN obligation are allowed under economic integration agreements but they are not permitted under taxation treaties and procedural issues (ISDS).

3-2-6-2. Hancal Holding B.V. and IPIC International B.V. v. Republic of Korea (ICSID Case No. ARB/15/17)[130]

Here, the applicable IIA is Republic of Korea-Netherlands BIT (2003). The respondent Stat is the Republic of Korea whereas the home State of investor is Netherlands. The Details of the Dutch company's investment is the majority shareholding in Hyundai Oilbank, a petroleum and refinery company based in the city of Seosan. The dispute arose out of the alleged tax levied on the 2010 sale of the claimants' controlling stake in Hyundai Oilbank, a petroleum and refinery company based in the city of Seosan. The amount of compensation claimed by the investor was 168 million US dollars.

The applicable arbitration rules are ICSID (International Centre for Settlement of Investment Disputes). Its administration institution is ICSID (International Centre for Settlement of Investment Disputes). It was registered on 20 May, 2015 and its Tribunal was constituted on 16 March, 2016. On 5 October, 2016, the Tribunal issues a procedural order taking note of the discontinuance of the proceeding pursuant to ICSID Arbitration Rule 44.

3-2-7. *LSF-KEB Holdings SCA & others v. Republic of Korea (ICSID Case No. ARB/12/37)*[131]

The applicable IIA is BLEU (Belgium-Luxembourg Economic Union)-Republic of Korea BIT (1974). The respondent State is the Republic of Korea whereas home States of the investor, a consortium of Belgian and Luxembourg, are Belgium and Luxembourg. It is the first known investment treaty case against Korea which took place in 2012. In this case, the investors led by the US-based private equity fund Lone Star filed a claim amounting to 4.7 billion US dollars at ICSID relating to the sale of a commercial bank.

The details of investment are the majority shareholding in a South Korean financial institution; shareholding in Seoul's Star Tower; and interests in an engineering and construction manufacturer. The claims arose out of the alleged failure by Korean regulatory authorities over a period of several years to approve the purchase by third parties of claimant's stake in Korea Exchange Bank, and the alleged imposition of arbitrary capital gains taxes on the sale by Korean tax authorities. The arbitration rules applied to this case is ICSID (International Centre for Settlement of Investment Disputes). The administration institution is ICSID (International Centre for Settlement of Investment Disputes). The amount of compensation claimed by the investor is 4700 million US dollars. The respondent requested to address the objections to jurisdiction as a preliminary question. The ICSID ruled out the respondent's request on 23 December 2013. The original proceedings are pending as of 10 May, 2019.[132] This case was noteworthy not only because it was filed under amended Belgium-Luxembourg BIT but also the amount in controversy is so high.

3-3. ISDS cases where the Republic of Korea is the Home State of Investor

3-3-1. *Baig v. Vist Nam (ICSID Case No. ARB (AF)/18/2)*[133]

The applicable IIA here is the Republic of Korea-Vietnam BIT (1993). The respondent is Socialist Republic of Vietnam whereas the claimant is Mr. Shin Dong Baig. This case was registered on 19 March, 2018 and its Tribunal was constituted on 5 July, 2018. It concerns real estate project in Vietnam. Its applicable rules is ICSID Additional Facility-Arbitration Rules and its administering institution is ICSID. On 1 March, 2019, the Tribunal issues Procedural Order No. 2 concerning the Respondent's request to address the objections to jurisdiction as a preliminary question. It is pending as of 10 May, 2019.

3-3-2. *Samsung Engineering Co., Ltd. v. Kingdom of Saudi Arabia (ICSID Case No. ARB/17/43)*[134]

The applicable IIA here is the Republic of Korea- Saudi Arabia BIT (2002). The respondent State is Saudi Arabia whereas the home State of the investor is Korea. The details of investment are investment in constructing an electric power plant. The claim arose out of the alleged termination of a power plant construction contract. The arbitration rules are the Arbitration Rules of ICSID (International Centre for Settlement of Investment Disputes). Its administering institution is ICSID. It was registered on 10 November, 2017 and its Tribunal was constituted on 14 March, 2018. On 29 October, 2018, the Claimant filed a memorial on the merits. Its original proceedings are pending as of 10 May, 2019.

3-3-3. *Samsung Engineering Co., Ltd. v. Sultanate of Oman (ICSID Case No. ARB/15/30)*[135]

Samsung Engineering filed a 1 billion USD case at ICSID against Oman. The applicable IIA is the Republic of Korea-Oman BIT (2003). The respondent State is Oman while the home State of the investor is the Republic of Korea. The details of investment concern deposit in connection with the bid for a refinery improvement project. The claims arose out of the alleged discriminatory treatment by the State towards the claimant in connection with the bidding process to undertake improvements to the Sohar refinery in northern Oman run by the state-owned Oman Refineries and Petroleum

Industries Company (ORPIC) in 2013. Its arbitration rules are Arbitration Rules of ICSID (International Centre for Settlement of Investment Disputes). Its administering institution is ICSID (International Centre for Settlement of Investment Disputes). The Claimant filed an international arbitration complaint against the Oman government over an oil refinery plant deal worth $1 billion on 20 July, 2015 and its Tribunal was constituted on 4 November, 2015. It was settled before decision on liability, so that IIA breach was not found.[136] On 17 January, 2018, the Tribunal renders its award.

3-3-4. *Ansung Housing Co., Ltd. v. People's Republic of China (ICSID Case No. ARB/14/25)*[137]

The details of investment are capital expenditure of over USD 15 million for the development of a golf and country club in China. The investor claims 100.00 mln CNY (16.30 mln USD) against China. The claim arose out of the provincial government's alleged actions in relation to Ansung's investment in the construction of a golf and country club and luxury condominiums in Sheyang-Xian, Jiangsu province. The respondent State is China whereas the home State of the investor is the Republic of Korea. The applicable IIA here is China - Republic of Korea BIT (2007). The BIT between China and Republic of Korea of 2007, which replaced the BIT between China and Republic of Korea of 1992, coexists with the FTA between Korea and China of 2015 and with the Trilateral Investment Agreement among China, Japan and Republic of Korea (2012).

Its arbitration rules is Arbitration Rules of ICSID (International Centre for Settlement of Investment Disputes). Its administering institution is ICSID (International Centre for Settlement of Investment Disputes).

The decision is in favor of People's Republic of China. On 9 March, 2017, the respondent is awarded its share of the direct costs of the proceeding in the amount of US$ 69,760.55, plus 75 percent of its legal fees and expenses in the amount of US$ 4853.25 plus EUR 267,443.10 plus CNY 1,387,500, plus interest.

3-3-5. *Lee John Beck and Central Asian Development Corporation v. Kyrgyz Republic*[138]

The applicable IIA in this case is CIS Investor Rights Convention (1997). The respondent State is Kyrgyzstan while the home State of the investor is the Republic of Korea. The details of investment concern the rights under certain lease agreements. The dispute arose out of the alleged expropriation of claimant's investment by terminating certain lease agreements with respect to various land plots to develop a theme park in Bishkek. The arbitral rules here is the Arbitration Rules of MCCI (Moscow Chamber of Commerce and Industry). Its administering institution is MCCI (Moscow Chamber of Commerce and Industry). Its decision on the original proceedings was rendered on 13 November 2013.[139] It was in favor of the investor and thus it was awarded 23 million US dollars because MCCI has found IIA breach based on indirect expropriation. The decision on its follow-on proceedings was made to set aside in its entirety.

4. CONCLUSION

The mechanism for investment dispute settlement is necessary for independent, depoliticized and effective dispute settlement. Its availability to investors and states helps to promote international investment by providing confidence in the dispute resolution process. Sometimes, some popular domestic policies can be subject to ISD. Hence, the Korean government and its officials need to be aware that its drastic policy change may be subject to ISD. Whenever the

Korean government drastically changes its policies, it needs to take into account its impact on foreign investors.[140] In this regard, this Article proposes the adoption of the mechanism forecasting and warning the potential ISD. Otherwise, politicians and governmental officials in Korea will likely to pursue popularity-driven policies without considering the ISD risks. Accordingly, the Ministry of Justice in Korea enacted the "Regulation Related to Prevention of and Countermeasures against International Investment Disputes" on 5 April, 2019.

Appendix

The BITs which Korea has concluded as of 30 April 2019 are as follows:

(1) **Albania** (signed on 15 December 2003 and effective since 18 May 2006); (2) **Algeria** (signed on 12 October 1999 and effective since 30 September 2001); (3) **Argentina** (signed on 17 May 1994 and effective since 24 September 1996); (4) **Austria** (signed on 14 March 1991 and effective since 1 November 1991); (5) **Azerbaijan** (signed on 23 April 2007 and effective since 25 January 2008); (6) **Bangladesh** (signed on 18 June 1986 and effective since 6 October 1988); (7) **Belarus** (signed on 22 April 1997 and effective since 9 August 1997); (8) **BLEU** (Belgium-Luxembourg Economic Union) (signed on 20 December 1974 and effective since 3 September 1976, but the effect of this BIT was terminated); (9) **BLEU** (Belgium-Luxembourg Economic Union)(signed on 12 December 2006 and effective since 27 March 2011); (10) **Plurinational State of Bolivia** (signed 1 April 1996 and effective since 4 June 1997); (11) **Brazil** (signed on 1 September 1995 but not in force); (12) **Brunei** Darussalam (signed on 14 November 2003 and effective since 30 October 2003); (13) **Bulgaria** (signed on 12 June 2006 and effective since 16 November 2006); (14) **Burkina Faso** (signed on 26 October 2004 and effective since 14 April 2010); (15) **Cambodia** (signed on 10 February 1997 and effective since 12 March 1997); (16) **Cameroon** (signed on 24 December 2013 and effective since 13 April 2018); (17) **Chile** (signed on 6 September 1996 and effective since 16 September 1999, but the effect of this BIT was terminated); (18) **China** (signed on 30 September 1992 and effective since 4 December 1992, but the effect of this BIT was terminated); (19) **China** (signed on 7 September 2007 and effective since 1 December 2007); (20) **Colombia** (signed on 6 July 2010 but not in force); (21)

Democratic Republic of the Congo (signed on 19 July 1990 but not in force); (22) **Democratic Republic of the Congo** (signed on 17 March 2005 but not in force); (23) **Congo** (signed on 8 November 2006 and effective since 13 August 2011); (24) **Costa Rica** (signed on 11 August 2000 and effective since 25 August 2002); (25) **Croatia** (signed on 19 July 2005 and effective since 31 May 2006); (26) **Czech Republic** (signed on 27 April 1992 and effective since 16 March 1995); (27) **Denmark** (signed on 2 June 1988 and effective since 2 June 1988); (28) **Dominican Republic** (signed on 30 June 2006 and effective since 10 June 2008); (29) **Egypt** (signed on 18 March 1996 and effective since 25 May 1997); (30) **El Salvador** (signed on 6 July 1998 and effective since 25 May 2002); (31) **Finland** (signed on 21 October 1993 and effective since 11 May 1996); (32) **France** (signed on 28 December 1977 and effective since 1 February 1979); (33) **Gabon** (signed on 10 August 2007 and effective since 9 August 2009); (34) **Germany** (signed on 4 February 1964 and effective since 15 January 1967); (35) **Greece** (signed on 25 January 1995 and effective since 4 November 1995); (36) **Guatemala** (signed on 1 August 2000 and effective since 17 August 2002); (37) **Guyana** (signed on 31 July 2006 and effective since 4 November 1995); (38) **Honduras** (signed on 24 October 2000 and effective since 20 August 2006); (39) **Hong Kong**, China SAR (signed on 30 June 1997 and effective since 30 July 1997); (40) **Hungary** (signed on 28 December 1988 and effective since 1 January 1989); (41) **India** (signed on 26 February 1996 and effective since 7 May 1996); (42) **Indonesia** (signed on 16 February 1991 and effective since 10 March 1994); (43) **Islamic Republic of Iran** (signed on 31 October 1998 and effective since 31 March 2006); (44) **Israel** (signed on 7 February 1999 and effective since 19 June 2003); (45) **Italy** (signed on 10 January 1989 and effective since 26 June 1992); (46) **Jamaica** (signed on 10 June 2003 and effective since 5 November 2007); (47) **Japan** (signed on 22 March 2002 and effective since 1 January 2003); (48) **Jordan** (signed on 24 July 2004 and effective since 25 December 2004); (49) **Kazakhstan** (signed on 20 March 1996 and effective since 26 December 1996); (50) **Kenya** (signed on 8 July 2014 and effective since 3 May 2017); (51) **Kuwait** (signed on 15 July 2004 and effective since 31 August 2007); (52) **Kyrgyzstan** (signed on 20 March 1996 and effective since 26 December 1996, but the effect of this BIT was terminated); (53) **Kyrgyzstan** (signed on 19 November 2007 and effective since 8 July 2008); (54) **Lao People's Democratic Republic** (signed on 15 May 1996 and effective since 14 June 1996); (55) **Latvia** (signed on 23 October 1996); (56) **Lebanon** (signed on 5 May 2006 and effective since 21 December 2006); (57) **Libya** (signed on 21 September 1993 and effective since 28 March 2007); (58) **Lithuania** (signed on 24 September 1993 and effective since 9 November 1993); (59) **Malaysia** (signed on 11 April 1988 and effective since 31 March 1989); (60) **Mauritania** (signed on 15 December 2004 and effective since 21 July 2006); (61) **Mauritius** (signed on 18 June 2007 and effective since 7 March 2008); (62) **Mexico** (signed on 14 November 2000 and effective since 27 June 2002); (63) **Mongolia** (signed on 28 March 1991 and effective since 30 April 1991); (64) **Morocco** (signed on 27 January 1999 and effective since 8 May 2001); (65) **Myanmar** (signed on 5 June 2014 and effective since 31 October 2018); (66) **Netherlands** (signed on 16 October 1974 and effective since 1 June 1975, but its effect was terminated); (67) **Netherlands** (signed on 12 July 2003 and effective since 1 March 2005); (68) **Nicaragua** (signed on 15 May 2000 and effective since 22 June 2001); (69) **Nigeria** (signed on 27 March 1998 and effective since 1 February 1999); (70) **Oman** (signed on 8 October 2003 and effective since 10 February 2004); (71) **Pakistan** (signed on 25 May 1988 and effective since 15 April 1990); (72) **Panama** (signed on 10 July 2001 and effective since 8 February 2002); (73) **Paraguay** (signed on 22 December 1992 and effective since 6 August 1993);

(74) **Peru** (signed on 3 June 1993 and effective since 20 April 1994), but its effect was terminated); (75) **Philippines** (signed on 7 April 1994 and effective since 25 September 1996); (76) **Poland** (signed on 1 November 1989 and effective since 2 February 1990); (77) **Portugal** (signed on 3 May 1995 and effective since 11 August 1996); (78) **Qatar** (signed on 16 April 1999 and effective since 16 May 1999); (79) **Romania** (signed on 7 August 1990 and effective since 30 December 1994, but its effect was terminated); (80) **Romania** (signed on 6 September 2006 and effective since 11 January 2008); (81) **Russian Federation** (signed on 14 December 1990 and effective since 10 July 1991); (82) **Rwanda** (signed on 29 May 2009 and effective since 16 February 2013); (83) **Saudi Arabia** (signed on 4 April 2002 and effective since 19 February 2003); (84) **Senegal** (signed on 12 July 1984 and effective since 2 September 1985); (85) **Slovakia** (signed on 27 May 2005 and effective since 7 February 2006); (86) **South Africa** (signed on 27 May 2005 and effective since 7 February 2006); (87) **Spain** (signed on 17 January 1994 and effective since 19 July 1994); (88) **Sri Lanka** (signed on 28 March 1980 and effective since 15 July 1980); (89) **Sweden** (signed on 30 August 1995 and effective since 18 June 1997); (90) **Switzerland** (signed on 7 April 1971 and effective since 7 April 1971); (91) **Tajikistan** (signed on 14 July 1995 and effective since 13 August 1995); (92) **United Republic of Tanzania** (signed on 18 December 1998 but not in force); (93) **Thailand** (signed on 24 March 1989 and effective since 30 September 1989); (94) **Trinidad and Tobago** (signed on 5 November 2002 and effective since 27 November 2003); (95) **Tunisia** (signed on 23 May 1975 and effective since 28 November 1975); (96) **Turkey** (signed on 14 May 1991 and effective since 4 June 1994); (97) **Ukraine** (signed on 16 December 1996 and effective since 3 November 1997); (98) **United Arab Emirates** (signed on 9 June 2002 and effective since 15 June 2004); (99) **United Kingdom** (signed on 4 March 1976 and effective since

4 March 1976); (100) **Uruguay** (signed on 1 October 2009 and effective since 8 December 2011); (101) **Uzbekistan** (signed on 17 June 1992 and effective since 20 November 1992); (102) **Viet Nam** (signed on 13 May 1993 and effective since 4 September 1993 but its effect was terminated); (103) **Viet Nam** (signed on 15 September 2003 and effective since 5 June 2004); and (104) **Zimbabwe** (signed on 24 May 2010 but not in force).

References

Amokura Kawharu & Luke Nottage, *Models for Investment Treaties in the Asia-Pacific Region: An Underview*, 34 Ariz. J. Int'l & Comp. L. 461, 476 (2017).

Charles N. Brower & Sadie Blanchard, *What's in a Meme? The Truth About Investor-State Arbitration: Why It Need Not, and Must Not, Be Repossessed by States*, 52 Colum. J. Transnat'l L. 689, 704-05 (2014).

David Williams et al., Williams & Kawharu on Arbitration 833-70 (2d ed. 2017).

Filippo Fontanelli & Giuseppe Bianco, *Converging Towards NAFTA: An Analysis of FTA Investment Chapters in the European Union and the United States*, 50 Stan. J. Int'l L. 211, 214-15 (2014).

Guk-Sang Hwang, *The reason why Korea suddenly became the respondent state in ISDS cases*, MONEYTODAY, 3 May, 2019, http://news.mt.co.kr/mtview.php?no=2019042917078291553&outlink=1&ref=http%3A% 2F%2Fsearch.daum.net (Access on 10 May, 2019).

Jeffrey L. Dunoff et al., International Law Norms, Actors, Process: A Problem-Oriented Approach 708 (4th ed. 2015).

Joongi Kim, *A Bellwether to Korea's New Frontier in Investor-State Dispute Settlement? The Moscow Convention and Lee Jong Baek v. Kyrgyz Republic*, 15 Pepp. Disp. Resol. L. J. 549, 550 (2015).

Julien Chaisse, *Exploring the Confines of International Investment and Domestic Health Protections-Is a General Exceptions Clause a Forced Perspective?*, 39 Am. J. L. & Med. 332, 333, n. 5 (2013).

Meredith Wilensky, *Reconciling International Investment Law and Climate Change Policy: Potential Liability for Climate Measures under the Trans-Pacific Partnership*, 45 Envtl. L. Rep. News & Analysis 10683, 10696 (2015).

Myung Seop Chung, *Will lowering mobile fees by most of telecommunication companies affect a bill providing universal fee system?*, KINEWS, 9 April, 2018, http://www.kinews.net/news/articleView.html?idxno=118372 (last visit on 2 March, 2019).

Spenser Karr, Comment, *A Battle for Choice: Selecting Investor-State Arbitrators under the RCEP*, 90 Temp. L. Rev. 127, 151 (2017).

Su-hyun Song, *Foreign investors may take Korea's mobile fee cut to ISD settlement*, 28 August, 2017. The Korea Herald, available at http:// www.koreaherald.com/view.php?ud=20170828000747 (last visit on 1 March, 2019).

http://globalarbitrationreview.com/article/1150100/saudi-arabia-hit-with-icsid-claim-by-samsung (last visit on 20 April, 2019).

http://globalarbitrationreview.com/news/article/33203/kyrgyzstan-quashes-cis-treaty-award-russia/ (last visit on 20 March, 2019).

http://globalarbitrationreview.com/news/article/33765/kyrgyzstan-overturns-stans-award-russia/ (last visit on 20 March, 2018).

http://globalarbitrationreview.com/news/article/34159/iranian-investors-sue-south-korea/ (last visit on 31 March, 2019).

http://hsfnotes.com/arbitration/2014/11/10/china-sued-by-south-korean-property-developer-at-icsid/ (last visit on 30 March, 2019)

http://www.iareporter.com/articles/20141106 (last visit on 10 April, 2019).

http://investmentpolicyhub.unctad.org/ISDS/CountryCases/111?partyRole=1 (last visit on 20 April, 2019).

http://investmentpolicyhub.unctad.org/ISDS/CountryCases/111?partyRole=2 (last visit on 20 April, 2019).

http://www.cisarbitration.com/2014/05/14/kyrgyz-republics-mixed-fortunes-in-investment-arbitration/ (last visit on 20 March, 2019).

http://www.debevoise.com/insights/news/2015/09/debevoise-and-kim (last visit on 20 March, 2019).

http://www.derainsgharavi.com/lawyers/hamid-gharavi/ (last visit on 30 March, 2019).

http://koreatimes.co.kr/www/news/biz/2015/11/488_187345.html (last visit on 30 March, 2019).

http://www.derainsgharavi.com/lawyers/hamid-gharavi/ (last visit on 30 March, 2019).

https://www.iareporter.com/articles/asia-round-up-china-and-vietnam-face-new-bit-claims-as-proceedings-against-korea-and-indonesia-move-forward/ (last visit on 30 March, 2019).

http://www.iareporter.com/articles/20141015_1 (last visit on 20 March, 2019).

http://www.iareporter.com/articles/20140923_2? (last visit on 20 March, 2019).

http://www.iareporter.com/articles/analysis-existence-of-investment-attribution-and-proportionality-likely-to-feature-in-iranian-claimants-newly-filed-arbitration-against-korea/ (last visit on 29 March, 2019).

http://www.iareporter.com/Korea+round-up%3A+Lone+Star+case+reaches+hearings%2C+as+at+least+two+other+investment+treaty+claims+loomarticles/23170/ (last visit on 30 March, 2019).

http://www.iareporter.com/articles/samsung-files-claim-against-oman-over-refinery-improvement-project/ (last visit on 20 April, 2019).

http://www.iareporter.com/Korea+round-up%3A+Lone+Star+case+reaches+hearings%2C+as+at+least+two+other+investment+treaty+claims+loomarticles/23170/ (last visit on 20 March, 2019).

http://www.italaw.com/cases/2022 (last visit on 20 April, 2019).

http://www.koreatimes.co.kr/www/news/biz/2015/07/488_183399.html (last visit on 20 April, 2019).

http://www.sidley.com/experience/recent-investor-state-arbitrations (last visit on 22 March, 2019).

http://www.atimes.com/atimes/Korea/HK21Dg01.html (last visit on 22 March, 2019).

http://www.arnoldporter.com/professionals.cfm?action=view&id=967 (last visit on 22 March, 2019).

https://icsid.worldbank.org/en/Pages/cases/casedetail.aspx?CaseNo=ARB/15/17 (last visit on 20 March, 2019).

http://globalarbitrationreview.com/news/article/34181/debevoise-joins-south-korea-counsel-team-icsid/ (requires subscription) (last visit on 20 March, 2019).

https://icsid.worldbank.org/en/Pages/cases/casedetail.aspx?CaseNo=ARB/12/37 (last visit on 22 March, 2019).

http://globalarbitrationreview.com/news/article/33240/lone-star-gets-tax-refund-south-korea-icsid-case-continues/ (last visit on 22 March, 2019).

http://www.iareporter.com/articles/20130513 (last visit on 22 March, 2019).
https://icsid.worldbank.org/en/Pages/cases/casedetail.aspx?CaseNo=ARB/17/43 (last visit on 20 April, 2019).
https://www.iareporter.com/articles/saudia-arabia-faces-a-second-bit-claim-within-days-as-korean-investor-turns-to-arbitration/ (last visit on 20 April, 2019).
https://icsid.worldbank.org/en/Pages/cases/casedetail.aspx?CaseNo=ARB/15/30 (last visit on 30 March, 2019).
http://globalarbitrationreview.com/news/article/34002/samsung-takes-oman-losing-refinery-deal/ (last visit on 20 April, 2019).
https://icsid.worldbank.org/en/Pages/cases/casedetail.aspx?CaseNo=ARB/14/25 (last visit on 30 March, 2019).
http://globalarbitrationreview.com/news/article/33143/%20china-faces-second-icsid-claim/ (last visit on 10 April, 2019).
https://icsid.worldbank.org/en/Pages/cases/casedetail.aspx?CaseNo=ARB/12/37 (last visit on 10 May, 2019).
https://investmentpolicyhubold.unctad.org/ISDS/Details/651 (last visit on 10 May, 2019).
https://investmentpolicyhubold.unctad.org/ISDS/Details/679 (last visit on 10 May, 2019).
https://investmentpolicyhubold.unctad.org/ISDS/Details/878 (last visit on 10 May, 2019)
https://icsid.worldbank.org/en/Pages/cases/casedetail.aspx?CaseNo=ARB(AF)/18/2 (last visit on 10 May, 2019).
https://investmentpolicyhubold.unctad.org/ISDS/Details/893 (last visit on 10 May, 2019).
https://investmentpolicyhubold.unctad.org/ISDS/Details/939 (last visit on 10 May, 2019).
https://investmentpolicyhubold.unctad.org/ISDS/Details/941 (last visit on 10 May, 2019).
https://pca-cpa.org/en/cases/198/ (last visit on 10 May, 2019).

Notes

1. Su-hyun Song, *Foreign investors may take Korea's mobile fee cut to ISD settlement*, 28 August, 2017. The Korea Herald, available at http://www.koreaherald.com/view.php?ud=20170828000747(last visit on 1 March, 2019).
2. *Id.*
3. Myung Seop Chung, *Will lowering mobile fees by most of telecommunication companies affect a bill providing universal fee system?*, KINEWS, 9 April, 2018, http://www.kinews.net/news/articleView.html?idxno=118372 (last visit on 2 March, 2019).
4. Joongi Kim, *A Bellwether to Korea's New Frontier in Investor-State Dispute Settlement? The Moscow Convention and Lee Jong Baek v. Kyrgyz Republic*, 15 Pepp. Disp. Resol. L. J. 549, 550 (2015).
5. Charles N. Brower & Sadie Blanchard, *What's in a Meme? The Truth About Investor-State Arbitration: Why It Need Not, and Must Not, Be Repossessed by States*, 52 Colum. J. Transnat'l L. 689, 704-05 (2014); Spenser Karr, Comment, *A Battle for Choice: Selecting Investor-State Arbitrators under the RCEP*, 90 Temp. L. Rev. 127, 151 (2017).
6. Meredith Wilensky, *Reconciling International Investment Law and Climate Change Policy: Potential Liability for Climate Measures under the Trans-Pacific Partnership*, 45 Envtl. L. Rep. News & Analysis 10683, 10696 (2015).
7. The appendix shows the BITs Korea has concluded as of 30 April, 2019.
8. Those treaties containing investment provisions are as follows:
   FTA between Republic of Korea and Republics of Central America (parties: Costa Rica, El Salvador, Honduras, Nicaragua and Panama) (signed on 21 February 2018 but not in force); (2) FTA between China and Republic of Korea (signed on 1 June 2015 and effective since 20 December 2015); (3) FTA between Republic of Korea and Viet Nam (signed on 5 May 2015 and effective since 20 December 2015); (4) FTA between Republic of Korea and New Zealand (signed on 23 March 2015 and effective since 20 December 2015); (5) Republic of Korea-Turkey Investment Agreement (2015) (signed on 26 February 2015); (6) Canada-Republic of Korea FTA (2014)(signed on 22 September 2014 and effective since 1 January 2015); (7) Australia-Republic of Korea FTA (2014) (signed on 8 April 2014 and effective since 12 December 2014); (8) Colombia-Republic of Korea FTA (signed on 21 February 2013 and effective since 15 July 2016); (9) China-Japan-Republic of Korea Trilateral Investment Agreement (2012) (parties: China, Japan)(signed on 13 May 2012 and effective since 17 May 2014)(Retaining international treaty arbitration for dispute settlement); (10) Korea-Peru FTA (signed on 14 November 2010 and effective since 1 August 2011); (11) EU-Korea FTA (signed on 6 October 2010 and effective since 1 July 2011); (12) EU-Korea Framework Agreement (signed on 10 May 2010 but not in force); (13) APTA Investment Agreement (2009)(parties: Bangladesh, China, Lao People's Democratic Republic, Sri Lanka) (signed on 15 December 2009 but not in force); (14) India-Republic of Korea CEPA (2009) (signed on 7 August 2009 and effective since 1 January

2010); (15) ASEAN-Korea Investment Agreement (signed on 2 June 2009 and effective since 1 September 2009); (16) Korea-US FTA (signed on 30 June 2007 and effective since 15 March 2012); (17) EFTA-Korea Investment Agreement (signed on 15 December 2005 and effective since 1 October 2006); (18) ASEAN-Korea Framework Agreement (signed on 13 December 2005 and effective since 1 July 2006); (19) Korea-Singapore FTA (signed on 4 August 2005 and effective since 1 July 2006); (20) Chile-Korea FTA (signed on 15 February 2003 and effective since 1 April 2004); (21) EC-Korea Cooperation Agreement (signed on 28 October 1996 and effective since 1 April 2001); (22) RECP (parties: ASEAN, Australia, China, India, Japan, New Zealand, Republic of Korea).

9. Those IRIs are as follows:
Fifth Protocol to GATS (1997); (2) Fourth Protocol to GATS (1997); (3) TRIPS (1994); (4) TRIMS (1994); (5) GATS (1994); (6) MIGA Convention (1985); (7) ICSID Convention (1965); (8) OECD Invisible Operations (1961); (9) OECD Capital Movements (1961); (10) New York Convention (1958); (11) MAI Draft (1998); (12) UN Code of Conduct on Transnational Corporations (1983); (13) OECD Convention on the Protection of Foreign Property (1967); (14) OECD Guidelines for Multinational Enterprises (2011); (15) UN Guiding Principles on Business and Human Rights (2011); (16) ILO Tripartite Declaration on Multinational Enterprises (2006); (17) Doha Declaration (2001); (18) OECD Declaration Multinational Enterprises (2000); (19) ILO Tripartite Declaration on Multinational Enterprises (2000); (20) OECD Principles of Corporate Governance (1999); (21) Singapore Ministerial Declaration (1996); (22) Pacific Basin Investment Charter (1995); (23) APEC Non-Binding Investment Principles (1994); (24) World Bank Investment Guidelines (1992); (25) ILO Tripartite Declaration on Multinational Enterprises (1977); (26) New International Economic Order UN Resolution (1974); (27) Charter of Economic Rights and Duties of States (1974); and (28) Permanent Sovereignty UN Resolution (1962).

10. The FTA between South Korea and USA includes ISDS in its investment chapter.

11. "While Australia claimed in 2011 that it would stop including ISDS in future trade treaties, it has since addressed the issue on a case-by-case basis, concluding a BIT as recently as 2014 with South Korea containing ISDS." (Jeffrey L. Dunoff et al., International Law Norms, Actors, Process: A Problem- Oriented Approach 708 (4th ed. 2015); Karr, *supra* note 5, at 137.

12. The FTA between New Zealand and Korea includes ISDS (Amokura Kawharu & Luke Nottage, *Models for Investment Treaties in the Asia-Pacific Region: An Underview*, 34 Ariz. J. Int'l & Comp. L. 461, 476 (2017); David Williams et al., Williams & Kawharu on Arbitration 833-70(2d ed. 2017)).

13. Article 1 of Foreign Investment Promotion Act (Act No. 14839, July 26, 2017).

14. Article 2 (1) 1 of FIPA.

15. Article 27 of FIPA prescribes that "(1) A Foreign Investment Committee shall be established under the Ministry of Trade, Industry and Energy to deliberate on the following:

1. Important matters concerning the basic policy and schemes for foreign investment;
2. Matters concerning integration and coordination of the measures by competent Ministry to improve an environment for foreign investment;
3. Matters concerning the criteria for tax reductions or exemptions for foreign-capital invested companies;
4. Matters concerning cooperation among, and coordination of different opinions of, central administrative agencies, 5. Special Metropolitan City, Metropolitan Cities, Metropolitan Autonomous City, *Do*s, and Special Self-Governing 6. Province with respect to foreign investment;
7. Matters concerning stimulus plans;
8. Matters concerning contributions to nonprofit corporations defined in Article 2 (1) 4 (d);
9. Matters concerning support for local governments under Article 14;
10. Matters concerning cash grants under Article 14-2;
11. Matters concerning the payment of monetary rewards for inducing foreign investment under Article 14-3 (2);
12. Matters concerning the designation of foreign investment zones and assistance thereto under Articles 18 and 19;
13. Matters concerning approval under Article 30 (7);
14. Other important matters concerning the inducement of foreign investment.
(2) The Minister of Trade, Industry and Energy shall be the Chairperson of the Foreign Investment Committee, and the following persons shall be its members:
1. The Vice Minister of Strategy and Finance, the Vice Minister of Education, the Vice Minister of Ministry of Science, ICT and Future Planning, the Vice Minister of Foreign Affairs, the Vice Minister of the Interior, the Vice Minister of Culture, Sport and Tourism, the Vice Minister of Agriculture, Food and Rural Affairs, the Vice Minister of Environment, the Vice Minister of Employment and Labor, the Vice Minister of Land, Infrastructure and Transport, the Vice Minister of Oceans and Fisheries, and the Vice Chairperson of the Financial Services Commission;
2. The Vice Ministers, vice chairpersons, or deputy administrators of central administrative agencies related to the agendas submitted to the Foreign Investment Committee, the Vice Mayor of Seoul Special Metropolitan City, Mayors/Do Governors (excluding the Seoul Special Metropolitan City Mayor) and the president of the Korea Trade-Investment Promotion Agency.
(3) A Foreign Investment Working Committee (hereinafter referred to as "Working Committee") shall be established to review and coordinate matters to be deliberated upon by the Foreign Investment Committee, and to deliberate on matters entrusted by the Foreign Investment Committee, as prescribed by Presidential Decree.
(4) The Minister of Trade, Industry and Energy shall report to the Foreign Investment Committee on the current status of improving an environment for foreign investment referred to in paragraph (1) 2.
(5) Except as otherwise expressly provided for in paragraphs (1) through (3),

matters necessary for the composition and operation of the Foreign Investment Commission and the Working Committee shall be prescribed by Presidential Decree."

16. Article 2 (1) 5 of FIPA.
17. Article 2 (1) 6 of FIPA.
18. Article 2 (1) 7 of FIPA.
19. Article 2 (1) 8 of FIPA.
20. Article 2 (1) 9 of FIPA.
21. Article 4 (2) of FIPA.
22. Article 4 (4) of FIPA.
23. Article 4 (1) of FIPA.
24. Article 2 (1) 4 (a) of FIPA prescribes that The term "foreign investment" means any of the following: (i) Acquisition of stocks, etc. newly issued by the Korean corporation or company run by the national of the Republic of Korea; (ii) Acquisition of stocks, etc. previously issued by the Korean corporation or company run by the national of the Republic of Korea (hereinafter referred to as "existing stocks, etc.").
25. According to Article 2 (1) 4 (c) and (d), The term "foreign investment" means any of the following: (a) and (b) (omitted); (c) Where a foreigner contributes to a nonprofit corporation pursuant to this Act in order to establish a continuous cooperative relationship with the corporation which satisfies the standards prescribed by Presidential Decree in terms of research personnel, facility, etc. and which is a corporation (including a corporation in the process of establishment) of the Republic of Korea in the field of science and technology; (d) Other contributions to a non-profit corporation by a foreigner, which the Foreign Investment Committee established under Article 27 (hereinafter referred to as the "Foreign Investment Committee") recognizes as a foreign investment in accordance with the standards prescribed by Presidential Decree regarding the business contents, etc. of the non-profit corporation.
26. Article 21 (1) of FIPA.
27. The term "foreign investment" means any of the following: (a) Where a foreigner holds stocks or shares (hereinafter referred to as "stocks, etc.") of a Korean corporation (including a Korean corporation in the process of establishment; hereafter the same shall apply in (i) below) or a company run by a national of the Republic of Korea, as prescribed by Presidential Decree, by any of the following methods in order to establish a continuous economic relationship with the Korean corporation or company, such as participating in the management of such Korean corporation or company in accordance with this Act: (i) Acquisition of stocks, etc. newly issued by the Korean corporation or company run by the national of the Republic of Korea; or (ii) Acquisition of stocks, etc. previously issued by the Korean corporation or company run by the national of the Republic of Korea (hereinafter referred to as "existing stocks, etc.").
28. Article 21 (2) of FIPA.

29. Article 5 (1) and (2) of FIPA prescribes as follows:
(1) A foreigner (including specially related personnel prescribed by Presidential Decree in cases falling under Article 2 (1) 4 (a) (ii); hereafter in this Article the same shall apply) who intends to make a foreign investment by either of the methods provided for in the items of Article 2 (1) shall, in advance, report thereon to the Minister of Trade, Industry and Energy, as prescribed by Ordinance of the Ministry of Trade, Industry and Energy.
(2) Notwithstanding paragraph (1), a foreigner who intends to make a foreign investment by any of the following methods may report thereon within 60 days from the acquisition of stocks, etc.: 1. Where the foreigner acquires existing stocks, etc. issued by a listed stock corporation under the Financial Investment Services and Capital Markets Act (excluding public purpose corporations defined under Article 152 (3) of the same Act and corporations that are restricted from acquiring stocks under separate Acts);
2. Where a foreign investor acquires stocks, etc. issued upon capitalizing reserves, revaluation reserves, or other reserves prescribed by Acts and other statutes of the relevant foreign-capital invested company;
3. Where a foreign investor acquires stocks, etc. of a surviving corporation or a newly incorporated corporation after a merger, all-inclusive stock swap or transfer, or spinoff by means of stocks he/she is holding at the time of the relevant foreign-capital invested company's merger, all-inclusive stock swap or transfer with another company, or spinoff;
4. Where a foreigner acquires stocks, etc. of a foreign-capital invested company registered under Article 21 by means of purchase, inheritance, testamentary gift, or gift from a foreign investor;
5. Where a foreign investor acquires stocks, etc. by investing the proceeds from the stocks, etc. acquired under the Acts of the Republic of Korea;
6. Where a foreigner acquires stocks, etc. using convertible bonds, exchangeable bonds, stock depositary receipts, and such similar ones as bonds or receipts that may be converted into, taken over as, or exchanged for stocks, etc.

30. According to Article 121-5 (2) 2 of the Restriction of Special Taxation Act under the title of "Additional Collection, etc. of Amount of Tax Reduced or Exempted on Foreign Investment," the director of a customs office or the head of a tax office shall additionally collect customs duties, individual consumption tax, and value-added tax exempted under Article 121-3 of the Restriction of Special Taxation Act, as prescribed by Presidential Decree in cases where the object of investment is used for any purpose other than the reported one, or is disposed, The director of a customs office or the head of a tax office shall additionally collect customs duties, individual consumption tax, and value-added tax exempted under Article 121-3 of the Restriction of Special Taxation Act, as prescribed by Presidential Decree.

31. Article 5 (Reporting on Foreign Investment) of FIPA prescribing that:
(1) A foreigner (including specially related personnel prescribed by Presidential Decree in cases falling under Article 2 (1) 4 (a) (ii); hereafter in this Article the same shall apply) who intends to make a foreign investment by either of the

methods provided for in the items of Article 2 (1) shall, in advance, report thereon to the Minister of Trade, Industry and Energy, as prescribed by Ordinance of the Ministry of Trade, Industry and Energy.
(2) Notwithstanding paragraph (1), a foreigner who intends to make a foreign investment by any of the following methods may report thereon within 60 days from the acquisition of stocks, etc.:
1. Where the foreigner acquires existing stocks, etc. issued by a listed stock corporation under the Financial Investment Services and Capital Markets Act (excluding public purpose corporations defined under Article 152 (3) of the same Act and corporations that are restricted from acquiring stocks under separate Acts);
2. Where a foreign investor acquires stocks, etc. issued upon capitalizing reserves, revaluation reserves, or other reserves prescribed by Acts and other statutes of the relevant foreign-capital invested company;
3. Where a foreign investor acquires stocks, etc. of a surviving corporation or a newly incorporated corporation after a merger, all-inclusive stock swap or transfer, or spinoff by means of stocks he/she is holding at the time of the relevant foreign-capital invested company's merger, all-inclusive stock swap or transfer with another company, or spinoff;
4. Where a foreigner acquires stocks, etc. of a foreign-capital invested company registered under Article 21 by means of purchase, inheritance, testamentary gift, or gift from a foreign investor;
5. Where a foreign investor acquires stocks, etc. by investing the proceeds from the stocks, etc. acquired under the Acts of the Republic of Korea;
6. Where a foreigner acquires stocks, etc. using convertible bonds, exchangeable bonds, stock depositary receipts, and such similar ones as bonds or receipts that may be converted into, taken over as, or exchanged for stocks, etc.
(3) Of the details reported under paragraph (1) or (2), where any of the matters prescribed by Ordinance of the Ministry of Trade, Industry and Energy, such as the foreign investment ratio (referring to the ratio of the stocks, etc. owned by a foreign investor to the total stocks, etc. of a foreign-capital invested company; hereinafter the same shall apply), is modified, a foreigner may reflect such modified matter when reporting to Minister of Trade, Industry and Energy.
(4) Upon receipt of a report filed under paragraphs (1) through (3), the Minister of Trade, Industry and Energy shall issue a certificate of completion of report to the relevant person without delay.

32. Article 6 (Permission of Foreign Investment, etc.) of FIPA stating that "(1) A foreigner (including specially related persons prescribed by Presidential Decree) who intends to make a foreign investment in a defense industry company prescribed by Presidential Decree by the method provided in Article 2 (1) 4 (a) (ii) shall obtain permission from the Minister of Trade, Industry and Energy in advance, as prescribed by Ordinance of the Ministry of Trade, Industry and Energy, notwithstanding Article 5 (1) and (2). The same shall also apply where the foreigner intends to modify any permitted details prescribed by Ordinance of the Ministry of Trade, Industry and Energy, such as the foreign investment

ratio.
(2) Upon receipt of an application for permission filed under paragraph (1), the Minister of Trade, Industry and Energy shall determine whether to grant permission or not, and notify the relevant applicant of his/her determination within a period prescribed by Presidential Decree.
(3) The Minister of Trade, Industry and Energy shall consult with the competent Minister before determining whether to grant permission or not under paragraph (2), as prescribed by Presidential Decree.
(4) The Minister of Trade, Industry and Energy may impose conditions on permission granted under paragraph (2) if deemed necessary to do so.
(5) No one who has acquired existing stocks, etc. without obtaining permission under paragraph (1) or in violation of conditions imposed under paragraph (4) shall exercise his/her voting rights in such existing stocks, etc.
(6) The Minister of Trade, Industry and Energy may order a person who has acquired existing stocks, etc. without obtaining permission under paragraph (1) or in violation of conditions imposed under paragraph (4) to transfer such existing stocks, etc. to a third party, as prescribed by Presidential Decree.
(7) Except as otherwise specifically provided for in paragraphs (1) through (6), matters necessary for permission of foreign investment shall be prescribed by Presidential Decree."

33. Article 21 (3) of FIPA.

34. Article 8 (business registrations) of the Value Added Tax Act prescribes that:
"(1) An entrepreneur shall file an application for business registration for each place of business with the head of the tax office having jurisdiction over each place of business, within 20 days from the commencement date of his/her business, as prescribed by Presidential Decree: Provided, That a person who intends to newly start a business may file an application for business registration even before the commencement date of the business.
(2) An entrepreneur may file an application for business registration under paragraph (1) with the head of any tax office other than the head of the tax office having jurisdiction over his/her place of business. In such cases, he/she shall be deemed to file an application for business registration with the head of the tax office having jurisdiction over his/her place of business.
(3) Notwithstanding paragraph (1), an entrepreneur who has two or more places of business may file an application for registration by his/her business unit with the head of the tax office having jurisdiction over his/her main office or principal office. In such cases, an entrepreneur so registered shall be treated as a per-business unit taxable entrepreneur.
(4) Where an entrepreneur who has filed for an application for business registration by his/her business unit under paragraph (1) intends to be converted to a per-business unit taxable entrepreneur under paragraph (3), he/she shall file an application for modification of registration with the head of the tax office having jurisdiction over his/her main office or principal office not later than 20 days before the commencement of the taxable period during which he/she intends to be treated as a per-business unit taxable entrepreneur. The same shall

also apply where a per-business unit taxable entrepreneur intends to register his/her business by his/her business unit.
(5) The head of the tax office having jurisdiction over the place of business who has received an application filed under paragraphs (1) through (4) (referring to the head of the tax office having jurisdiction over the main office or principal office in cases falling under paragraphs (3) and (4); hereafter the same shall apply in this Article) shall, upon registration of the business, issue a certificate of registration with a registration number assigned (hereinafter referred to as "business registration certificate") to the relevant entrepreneur, as prescribed by Presidential Decree.
(6) Where an entrepreneur registered under paragraph (5) suspends or closes his/her business or is subject to any modification of his/her registration, he/she shall promptly report such fact to the head of the tax office having jurisdiction over his/her place of business, as prescribed by Presidential Decree. The same shall also apply where a person who has filed an application for business registration under the proviso to paragraph (1) turns out, in fact, not to start the business.
(7) to (10) [Omitted]."

35. Article 21 (4) of FIPA.
36. Article 4 (2) and (3) of FIPA stating that "(2) No foreigner shall be restricted from making any foreign investment prescribed in this Act, except in the following circumstances:
1. Where he/she threatens national security and public order;
2. Where he/she has harmful effects on public health and sanitation or environmental preservation or is against Korean morals and customs;
3. Where he/she violates any Act or statutes of the Republic of Korea.
(3) The categories of businesses in which foreign investment is restricted in accordance with any of the subparagraphs of paragraph (2) and the details of restrictions shall be prescribed by Presidential Decree."
37. *Id.*
38. Article 21 (5) of FIPA.
39. Article 21 (6) of FIPA.
40. Article 2 (1) 4 (b) of FIPA prescribing that The term "foreign investment" means any of the following: (a) [omitted];
(b) A loan with maturity of not less than five years (based on the loan maturity prescribed in the first loan contract), which is provided to a foreign-capital invested company by any of the following entities: (i) The overseas parent company of the foreign-capital invested company; (ii) A company that has a capital investment relationship prescribed by Presidential Decree with the company prescribed in (i); (iii) A foreign investor; (iv) A company that has a capital investment relationship prescribed by Presidential Decree with the investor prescribed in (iii); or
(c) and (d) [omitted].
41. Article 3 (1) of FIPA.

42. Article 3 (2) of FIPA.
43. Article 2 (1) 4 (b) of FIPA prescribing that The term "foreign investment" means any of the following: (a) [omitted];
(b) A loan with maturity of not less than five years (based on the loan maturity prescribed in the first loan contract), which is provided to a foreign-capital invested company by any of the following entities: (i) The overseas parent company of the foreign-capital invested company; (ii) A company that has a capital investment relationship prescribed by Presidential Decree with the company prescribed in (i); (iii) A foreign investor; (iv) A company that has a capital investment relationship prescribed by Presidential Decree with the investor prescribed in (iii); or
(c) and (d) [omitted].
44. Article 3 (3) of FIPA.
45. Article 3 (4) of FIPA.
46. Article 14 of FIPA prescribes that:
(1) Where a local government requests the State to provide funds necessary for the formation of a foreign investment zone prescribed in Article 18, loan for the purchase of land to be leased to any foreign-invested company, etc., reduction or exemption of the rental payments of land, etc., reduction of lot prices (including such cases where a local government provides the money, where any person prescribed by Presidential Decree leases the land, etc. to any foreign invested company, etc. with the rental payments reduced or exempted or sells at a price lower than the land preparation costs, for the portion equivalent to the amount of the rental payments reduced or exempted as such or to the difference between the land preparation costs and the lot prices), payment of various kinds of subsidies, such as the education and training subsidy, and other foreign investment inducement projects, the State shall provide such funds to the maximum extent possible.
(2) The criteria and procedures for the provision of funds by the State to a local government in accordance with paragraph (1) shall be determined by the Foreign Investment Committee, as prescribed by Presidential Decree. For determining the criteria for the provision of funds in such cases, efforts made by a local government for the inducement of foreign investment and the actual outcomes thereof shall be taken into consideration.
(3) The State shall estimate the amount of funds to be provided in accordance with paragraph (1) each year and include the estimated amount in its budget.
(4) Where necessary for the purpose of promoting the inducement of foreign investment or improving foreign investment environment, a local government may pay a foreign-capital invested company an employment subsidy, etc. determined by Presidential Decree, as prescribed by municipal ordinances.
47. Article 13 (1) of FIPA.
48. It prescribes that "Foreign investment for operating any of the following businesses (referring to foreign investment defined in Article 2 (1) 4 of FIPA; hereafter in this Chapter, the same shall apply), shall be eligible for a reduction

of, or exemption from, corporate tax, income tax, acquisition tax, and property tax (referring to the amount of tax levied under Article 111 of the Local Tax Act; hereinafter the same shall apply), respectively, as prescribed in paragraphs (2), (4), (5), and (12), if the investment meets the conditions prescribed by Presidential Decree:
(1) Foreign investment for operating any of the following businesses (referring to foreign investment defined in Article 2 (1) 4 of FIPA; hereafter in this Chapter, the same shall apply), shall be eligible for a reduction of, or exemption from, corporate tax, income tax, acquisition tax, and property tax (referring to the amount of tax levied under Article 111 of the Local Tax Act; hereinafter the same shall apply), respectively, as prescribed in paragraphs (2), (4), (5), and (12), if the investment meets the conditions prescribed by Presidential Decree:
A business that requires any of the technologies prescribed by Presidential Decree and belongs to the new growth engine industry essential for upgrading domestic industrial structures and strengthening international competitiveness; 2 to 3 [Omitted]."

49. Article 13 (2) of FIPA.

50. Article 35 (1) of the State Property Act prescribing that "The period for permission for use of any administrative property shall be five years or less: Provided, That in cases under Article 34 (1) 1, it shall be within the period wherein the total sum of usage fees reaches the value of the property donated."; Article 46 (1) of the same Act stating that "The loan period for general property shall not exceed any of the following: Provided, That in cases of constructing permanent facilities under the proviso to Article 18 (1), it shall not exceed ten years:
1. Land and its fixtures to be afforested: Ten years;
2. Land and its fixtures, other than those in subparagraph 1: Five years;
3. Any other property: One year."

51. Article 69 (Lease of State-owned land and public land, etc.) prescribing that "(1) In cases of an implementer referred to in Article 11 (1) 7, the Minister of Strategy and Finance, the managing agency of the state-owned assets or the head of a local government may use, profit from or lend (hereinafter referred to as "lease"), through free contract, the land, factories and other state-owned land and public land owned by the State or local governments in an urban development zone, notwithstanding the State Property Act and the Public Property and Commodity Management Act.
(2) The period of lease in cases where land, etc. owned by the State or local governments is leased under paragraph (1) may be set within 20 years, notwithstanding the State Property Act and the Public Property and Commodity Management Act."

52. Article 13 (3) of FIPA.

53. Article 18 (Prohibition on Constructing Permanent Facilities) of the State Property Act prescribing that: "(1) Every person other than the State shall be prohibited

from constructing any types of structures, such as buildings and bridges, and other permanent facilities on State property: Provided, That the same shall not apply to any of the following cases:
1. Where they are constructed on the condition that they be donated;
2. Where they are constructed as public facilities, the ownership of which shall revert to the State pursuant to other statutes;
2-2. Where the relevant property is general property, the purchase price of which is being paid in installments pursuant to Article 50 (2), as prescribed by Presidential Decree;
3. Where they enhance the utility of the State property without disrupting any use of it, and they are deemed necessary by the head of a central government agency, etc. to achieve the purposes of use for the State property under the loan contracts;
4. Where they are developed pursuant to Article 59-2.
(2) Where the construction of permanent facilities is allowed under the proviso to paragraph (1), measures for having such person guarantee the payment of an amount equivalent to the expenses and costs to be incurred in restoring the State property to its original state, including removal of such permanent facilities, shall be taken pursuant to the standards and procedures prescribed by Presidential Decree."

54. Article 13 (4) of FIPA.

55. Article 32 (1) of the State Property Act prescribing that "When permission for use of administrative property is granted, the usage fees shall be collected each year in accordance with the rates and calculation methods specified by Presidential Decree: Provided, That where the annual fees are less than the amount specified by Presidential Decree, the fees for the period of permission for use may be entirely collected at the same time."; Article 47 of the same Act stating as follows:
"Article 47 (Rent, Rescission of Contracts, etc.)
Articles 30 (2), 31 (1) and (2), 32, 33, 34 (1) 2 and 3, 34 (2), 36 and 38 shall apply mutatis mutandis to the restriction on loan, rent, exemption of rent, and rescission or termination of loan contracts, etc., for any general property.
Despite paragraph (1), with respect to rent, all or part of annual rent may be received after converting it into loan deposit, as prescribed by Presidential Decree.
Where the term of a loan expires or a loan agreement is rescinded or terminated, the head of the relevant central government agency, etc., shall return the loan deposit prescribed under paragraph (2). In such cases, if there are rents or utility bills, etc., that the person who made the loan failed to pay, the head of a central government agency shall return the loan deposit after excluding the unpaid amount."

56. "Article 26 (Supply Plans of Developed Land, etc.) (1) When any implementer (excluding where the designating authority is an implementer) intends to supply developed land, etc., he/she shall prepare or amend a supply plan of such land, etc. to submit it to the designating authority. In such cases, an implementer who

is not an administrative agency shall submit it through the head of a Si (excluding the head of a Large Si)/Gun/Gu.
Details of a supply plan, procedures and standard for supply, appraisal price of the developed land, etc. and other necessary matters shall be prescribed by Presidential Decree."

57. Article 69 (Lease of State-Owned Land and Public land, etc.) of the Urban Development Act prescribes as follows:
(1) In cases of an implementer referred to in Article 11 (1) 7, the Minister of Strategy and Finance, the managing agency of the state-owned assets or the head of a local government may use, profit from or lend (hereinafter referred to as "lease"), through free contract, the land, factories and other state-owned land and public land owned by the State or local governments in an urban development zone, notwithstanding the State Property Act and the Public Property and Commodity Management Act.
(2) The period of lease in cases where land, etc. owned by the State or local governments is leased under paragraph (1) may be set within 20 years, notwithstanding the State Property Act and the Public Property and Commodity Management Act.
(3) Where the land owned by the State or local government is leased under paragraph (1), construction of factories or other permanent facilities on such land may be permitted, notwithstanding the State Property Act and the Public Property and Commodity Management Act. In such cases, the land may be leased, in consideration of the types, etc. of such facilities, on condition that they shall be donated to the State or a local government or be returned by restoring to their original state when the period of lease expires.
(4) Rent for land, etc. leased under paragraph (1) shall be prescribed by Presidential Decree, notwithstanding the State Property Act and the Public Property and Commodity Management Act.
(5) The period of lease under paragraph (2) may be renewed. In such cases, whenever renewed, the period shall not exceed the period under paragraph (2).

58. Article 50 of the Act on the Development and Management of Logistics Facilities (Disposition of Developed Land, Facilities, etc.) is as follows:
Any project implementer may sell or lease land, facilities, etc. (in cases of an urban advanced logistics complex development project, excluding land on which installation of facilities has not been complete) developed under a logistics complex development project.
Matters necessary for the methods and procedures for disposition of land, facilities, etc. prescribed in paragraph (1) and guidelines for prices thereof shall be prescribed by Presidential Decree.

59. Article 13 (5) of FIPA.

60. It states that "Proceeds from the sale of any general property shall be paid, as prescribed by Presidential Decree: Provided, That the period for payment may be extended as permitted by Presidential Decree."

61. It prescribes that "Necessary matters concerning the accounting principles and

restrictions on the qualification for bidding under the provisions of paragraphs (1) and (2) shall be prescribed by Ordinance of the Ministry of Strategy and Finance."

62. Article 13 (6) of FIPA.

63. Article 38 of the Industrial Sites and Development Act prescribes that:
"(1) Where a project operator intends to sell, lease, or transfer (hereafter referred to as "disposal" in this Article) land, facilities, etc. in an area for which a master plan for industrial complex management has been formulated among land, facilities, etc. he/she has developed, he/she shall formulate a disposal plan and consult with the managing agency (hereafter referred to as "managing agency" in this Article) under Article 30 of the Industrial Cluster Development and Factory Establishment Act, and the managing agency shall notify him/her of its opinion within 20 days from the receipt of a request to consult.
(2) A project operator may dispose of land, facilities, etc. in an area other than the management area according to the master plan for industrial complex management under paragraph (1), among the developed land, facilities, etc., as prescribed by Presidential Decree.
(3) Where a project operator deems it necessary for efficiently performing disposal affairs and the Korea Industrial Complex Management Corporation under Article 31 of the Industrial Cluster Development and Factory Establishment Act has been established, he/she may enter into a contract with the Korea Industrial Complex Management Corporation and entrust the affairs concerning sale or lease of the developed land, facilities, etc.
(4) Before formulating a disposal plan under paragraph (1), a project operator may request the managing agency to amend the master plan for industrial complex management to ensure that the scope of buildings by each district, as permitted in the master plan for industrial complex management, coincides with the development plan under Articles 6, 7, and 7-2.
(5) Where a building project is included in an industrial complex development project, the project operator shall use earnings from sale accrued from the building project to reduce the prices of industrial facility sites, such as installation of infrastructure, as prescribed by Presidential Decree.
(6) Where a project operator entitled to perform a building project among industrial complex development projects, constructs a knowledge industry center defined in subparagraph 13 of Article 2 of the Industrial Cluster Development and Factory Establishment Act, he/she shall rent out part of the knowledge industry center at the rate prescribed by Presidential Decree, within the limits of 50 percent: Provided, That the same shall not apply to cases of constructing knowledge industry centers by December 31, 2018.
(7) The details of a disposal plan, methods of disposal, procedures for disposal, price standards under paragraph (1) and other necessary matters shall be prescribed by Presidential Decree. In such cases, where a project operator who is the State or a local government leases land, facilities, etc., the related provisions of the State Property Act and the Public Property and Commodity Management Act shall not apply to the terms of lease, methods of lease,

procedures for lease, criteria for the calculation of rent, etc.
(8) Where a project operator falling under paragraph (1) sells a site for a factory to a person who intends to purchase such site to lease it to a small and medium enterprise, price standards for such site, methods of payment, etc. may be separately prescribed by (9) Ordinance of the Ministry of Land, Infrastructure and Transport.
(9) Among project operators provided for in Article 16 (1) 3, a person who intends to install and take occupancy in facilities in compliance with the relevant industrial complex development plan intends to dispose of land, facilities, etc. he/she has directly developed and uses, may dispose of such land, facilities, etc. when five years have passed before or after filing a report on completion of establishing a factory, etc. under Article 15 (1) of the Industrial Cluster Development and Factory Establishment Act and before or after filing a report on commencement of a project under Article 15 (2) of the same Act: Provided, That in any of the following cases, a project operator may directly dispose of them with an approval from the authority designating industrial complexes.
1. Where the ownership is transferred by inheritance, or a split-off or merger of a corporation;
2. Where the ownership is transferred due to an investment in kind in a corporation, and thereby, the original project operator becomes to hold at least 50 percent of the total amount of investment or total number of stocks issued by investment in kind in the corporation;
3. Where a project operator is an enterprise subject to restructuring under Article 21 of the Industrial Development Act;
4. Other cases prescribed by Presidential Decree.
(10) Notwithstanding the main sentence of paragraph (9), if a project operator intends to dispose of land, facilities, etc. within five years before or after filing a report on completion of establishing a factory, etc. and before or after filing a report on commencement of a project, he/she shall transfer such land, facilities, etc. to a management agency: Provided, That where the management agency is unable to purchase such land, facilities, etc., he/she may directly dispose of such land, facilities, etc. with approval from the authority designating industrial complexes.
(11) Where a project operator transfers land, facilities, etc, to a management agency pursuant to paragraph (10), Article 39 (5) of the Industrial Cluster Development and Factory Establishment Act shall apply mutatis mutandis to the transfer price thereof."

64. Article 13 (7) of FIPA.

65. Article 32 (1) of the State Property Act prescribing that "When permission for use of administrative property is granted, the usage fees shall be collected each year in accordance with the rates and calculation methods specified by Presidential Decree: Provided, That where the annual fees are less than the amount specified by Presidential Decree, the fees for the period of permission for use may be entirely collected at the same time."; Article 47 of the same Act

stating as follows:
"Article 47 (Rent, Rescission of Contracts, etc.)
Articles 30 (2), 31 (1) and (2), 32, 33, 34 (1) 2 and 3, 34 (2), 36 and 38 shall apply mutatis mutandis to the restriction on loan, rent, exemption of rent, and rescission or termination of loan contracts, etc., for any general property.
Despite paragraph (1), with respect to rent, all or part of annual rent may be received after converting it into loan deposit, as prescribed by Presidential Decree.
Where the term of a loan expires or a loan agreement is rescinded or terminated, the head of the relevant central government agency, etc., shall return the loan deposit prescribed under paragraph (2). In such cases, if there are rents or utility bills, etc., that the person who made the loan failed to pay, the head of a central government agency shall return the loan deposit after excluding the unpaid amount."

66. Article 13 (8) of FIPA.
67. Article 13 (9) of FIPA.
68. Article 13 (10) of FIPA.
69. Article 13 (11) of FIPA.
70. Article 15.2 (1) of FIPA.
71. Article 15.2 (2) of FIPA.
72. Article 15.2 (3) of FIPA.
73. Article 15.2 (4) of FIPA.
74. Article 15.2 (5) of FIPA.
75. Article 15.2 (6) of FIPA.
76. Article 15.2 (7) of FIPA.
77. Article 15.2 (8) of FIPA.
78. Article 15.2 (9) of FIPA.
79. Article 15.2 (10) of FIPA.
80. Article 15 (1) of FIPA.
81. Article 15 (2) of FIPA.
82. Article 15 (3) of FIPA.
83. Article 15 (4) of FIPA.
84. Article 15 (2) of FIPA prescribes that:
"Where necessary to properly perform foreign investment-related affairs, the president of the Korea Trade-Investment Promotion Agency may request the relevant administrative agencies, corporations or organizations related to foreign investment (hereinafter referred to as "foreign-investment related agencies") to dispatch their public officials or executives and employees to render service at the Investment Support Center: Provided, That where the service of public officials is required, prior consultation with the competent minister shall be made."
85. Article 15 (5) of FIPA.
86. Article 15 (6) of FIPA.

87. Article 15 (7) of FIPA.
88. Article 15 (9) of FIPA.
89. Article 30 (1) of FIPA.
90. Article 462-2 (1) of the Commercial Act stating under the title of "Stock Dividends" that "A company may pay dividends by issuing new shares by a resolution adopted at a general meeting of shareholders: Provided, That such stock dividends may not exceed the amount equivalent to half of the total amount of dividends."
91. Article 434 of the Commercial Act prescribing that "Article 434 (Special Resolutions for Amending Articles of Incorporation) A resolution under Article 433 (1) shall be adopted by the affirmative votes of at least two thirds of the voting rights of the shareholders present at a general meeting of shareholders and of at least one third of the total number of issued and outstanding shares." Also, Article 433 (1) states that "Articles of incorporation shall be amended by a resolution at a general meeting of shareholders."
92. Article 30 (2) of FIPA.
93. The capital goods refer to the term defined in Article 2 (1) 8 (b) of FIPA.
94. Article 299 (Investigation and Reporting by Inspectors) stipulating that "(1) An inspector shall investigate the matters listed in the subparagraphs of Article 290 and whether or not the investment in kind pursuant to Article 295 has been made and shall report the outcomes thereof to the court.
(2) The provisions of paragraph (1) shall not apply in cases falling under any of the following subparagraphs:
1. In cases where the total amount of assets under subparagraph 2 or 3 of Article 290 does not exceed both one fifth of the amount of capital and the amount determined by Presidential Decree;
2. In cases where the assets under subparagraph 2 or 3 of Article 290 constitute securities for which there is an exchange based market, and the price stated in the articles of incorporation does not exceed the price calculated by the method determined by Presidential Decree;
3. Other cases determined by Presidential Decree as equivalent to those under subparagraph 1 or 2.
(3) An inspector shall, without delay after he/she has prepared a report of investigation under paragraph (1), deliver a copy thereof to each incorporator.
(4) Where any statement in the report of investigation is contrary to the facts, incorporators may submit an explanatory document thereon to the court."
Article 290 (Particulars of Exceptional Incorporation) prescribes that "The following shall take effect upon entry in the articles of incorporation:
1. Any special benefits to be received by incorporators and names of such incorporators;
2. The name of a person who is to make an investment in kind, the type, quantity and value of the subject matter of such investment in kind and the class and number of shares to be given in consideration thereof;
3. The class, number and value of the assets agreed to be transferred to the

company after its incorporation and the name of the transferor;
4. The expenses for incorporation to be borne by the company and the amount of remunerations for the incorporators." Also, Article 295 of the Commercial Act states that "(1) Where incorporators subscribe to the total number of shares to be issued at the time of incorporation, they shall without delay make full payment of the subscription price. In such cases, they shall designate a bank or other financial institutions at which the subscription price is to be paid as well as the place for payment.
(2) An incorporator who is to make an investment in kind shall, without delay, provide all of the asset which is the subject matter of the investment on the date designated for the payment of the subscription price, and if registration, records, or the creation or transfer of rights is required, he/she shall prepare completely the relevant documents and deliver them to the company."

95. Article 30 (3) of FIPA.

96. Article 299-2 (Certification of Investments in Kind, etc.) of the Commercial Act prescribing that "With respect to matters listed in subparagraphs 1 and 4 of Article 290, investigations and reporting by a notary public may replace the investigation of an inspector under Article 299 (1) and with respect to matters listed in subparagraphs 2 and 3 of Article 290 and the investments in kind pursuant to Article 295, appraisal by a certified appraiser may replace the investigation of an inspector under Article 299 (1). In such cases, the notary public or appraiser shall report on the outcomes of the investigation or appraisal to a court."

97. Article 30 (4) of FIPA.

98. Article 2 (1) 4 (a) (i) prescribes that foreign investment means "acquisition of stocks, etc. newly issued by the Korean corporation or company run by the national of the Republic of Korea where a foreigner holds stocks or shares (hereinafter referred to as "stocks, etc.") of a Korean corporation (including a Korean corporation in the process of establishment) or a company run by a national of the Republic of Korea, as prescribed by Presidential Decree, by any of the following methods in order to establish a continuous economic relationship with the Korean corporation or company, such as participating in the management of such Korean corporation or company in accordance with FIPA."

99. Article 30 (5) of FIPA.

100. Article 30 (6) of FIPA.

101. Article 30 (7) of FIPA.

102. Article 30 (8) of FIPA.

103. Article 30 (9) of FIPA.

104. Filippo Fontanelli & Giuseppe Bianco, *Converging Towards NAFTA: An Analysis of FTA Investment Chapters in the European Union and the United States*, 50 Stan. J. Int'l L. 211, 214-15 (2014).

105. Julien Chaisse, *Exploring the Confines of International Investment and Domestic Health Protections-Is a General Exceptions Clause a Forced Perspective?*, 39 Am. J. L. & Med. 332,

333, n. 5 (2013).

106. KORUS FTA Final Text art. 11.15.

107. *Id.* at art. 11.16(3).

108. *Id.* at art. 11.20(1).

109. *Id.*

110. *Id.* at art. 11.20(2).

111. *Id.* at art. 11.20(3).

112. *Id.* at art. 11.20(6)(c).

113. *Id.*

114. *Id.* at art. 11.22(2)(b)(i).

115. *Id.* at art. 11.22(2)(b)(ii).

116. *Id.* at art. 11.22(3).

117. *Id.*

118. Colt Indus. Operating Corp., Firearms Div. v. Republic of Korea, ICSID Case No. ARB/84/2 (Feb. 21, 1984).

119. Joongi Kim, *supra* note 4, at 553.

120. https://investmentpolicyhubold.unctad.org/ISDS/Details/893 (last visit on 10 May, 2019).

121. https://investmentpolicyhubold.unctad.org/ISDS/Details/941 (last visit on 10 May, 2019).

122. The PCA acts as registry in this arbitration, which is being conducted under the UNCITRAL Arbitration Rules 1976 pursuant to the Free Trade Agreement between the Republic of Korea and the United States of America of 30 June 2007.

123. https://pca-cpa.org/en/cases/198/ (last visit on 10 May, 2019).

124. https://investmentpolicyhubold.unctad.org/ISDS/Details/939 (last visit on 10 May, 2019).

125. *Id.*

126. https://investmentpolicyhubold.unctad.org/ISDS/Details/896 (last visit on 10 May, 2019).

127. *Id.*

128. https://investmentpolicyhubold.unctad.org/ISDS/Details/679 (last visit on 10 May, 2019);
http://www.iareporter.com/articles/analysis-existence-of-investment-attribution-and-proportionality-likely-to-feature-in-iranian-claimants-newly-filed-arbitration-against-korea/ (last visit on 29 March, 2019);
http://www.iareporter.com/Korea+round-up%3A+Lone+Star+case+reaches+hearings%2C+as+at+least+two+other+investment+treaty+claims+loomarticles/23170/ (last visit on 30 March, 2019);
http://globalarbitrationreview.com/news/article/34159/iranian-investors-sue-south-korea/ (last visit on 31 March, 2019);
http://www.derainsgharavi.com/lawyers/hamid-gharavi/(last visit on 30 March,

2019); http://koreatimes.co.kr/www/news/biz/2015/11/488_187345.html (last visit on 30 March, 2019);
http://www.derainsgharavi.com/lawyers/hamid-gharavi/ (last visit on 30 March, 2019);
https://www.iareporter.com/articles/asia-round-up-china-and-vietnam-face-new-bit-claims-as-proceedings-against-korea-and-indonesia-move-forward/ (last visit on 30 March, 2019).

129. https://www.italaw.com/sites/default/files/case-documents/italaw9847.pdf (last visit on 10 May, 2019).

130. https://icsid.worldbank.org/en/Pages/cases/casedetail.aspx?CaseNo=ARB/15/17 (last visit on 20 March, 2019);
http://globalarbitrationreview.com/news/article/34181/debevoise-joins-south-korea-counsel-team-icsid/ (requires subscription) (last visit on 20 March, 2019);
http://www.iareporter.com/Korea+round-up%3A+Lone+Star+case+reaches+hearings%2C+as+at+least+two+other+investment+treaty+claims+loomarticles/23170/ (last visit on 20 March, 2019);
http://www.debevoise.com/insights/news/2015/09/debevoise-and-kim (last visit on 20 March, 2019).

131. https://icsid.worldbank.org/en/Pages/cases/casedetail.aspx?CaseNo=ARB/12/37 (last visit on 22 March, 2019);
http://globalarbitrationreview.com/news/article/33240/lone-star-gets-tax-refund-south-korea-icsid-case-continues/ (last visit on 22 March, 2019);
http://www.iareporter.com/articles/20130513 (last visit on 22 March, 2019);
http://www.sidley.com/experience/recent-investor-state-arbitrations (last visit on 22 March, 2019); http://www.atimes.com/atimes/Korea/HK21Dg01.html (last visit on 22 March, 2019);
http://www.arnoldporter.com/professionals.cfm?action=view&id=967 (last visit on 22 March, 2019).

132. http://www.italaw.com/cases/2022 (last visit on 20 April, 2019); https://icsid.worldbank.org/en/Pages/cases/casedetail.aspx?CaseNo=ARB/12/37 (last visit on 10 May, 2019).

133. https://investmentpolicyhubold.unctad.org/ISDS/Details/878 (last visit on 10 May, 2019);
https://icsid.worldbank.org/en/Pages/cases/casedetail.aspx?CaseNo=ARB(AF)/18/2 (last visit on 10 May, 2019).

134. https://icsid.worldbank.org/en/Pages/cases/casedetail.aspx?CaseNo=ARB/17/43 (last visit on 20 April, 2019);
https://www.iareporter.com/articles/saudia-arabia-faces-a-second-bit-claim-within-days-as-korean-investor-turns-to-arbitration/ (last visit on 20 April, 2019);
http://globalarbitrationreview.com/article/1150100/saudi-arabia-hit-with-icsid-claim-by-samsung (last visit on 20 April, 2019).

135. https://icsid.worldbank.org/en/Pages/cases/casedetail.aspx?CaseNo=ARB/15/30 (last visit on 30 March, 2019);
http://globalarbitrationreview.com/news/article/34002/samsung-takes-oman-losing

-refinery-deal/ (last visit on 20 April, 2019);
http://www.iareporter.com/articles/samsung-files-claim-against-oman-over-refinery-improvement-project/ (last visit on 20 April, 2019);
http://www.koreatimes.co.kr/www/news/biz/2015/07/488_183399.html (last visit on 20 April, 2019).

136. https://investmentpolicyhubold.unctad.org/ISDS/Details/651 (last visit on 10 May, 2019).

137. https://icsid.worldbank.org/en/Pages/cases/casedetail.aspx?CaseNo=ARB/14/25 (last visit on 30 March, 2019);
http://globalarbitrationreview.com/news/article/33143/%20china-faces-second-icsid-claim/ (last visit on 10 April, 2019);
http://hsfnotes.com/arbitration/2014/11/10/china-sued-by-south-korean-property-developer-at-icsid/ (last visit on 30 March, 2019);
http://www.iareporter.com/articles/20141106 (last visit on 10 April, 2019);
https://www.transnational-dispute-management.com/downloads/17550_case_report_ansung_housing_v_china_-_award.pdf (last visit on 30 March, 2019);
https://www.iareporter.com/articles/china-prevails-as-arbitrators-dismiss-korean-investors-icsid-claim-for-non-compliance-with-bits-3-year-claims-window-mfn-argument-also-fails/ (last visit on 10 April, 2019);
http://globalarbitrationreview.com/article/1137853/off-the-tee-but-out-of-bounds-%E2%80%93-icsid-tribunal-dismisses-claim-against-china (last visit on 10 April, 2019).

138. http://www.cisarbitration.com/2014/05/14/kyrgyz-republics-mixed-fortunes-in-investment-arbitration/ (last visit on 20 March, 2019);
http://globalarbitrationreview.com/news/article/33765/kyrgyzstan-overturns-stans-award-russia/ (last visit on 20 March, 2019);
http://globalarbitrationreview.com/news/article/33203/kyrgyzstan-quashes-cis-treaty-award-russia/ (last visit on 20 March, 2019);
http://www.iareporter.com/articles/20141015_1 (last visit on 20 March, 2018);
http://www.iareporter.com/articles/20140923_2? (last visit on 20 March, 2019).

139. Judgment of the Moscow Arbitrazh Court on Application to Set Aside Award dated 24 June 2014 (last visit on 22 March, 2019); Judgment of the Moscow Arbitrazh Court on Application to Set Aside Award dated 5 June 2015 (last visit on 20 March, 2019).

140. Guk-Sang Hwang, *The reason why Korea suddenly became the respondent state in ISDS cases*, MONEYTODAY, 3 May, 2019, http://news.mt.co.kr/mtview.php?no=2019042917078291553&outlink=1&ref=http%3A%2F%2Fsearch.daum.net (Access on 10 May, 2019).

International Human Rights Legal Challenges to Solve Japanese Military 'Comfort Women' Issue

DOH See-Hwan
Director of Research Center for Japanese Military Comfort Women
Northeast Asian History Foundation, Seoul, Korea

Abstract

Today the issue surrounding Japanese military 'comfort women' as the most serious historical conflict in Northeast Asia and the biggest human rights issue in the international community has become a challenge of historical justice that needs sincere resolution. However, the Japanese government has avoided its responsibility for the comfort women issue by framing the "legitimate theory of 1910 colonization" and the "completion theory of the 1965 Korea-Japan treaty" at both of the historical moments of the centenary of Japan's forced annexation of Korea in 2010 and the 50-year anniversary of the Korea-Japan treaty in 2015.

In this respect, it is notable that the Korean government proclaimed the restoration of the dignity and honor of sexual slavery victims of Japanese military as a national challenge by remembering August 14, the day when Kim Hak-sun, a former comfort woman, testified her victimization for the first time, just before the 73rd anniversary of the National Liberation Day in 2018. It was within same context of the victim-centered approach principle stipulated under the "Basic Principles and Guidelines on the Right to a Remedy and Reparation for Victims of Gross Violations of International Human Rights Law and Serious Violations of International Humanitarian Law" adopted unanimously in the United Nations General Assembly in 2005.

Marking the 70th anniversary of Japan's surrender in August 2015, Prime Minister Shinzo Abe gave a speech denying responsibility for colonial rule and the wars of aggression. He thus invited criticism for turning a blind eye to the victims of sexual slavery. His denial seems to stem from Japan's tilting toward the right and its attempts to revive militarism, boosted by historical revisionism. Following an agreement reached by the foreign ministers of Korea and Japan on Dec. 28, 2015, Japan has publicly denied that it forcefully took women into sexual slavery. The country has made the same denial international human rights organizations, including the U.N. Commission on Human Rights even though what Japan's actions undoubtedly constituted a crime against humanity.

One of the striking illustrations of this is the statement of Masato Otaka, Japanese ambassador to the U.N., who said that "the issue of the comfort women was resolved with the 2015 agreement between Korea and Japan." This statement was made at the Committee on the Elimination of Racial Discrimination held in Geneva on Aug. 16 in order to deflect criticism from human rights advocates. These included U.N. Special Rapporteur Gay McDougall, who wrote the 1998 report stating that an agreement between governments without apologies to victims cannot resolve human rights issues.

Additionally, in a report released on Nov. 19 the U.N. Committee on Enforced Disappearances expressed deep regret about the 2015 Korea-Japan agreement that calls for the two nations to resolve the sexual slavery issue "finally and irreversibly." The report stated that there was a lack of adequate reparations for the victims of sexual slavery. It even recommended that the truth should be uncovered and the perpetrators be held accountable. This demonstrates a contradiction between the Japanese assertion and international human rights organizations.

Most of all, legal principles should be established to better protect human rights and renounce the militarism and imperialism that were used to justify Japan's colonial rule of Korea and Japan's aggressions. Now is the time for the Japanese government to make a sincere and genuine effort to resolve the 'comfort women' issue. It should respond to the call of the international community for "irreversible historical reconciliation" to heal the comfort women's scars based on victims-centered approach.

Key Words

International human rights law, comfort women, colonial rule, war of aggressions, sexual slavery, victims-centered approach, irreversible historical reconciliation

1. INTRODUCTION

As we celebrate the meaningful centennial of the March 1st Movement and the establishment of the Provisional Government, we come to reconsider the challenges that stem from historical events and that have been handed to us today. This should begin with sincerely wiping the tears of victims of crimes against humanity by being forcibly mobilized during the aggressive war under Japan's colonial rule, the effects of which are still today in the 21st century. In this respect, it is notable that the Korean government proclaimed the restoration of the dignity and honor of sexual slavery victims of Japanese military as a national challenge by remembering August 14, the day when Kim Hak-sun, a former comfort woman, testified her victimization for the first time, just before the 73rd anniversary of the National Liberation Day in 2018. It was within same context of the victim-centered approach principle stipulated under the "Basic Principles and Guidelines on the Right to a Remedy and Reparation for Victims of Gross Violations of International Human Rights Law and Serious Violations of International Humanitarian Law (Basic Principles and Guidelines on Victims' Rights)" adopted unanimously in the United Nations General Assembly in 2005.

Today the issue surrounding 'comfort women' as the most serious historical conflict in Northeast Asia and the biggest human rights issue in the international community has become a challenge of historical justice that needs sincere resolution, However, the

Japanese government has avoided its responsibility for the comfort women issue by framing the "legitimate theory of 1910 colonization" and the "completion theory of the 1965 Korea-Japan treaty" at both of the historical moments of the centenary of Japan's forced annexation of Korea in 2010 and the 50-year anniversary of the Korea-Japan treaty in 2015.

In the process of seeking the challenge of historical justice for the relief of gross and serious violations of human rights sacrificed as sex slaves by forced mobilization of 'comfort women' in the war of aggression under Japanese illegal colonial rule, the Korean Constitutional Court in 2011 and the Korean Supreme Court in 2012 responded with a verdict based on the historical truth and justice based on international human rights law that had been rejected by Japan.

The two top Courts in Korea held Japan fully accountable for its colonial rule by ruling that "the state's intentions and obligations to restore the damaged dignity and worth of comfort women abused during Japan's colonial rule are constitutional duties,"[1] and that "claim rights for tort against humanity involving Japanese government power or colonial rule tort damages were not addressed in the Claims Agreement. Thus, individual damages claim right has not expired due to the Claims Agreement."[2] They went a step further to make the ruling beneficial for historical justice by pursuing positive peace through the assurance of human rights as a universal value of mankind.

2. JAPAN'S POSTWAR COMPENSATION TRIALS'S LIMITATION

2-1. Japan's Nationalistic Postwar Trials

Since the 1990s when the cold war ended, calls for 'postwar claims' escalated into lawsuits in global solidarity across Asia along amid the changes in the international situation following democratization of many Asian countries.[3] Japan only compensated for the lawsuit filed against the state through the San Francisco Peace Treaty and bilateral agreement but did not agree to personal 'reparation' at all, prompting a great number of war victims in Asia to file suit against the Japanese government.[4]

Nevertheless, Japan has not recognized its responsibility for colonial rule and invasion war and only proceeded with postwar claims trials. The number of lawsuits relevant to 'postwar claims' in Japan stands at 100 as 2019.[5] Of these lawsuits, 10 were filed by former 'sexual slaves' with three of them made by Korean women.[6]

Lawsuits filed by former Korean comfort women as follows; 'Lawsuit for Korean Victims' Claims of the Asia-Pacific War' made by Kim Hak-soon on December 6, 1991; 'Lawsuit for Official Apology for Busan Comfort Women and Women's Labor Corps' on December 25, 1992; and 'Former Korean-Japanese Sex Slave Song Sin-do's Lawsuit' on April 5, 1993. However, the judiciary solution in Japan came to an end when the Supreme Court of Japan dismissed the suits on November 19, 2004 citing the amount of time passed since those atrocities were committed and the lack of response or solution from the state.[7]

Meanwhile, the lawsuits filed by Korean victims ofover the forced labor are 'Lawsuit against Mitsubishi Heavy Industries over the Unpaid Wage' on December 11, 1995 and Damages for Forced Laborers in Nippon Steel & Sumitomo Metal Corporation on December 24, 1997. However, the two suits were also dismissed by the Supreme Court of Japan based on based on the expiration of the statute of limitations and Korea-Japan Basic Relations Treaty in 1965 on November 1, 2007 and October 9, 2003 respectively.

Japanese lawyer Shuichi Adachi who led the 'postwar claim' suit in Japan analyzed the rulings rendered by the Supreme Court of Japan and presented ‘four obstacles,’ pointing out that the interpretation of law was justifiable nowhere but Japan.[8] The first obstacle is Japan’s failure to acknowledge the truth. The second one is the ‘lack of response or solution from the state’ where the state is not held liable for damages under the Constitution of the Empire of Japan. The third one, the amount time passed since those atrocities were committed. The fourth one is political obstacle as an extinguishment of right by Korea-Japan Basic Relations Treaty in 1965 and law of property rights.

In the meantime, since 2000, the Japanese government has held a stance that individual’s rights to compensation are extinguished and thus solved completely by expanding the meaning of ‘waiver of claims’ to ‘waiver of rights to diplomatic protection.’ This stance was initially devised to respond to the lawsuit[9] filed by Hwang Geum Joo and other 18 former sexual slaves in China, Taiwan, and the Philippines with District Court of Washington on September 18, 2000.

To put it in another way, the Japanese government did so because it knew it would be difficult to have legal advantage with principles like the amount of time allowed to bring a legal action since those atrocities were committed and the lack of response or solution from the state in lawsuits filed in the U.S. Afterwards, the Japanese government reversed its existing claim regarding Korea-Japan Basic Relations Treaty in 1965. It put forward as a core defense by invoking Article 2 paragraph 1 of the Treaty, the problem concerning claims...is settled and finally,[10] and Article 2 paragraph 3 ‘No contention shall be made.’

2-2. Japanese Government’s Refusal to Accept the Accusation

On December 28, 2016, a group of 20 plaintiffs, including 11 comfort women survivors and family members of six others who had passed away, filed suit against the Japanese government,[11] claiming "enormous psychological and physical suffering due to the Japanese government forcing [the survivors] to live as comfort women." In the two years and three months since the complaint was received by the court, no full-fledged hearings have yet taken place. The reason stems from the Japanese government's repeated refusals to accept the documents in connection with the case. The civil suit in a Korean court can only begin once the complaint has been delivered to a Japanese court.

The 15th civil division of Seoul Central District Court, which is handling the comfort women compensation case, announced on March 12 that it had served translated copies of the accusation and a lawsuit guidance document to the Japanese government on March 8. Under the service by publication format, legal and other documents are regarded as having been served once posted on the court website or elsewhere for a certain period of time. It is used when one of the parties has an unknown address or refuses to accept the documents in question. According to the terms of the Civil Procedure Act, the service by publication in this case is to enter effect in two months as of midnight on May 9.

"As a rule, legal documents are delivered directly to the party, but the court appears to have ultimately decided on service by publication after repeated attempts at delivery revealed that this approach would not be possible," explained a court official.

According to the established rules regarding international judicial assistance on civil cases, documents in connection with the lawsuit are to proceed from Korean court to the court president, the court administration, the Korean Ministry of Foreign Affairs, the Korean embassy in Japan, the Japanese Ministry of Foreign Affairs and on to a Japanese court. But the Japanese government has repeatedly refused to accept the documents, with the Minister of Justice declaring in April and August 2017 and again in November 2018 that the case was regarded as "violating sovereignty."[12]

3. THE SOLUTIONS OF INTERNATIONAL HUMAN RIGHTS ORGANIZATION'S AND THE DISSOLUTION OF THE RECONCILIATION AND HEALING FOUNDATION

3-1. Committee on the Elimination of Racial Discrimination (hereinafter, "the CERD")'s "Victim-Centered Solution"

While noting information provided by Japan on the efforts to resolve the issue of 'comfort women,' including the recent agreement with the Republic of Korea in 2015, the CERD is concerned at reports that these efforts do not take a fully victim-centered approach, that the surviving comfort women were not adequately consulted and that this solution did not acknowledge unequivocal responsibility for the human rights violations committed against these women by the Japanese military before and during the Second World War. The CERD is also concerned by statements of some public officials, minimizing the responsibility of the Government with respect to comfort women, and their potential negative impact on survivors.

The CERD recommends that the State party ensure a lasting solution to the issue of comfort women with a victim-centered approach, inclusive of comfort women of all nationalities, accepting responsibility for its role in the violation of the human rights of these women. The CERD requests detailed information in its next periodic report on efforts to resolve the issue of comfort women, including adequate measures addressing surviving comfort women and their families.[13]

3-2. Committee on Enforced Disappearances (hereinafter, "the CED")' Expression of Regret on "Final and Irreversible Resolution"

Recalling Articles 8, 12 and 24 of the Convention, the CED

wishes to emphasize the continuous nature of the crime of enforced disappearance and to reaffirm the rights of victims to justice, reparation and to know the truth about the circumstances of an enforced disappearance, the progress and results of the investigation and the fate of the disappeared person, regardless of when the enforced disappearance was committed. In this respect, the CED is concerned about the lack of statistical information on the number of so-called 'comfort women' who may have been subjected to enforced disappearance, and about the absence of investigations, prosecutions and convictions of perpetrators of these cases. It is further concerned at reports of the removal of children born to these women and the refusal of the State to investigate such cases. The CED remains concerned at reports of the concealment or failure by the State party to disclose related facts and materials on the issue of the so-called 'comfort women.'

It is further concerned at the lack of adequate reparations to the victims in accordance with Article 24 (5) of the Convention and regrets the State party's position that the issue "is resolved finally and irreversibly." This perpetuates impunity and denies victims their right to know the truth and to obtain justice, reparation and guarantees of non-repetition (Art. 1, 8, 12, 24 and 25).

The CED recalls the continuous nature of the offence of enforced disappearance and recommends the State party to: (a) Generate accurate statistics on the number of the so-called 'comfort women' who may have been subjected to enforced disappearance to conduct investigations and guarantee the rights to the truth and reparation; (b) Ensure that all cases of so-called 'comfort women' who may have been subjected to enforced disappearance, including the removal of children born to these women, are investigated thoroughly and impartially without delay, regardless of the time that has elapsed since they took place and even if there has been no formal complaint; (c) Ensure that the alleged perpetrators are prosecuted and, if found guilty, punished in accordance with the gravity of their acts; (d) Take the necessary measures to search for and identify any children born to 'comfort women' who may have been victims of wrongful removal, enforced disappearance and/or identity substitution and that they are returned to their families of origin, in conformity with article 25, paragraph 2, of the Convention; (e) Ensure the disclosure of any information related to facts and materials; (f) Ensure that all victims receive adequate reparation in accordance with article 24 (4) and (5) of the Convention and that it takes account of gender issues; (g) Guarantee the right to truth.[14]

3-3. The Dissolution of the Reconciliation and Healing Foundation

The Reconciliation and Healing Foundation was launched in July 2016 according to an agreement which the Korean government signed with the Japanese government in December 2015.[15] The purpose of the foundation was to heal the wounds and restore the honor of the comfort women victims, and it was funded with 1 billion yen paid by the Japanese government. But The comfort women victims, the bereaved families and Korean civic society had from the start demanded the dissolution of the foundation claiming that it was one based on an agreement that the victims had no part in.[16]

The Korean government officially announced on November 21, 2018 that it plans to go ahead with legal procedures to dissolve the Reconciliation and Healing Foundation. This comes two years and four months after the foundation was established in July 2016 to pay compensation to comfort women survivors and surviving family members following the Park Geun-hye administration's agreement with the Japanese government on the comfort women issue the preceding December.

Japan argues that this was a legitimate intergovernmental agreement that represents a "final and irreversible solution" to the comfort women. But Japan ought to reflect upon the fact that even international human rights organizations have been very critical of its position. In November 2018, the UN Committee on Enforced Disappearances stated that the comfort women agreement denied the rights of the victims and that Japan's compensation was inadequate. And back in August 2018, the UN's Committee on the Elimination of Racial Discrimination criticized the agreement for neither failing to specify responsibility for human rights violations against women nor taking a victim-centered approach.

In the end, these international bodies share the view that the comfort women issue will not be resolved until the victims have received relief from their emotional wounds and lingering resentment. Despite that, the Japanese government gave Korea 1 billion yen and told it to handle things on its own while repeatedly attempting to wash its hands of the whole matter. Such behavior disregards universal human rights standards. In order to truly resolve the comfort women issue, Japan should hurry to show contrition and make a heartfelt apology while willingly assuming legal responsibility.[17]

4. VICTIM-CENTERED APPROACH TO SOLVE 'COMFORT WOMEN' ISSUE

4-1. International Legal Shift from Nationalism to Human Rights Centralism

In the traditional international law, an individual was regarded as a citizen of a specific state. Therefore, if an individual suffered damage by a foreign state, protection was confined to the scope of diplomatic range in his/her originating country. However, it is important to note that the international human rights law came from the reflection that the atrocities committed by Germany and Japan right after the Second World War were derived from the traditional nationalism that despised human rights. International human rights law led to the idea that an individual should be protected not as a member of a state or a group but as an individual human being him/herself.

In this regard, the Constitutional Court of Korea quotes in its decision verdict ILC's 2006 Draft article on Diplomatic Protection which was also quoted in ICJ's[18] Case concerning Ahmadou sadio Diallo in 2007. The draft pointed out that the view that violation of individual rights as a violation against his/her belonging state according to international law is nothing but unfounded and agenda and should not call for sacrifice from an individual on behalf of national friendship. This is an important change in the international law in the context of the essence of diplomatic protection and individual rights to claims.

In the meantime, with regard to the termination of individual rights to claims, there do not exist adequate grounds for agreement between Korea and Japan. Therefore, even if plaintiff's rights to claims are covered in the Korea-Japan Basic Relations Treaty in 1965, the rights itself shall not be deemed terminated by the treaty only. Instead, as Republic of Korea's diplomatic protection rights to the claims are waived, Korea will only lose the tool for diplomatic protection even if the rights to claims are extinguished in Japan by domestic measures. Therefore, as plaintiff's rights to compensation are not terminated, plaintiffs can exercise their rights to compensation.

4-2. Victims' Right to Claim Damages from Crime Against Humanity

The damage done to comfort women is unprecedented and unique, as it stems from forced mobilization and sexual slavery by the Japanese government and military.

The particularity of comfort women has been affirmed not only by the international community but also by the Japanese courts. The report of a non-governmental organization named International Commission of Jurists released on September 2, 1994 and the "Coomaraswamy Report" of the U.N. Sub-Commission on Human Rights published on February 6, 1996 defined it as "sexual slavery by the military." The report of August 12, 1998 submitted by Special Rapporteur Gay J. McDougall of the U.N. Sub-Committee on Prevention of Discrimination and Protection of Minorities concluded that the act of coercing sexual slavery amounts to a crime against humanity.

The resolution adopted by the U.S. House of Representatives in July 2007 also described Japanese military's sexual slavery as "forced military prostitution by the government of Japan, considered unprecedented in its cruelty and magnitude" and "one of the largest cases of human trafficking in the 20th century." Furthermore, in its ruling on April 27, 1998, the Shimonoseki Branch of the Yamaguchi District Court admitted to the liability of legislative inaction in the comfort women issue and ordered to pay compensation, stating that it is a "clear case of sexual and ethnic discrimination, fundamental violation of the dignity of women, and undermining of national pride."

The comfort women victims' right to claim damages from the government of Japan for its extensive crime against humanity is not just part of the property rights enshrined under Korean constitution, but also implies the post-facto restoration of dignity and value and personal liberty that has been ruthlessly and continuously violated. Therefore, blocking the repayment of damage claims is not just confined to a constitutional property issue but is also directly associated with the infringement of fundamental dignity and value of human beings.[19]

4-3. Victims' Right to Claim had not Expired due to Claim Agreement

The "Agreement between Japan and the Republic of Korea Concerning the Settlement of Problems in Regard to Property and Claims and Economic Cooperation"("Claims Agreement") did not negotiate for compensation for Japanese colonial rule. Based on Article 4 of San Francisco Treaty, it attempts to solve financial and civil debt relation between Korea and Japan with political agreement.

Under Article 1 of the Claims Agreement, Japan government's economic cooperation fund payment to Korea government is unrelated legally to rights issue solution under Article 2. During the course of negotiation for the Claims Agreement, Japanese government did not acknowledge colonial rule's unlawfulness and denied legal compensation for forced mobilization victims. Korean and Japanese government did not agree on the nature of Japanese Korean peninsula rule. In this circumstance, claim rights for tort against humanity involving Japanese government power or colonial rule tort damages were not addressed in the Claims Agreement. Thus, victims' right to claim damages have not expired due to the Claims Agreement.

Korea's diplomatic protection right was also not abandoned. Further, a country may not expire a citizen's individual right to claim without consent of an individual citizen by treaty where a diplomatic protection right is abandoned. It is against the principle of modern law. If a country may expire citizen's individual right to claim by treaty under the international law, unless explicitly expressed in the treaty, citizen's individual right to claim cannot be seen as expired together with the country's diplomatic protection right since the country and individual citizen are separate legal entity. The Claims Agreement does not have a sufficient basis to show agreement between Korea and Japan government as to whether an individual right to claim expired. Japan enacted and enforced the Property Right

Settlement Act after the Claims Agreement in order to expire Korea citizen's right against Japan and her citizens with in Japan under the premise that the Claims Agreement alone did not expire Korea citizen's individual right to claim.

Even if victims' rights to claim are subject to the Claims Agreement, the individual right to claim itself did not expire just based on the Claims Agreement as a matter of course. With the Claims Agreement, Korea's diplomatic protection right for claims was abandoned. Korea lost means to protect the pertinent right diplomatically if it expired within Japan by Japanese measures. Thus, victims' rights to claim against Japan had not expired due to the Claims Agreement.[20]

4-4. "Victim-Centered Approach" for "Final and Irreversible Resolution"

In regard to relief overlapped and serious violations of human rights as crimes against humanity by forced mobilization of 'comfort women' in the war of aggression under illegal Japanese colonial rule, The UN General Assembly adopted the following basic Principles and Guidelines on the Right to a Remedy and Reparation for Victims of Gross Violations of International Human Rights Law and Serious Violations of International Humanitarian Law.

In cases of gross violations of international human rights law and serious violations of international humanitarian law constituting crimes under international law, States have the duty to investigate and, if there is sufficient evidence, the duty to submit to prosecution the person allegedly responsible for the violations and, if found guilty, the duty to punish her or him. Moreover, in these cases, States should, in accordance with international law, cooperate with one another and assist international judicial organs competent in the investigation and prosecution of these violations (Article 4).

To that end, where so provided in an applicable treaty or under other international law obligations, States shall incorporate or otherwise implement within their domestic law appropriate provisions for universal jurisdiction. Moreover, where it is so provided for in an applicable treaty or other international legal obligations, States should facilitate extradition or surrender offenders to other States and to appropriate international judicial bodies and provide judicial assistance and other forms of cooperation in the pursuit of international justice, including assistance to, and protection of, victims and witnesses, consistent with international human rights legal standards and subject to international legal requirements such as those relating to the prohibition of torture and other forms of cruel, inhuman or degrading treatment or punishment (Article 5).

Remedies for gross violations of international human rights law and serious violations of international humanitarian law include the victim's right to the following as provided for under international law: (a) Equal and effective access to justice; (b) Adequate, effective and prompt reparation for harm suffered; (c) Access to relevant information concerning violations and reparation mechanisms (Article 11).

A victim of a gross violation of international human rights law or of a serious violation of international humanitarian law shall have equal access to an effective judicial remedy as provided for under international law. Other remedies available to the victim include access to administrative and other bodies, as well as mechanisms, modalities and proceedings conducted in accordance with domestic law. Obligations arising under international law to secure the right to access justice and fair and impartial proceedings shall be reflected in domestic laws. To that end, States should: (a) Disseminate, through public and private mechanisms, information about all available remedies for gross violations of international human rights law and serious violations of international humanitarian law; (b) Take measures to minimize the inconvenience to victims and their representatives, protect against unlawful interference with their privacy as appropriate and ensure their safety from intimidation and retaliation, as well as that of their families and witnesses, before, during and after judicial, administrative, or other proceedings that affect the interests of victims; (c) Provide proper assistance to victims seeking access to justice; (d) Make available all appropriate legal, diplomatic and consular means to ensure that victims can exercise their rights to remedy for gross violations of international human rights law or serious violations of international humanitarian law. In addition to individual access to justice, States should endeavour to develop procedures to allow groups of victims to present claims for reparation and to receive reparation, as appropriate (Article 12).

5. CONCLUSION

The comfort women issue has yet to be resolved due to Japan's lack of a sincere apology and compensation for the crime against humanity. The situation, which has caused the historical conflicts between Korea and Japan, has also emerged paradoxically as an international human rights issue that calls for a resolution by laying bare the truth and letting Japan take legal responsibility for its misdeeds.

Marking the 70th anniversary of Japan's surrender in August 2015, Prime Minister Shinzo Abe gave a speech denying responsibility for colonial rule and the wars of aggression. He thus invited criticism for turning a blind eye to the victims of sexual slavery. His denial seems to stem from Japan's tilting toward the right and its attempts to revive militarism, boosted by historical revisionism. Following an agreement reached by the foreign ministers of Korea and Japan on December 28, 2015, Japan has publicly denied that it forcefully took women into sexual slavery. The country has made the same denial international human rights organizations, including the U.N. Commission on Human Rights even though what Japan's actions undoubtedly constituted a crime against humanity.

One of the striking illustrations of this is the statement of Masato Otaka, Japanese ambassador to the U.N., who said that "the issue of the comfort women was resolved with the 2015 agreement between Korea and Japan." This statement was made at the Committee on the Elimination of Racial Discrimination held in Geneva on August 16 in order to deflect criticism from human rights advocates. These included U.N. Special Rapporteur Gay McDougall, who wrote the 1998 report stating that an agreement between governments without apologies to victims cannot resolve human rights issues. The Supreme Court of Korea ruled on October 30 this year that the victims of forced labor should get compensation, which reconfirmed a historic ruling made on May 24, 2012, that set a milestone in international human rights law. Additionally, in a report released on November 19 the U.N. Committee on Enforced Disappearances expressed deep regret about the 2015 Korea-Japan agreement that calls for the two nations to resolve the sexual slavery issue "finally and irreversibly."

The report stated that there was a lack of adequate reparations for the victims of sexual slavery. It even recommended that the truth should be uncovered and the perpetrators be held accountable. This demonstrates a contradiction between the Japanese assertion and international human rights organizations. The international community needs to be more active in discussing such issues as comfort women, forced laborers and other victims of human rights violations committed by Japan during the colonial period. Such discussions could lay the groundwork for reparations for those victims. Most of all, legal principles should be established to better protect human rights and renounce the militarism and imperialism that were used to justify Japan's colonial rule of Korea and Japan's aggressions.

Japan's coercion of young Korean women into sexual slavery for its frontline troops was a grave violation of human rights. It cannot be resolved by distorting the historical facts and describing those victims as prostitutes bent on making money. Now is the time for the Japanese government to make a sincere and genuine effort to resolve the 'comfort women' issue. It should respond to the call of the international community for "irreversible historical reconciliation" to heal the comfort women's scars based on victims-centered approach.[21]

Notes

1. Constitutional Court Decision 2006HunMa788, August 30, 2011.
2. Supreme Court Decision 2009Da22549, May 24, 2012.
3. Jong-won Lee, "A Reexamination of the Policy of Post-War Compensation from the Japanese," *Reexamination Court Rulings on Colonial Responsibilities and the System of the Korea-Japan Agreement of 1965*, Northeast Asian History Foundation, International Conference on Revisiting the fifty years of the Agreement between Korea and Japan, June 21, 2013, p. 115.
4. Won-deog Lee, "A Study on the Japan's Post-war Reparations Diplomacy : the Perspective of the International Comparisons," *Northeast Asian History Journal*, Vol. 22, Northeast Asian History Foundation, December 2008, p. 32.
5. Hiroshi Tanaka · Taketoshi Nakayama · Ken Airimitsu, Unresolved Postwar Compensation - Judgment of Japan's Past and Future (Sousisha, 2012), pp. 208~213; Seita Yamamoto, Overview of Japan's postwar trials (http://justice.skr.jp/souran-jp-intro.html).
6. Refer to documents related to lawsuits on victims of rape by Japanese soldiers in Japan at WAM website http://wam-peace.org/ianfu-mondai/lawsuit.
7. The wartime rape lawsuit the last lawsuit to be related to 'sexual slavery' on July 16, 2001 was eventually dismissed by the Supreme Court of Japan on March 2, 2010.
8. Shuichi Adachi, "An Evaluation of the Limitations and Issues of the Rulings of the Supreme Court of Japan," *Revisiting the fifty years of the Agreement between Korea and Japan*, Northeast Asian History Foundation International Conference, June 21, 2013, pp. 3~16.
9. Hwang Geum Joo, et al. v. Japan, 172F. Suppp. 2d 52 (D.D.C. Oct. 4, 2001); Hwang Geum Joo et al. v. Japan, 332 F.3d 679 (C.A.D.C.,2003); Hwang Geum Joo et al. v. Japan, 413 F.3d 45 (C.A.D.C.,2005); Hwang Geum Joo et al. v. Japan, 546 U.S. 1208, 126 S.Ct. 1418 (U.S.,2006); For more detail for this lawsuit, refer to Tae-Hyun Choi, "A Study on the Comfort Women Litigations in the United States," *New Perspectives on Historical Issues in Korean-Japanese Relations-from the Point of International Law*, Northeast Asian History Foundation, 2009, pp. 603~662.
10. On July 15, 1960, Germany and France signed a treaty to compensate French people for the suffering under German Nazism and paid 400 million mark. Despite Paragraph 3 which stipulated that all claims are completed, Germany accepted France' additional compensation for forced labor. In 1981, Germany and France signed a treaty to establish a foundation to promote mutual understanding and in 2000, the two countries created 'Memory, Responsibility, and Future Foundation.' In 2012, Germany announced a plan to compensate for those who were excluded from the compensation living in former communist states. "Japan Should Respond Comfort Women Issue in the International Community," See-hwan Doh, *Dong-A Daily*, March 19, 2013, p. 29.

11. Seoul Central District Court 2016GaHab580239, December 28, 2016.
12. While the Japanese government has refused to cooperate with the trial, five comfort women survivors and plaintiffs have passed away: Lee Sang-hee in 2017, An Jeom-soon and Kim Bok-deuk in 2018, and Kim Bok-dong and Gwak Ye-nam in 2019. "Japanese government has delayed trial by refusing to accept documents over 2 years," *The Hankyoreh*, March 13, 2019, p. 12.
13. U.N. Doc. CERD/C/JPN/CO/10-11(26 September 2018), paras. 27~28.
14. U.N. Doc. CED/C/JPN/CO/1 (19 November 2018), paras. 25~26.
15. After inter-governmental consensus between Korea and Japan in 2015, Deputy Director-general of Japanese Foreign ministry, Sugiyama Shinsuke, denied the compulsory mobilization of comfort women during CEDAW in February 16th 2016, and uploaded this statement to the homepage. Foreign Minister, Kishida Humio, emphasized the completion of the deal in 1965 and Prime Minister Abe opposed to write apology letter to the victims. Seen from this process. it is a typical case of denial of comfort women, the atrocity against women, and damage to fundamentals of the inter-governmental consensus. See-hwan Doh, "Women Policy in East Asia -Focusing on 'Comfort Women' Policy of Japanese Government-," *Justice*, Vol. 158, No. 2, 2017, p. 469.
16. "Dissolution of the Reconciliation and Healing Foundation According to the Wishes of the Comfort Women Victims," *The Kyunghyang Shinmun*, November 22, 2018, p. 1.
17. "There is no "reconciliation" or "healing" without a sincere apology," *The Hankyoreh*, November 22, 2018, p. 23.
18. Dae-Soon Kim, "Selected Issues concerning Diplomatic Protection: centering around the UN ILC's draft articles of 2006 on Diplomatic Protection," *Law Review*, Vol. 48, No. 1, August 2007, pp. 204~205.
19. Constitutional Court Decision 2006HunMa788, August 30, 2011.
20. Supreme Court Decision 2009Da22549, May 24, 2012.
21. See-hwan Doh, "Comfort Women and Human Rights," *The Korea Times*, December 13, 2018, p. 9.

KYIL

The Establishment of Screening Systems of Foreign Directive Investment on National Security Grounds: A South Korean Perspective

Carlos Esplugues*
Professor, University of Valencia, Valencia, Spain

Abstract

The process of liberalization of international trade and of Foreign Direct Investment (FDI) has constituted a broadly accepted trend during the last few decades and FDI inflows have expanded constantly since the end of the 1980's. However, signs of a certain crisis of the positive and one-way attitude towards international trade and FDI exist nowadays. The financial crisis, the change in the origin of the FDI derived from the new geo-strategic reality arising out of the crisis, the growing participation of foreign sovereign actors in international trade and investment, the changing environment for national security or the quest to protect technologies and sectors of the economy considered vital for the host country, its sovereignty and competitiveness have led many countries to set forth mechanisms to evaluate FDI proposals before they are implemented. Korea is not alien to this trend.

As a matter of principle, the protection of national security is a legitimate goal of any state. However, there is a risk of these kinds of instruments being politicised, and the potential negative consequences of a broad interpretation of the notion of

* Dr. Dr. h.c. Carlos Esplugues LLM (Harvard), MSc (Edinburgh) is full Professor of Private International Law and International Trade Law at the University of Valencia (Spain), Spanish Delegate to UNCITRAL's WGII (Dispute Resolution) and former President of the Spanish Association of Professors of International Law and International Relations.

national security remain. The creation of these screening systems has taken place in an atmosphere of liberalisation of investment, and their introduction has ultimately constituted a sort of exception to it. But this atmosphere is changing negatively very quickly and the peril to use these screening systems as an excuse to impose hidden limitations on free trade and investment increases. The Republic of Korea, as many other countries in the world, is not vaccinated against this danger.

Key Words

Foreign Direct Investment (FDI), Foreign investment and national security, Freedom of Investment, Control of FDI, Barriers to foreign investment, Screening systems of control of FDI, Restrictions to foreign investment, Republic of Korea

1. FOREIGN DIRECT INVESTMENT UNDER DEBATE··· ONCE AGAIN!

The process of liberalization of international trade and of Foreign Direct Investment (FDI) has constituted a broadly accepted trend during the last few decades.[1] However, signs of a certain crisis of the positive and one-way attitude towards international trade and FDI exist today.[2] The atmosphere of growing prevention as regards some of the consequences arising out of globalization is rapidly favouring protectionism and creating a new element of pressure on the freedom of FDI. Liberalization of FDI constitutes a strong trend that will probably continue in the future. However some signs of "backlash against FDI"[3] exist that make the regulatory framework less welcoming in certain countries as regards foreign investments or, at least, as regards foreign investments coming from certain countries, sovereign-driven FDI or FDI directed to certain areas of the economy.

A double-edged attitude towards FDI is growing nowadays in

many parts of the world. As a matter of principle most states encourage FDI, but at the same time many of them are increasingly beginning to adopt a more selective approach in relation to it. That finally means that FDI is welcomed as a general rule, but some FDI or some kinds of FDI are not that welcome in certain cases or as regards particular targets. National security, national essential security interests or similar vague and elusive terms are some of the grounds used to protect the host state from undesired FDI.[4]

The changing environment for national security or the quest to protect technologies and sectors of the economy considered vital for the host country, its sovereignty and competitiveness are creating a new reality that will necessarily affect both, the legal framework and the global fluxes of FDI. This becomes especially manifest as regards the protection of certain strategic industries and of some critical infrastructures.[5] The changing origin of FDI and the possibility of certain areas of the economy to be dominated by foreigners have raised national security anxieties in many western economies as well as have fostered economic nationalism.[6] This dissatisfaction increases in relation to sovereign driven FDI.

The traditionally rather innocuous area of investment law is nowadays under pressure.[7] FDI both inwards and outwards is not as welcome as before.[8] More and more some developed countries are starting to feel disquiet with respect to the FDI regime that they have helped construct for decades.[9] And the contradictions and tensions that have traditionally accompanied FDI are now superseded by the rising mistrust towards globalization and free trade that is arising in certain countries.[10] There is a strong trend to provide governments with broader powers to decide what FDI they want, and which one they don't. These objectives are ensured and reached through different mechanisms and policies fixed by the state itself. And it may lead governments, now also from developed countries, to pay more attention, among other things, to some competing objectives like the safeguard of special national interests or of essential security interests, the promotion of national champions or the protection of certain national industries and critical infrastructures.[11]

2. THE BUILDING OF A MORE CAUTIOUS APPROACH TOWARDS FOREIGN INVESTMENT

FDI legislation reflects the balance between the benefits that host and home countries expect from foreign capital and the potential risks that FDI has for them.[12] And it is increasingly under pressure, especially in many western countries, which are currently re-evaluating the cost-benefit trade-off of certain types of FDI. Consequently, in certain places not all FDI is considered welcome but only some types of FDI and different instruments and devices are used to control it.[13]

No state has ever granted unrestricted entry to foreign investors and some limits to them have always existed. But nowadays some states and political actors are starting to think of whether they have relinquished "too much 'policy space'" in signing International Investment Agreements (IIAs) that through their interpretation by international arbitration panels may cast a "regulatory chill" over domestic measures that are considered to be needed to achieve legitimate, non-investment policy objectives, not only in the economic field but also as regards other ambits like health and safety policy objectives, or national security as well as human rights or environmental protection.[14]

Fears increase further when the investment is undertaken by multinational enterprises (MNEs) belonging to emergent countries, some of them with a high participation of foreign governments in their control, governance and determination of their final aims.[15] More and more, some states wonder whether it is acceptable that key elements of the economy or prominent industries become controlled by foreign investors, some of them sovereign driven investors belonging to countries that do not always fully share their social, economic or democratic ideas. There are growing concern by states and public opinion about the compatibility of FDI, or at least of FDI coming from certain countries and targeting certain areas of the economy, with the protection and safeguarding of some values, policies and objectives of the host state in certain areas.[16]

2-1. Potential Threats related to National Security Issues Generated by FDI

In addition to certain purely social and economic problems related to the potential change of domicile of the acquired enterprise, the loss of jobs that it can imply or the change in its management, some particular fears specifically related to national security issues exist in relation to FDI. Authors speak of at least three threats of diverse kinds potentially generated by FDI: the dominance of supply that penalizes the host country, the transfer of technology that harms host country interests, or the possibility of engaging in sabotage or espionage.[17]

In any case, taking these three different threats into account and leaving aside the potential political and media impact of some of the mergers and acquisitions (M&As) undergone in recent times, it is necessary to differentiate when approaching particular FDI proposals between genuine threats and generic which in some cases may be just excuses for the host state to adopt hidden protectionist measures. This is something to be determined on case by case bases. However, and generally speaking, all those countries endorsing these kinds of measures on security related grounds should share the challenge of ensuring that these security-related objectives are duly achieved at the same time that unnecessarily restrictive measures are not endorsed.[18]

Acquisitions of national corporations by foreign investors either private or public coming on many occasions from emerging markets and targeted at different sectors of the economy or firms of the host state has spread social alarm and regulatory reactions against FDI in many places of the world, or at least against FDI coming from certain countries or that which is targeting certain areas of the national economy. This refers to developing countries -the extractive industry is a good example of that- but also increasingly to developed ones. Developed countries fear they will lose control of strategic sectors of the economy and national champions in favour of foreign corporations coming in many cases from geopolitical or economic competitors.[19]

In this scenario it is indispensable to distinguish between the protection of the state and its economic and social viability, through the reference to terms like national security or essential security interests and the protection of the economic interests of the state, of its economic development or any other critical objective which may or may not be linked to the previous idea of national security and that in certain cases may even run against the notion of the free market. The line between protecting legitimate public policy objectives and protectionism is very fine and not always easy to be determined.

2-2. Some Factors to be Taken into account in Evaluating the Potential Threat

The acceptance of FDI on national security grounds becomes increasingly qualified and made dependent on factors such as the sector or specific industry targeted by the investment, its nature -either greenfield or through M&A of an already existing undertaking, its condition -purely private or sovereign driven- or its origin. Reference to these factors opens the question of determining which foreign investment can be dangerous for the host state, in other words, to specify against "what" or against "whom" is protection sought. And this is done by every state on its own. Any of these factors, alone or a combination of some of them, activate in most cases the national system of evaluation of FDI on national security or related grounds.

1) The origin of the FDI constitutes an essential element in the current security related discourse towards foreign investmen t.[20] Against whom is protection sought? The primary response to this question is: against certain investors who come from individual countries, those which are perceived as hostile or with which the host country has an unfriendly relationship.[21]

2) The nature of FDI constitutes an additional element of concern and potential control. Many cases of acquisitions of existing firms by some Sovereign Wealth Funds (SWFs) and, mostly by, State Owned Enterprises (SOEs)[22] since the beginning of the financial crisis in 2007 have been published.[23] This growing role played by SWFs and SOEs in recent times, and the wide potential for influence over their objectives and activities by foreign governments directly or indirectly owning or controlling them, has created certain concerns in host states regarding the real purpose of the investment to be made: whether it is purely commercial or it primarily responds to some political and geo-strategic reasons.[24]

3) Also the particular sector where it is to be made or the specific firm targeted constitute a landmark for the evaluation and acceptance of FDI proposals. For different reasons, the host country may wish to retain control over certain key areas of its economy or to prevent "flagship" companies falling under the control of foreigners, even if they come from friendly countries.[25]

4) In addition to the origin or nature of the foreign investment and to the target of the investment, the amount of the investment or the future degree of involvement of the foreign investor in a specific firm is relevant. Thresholds for invoking national security concerns are usual fixed in some FDI review systems on national security grounds. It is important to specify how much involvement a foreign investor must have in a specific firm in the host state before it is considered to be a risk for its national security. If it is necessary for the foreign investor to fully own the firm in order to become a risk for the host state or whether it is enough when an effective control or just certain voting rights exist, and how this is actually determined. All these elements are for states to determine and different responses to them are found worldwide.[26]

2-3. Measures a State could Adopt

The study of FDI has been traditionally very much linked to the analysis of International Investment Agreements (IIAs), especially of Bilateral Investment Treaties (BITs) and, consequently, to the dimension of its protection *ex post*; once the specific investment project has already been implemented in the host country. Only some isolated BITs, mostly those entered into by the US and Canada and more recently Japan,[27] cover both the pre-establishment and the post-establishment phase of FDI.[28] Habitually, the majority of them, irrespective of their bilateral and multilateral dimension, basically include rules referring to the traditional dimension of the promotion and protection of FDI.[29]

Nevertheless, this traditional *ex post* approach linked to the IIAs entered into worldwide is now combined in many states with an increased focus on the phase previous to the actual implementation of the investment in the host country. The goal to balance the commitment towards the free circulation of FDI with the preservation of certain areas of the national economy and firms from control by foreign investors has not -always or only- given place to broader areas where access of FDI is not allowed, but to the establishment of mechanisms aimed to control *ex ante* foreign investment in certain fields or coming from certain countries on national security or national interests' bases.

3. THE ESTABLISHMENT OF MECHANISMS TO CONTROL FDI (*ex ante*) ON NATIONAL SECURITY OR RELATED GROUNDS

Despite the generally positive attitude maintained as regards FDI flows a truly "open door policy" towards foreign investment does not seem to exist, or to have ever existed, anywhere. No country accepts foreign capital to enter its economy with total freedom and to be freely invested in any area of the country.[30] In fact, and despite the maintenance of a global trend in favour of the liberalization of FDI, many national regulations that include provisions aimed to enhance the entrance of FDI and which usually grant investors many benefits and guarantees, now increasingly vest at the same time in host states the possibility to control FDI and to prevent it from entering their economy or some firms on certain different grounds.[31] Some of these changes relate to the introduction of control systems on the entry of FDI into their economies on national security or related grounds.[32]

The state is granted the power to regulate and to stop some FDI proposals, at least those that, according to it, pose national security concerns.[33] In some cases the final consequence is that the investment policy of the country and its investment law are becoming increasingly considered and treated as an additional tool to foster national security policies amid an increasingly securitized world.[34] In fact, the OECD already stated in 2006 that "(I)ssues of security and other strategic concerns have moved to the forefront of domestic and international investment policy making,"[35] and recently warned of the rise of "hidden protectionism" and protectionism abuse based, among other factors, on national security and related grounds.[36]

No specific rules controlling the entrance of foreign investment on national security, national essential security interests and related grounds existed for a long time in many countries.[37] But this has changed in the last few decades and now more and more specific rules on FDI govern this issue in many countries. States are nowadays fully concerned about the problems that FDI may cause to them in some cases and special relevance is being given to sovereign FDI. Even countries that are investing abroad are progressively aware of the national security aspects of FDI.

Governments are increasingly eager to screen, and in some cases even restrict, condition or block foreign investment implemented through takeovers of already existing domestic corporations on grounds of national security or related grounds. FDI is still wanted and encouraged as a general rule, and policies in favour of attracting FDI are implemented almost worldwide. But this fact does not supersede the increasing desire of many states to preserve certain areas of their economies or firms from foreign control or, in a less invasive way, to control certain FDI of a particular nature -basically sovereign driven FDI-, coming from certain countries or targeting particular firms or sectors of the national economy.

According to the World Bank's Survey Investing Across Borders in 2010, a fifth of the 87 countries analysed require foreign companies to go through a foreign investment approval process before proceeding with investment in certain areas of their economy. And almost 90 per cent limit foreign companies' ability to participate in some specific sectors of their economies, with stricter limits to their participation in services.[38] Different measures may be adopted by the host state to protect itself -*ex ante*- from foreign investment on national security or similar grounds.[39] Some of this measures, as we will see in 5 *supra*- are also present in Korea.

3-1. Market Access Measures

Prohibiting, fully or partially, foreign investment in particularly sensitive sectors is the most obvious *ex ante* restriction to FDI. National governments may foresee exclusive national ownership in certain sectors that are considered strategic on different grounds and therefore ban FDI in several areas of the economy.[40]

The state has the right to protect its "essential security interests,"[41] and practice shows that the "most heavily restricted sectors" are those considered "highly sensitive to national security or national sovereignty considerations."[42] However, a total ban of FDI is almost unrealistic nowadays. Habitually, the prohibition refers to certain specific areas of the economy or industries and affects both developed and developing countries.[43] In fact, this limited prohibition constitutes a rather habitual measure usually drafted "in grandiose, but vague terms."[44]

Full or partial foreign ownership restrictions usually exist in the defence industry (both production of weapons and war materials); air and maritime cabotage services and air traffic control or the purchase of real estate by foreigners in border areas or near other sensitive sites.[45] Border restrictions, for instance, constitute the most obvious example of limitation of ownership which has existed for a long time in many countries of the world. Foreigners are prevented -or face limitations- from owing real estate near territorial borders or in areas of strategic significance. Additionally restrictions may also concern electricity power grids and exchanges, seaport or airport management, or oil and gas extraction activities.[46] However, these potential restrictions may have different degrees.

However, the degree of restrictiveness is generally higher in the latter group of countries.[47] In some cases no explicit rule exists and a more subtle position is maintained.[48]

In addition to this ban, either total or sectoral, of foreign ownership in certain areas of the economy, also the number of foreign investors admitted into a certain sector of the economy can be limited by certain states.[49]

3-2. Maintenance of State's Monopolies

Another way of preserving some strategic sectors of the economy from foreign investment is through the maintenance of state monopolies in particularly sensitive sectors usually linked to the provision of basic public services and communications in a certain state; railway transport and infrastructure maintenance, landline telecommunications, oil and gas transportation, or electricity and water transmission are usual examples of them.[50]

3-3. Equity Limitation

Some countries have also introduced the requirement of joint ventures or equity restrictions in certain areas of their economy. In fact it is said to be one of the most common forms of discrimination against foreign investors, although their effectivity is, once again, under question.[51]

The amount and final transcendence of the FDI implemented in the host state can be controlled in order to ensure local control of the sector or firm affected. For instance, the Open Air Agreement between the EU and USA of 2007 explicitly limits the possibility of foreign ownership, even by an EU citizen or corporation, of US airlines to no more than 25 per cent of the corporation´s voting equity.[52] Similar limitations in other areas of the economy like banking, natural resources and energy,[53] nuclear energy and mining and mineral leases or telecommunications exist in many countries of the world.[54]

In some countries the possibility of golden shares to prevent the acquisition of local firms, usually privatized firms, by unwanted foreign investors also exists.[55]

3-4. Imposition of Certain Conditions on the Future Implementation of the FDI

In addition to the previous systems and not always fully independent of them, the host government can also subject the acceptance of the proposal to the meeting of certain specific conditions for its future implementation. These conditions can be independent of the existence of a screening systems or be included in a prospective conditionality agreement reached as a consequence of the evaluation of the FDI project on national security or related grounds.[56]

Through these mechanisms, host states may try to maximise the benefits of FDI or to control FDI flows by imposing on the investor some performance requirements, although their effectiveness is still a controversial issue.[57] Specific measures can be very different and vary from country to country.

Whether all these measures are adopted to preserve some sectors of relevant national interests from foreign control in general or from certain investors coming from particular countries or with the hidden goal of safeguarding particular areas of the economy from competition is something to be determined on case by case bases. However, and generally speaking, all those countries endorsing these kinds of measures on security related grounds share the challenge of ensuring that these security-related objectives are duly achieved at the same time that unnecessarily restrictive measures are not endorsed.[58]

3-5. The Rising Star: Screening Systems of Evaluation on National Security Grounds

Screening mechanisms of FDI on national security, national essential interests or related grounds are the rising star in this area. Screening and notification procedures constitute mechanisms to control the flux of FDI that are becoming very popular nowadays around the world. Many countries, both developing and developed states, are aware of the need to protect some industries and areas of their economy from certain FDI or FDI coming from certain countries and are progressively referring to this kind of device. States are increasingly designing this kind of instruments which provide the host state administration with the ability to evaluate FDI proposals and decide upon their acceptability or rejection. The recent enactment by the European Union of the Regulation (EU) 2019/452 of the European Parliament and of the Council of 19 March 2019 establishing a framework for the screening of foreign direct investments into the Union[59] or the enactment in the US of the Foreign Investment Risk Review Modernization Act of 2018 (FIRRMA)[60] are, among many others, good examples of this trend.

These mechanisms are based either on the nature of the specific sector where the FDI project is envisaged, on the existence of a certain threshold or on the nature of the investor, among other potential grounds. States are certainly sovereign to control FDI flows in an absolute manner. However, authors cast some doubts as regards the all-embracing scope of this power and subject the validity of these potential measures to the fact that they are adopted on rational grounds.[61] A case-by-case evaluation of proposed FDI projects by the government of the host country or by a specialized -and, in some cases, independent- body is undertaken with the goal of establishing whether the project is in accordance with the very basic economic or social policies of the host state or runs against its national security.

As a matter of principle, the development of a screening system does not in many cases hamper the openness of the country that designs it towards FDI. At least most developed countries and many emerging economies are clearly aligned with the free movement of FDI. Nevertheless, as practice shows, these kinds of systems have also in many cases the tangential effect of dissuading potential FDI projects that are abandoned by their promotors after some concerns are expressed by public authorities.[62]

4. SCREENING SYSTEMS ON NATIONAL SECURITY, NATIONAL ESSENTIAL SECURITY INTERESTS OR RELATED GROUNDS AND THEIR FOUNDATIONS

Rules on market access or ownership limitation certainly remain in some countries, and mechanisms to control the future activity and functioning of foreign acquired national firms are also designed in some places. But, as stated, the very novelty nowadays is the growing development of screening systems of FDI on national security or related grounds by developed and emerging countries which, as a matter of principle and due to their limited scope, do not limit the full support of many of these countries to the idea of free movement of investment. National states may impose conditions on the entrance of aliens and they can also impose conditions on the entrance of FDI. All these screening systems stand on different grounds but share the same idea of providing the state with a tool to protect certain industries or areas of the economy from FDI that either because its nature or origin can potentially generate threats to the national security of the host state.[63]

4-1. Goals and Key Principles of any Screening System

Screening systems are usually mechanisms with a rather limited scope: the control of those particular FDI proposals that can threaten the national security of a specific host country. Because of their own nature they do not target all FDI and they habitually do not put under question the validity of the premise in favour of the free movement of FDI. They only refer to some specific FDI projects that encompass certain traits and that therefore are subject to evaluation on national security grounds by the public authorities of the host state. Which traits those are varies from country to country as does the philosophy on which the evaluation is undertaken and its results do too.[64]

Screening mechanisms of evaluation of FDI on national security grounds are becoming rather popular worldwide. And their popularity poses certain issues as regards the principles and grounds on which they must be drafted for them to be compatible with the freedom of movement of capital and investment. Thus, the OECD identifies four key principles to be taken into account in relation to the development of any evaluation system of FDI on grounds of safeguard of national security interests, public order or related notions: non-discrimination,[65] transparency and predictability of the system developed,[66] proportionality,[67] and accountability.[68]

The final relevance of the screening system designed by a particular country will depend on the grounds and goals on which the system stands and on the flexibility of its application. Usually, either specific industries or all sectors of the economy in relation, habitually, to FDI projects over certain thresholds are subject to review by an entitled authority.[69] But many possibilities and combinations exist and the revision, like in the US, may also be done simple on grounds of national security implications of the FDI proposal without taking into account the final amount of the investment foreseen or the sector of the economy targeted. Or combine thresholds and other requirements like the need for the FDI proposals to render "net benefit to Canada" in the case of FDI targeting this country.[70] The case of Japan, for instance, is significant of this trend. Article 27(3)(i)(a) & (b) of the Foreign Exchange and Foreign Trade Act[71] allows the Minister of Finance to screen any FDI that may potentially impair "*national security*," disturb the maintenance of "*public order*," hinder the protection of "*public safety*" or have an adverse effect on the "*smooth management of the Japanese economy*." None of these very broad and vague terms are defined and a large amount of discretion is granted to the government to evaluate the acceptance or not of the FDI project. It is finally for it to balance its positive stance towards FDI and its desire to have enough flexibility to stop non-desired FDI.

4-2. Existence of Different Models

Remarkable differences exist among the several screening systems designed. In some cases, the screening system is solely designed to protect the national security of the country against potential harmful FDI; this would be the case of the US. On the contrary, other states refer to broader goals, such as the protection of "national interest," like in Australia.[72] Or require the investment to be of "the net benefit" of the host country, as happens in Canada. In other nations, like France, the freedom of movement of capital and of investment coexist with the existence of some ideas of "economic patriotism" applied to filter some FDI projects. Some countries, like Germany do not have any special rule as regards sovereign driven FDI, whereas this kind of FDI is subject to a particular treatment in countries like Canada or the US.[73]

Also the designation of specific independent organisms in some countries -CFIUS in the US- contrasts with the broad powers granted to the government in some other systems -Australia, Germany, France or the UK- in order to implement the process of evaluation of FDI on national security or related grounds.[74]

The legal basis referred to for this evaluation on national security grounds varies from country to country too; reference to competition law as a mechanism to control FDI on national security grounds in some countries -in the PRC- is in contrast with the enactment of special rules as regards this issue -US, Germany, France, Australia or, Canada-. Also, these systems are envisaged in certain countries as a last resort instrument only applicable when no other legal device is available -the US-. As a matter of principle these tools should be considered as last resort mechanisms usually dependent on the application of other provisions and systems foreseen in the host state to monitor the market or some specific areas of it.[75]

The 2009 OECD Recommendation on Guidelines for Recipient Country Investment Policies Relating to national security explicitly supports this point. These instruments should then be avoided when there are other existing measures adequate and appropriate to address national security concerns.[76] Consequently, any system designed to control the entrance of foreign capital into the country should then come into play only when those other systems designed to monitor the normal activity of the market -free competition, transparency of the financial market…- have already been applied and not previously or in addition to them, as if it were a fully independent system applicable at the same time and level than the other ones.

But this is not the case in many other countries in which the system interplays in different ways with other legal mechanisms designed in the host country. For instance, on the one hand FDI in companies' shares that are listed on a stock or security exchange system will usually be subject to specific regulations and some conditions may be imposed to them. Additionally they may be subject to other applicable rules like those of competition law which are used to prevent dominant firms -national and, in this case, foreign- to enter the market of the host country,[77] or in the case of greenfield FDI the request for the investment to be made only through joint-ventures. They can also be submitted to the existing legislation on the privatization of certain formerly public owned enterprises which may bar certain FDI from state controlled enterprises or allow it only after approval by certain institutions or those that create a certain kind of shares with no sufficient voting rights to control the enterprise object of the investment.[78]

As a matter of fact, only when these rules have been implemented should national systems on control of FDI become applicable. However, reality seems to be rather different. For instance, the rejection in 2011 of the bid by the Singapore Exchange Ltd. to acquire a major interest in the Australian Stock Exchange, both of them private entities, was made not only on the basis of the '*FATA*' but also taking into account that the *Corporations Act 2001*[79] limits ownership by a person in the Australian Stock Exchange to a maximum of 15 per cent unless a special regulation is passed to increase this threshold.[80]

In addition to the existence of different bases and goals in the designation of the several existing national screening systems, as well as relevant disparities as regards their institutional structures, also the concept of national security or security related industries on which they habitually stand varies from country to country; from narrow definitions to broader interpretations that extend investment review procedures to critical infrastructure and strategic industries. Countries do not provide a "clear-cut definition" of national security in relation to foreign investment. Instead, in some cases only a number of sectors or activities that may potentially pose national security-related threats from a national security stand-point are identified.[81]

Finally, the content and depth of the screening procedure and the degree and amount of information required from the investor is different from jurisdiction to jurisdiction.[82] In addition to these factors, potential consequences for investments considered to be problematic from a national security perspective vary and include full or partial investment prohibitions and the possibility of final approval under certain -present or future- conditions.

4-3. Systems in Practice

Screening systems developed by national legislators have mainly focussed in relation to M&As proposals, mostly in the infrastructure, telecommunications, finance and energy sectors, with special intensity in those cases in which the foreign acquirer is controlled or owned by a foreign state.[83] As figures of the practical implementation of national screening systems show, these systems should not "strike terror into the hearts of foreign direct investors."[84] However, and despite existing statistics, they are said to play an additional subtle role as regards potential foreign direct investors in so far they both foster the self-constraint and control by foreign investors as regards the goals and conditions of their prospective investment operations, as well as their willingness to enter potential agreements with the administration of the host country.[85]

States are increasingly imposing national security or related conditions on the entrance of foreign investment into their territory on specific areas of the economy or firms, or coming from certain countries or investors. Theoretically speaking these mechanisms should combine procedural fairness with the protection of sensitive information, and to ensure a level of flexibility which is enough to offer protection from investments that generate legitimate concerns at the same time that avoid political interference.[86] However, and significantly, the different screening systems introduced usually correspond with each other in the lack of clear definitions of some relevant notions on which they stand -national essential security interests, national security, control, critical infrastructure…-, in the use of some very vague guidelines or criteria to assert whether the investment is acceptable or not, and in the granting of a broad power to the administration in order to perform the requested evaluation.[87]

The drafting of these screening systems has taken place in an atmosphere of liberalization of investment and their introduction has finally constituted a sort of exception to it. Consequently, any security related condition imposed on foreign investment or any system designed to evaluate it on national security grounds should be narrowly-tailored, focussing only on really genuine national security risks.[88] And their use as an excuse to impose hidden limitations to free trade and investment should be prevented. Therefore, it is not the potential benefits for the host country arising out of the FDI project but the risks for the host state that it may generate that should finally be taken into account by these sorts of schemes of evaluation of FDI proposals. However, the peril of politicisation of these kinds of instruments exists and the potential negative consequences derived from a broad interpretation of the notion of national security remain.[89]

5. SOUTH KOREA AS A PARADIGM OF THIS EVOLUTION

South Korea is a very open economy and a very relevant economic actor worldwide. After the Asian financial crisis in 1997, Korea was forced to finish with its less than receptive attitude towards FDI and to pursue a FDI-friendly policy.[90] Reforms designed were considered both rapid and far-reaching and the "aggressive FDI inducement policy" implemented has fostered a continuous increase in the flows of FDI in the country ever since.[91]

5-1. General Principle: Openness towards FDI

The Korean Government enacted the Foreign Investment Promotion Act (FIPA) in 1998.[92] Its main goal was to regain the confidence of foreign investors and to attract FDI: "*(T)he purpose of this Act is to promote foreign investment in this nation by providing incentives and inducements with the ultimate view of contributing to the sound development of this nation's economy.*"[93] At the same time, and with the aim of attracting FDI, the Korea Trade-Investment Promotion Agency (KOTRA)[94] established the Korea Investment Service Center (KISC) in July 1998. The Center was relaunched in December 2003 as Invest KOREA (IK), Korea's national investment promotion agency.[95]

5-2. Existence of some Mechanisms of Controlling FDI

This extremely open attitude towards FDI does not impede the existence of certain limitations on FDI in Korean Law on national security or related grounds. The country has not closed any sector of its economy to FDI based on these grounds, but two review mechanisms of prospective investments -a general one and another targeting specific sectors of the economy- are designed.[96]

5-2-1. *Mechanisms targeting specific sectors of the Korean economy*

The Korean legislation sets forth two compulsory systems of control of FDI targeting some specific sectors of the economy. Firstly, screening systems operate as regards FDI proposals targeting Korean entities holding key national technologies, or that have received funding from the Korean Government. Additionally FDI proposals affecting the Defence sector are also subject to control.[97]

1) The first of these two mechanisms is designed by the Act on Prevention of Divulgence and Protection of Industrial

Technology (APDPIT) of 2006.[98] Article 1 APDPIT states that the purpose of the Act, "*is to prevent undue divulgence of industrial technology and protect industrial technology in order to strengthen the competitiveness of Korean industries and contribute to national security and development of the national economy.*"

Article 7(1) of the Act compels the Government to establish the Industrial Technology Protection Committee with the goal of deliberating on certain matters which concern preventing divulgence of industrial technology and protecting industrial technology. The Committee shall deal with matters concerning the formulation and implementation of comprehensive plans; matters concerning the designation, change and cancellation of national core technology under article 9 APDPIT; matters concerning the export, etc. of national core technology under article 11 APDPIT; matters concerning overseas acquisition, merger, etc. of an institution possessing industrial technology which possesses national core technology under article 11(2) APDPIT and any other matters determined by Presidential Decree as necessary to prevent the divulgence of, and protect industrial technology.[99] The provision establishes the composition of the Committee and the way in which it will develop its activities.

Focussing on the functioning of the Committee, article 9(1) of the Act grants on it the power to designate National Core Technology (NCT). The Committee can also change the scope or substance of the NCT or to cancel the designation thereof.[100] In designating NCT, the Committee shall take into "*account the ripple effect of the technology in question on national security and the national economy, market share of relevant products in the Korean and overseas markets, harmony between trends in research in the areas concerned and the spread of technology, etc. in a comprehensive manner.*"[101]

The APDPIT does not provide any definition of "national security or national economy" of Korea or similar notions referred to in the provision.[102] However, the definition of "National Core Technology" provided by article 2(2) APDPIT offers some guidance to this respect. According to article 2(2), NCT means "*industrial technology designated under Article 9, which has high technological and economic values in the Korean and overseas markets or brings high growth potential to its related industries and is feared as a technology to exert a significantly adverse effect on the national security and the development of the national economy in the event that it is divulged abroad.*"

The designation of NCT directly leads to the establishment in the APDPIT of certain measures for its protection, irrespective of the amount of the investment.[103]

A) Thus, article 10(1) APDPIT states that the "*head of institutions possessing industrial technology which possesses and manages national core technology shall take measures necessary to establish infrastructure to prevent the divulgence of national core technology such as designation of protection zones, approval of admission, or inspection of personal belongings at the time of entry.*" No person is allowed to refuse, interfere with or challenge any of these measures for protection without any justifiable ground.[104]

B) Article 11 APDPIT deals with the exportation of NCT developed with government subsidies for research and developments. Depending on the nature of the NCT to be exported previous approval by the Minister or only a previous report to it is considered necessary:

a) Article 11(1) estates that in those cases in which an institution holding this kind of industrial technology which holds NCT intends to export it to a foreigner by means of sale, transfer or similar it is requested to obtain approval from the Minister of Knowledge Economy. The Minister will grant -or deny- approval "*taking into account the ripple effect of the export of national core technology on national security, the national economy, etc.*"[105]

b) In case of institutions possessing industrial technology "*which possesses and manages national core technology, other than that approved pursuant to paragraph(1)*" of article 11 APDPIT and intends to export it, it is obliged to report it to the Minister of Knowledge Economy in advance.[106] When the Minister deems that this exportation "*may seriously affect national security, he or she may, after consulting with the head of the relevant central governmental administrative agency, order institutions possessing industrial technology to take measures such as suspension or prohibition of export of such national core technology, restoration to original state, etc.*"[107]

In both cases, article 11(7) APDPIT estates that should the NCT be exported without obtaining valid approval or making a valid report, the Minister of Knowledge Economy may order institutions possessing industrial technology to take measures, such as suspension and prohibition of export of the national core technology in question, restoration to original state, etc.

C) Finally, article 11-2 APDPIT refers to the overseas acquisition, merger, joint venture or similar of institutions possessing industrial technology which possess NCT developed with government subsidies for research and development. In accordance to paragraphs 1 and 2 of this provision, these institutions are obliged to report them in advance to the Minister of Knowledge Economy.[108]

Where the Minister of Knowledge Economy deems that the divulgence of national core technology under paragraphs (1) and (2) of article 11-2 APDPIT may seriously affect national security, he or she may, "*order institutions possessing industrial technology to take measures, such as suspension, prohibition, restoration to original state, etc. with respect to overseas acquisition, merger, etc.*"[109]

In case the institution possessing industrial technology which holds NCT fails to file a report under article 11-2(1) and (2) or submits a false or unlawful means of report, and proceed overseas acquisition, merger, joint-venture etc., the Minister of Knowledge Economy may request an examination to the head of the intelligence and investigation agency and order the institution possessing industrial technology to take necessary measures, such as suspension, prohibition, restoration to original state, etc. with respect to overseas acquisition, merger, etc.[110]

2) Also FDI proposals affecting the Defence sector are subject to control. Article 6(3) of the Foreign Investment Promotion Act (FIPA) sets forth a specific review mechanism as regards defence industry companies. The provision states that in case a "*foreigner intends to make a foreign investment by means of acquiring the existing stocks, etc. of a defense industry company prescribed by Presidential Decree, the foreigner shall, notwithstanding the provisions of paragraph (1), obtain in advance permission of the Minister of Knowledge Economy as prescribed by Ordinance of the Ministry of Knowledge Economy. The same shall also apply in cases of modifying any permitted details prescribed by Presidential Decree, such as the amount of foreign investment and the ratio thereof.*" Article 3 of the Defense Acquisition Program Act defines the meaning of "*defense industry*": "*8. The term "defense industry" means the manufacture, repair, processing, assembling, testing, maintenance, recycling, betterment, or remodeling (hereinafter referred to as "manufacture"), or research and development of defense materials.*"[111]

The review is triggered if the acquisition provides the foreign acquirer with 10% or more of the voting shares.[112] The Minister of Knowledge Economy, when he/she receives an application for permission in accordance to article 6(3) FIPA shall determine whether to give the permission or not, and notify the applicant of his/her determination within a period prescribed by the law.[113] Should it be considered necessary, the Minister may attach conditions to the permission granted.[114]

In any case, any person who may have acquired existing stocks in violation of article 6(3) and (6) FIPA shall not exercise his/her voting rights of such existing stocks, and the Minister of Knowledge Economy may order the said person to transfer the relevant existing stocks, etc. to a third party.[115]

5-2-2. *General restriction on FDI based on national safety concerns*

In addition to these two sectoral systems, Korean legislation designs a general review mechanism of FDI based on national security, national safety and public order.

As a matter of principle, article 4(1) FIPA states that "*(E)xcept as otherwise prescribed by any relevant Act of the Republic of Korea, a foreigner may conduct, without restraint, various activities of foreign investment in the Republic of Korea.*" However, this statement in favour of the free entrance of FDI is qualified in the next paragraphs of the provision, and some entry conditions and limitations are set forth:

> *"(2) Except for the following cases, a foreigner shall not be restricted in the investments prescribed in this Act:*
>
> *1. Where it threatens the maintenance of national safety and public order;*
>
> *2. Where it has harmful effects on public hygiene or the environmental preservation of the Republic of Korea, or is against Korean morals and customs; and*
>
> *3. Where it violates any relevant Act of the Republic of Korea."*

As a matter of principle, no prior authorization or notification are required as regards FDI proposals. Filling a prior report is required in case the foreign investor seeks to acquire either 10% or more of the total voting shares or equity of a Korean company. Or in case the FDI proposal will grant the investor less than 10% but would assure him the participation in the company's management.[116]

The FIPA does not provide any meaning for "*national safety and public order··· public hygiene or··· Korean morals and customs.*" However, in accordance to article 4(3) FIPA, the categories of business in which foreign investment is restricted in accordance with any of the subparagraphs of paragraph (2) and the details of the restriction, are prescribed by article 5(1)2 EDFIPA: "*(a) In cases where a foreign entity intends to acquire de facto control over the management of an existing domestic enterprise, by acquiring stocks, etc. in such enterprise; and (b) Any of the following cases where: (i) Manufacturing of defence supplies under subparagraph 7 of Article 3 the Defense Acquisition Program Act may be impeded; (ii) Goods or technologies, subject to permission or approval for export under Article 19 of the Foreign Trade Act and Article 13 of the Technology Development Promotion Act, are considerably likely to be misappropriated for military purposes; (iii) Contracts, which are classified as State secrets Article 13 (4) of the National Intelligence Service Act, may be disclosed; or (iv) International efforts of the United Nations, etc. for world peace and security assurance may considerably be impeded.*"

The meaning and scope of the restriction are prescribed by articles 5 and 5-2 EDFIPA.[117] Both provisions deal with the areas in which foreign investment may be restricted or prohibited, the ratio of total foreign investment permissible in certain areas or the qualification of foreign investors, among other issues. They also set forth rules on the potential request of review of the investment by the Korean Government and the dates to carry them out. In addition to that, article 4(4) FIPA establishes an obligation for the Minister of Commerce, Industry and Energy to inform on yearly basis about additional restrictions on foreign investors.[118]

As a matter of principle, and in line with other national regulations, the Government is granted broad power to control FDI on certain cases that may impede national security as set forth in article 4(2)(1) FIPA. This is done without establishing a clear-cut definition of national security in relation to foreign investment.[119] Should the approval process result in the blocking of an investment on national safety and public order grounds a public disclosure shall be made in accordance to article 5(8) EDFIPA.[120]

5-2-3. *Other applicable provisions*

As in many other nations, some other pieces of Korean legislation may also affect the entry of FDI in Korea. The Foreign Exchange Transaction Act (FETA) of 2010,[121] the Foreigner's Land Acquisition Act (FLAA) of 2008,[122] or the Monopoly Regulation and Fair Trade Act (MRFTA) of 2009,[123] among others, cast some potential limitations on the implementation of FDI in the country.

1) As a matter of principle the FETA liberalizes the payment and receipt for current transactions -the object of the Act is, among others, "to facilitate foreign transactions"-[124] but, at the same time, certain transactions are subject to notification, confirmation or, even, suspension.[125] Although article 4(1) FETA requires to impose any restrictions as referred to in the Act "only within the minimum extent necessary."

2) The FLAA -art. 4- requires the submission of a report of the land acquisition -art. 4(1) & art. 5-, continuous possession -art. 6- or authorization when the land is located near military basis or has some cultural and ecologic relevance -art. 4(2)-. In accordance to articles 7 to 9 FLAA, failure to comply with the obligations set forth by article 4 may entail a fine for negligence -in the case of art. 4(2)- or, even, imprisonment -in case of

breaching art. 4(2)-.

3) Finally, the prohibition of cartel practices and cross-border equity investment among affiliated companies may lead to the application of the MRFTA and affect the prospective FDI project.[126]

6. AN UNCERTAIN AND UNCLEAR FUTURE

The process of liberalization of international trade and of Foreign Direct Investment has constituted a broadly accepted trend during the last few decades and FDI inflows have expanded constantly since the end of the 1980's. However, signs of a certain crisis of the positive and one-way attitude towards international trade and FDI exist nowadays. The financial crisis, the change in the origin of the FDI derived from the new geo-strategic reality arising out of the crisis, the growing participation of foreign sovereign actors in international trade and investment, the changing environment for national security or the quest to protect technologies and sectors of the economy considered vital for the host country, its sovereignty and competitiveness have led many countries to set forth mechanisms to evaluate FDI proposals before they are implemented. Korea is not alien to this trend.

As a matter of principle the protection of national security is a legitimate goal of the state. However, there is a risk of these kinds of instruments being politicised, and the potential negative consequences of a broad interpretation of the notion of national security remain. The creation of these screening systems has taken place, so far, in an atmosphere of liberalisation of investment, and their introduction has ultimately constituted a sort of exception to it. But this atmosphere is changing negatively very quickly and the peril to use these screening systems as an excuse to impose hidden limitations on free trade and investment increases. The Republic of Korea, as many other countries in the world, is not vaccinated against this danger.

States have the power to control FDI and its imposition does not necessarily have a negative impact on foreign investment flows. However, many of these systems are opaque and susceptible to political influence. And in many cases, the combination of the vast powers granted on the administration, the absence of clear-cut definitions of some basic notions like national security, the changing attitude towards multilateralism or the fast geostrategic changes that are taking place in the world -also in Asia- may support the temptation to use these screening systems both to control the functioning of the market or to adopt hidden economic or strategic goals. The more international trade, FDI and globalization are attacked, the more this temptation will grow.

Notes

1. Stephen S. Golub, *Measures of Restrictions on Inward Foreign Direct Investment for OECD Countries*, OECD Economic Department Working Papers, No. 357, OECD Publishing, Paris, 2003, 1; Karl P. Sauvant, *FDI Protectionism Is on the Rise*, Policy Research Working Paper 5052, The World Bank Poverty Reduction and Economic Management Network (International Trade Department World Bank, Washington, September 2009) 3.
2. Note Carlos Esplugues, *Foreign Investment, Strategic Assets and National Security*, Cambridge, intersentia, 2018, 3 ff.
3. Lisa E. Sachs and Karl P. Sauvant, 'BITs, DTTs, and FDI Flows: An Overview,' in Karl P. Sauvant and Lisa E. Sachs, *The Effect of Treaties on Foreign Direct Investment: Bilateral Investment Treaties, Double Taxation Treaties, and Investment Flows* (OUP, Oxford, 2009) xxvii & lix.
4. As regards the meaning of these terms, note Carlos Esplugues, above n 2, 76 ff.
5. UNCTAD, *The Protection of National Security in IIAs.* UNCTAD Series on International Investment Policies for Development, UNCTAD/DIAE/IA/2008/5 (UNCTAD, New York/Geneva 2009), xiv.
6. Stuart S. Malawer, 'Global Mergers and National Security' (2006) December *Virginia Lawyer Magazine* 33, 34.
7. José E. Alvarez, 'Contemporary Foreign Investment Law: An "Empire of Law" or the "Law of Empire"?' (2009) 60 *Alabama Law Review* 943, 970.
8. Crispin Waymouth, 'Is 'Protectionism' a Useful Concept for Company Law and Foreign Investment Policy? An EU Perspective' in Ulf Bernitz and Wolf-Georg Ringe (eds), *Company Law and Economic Protectionism New Challenges to European Integration* (OUP, Oxford, 2010) 35-6.
9. José E. Alvarez, above n 7, 972 & 975.
10. Note Karl P. Sauvant, 'Driving and Countervailing Forces: A Rebalancing of National FDI Policies' (2008-9) *Yearbook on International Investment Law & Policy* 215, 234.
11. *Vid.*, OECD, *Building Trust and Confidence in International Investment. Report by countries participating in the "Freedom of Investment" Process March 2009* (OECD, Paris, 2009) 10.
12. Karl P. Sauvant, 'Driving and Countervailing Forces: A Rebalancing of National FDI Policies" (2008-9) *Yearbook on International Investment Law & Policy* 215, 233.
13. *Vid.*, Carlos Esplugues, above n 2, 221 ff.
14. Suzanne A. Spears, 'The Quest for Policy Space in a New Generation of International Investment Agreements' (2010) 13:4 *Journal of International Economic Law* 1037, 1039-1040. Also consider, OECD, *Interim report approved by the OECD Investment Committee at the fourth OECD Roundtable on Freedom of Investment, National Security and "Strategic" Industries on 30 March 2007* (reproduced in OECD, *International Investment Perspectives: Freedom of Investment in a Changing World* (OECD, Paris, 2007) 55.
15. Note, Carlos Esplugues, above n 2, 178 ff.

16. OECD, *Novel Features in OECD Countries' Recent Investment Agreements: An Overview*, OECD, Paris 2005, 4 at No. 11; Albertina Sara Vadi, 'Fragmentation or Cohesion? Investment versus Cultural Protection Rules' (2009) 10 *Journal of World Investment and Values* 573, 579ff.
17. Theodore H. Moran, 'Foreign Acquisitions and National Security: What are Genuine Threats? What Are Implausible Worries?' in Zdenek Drabek and Petros C. Mavroidis (eds), *Regulation of Foreign Investment Challenges to International Harmonization* (Singapore World Scientific, World Studies in International Economics (Vol. 21), Columbia University, (New York, 2013) 372-373.
18. OECD, above n 11, 10.
19. *See* Carlos Esplugues, above n 2, 63-67.
20. Carlos Esplugues, above n 2, 166 ff.
21. Note UNCTAD, above n 5, 17.
22. George Gilligan, Megan Bowman and Justin O'Brien, *The Global Impact of State Capital* (The University of New South Wales School of Law, Centre for Law, Markets and Regulation, CLMR Research paper series, Working Paper No. 13-2, Sydney, July 2013) 16.
23. Note Thomas Jost, 'Sovereign Wealth Funds and the German Reaction' in Karl P. Sauvant, Lisa E. Sachs and Wouter P.F. Schmit Jongbloed (eds), *Sovereign Investment. Concerns and Policy Reactions* (OUP, Oxford, 2012) 453.
24. Vid. Carlos Esplugues, above n 178-219.
25. UNCTAD, above n 5, 18.
26. UNCTAD, above n 5, 24-5; Carlos Esplugues, above n 2, 177.
27. Consider, Peter T. Muchlinski, 'Corporations and the Uses of Law: International Investment Arbitration as a "Multilateral Legal Order" (2011) 1:4 *Oñati Socio-Legal Series* 3, 3-4.
28. Also the OECD Code of Liberalization of Capital Movements (OECD, Paris, 2013) and the OECD Code of Current Invisibles Operations (OECD, Paris, 2013) consider the pre-establishment phase, note Katia Yannaca-Small, 'Essential Security Interests under International Investment Law' in OECD, *International Investment Perspectives: Freedom of Investment in a Changing World* (OECD, Paris, 2007) 94.
29. Note Leon E. Trakman and Nicola W. Ranieri, 'Foreign Direct Investment: A Historical Perspective' in Leon E. Trakman and Nicola W. Ranieri (eds), *Regionalism in International Investment Law* (OUP, Oxford, 2013) 19.
30. Jeswald W. Salacuse, *The Three Laws of International Investment. National, Contractual and International Frameworks for Foreign Capital* (OUP, Oxford, 2013) 87.
31. In fact, when UNCTAD analysed the legislative changes on FDI implemented between 1990 and 2009 it stressed the incidence of the promotion and liberalization of FDI during this period UNCTAD, *World Investment Report 2010. Investing in a Low-Carbon Economy* (United Nations, New York and Geneva, 2010) 76-7.
32. As well as, significantly, to the promotion and incentives of FDI, note Andrew

Sumner, 'Foreign Direct Investment in Developing Countries: Have We Reached a Policy 'Tipping Point'?' (2008) 29:2 *Third World Quarterly* 239, 242.

33. J. Anthony Vanduzer, Penelope Simons and Graham Mayeda, *Integrating Sustainable Development into International Investment Agreements: A Guide for Developing Countries (prepared for the Commonwealth Secretariat by the authors)* (London, 2012) 39 & 224; UNCTAD, *Investment Policy Framework for Sustainable Development*, Doc. UNCTAD/DIAE/PCB/2015/5 (UNCTAD, Geneva, 2015) 8.

34. OECD, *Protection of "Critical Infrastructure" and the Role of Investment Policies Relating to National Security* (OECD, Paris 05.2008) 9.

35. OECD, *International Investment Perspectives. 2006 Edition* (OECD, Paris, 2006) 32.

36. OECD, above n 14, 9.

37. Muthucumaraswamy Sornarajah, *The International Law on Foreign Investment* (CUP, Cambridge, 3rd ed., 2010) 97.

38. Investment Climate Advisory Services World Bank Group, *Investing Across Borders 2010. Indicators of foreign direct investment regulation in 87 economies* (World Bank, Washington, 2010) 8.

39. For instance, imposition of other emergency measures, forced disinvestment, denial of benefits based on the existence of a clause in the agreement, see UNCTAD, above n 5, 30-3.

40. *See* Thomas Pollan, *Legal Framework for the Admission of FDI* (Eleven International Publishing, Utrecht, 2006) 58-61.

41. James K. Jackson, *Foreign Investment and National Security: Economic Considerations*, Congressional Research Service, 7-5700, RL34561 (Washington, 4 April 2013) 6.

42. Golub, above n 1, 24.

43. Jürgen Kurtz, 'A General Investment Agreement in the WTO? Lessons from Chapter 11 of NAFTA and the OECD Multilateral Agreement on Investment' (2002) 243:3 *University of Pennsylvania Journal of International Economic Law* 713, 725-726.

44. Peter T. Muchlinski, *Multinational Enterprises & the Law* (OUP, Oxford, 2nd ed, 2007) 179-180.

45. Julien Chaisse, Debashis Chakbaborty and Jaydeep Mukherjee, 'Emerging Sovereign Wealth Funds in the Making: Assessing the Economic Feasibility and Regulatory Strategies' (2011) 45:4 *Journal of World Trade* 837, 854; UNCTAD, *World Investment Report 2016. Investor Nationality: Policy Challenges* (United Nations, New York and Geneva, 2016) 97-8.

46. *Ibid.*, 98.

47. Stephen Thomsen and Fernando Mistura, *'Is investment protectionism on the rise? Evidence from the OECD FDI Regulatory Restrictiveness Index' OECD Global Forum on International Investment* (OECD, Paris, 2017) 16.

48. In Canada, for instance, the health care sector is considered to be de facto closed to FDI because private hospitals and clinics may not receive payments from provincial health insurance funds, which are deemed critical for the financial viability of operators in the sector. Vid. Investment Climate Advisory Services World Bank Group, above n 38, 98.

49. Kurtz, above n 43, 725.
50. UNCTAD, above n 45, 98.
51. Thomsen and Mistura, above n 47, 4.
52. REFERENCE "ANNEX 4: *Concerning Additional Matters Related to Ownership, Investment and Control.* Article 1: Ownership of Airlines of a Party. 1. Ownership by nationals of a Member State or States of the equity of a U.S. airline shall be permitted, subject to two limitations. First, ownership by all foreign nationals of more than 25 percent of a corporation's voting equity is prohibited. Second, actual control of a U.S. airline by foreign nationals is also prohibited. ···." Note also, United States Government Accountability Office, *Report to the Committee on Banking, Housing, and Urban Affairs, U.S. Senate, Sovereign Wealth Funds. Laws Limiting Foreign Investment Affect Certain U.S. Assets and Agencies Have Various Enforcement Processes,* GAO-09-608 (Washington DC, 05.2009), 15 and Appendix II.
53. Note Edward M. Graham and David M. Marchick, *U.S. National Security and Foreign Direct Investment* (Institute for International Economics, Washington, 2006), 13-4.
54. Efraim Chalamish, 'Global Investment Regulation and Sovereign Funds' (2012) 13:2 *Theoretical Inquiries in Law* 645, 651.
55. *See* Thomas Pollan, *Legal Framework for the Admission of FDI* (Eleven International Publishing, Utrecht, 2006) 61-2.
56. Carlos Esplugues, above n 2, 236-238.
57. Guoquiang Long, 'China's policies on FDI: review and evaluation' in Theodore H. Moran, Edward M. Graham and Magnus Blomström (eds), *Does foreign direct investment promote development?* (Institute for International Economics, Washington, 2005) 315.
58. OECD, above n 11, 10.
59. *OJ* L 79, of 21.3.2019. As regards the Regulation, note, Carlos Esplugues, "A Future European FDI Screening System: Solution or Problem?," *Columbia FDI Perspectives. Perspectives on topical foreign direct investment issues,* No. 245, February 11, 2019 (http://ccsi.columbia.edu/files/2018/10/No-245-Esplugues-Final.pdf,accessed 19.04.2019).
60. H. R. 5515—538.
61. *See* Muthucumaraswamy Sornarajah, above n 37, 137.
62. *See* Andreas Heinemann, 'Government Control of Cross-Border M&A: Legitimate Regulation or Protectionism? Control of Cross-Border M&A' (2012) 15:4 *Journal of International Economic Law* 843, 851.
63. *See* Carlos Esplugues, "La Propuesta de Reglamento estableciendo un marco para la evaluación de las inversiones extranjeras directas en la Unión Europea de septiembre de 2017," *Cuadernos de Derecho Transnacional,* 2018, vol. 10:1, 177-179.
64. Vid. Carlos Esplugues, above n 2, 254-263.
65. OECD, *Recommendation of the Council on Guidelines for Recipient Country Investment Policies relating to National Security* C(2009)63 (OECD, Paris, 25 May 2009) Annex 1.
66. OECD, *Accountability for Security-Related Investment Policies* (OECD, Paris, November 2008) 4.

67. OECD, above n 65, Annex 3.
68. OECD, above n 66, 4. Four additional principles are mentioned by the World Bank Guidelines on the Treatment of Foreign Direct Investment: 1) Firstly, that the burden of proof should fall on those calling for restricting access to national markets and not the other way round; that is, on the host state. 2) Secondly, that SWFs -as well as SOEs- do not constitute a homogeneous category and that these kinds of actors may vary deeply in major issues like size, funding, objectives, investment styles or sophistication. 3) Thirdly, that instead of stigmatizing the whole category of SWFs -and SOEs- by referring globally to all of them as negative FDI actors and subjecting all their FDI proposals to controls, only those SCEs that actually misbehave should be subject to control and evaluation. And, 4) Fourthly, in addition to all these requirements the World Bank recognizes the right of every state to draft legislation to govern the admission of FDI and the possibility of drafting a restricted list of investments (World Bank Guidelines on the Treatment of Foreign Direct Investment, No. II(3) <https://www.italaw.com/documents/WorldBank.pdf> accessed 18.04.2019). A general approach to all these principles may be found in Carlos Esplugues, above n 2, 245-254.
69. Mark A. Clodfelter and Francesca M. S. Guerrero, 'National Security and Foreign Government Ownership Restrictions on Foreign Investment: Predictability for Investors at the National Level,' in Karl P. Sauvant, Lisa E. Sachs and Wouter P. F. Schmit Jongbloed (eds), above n 23, 175-7.
70. Carlos Esplugues, above n 2, 277 & 334.
71. Foreign Exchange and Foreign Trade Act, Act No. 228 of December 1, 1949, available at: http://www.cas.go.jp/jp/seisaku/hourei/data/FTA.pdf (accessed 14.04. 2019).
72. John Cobau, 'Legal Developments in U.S. National Security Reviews of Foreign Direct Investment (2006-2008)' in Sauvant, Sachs and Schmit Jongbloed (eds), above n 23, 107.
73. Carlos Esplugues, above n 2, 239-243.
74. James K. Jackson, *The Committee on Foreign Investment in the United States (CFIUS)*, Congressional Research Service, 7-5700, RL33388 (Washington, six March 2014), 30; UNCTAD, above n 100, 94ff.
75. Carlos Esplugues, above n 2, 239-243.
76. OECD, above n 65, Annex 3.
77. Muthucumaraswamy Sornarajah, above n 37, 92.
78. Jeswald W. Salacuse, above n 30, 121-2.
79. *Corporations Act 2001*, No. 50, 2001 s 850B.
80. Note, *Singapore finally walks from ASX bid, The Sydney Morning Herald* (on line), 08.04.2011 <http://www.smh.com.au/business/singapore-finally-walks-from-asx-bid-20110407-1d6o4.html> accessed 16.04.2017. *See* Vivienne Bath, 'Foreign Investment, the National Interest and National Security - Foreign Direct Investment in Australia and China' (2012) 34:5 Sydney Law Review 5, 8.

81. UNCTAD, above n 45, 94-5.
82. *Ibid.*, 99-100.
83. OECD, *Interim report approved by the OECD Investment Committee at the fourth OECD Roundtable on Freedom of Investment, National Security and "Strategic" Industries on 30 March 2007* (reproduced in OECD, *International Investment Perspectives: Freedom of Investment in a Changing World* (OECD, Paris, 2007) 55.
84. David Zaring, 'CFIUS as a Congressional Notification Service' (2009) 83 *Southern California Law Review* 81, 106, as regards the US screening system before its reform in 2018.
85. David Zaring, above n 84, 106-9 or John B. III Bellinger and Nicholas L. Townsend, 'Inside 'the CFIUS': US National Security Review of Foreign Investments' (2011) 6:1 *Global Trade and Customs Journal* 1, 2 -stating certain operations that failed because of CFIUS- also as regards the US screening system. In the particular case of the US, the delays derived from a CFIUS investigation and the potentially negative publicity that can be associated to such an investigation have negatively affected some operations and have led the investor to withdraw them. *See* James K. Jackson, *The Exon-Florio National Security Test for Foreign Investment*, Congressional Research Service, 7-5700, RL33312 (Washington, 29 March 2013), 10 & 14 providing some examples.
86. Jackie Vandermeulen and Michael J. Trebilcock, 'Canada´s Policy Response to Foreign Sovereign Investment: Operationalizing National Security Exceptions' (2009) 47 *Canadian Business Law Journal* 392, 394.
87. Jackie Vandermeulen and Michael J. Trebilcock, above n 86, 394; Jackie Vandermeulen and Michael J. Trebilcock, above n 86, 394; A. Edward Safarian, 'The Canadian Policy Response to Sovereign Direct Investment' in Sauvant, Sachs and Schmit Jongbloed (eds), above n 23, 446.
88. *Statement of the European Union and the United States on Shared Principles for International Investment* of April 2012 <http://trade.ec.europa.eu/doclib/press/index.cfm?id=796&title=EU-and-US-adopt-blueprint-for-open-and-stable-investment-climates> accessed 18.04.2019.
89. Thus, the White House statement on the US-China economic relations of 2015, explicitly states that, "*The United States and China commit to limit the scope of their respective national security reviews of foreign investments (for the United States, the CFIUS process) solely to issues that constitute national security concerns, and not to generalize the scope of such reviews to include other broader public interest or economic issues. The United States and China commit that their respective national security reviews apply the same rules and standards under the law to each investment reviewed, regardless of country of origin*…." (The White House. Office of the Press Secretary, Fact Sheet: U.S.-China Economic Relations, Washington D.C., 25 September 2015, <https://obamawhitehouse.archives.gov/the-press-office/2015/09/25/fact-sheet-us-china-economic-relations> accessed 19.04.2019).
90. Choong Yong Ahn, *New Direction of Korea's Foreign Direct Investment Policy in the Multi-Track FTA Era: Inducement and Aftercare Services*, OECD VII Global Forum on International Investment, 27-28 March 2008, OECD Investment Division, 2;

Charles Harvie & H.H. Lee, Korea's Fading Economic Miracle 1990-97, Working Paper 05-09, Department of Economics, University of Wollongong, 2005, 9-11.

91. Françoise Nicolas, Stephen Thomsen & Mi-Hyun Bang, *Lessons from Investment Policy Reform in Korea*, OECD Working Papers on International Investment, 2013/02, Paris, OECD Publishing, 2013, 18; Choong Yong Ahn, above n 90, 7. As regards current figures of FDI in Korea, note https://tradingeconomics.com/south-korea/foreign-direct-investment, accessed 20.04.2019.

92. Official English version available at http://legal.un.org/avl/pdf/ls/Shin_RelDocs.pdf, accessed 19.04.2019.

93. Art. 1 FIPA. Note Gyooho Lee, "The Korean Foreign Investment Law and Investor-State Dispute Settlement," in Carlos Esplugues (ed), *Foreign Investment and Investment Arbitration in Asia*, Cambridge, intersentia, 2019, 139, 141. Also, Françoise Nicolas, Stephen Thomsen & Mi-Hyun Bang, above n 91, 19 ff.

94. https://www.kotra.or.kr/foreign/kotra/KHENKT010M.html, accessed 19.04.2019.

95. http://www.investkorea.org/en/ik/investkorea.do, accessed 19.04.2019.

96. *See* Frédéric Wehrlé & Joachim Pohl, Investment Policies Related to National Security: A Survey of Country Practices, OECD Working Papers on International Investment 2016/02, Paris, OECD, 2016, 61.

97. *Ibid.*

98. http://elaw.klri.re.kr/eng_service/lawView.do?lang=ENG&hseq=24351, accessed 21.04.2019.

99. Art. 7(1) numbers 1-5 APDPIT.

100. Art. 9(3) APDPIT.

101. Art. 9(2) APDPIT.

102. *See* Frédéric Wehrlé & Joachim Pohl, above n 96, 63.

103. No numerical thresholds are established as regards this kind of investment. See Frédéric Wehrlé & Joachim Pohl, above n 96, 62. Additionally, no specific time frames to carry out the revision by the Government are established by law (*ibid.*, 64).

104. Art. 10(3) APDPIT.

105. Art. 11(2) APDPIT. Also, note paragraph (3) as regards permission of transferal of NCT which, in accordance to art. 19 (1) of the Foreign Trade Act (available at: http://elaw.klri.re.kr/kor_service/lawView.do?lang=ENG &hseq=37529&joseq=JO0019000, accessed on 18.08.2019), is considered technology: "*on which restriction, such as export permission, is required for maintaining international peace and security as well as national security,*" or which is considered defense science and technology and defense articles under articles 30 and 34 of the Defense Acquisition Program Act (available at: http://elaw.klri.re.kr/kor_service/law View.do?lang=ENG&hseq=46900&joseq=JO0057000, accessed 18.08.2019).

106. Art. 11(4) APDPIT. The possibility of filling an application for prior review with the Minister of Knowledge Economy as to whether the national core technology in question is related to national security is envisaged in paragraph (6) of art. 11 APDPIT.

107. Art. 11(5) APDPIT.

108. Art. 11-2(4) APDPIT admits the possibility of requesting the Minister of Knwoledge Economy to examine in advance whether the NCT in question is related to national security; whether the overseas acquisition, merger, etc. in question is subject to the reporting of paragraphs (1) and (2); or any other questionable matters with regard to relevant overseas acquisition, merger, etc.

109. Art. 11-2(3) APDPIT.

110. Art. 11-2(5) APDPIT.

111. Note to this respect, art. 7(2) Enforcement Decree of the Foreign Investment Promotion Act (EDFIPA), available at: http://www.investkorea.org/InvestKoreaWar/data/bbs/20081006/fdi_law2.pdf, accessed 18.04.2019.

112. *See* Frédéric Wehrlé & Joachim Pohl, above n 96, 62.

113. The period for decision on and issuance of the permission are established by art. 6(3) & (4) EDFIPA.

114. Art. 6 (4) & (6) FIPA.

115. Art. 6(7) FIPA.

116. *See* Frédéric Wehrlé & Joachim Pohl, above n 96, 63.

117. Vid. Gyooho Lee, above n 93, 144 ff.

118. *See* Frédéric Wehrlé & Joachim Pohl, above n 96, 62.

119. Vid. Carlos Esplugues, above n 2, 240.

120. Art. 5(8) EDFIPA. Note Frédéric Wehrlé & Joachim Pohl, above n 96, 63-64.

121. http://www.moleg.go.kr/images/common/ico_pdf.gif, accessed 20.04.2019.

122. http://www.moleg.go.kr/FileDownload.mo?flSeq=34253, accessed 20.04.2019.

123. http://www.moleg.go.kr/FileDownload.mo?flSeq=34252, accessed 20.04.2019.

124. Art. 1 FETA.

125. PWC /SAMIL, *Doing Business and Investing in Korea*, Seoul, PWC, 2012, 18.

126. Françoise Nicolas, Stephen Thomsen & Mi-Hyun Bang, above n 91, 26.

KYIL

The Distortion of History regarding the Dokdo Territory in Japanese History Textbook and the Truth under International Law & History

LEE Jang-Hie
Emeritus Professor, Law School, Hankuk Univ. of Foreign Studies, Seoul, Korea
Judge, Permanent Court of Arbitration(PCA), Hague

Key Words

Distortion, School History Textbooks, the Truth of Dokdo, the Japanese Dajokan Order. Imperial Decree No.41, An Yong-bok, 'Woosan island,' the Shimane Prefecture, the San Francisco Peace Treaty, SCAPIN 677, legal apology and legal compensation, multiple choice method in Elementary School, terra nullius, Sim Hueng-taek, Syngman Rhee Lee Line, the Potsdam Declaration, the Russo-Japanese war

1. INTRODUCTION

As of 2018, it has been 73 years since Korea has become a free and independent state from Japanese illegal colonial rule after the end of WW II on August 15, 1945. However, Korea and Japan still have numerous unresolved colonial issues such as the Dokdo territorial issues, Comfort Women issues, Forced Labour issues, and so on. The main concern is that Japan has not yet accepted its actions committed during its illegal colonial rule, and subsequently assumed responsibility for giving a legal apology and legal compensation.

When Abe Shinzo in Japan came into power again in 2012, he denied Japan's colonial history and colonial atrocities such as wartime sex slavery between 1910 and 1945. The Shinzo Abe government has since its inauguration stood by its policy to intensify its territorial claims, which has included revising school textbooks on territory and history education.

Prime Minister Abe sent a high-ranking official to participate in the country's Takeshima Day on February 22. The event has been held in Shimane Prefecture since 2005, and was devised to stress Japan's territorial claims over the Dokdo islets.

One of the most contentious issues, which continue to strain Japan-Korea relations involves a group of tiny islets in the East Sea referred to as Dokdo in Korea and Takeshima in Japan. Since the end of Japanese colonialism in Korea in 1945, both Japan and Korea have made claims of sovereignty over Dokdo(Takeshima) taking various actions to buttress their claims.

The earliest recorded reference of Dokdo in Korean history is traced to 512 AD when a Silla general (Yi Sa Bu,吏史夫) conquered the kingdom of Usan which had possession of both Ulleundo and Dokdo.[1]

The Korean government has never renounced the territorial sovereignty over Dokdo Islets ever since A.D. 512 in which the Islets became as part of the Korean territory.

Dokdo is Korea's inherent territory historically, geographically and by international law. However, Japan claims that Korea is "illegally occupying" Korea's easternmost territory, the Dokdo islets.

Japan has systematically begun to distort high school textbooks since 2012, claiming that Korea has illegally occupied Dokdo.

Every year the two countries has waged history wars regarding distortion of history textbooks[2] issued since 2012.

2. SHORT HISTORY OF THE DOKDO TERRITORY[3]

Korea has a long historical claim, going back, according to some reports, 1500 years into the Sila Kingdom period. Maps drawn by prominent Japanese cartographers in the 1700s and early 1899s seemed to recognize that Dokdo was part of Korea.

- AD/512: Subjugation to Usan-guk
- 1454: Sejong Sillok, Jiriji; Geography Section of the Annals of King Sejong's Reign.
- 1625: Passage License to Takeshihma (Ulleungdo)
- 1693: Abduction of An Yong-bok by Japanese Fishermen.
- 1694: Instruction to Inspect Ulleungdo
- 1695: The Tottori-han's Submission
- 1696: January, Order Banning Passage to Ulleungdo
- 1695: May, An Yong-bok's Voyage to Japan.
- 1770: Dongguk Munheon Bigo (Reference Compilation of Documents on Korea)
- 1870: Confidential Inquiry into the Particulars of Relations with Joseon (1870)
- 1877: The Japanese Dajokan Order.

It instructed the Home Ministry that "our country has nothing to do with" Dokdo and Ulleungdo.

- 1900: Imperial Decree No.41.

The Korean government promulgated Imperial Decree No.41, which established the county of Ulleungdo and clearly included Dokdo within its boundaries.

- 1905: The Shimane Prefecture, Public Notice No.40.

Japan claimed sovereignty over Dokdo on January 28,1905, stating that this territory was "terra nullius." Japan's 1905 claim to Dokdo was made during the period when Japan engaged in unrelenting efforts to exert increasing military and civilian control over Korea, which led to establishment of a protectorate over Korea in November 1905 and form annexation in 1910.[4]

- 1906: March, County Magistrate Sim Heung-Taek's Report May, Uijeongbu Directive No.3.

The Korean government did attempt to protest Japan's claim to Dokdo in 1906, but its independence had been swallowed up by Japan by then, and its voice was muffled.

- 1946: January 29, SCAPIN 677
  June 22, SCAPIN 1033

In 1946, after World War II, the Allied Powers occupying both Japan and Korea issued instructions that separated Dokdo from Japanese territory.

- 1951: Conclusion of the Treaty of Peace with Japan.[5]

But the 1951 Peace Treaty between Japan the Allied Powers made no specific mention of Dokdo(perhaps because of the Korean War and the dynamics of Cold War politics). Article 2(a) of the San Francisco Treaty has been invoked by Japan to claim sovereignty over Dokdo and to argue that the paragraph does not specify Dokdo. But Korea did not sign on the treaty.

- 1952: January 18. Proclamation of Korean Jurisdiction over waters within a line an average of 60 nautical miles from the Korean coast. (so-called, Syngman Rhee Lee Line)[6]
- 1965: Diplomatic Normalization between Korea and Japan.

Dokdo was never listed as an official agenda item for discussion during the negotiations.

3. DISTORTION OF HISTORY IN JAPANESE TEXTBOOKS ON THE DOKDO TERRITORY

Japanese textbooks intensified Dokdo claim. On March 18, 2016 Japan's Ministry of Education, Culture, Sports, Science and Technology announced the results of its review of high school textbooks, in which some 77 percent of the textbooks mention that Dokdo is Japanese sovereign territory or that Korea's occupation of the islets is illegal.[7]

Korea issued a strong protest after Japan authorized dozens of updated high school textbooks on March 18, 2016, all of which renewed territorial claims to the South's easternmost islets of Dokdo in a move sure to aggravate historical tensions between the two neighbors.

Tokyo approved updated high school textbooks which claimed that Korea illegally occupied Takeshima without any basis upon international law. The Japan government says no measures that taken by Korea with regard to Takeshima during illegal occupation has any legal justification.

Furthermore, Korea denounced Japan after Tokyo issued a diplomatic report renewing the country's claims to the South's easternmost islets of Dokdo on April 15, 2016. This annual report, Diplomatic Bluebook 2016, was reported to the Cabinet with claims that Dokdo was clearly Japanese territory both historically and under international law.

The Japanese Ministry of Education began the first screenings for all social studies textbooks in 2015 since the government revised textbook screening guidelines in January 2014 to require textbooks to reflect its stances on history and territorial issues.[8]

Stressing that Dokdo is Korea's inherent territory historically, geographically and by international law, Seoul's Foreign Ministry "strongly deplored" Tokyo's approval of the textbooks and demanded an "immediate" rectification.

"The Japanese government should never forget that teaching correct history is its grave responsibility for its future generations and neighboring countries suffering from Japan's history of invasion," the Ministry said in a press release.

"We once again urge Japan to show its efforts to open a new chapter of Korea-Japan relations through sincere action, while squarely facing historical truths."

The Ministry called on Hideo Suzuki, a minister at the Japanese Embassy in Seoul, to lodge a protest. Chung Byung-won, Director-General handling Northeast Asian affairs at the ministry, met with him.

The authorization of the textbooks to be used from April 2017 represented a bolstering of Tokyo's claims to Dokdo because 27 of the newly approved 35 social studies textbooks -- or nearly 80 percent -- claim that the Korea is "illegally occupying" the islets.[9]

In the previous screening in 2012, 27 of the 39 total textbooks -- or 69.2 percent -- included Tokyo's territorial claim to the islets, called "Takeshima" in Japanese. This number has increased to 77.1 percent this year from 69.2 percent, or 27 of the 39 total textbook in 2012.

Many of the updated textbooks state that Dokdo is Japan's "inherent" territory, while some others highlight that the Tokyo government has proposed taking the simmering territorial issue to the International Court of Justice.

The Korean Ministry of Education also released a statement of protest and denounced Japan's new textbooks as "un-educational," and said that "teaching a distorted view of history to students who are yet immature in historical perception and making judgments can lead to a repeated history of aggression, which could jeopardize peace in Northeast Asia."

The Ministry of Education said it will distribute reference

materials and textbooks in April 2016, explaining South Korea's position on the issue of Dokdo and emphasizing the description of the islet in its new state history textbooks. It is also planning to send a request for a correction to Japan's Foreign Ministry in June.

The issue of Dokdo has been one of the thorniest issues that have fueled historical enmities between the two countries. Korea has been in effective control of the islets with a small police detachment since its liberation from Japan in 1945. The content about the controversial deal was not reflected in the new history textbooks as the publishers' applications for the state authorization process were made before the deal was reached. Private Japanese publishers must go through an authorization process to get state approval to publish textbooks for use in Japanese schools.

Tokyo says the process, which is conducted every four years, is necessary to ensure the "objectivity and impartiality" of textbooks, but critics here argue it is intended to whitewash and gloss over Japan's colonial-era wrong doings. The Japanese government's conservative swing seems to have been reflected in the textbooks. The Korean Civil Society urged Japan to withdraw its policy of writing distorted history textbooks.

Dokdo issue was prepared in the Sham Examination question of multiple choice method[10] in Elementary School for admission to Japanese Middle School, although it was made by Japanese private academy on June 20, 2016 (See Material 1). The Korean government strongly denounced Japan on March 30, 2018 for Japan's claiming sovereignty over Dokdo in its guidelines for high school textbooks. Protesting the move, South Korean Foreign Minister Kang Kyung-wha lodged a complaint in a phone call with Japanese counterpart Taro Kono on the same day. Earlier, the Korean Ministry of Foreign Affairs summoned in Japanese Ambassador to Korea Yasumasa Nagamine.

The Ministry said in a statement issued by its spokesman, Noh Kyu-duk that "the Korean government strongly criticizes the Japanese government for confirming the guidelines that include an inappropriate argument about Korea's inherent territory of Dokdo, and urges immediate withdrawal of the guidelines" and that "the islets are clearly the territory of Korea which Japan first occupied when it began invading the Korean Peninsula."[11]

The legally binding guidelines are scheduled to be applied for Japanese high school textbooks from 2022. In the section about territory, the textbooks stipulate that Takeshima, the Kuril Islands and the Senkaku Islands are Japanese territory. For years, Japan has intensified the long-standing territorial disputes through textbook guidelines. In 2017, the Japanese government claimed its sovereignty of Dokdo and Diaoyudao Islands, in the revised textbook guidelines for elementary and middle school students.[12] Korea's concern is that every year the two countries would waged history wars regarding distorted history textbooks. The wars over historical distortion happened again in 2017[13] and in 2018.[14]

Japan repeated its territorial claims to Dokdo its annual diplomatic report, Tokyo claimed the islets are clearly Japanese territory historically and under international law. The Diplomatic Bluebooks 2016, 2017 and 2018 were reported to the Cabinet by Foreign Minister Fumio Kishida. These kind of distortions of history distortion would not be instructive for future young generation.

Material 1.	
	The Sham Examination question of multiple choice method in Elementary School for admission to Japanese Middle School

4. LOCATION & NAMES OF DOKDO

4-1. The Location

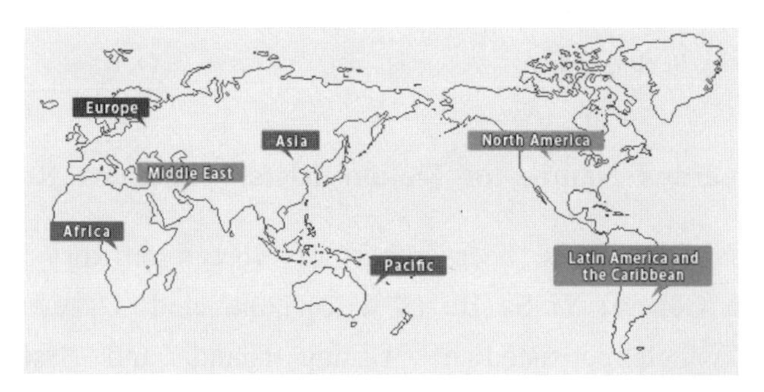

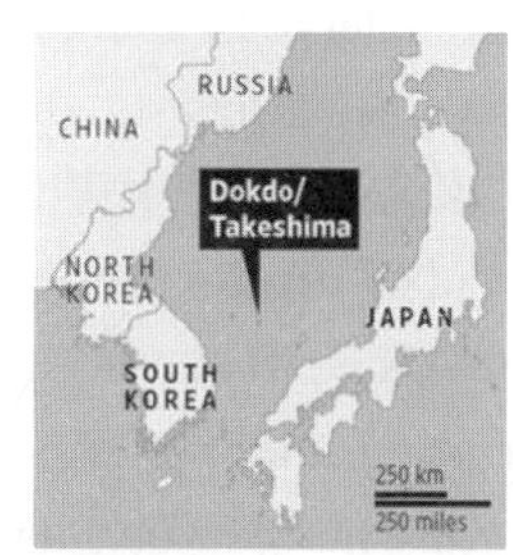

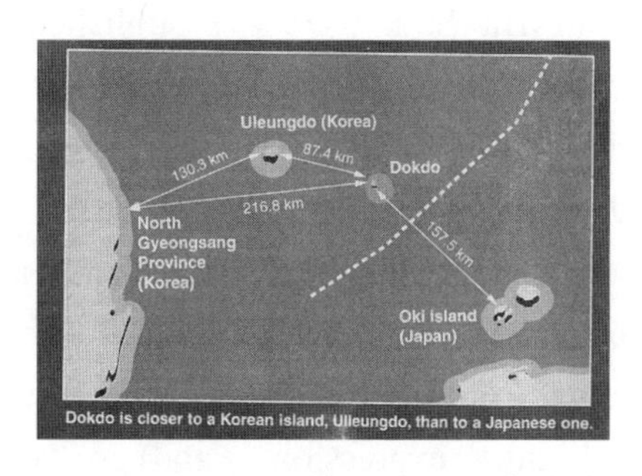

Dokdo is closer to a Korean island, Ulleungdo, than to a Japanese one.

Dokdo Islets consist of two big Islets (East, West) and numerous rocks surrounding the Islets.

Coordinates	Height
North Latitude 37° 14′ 12″	East Islet: 98m
East Longitude 131° 52′ 17″	West Islet: 186m

Area of the Islets	A total of 186,173㎡
East Islet	64,698㎡
West Islet	91,740㎡
Subordinate Rocks(East)	6,075㎡
Subordinate Rocks(West)	19,855㎡
Reefs(East)	71,5578㎡
Reefs(West)	114,595㎡

4-2. Numerous Names for Dokdo Islets (Liancourt Rocks)

Dokdo Islets have been a part of Korean territory since A.D. 512 when General Yi Sa Bu (吏史夫) conquered 'Usanguk' country (于山國) which consisted of 'Ullung Island' and 'Usando Islet' (Dokdo Islets) in the 13th year of King Ji Jeng's rein of the Shilla dynasty, according to the History of Three Early Korean Kingdoms 'Sam Kugsagi' (三國史記) by Kim Bu Shik (金富軾) published in A.D. 1145 under the endorsement of the Government of the Korea Dynasty.

During the period of 1,500 years, the Dokdo Islets have had numerous names such as 'Woosan island' (于山島, Steep Rocks and Water Island), 'Jasando' (the subordinate islets), 'Sambongdo' (Three Summits Island), 'Gajido' (Sea lion Island), 'Sukdo' (Rocks Island) and 'Dokdo' (Rocks in Korean colloquial expression Island) in Korea while Dokdo appeared in Japan as 'Matsushima island' (松島) for the first time in a local officer's territorial boundary patrol report (隱州視聽合記) in A.D. 1667, preceding to the current name 'Takeshima island' given in 1905 during the Russo-Japanese war.[15]

Ulleungdo is located due east of the county. During the Silla period,it was referred to as "Usanguk." Its extent is 100 ri ... According to some, Usan and Mureung are two separate islands situated adjacent to each other, which are visible from each other on a clear day.[16] This group of two islands (Usando. Ulleungdo) is also known as "Mureung" or "Ureung." They are located in a sea area due east of the county ..... According to some sources, the two are one same island.[17] But Jiriji of Goryeosa mentions the notion that Ulleungdo couldbe two separate islands.[18]

5. WHAT IS THE TRUTH ABOUT DOKDO?

1. Japan's Claims: There is no evidence that Korea recognized the existence of Dokdo in the past. Korea claims that Usando is the current island of Dokdo. However, Usando is either the same island as Ulleungdo or non-existent.[19]

1-1. Korea's Response

It is not true because Korea's clear recognition of Dokdo is proven by ancient documents and maps. The truth is as follows: two islands means that their existence had been clearly recognized at the time when the map was drawn. And all the maps produced after the eighteenth century, including the "Map of Korea" (Donggukjido), place Usando to the east of Ulleungdo, showing that the location and formation of Dokdo had also become more precisely.

On fine days, Dokdo is visible to the naked eye from Ulleungdo. One can safely conclude that Korea recognized Dokdo's existence as early as when Ulleungdo was first inhabited, because in fair weather, Dokdo is within an easy range of the naked eye from Ullengdo (See Material 2). Dokdo has historically been recognized as a part of Ulleungdo due to this geographical characteristic. The Geographical Appendix to the Veritable Records of King Sejong (*Sejong sillok jiriji*, 1454) states, "Usan [that is, Dokdo] and Mureung [that is, Ulleungdo] are located in the middle of the sea, due east of this county. The two islands are visible from each other on fine days, as they are not far apart. The island was called Usan-guk in the Silla period, and it is also known as Ulleungdo." This clarifies that Ulleungdo is visible from Dokdo, and Usando belonged to Usan-guk.[20]

Numerous historical documents issued by the Korean government, including the Newly Enlarged Geographical Survey of Korea (*Sinjeung Dongguk yeoji seungnam*, 1531), Reference Compilation of Materials on Korea (*Dongguk munheon bigo*, 1770), the Book of Ten Thousand Techniques of Governance (*Mangi yoram*, 1808), and Revised and Enlarged Edition of the Reference Compilation of Documents on Korea (*Jeungbo Munheon bigo*, 1908), record that Usando is the same as Dokdo.[21]

In particular, descriptions in documents such as "Considering Maps" in Reference Compilation of Materials on Korea ("*Yeojigo*," in Dongguk munheon bigo) which state that both Ulleung (Ulleungdo) and Usan (Dokdo) are territories of Usanguk, and Usan (Dokdo) is what Japan calls Matsushima, clearly indicate that Usando is Dokdo.

"The Map of the Eight Provinces of Korea" (*Paldo chongdo*), in The Newly Enlarged Geography of Korea (*Sinjeung Dongguk yeoji seungnam*) has the two islands of Ulleungdo and Usando [Dokdo] in the East Sea (See Material 3, 3-1). The locations are not precise, but the presence of the two islands means that their existence had been again clearly recognized at the time when the map was drawn. And all the maps produced after the eighteenth century, including the "Map of Korea" (*Dongguk jido*), place Usando east of Ulleungdo, showing that the location and formation of Dokdo was precisely located.[22]

<table>
<tr><th colspan="2">Material 2.</th></tr>
<tr><td></td><td>Dokdo Seen from Ulleungdo</td></tr>
</table>

Material 3.	
	The Map of the Eight Provinces of Korea (Paldo chongdo)

Material 3-1.	
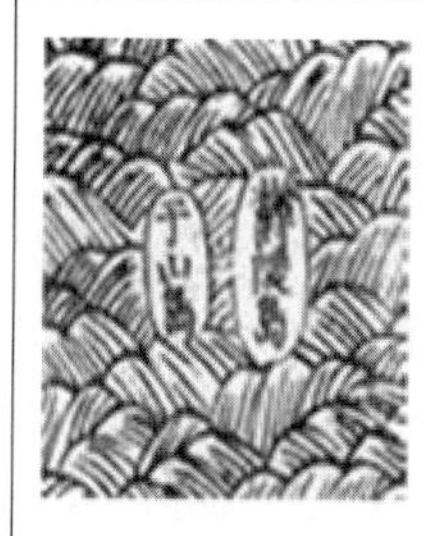	This map of Joseon was included at the beginning of The Newly Enlarged Geographical Survey of Korea (Sinjeung Dongguk yeoji seungnam) published by the Joseon government. Ulleungdo and Dokdo are clearly marked in the East Sea.

2. Japan's Claims: Japan reaffirmed its intention to claim sovereignty over Dokdo by incorporating the island into Shimane Prefecture in 1905 through a Cabinet decision. After receiving a request from Nakai Yozaburo, a resident of Oki Islands in Shimane Prefecture, to incorporate Dokdo into Japanese territory, the Japanese government reaffirmed, through a Cabinet decision made in January of 1905, its intention to claim sovereignty over the island. Consequently, in February of that year, the governor of Shimane Prefecture issued an official notification that Dokdo was to be put under the jurisdiction of the Okinoshima office of Shimane Prefecture.[23]

2-1. Korea's Response

It is not true because Japan illegally occupied Dokdo during the Russo-Japanese War of 1904-1905. The truth is as follows: in January of 1905, during the Russo-Japanese War, Japan incorporated Dokdo under the rationale of the acquisition of sovereignty over *terra nullius*. However, such an excuse was modified as "a reaffirmation of Japan's intention to claim sovereignty over Dokdo" because Japan realized that its own rationale of "Dokdo has always been Japanese territory" and "occupation of terra nullius" conflicted with each other. Its claim, "occupation of *terra* nullius," contradicted Japan's previous argument that Dokdo had no relationship with Japan, which is also shown in the State Council (Dajokan) Directive of 1877 (Material 4).

Japan did not "reaffirm its intention of claim Dokdo in 1905," and it certainly was not "broadly publicized" at all. The Japanese Government clandestinely annexed Dokdo Island in a sub rosa cabinet meeting. This was without external notification beyond a minuscule ad on a second page of a local newspaper that didn't even mention the island's name.

Furthermore, the Korean government contested Japan's annexation of Dokdo at different governmental levels and through local media immediately upon being informed in 1906. However, by this time, the Japanese had assumed control over Korea's foreign affairs office.

The Russo-Japanese War began in 1904 when the Japanese Navy launched a surprise attack against the Russian Pacific Fleet at Port Arthur and at Jemulpo. The Japanese Navy built watch towers at Jeju Island, Geomun Island, and Ulsan in order to monitor the movement of the Russian fleet. In August of 1904, two watch towers were also installed in Ulleungdo, actions which stressed the strategic value of Dokdo.

Nakai Yozaburo[24] was aware that Dokdo belonged to Joseon. He intended to submit a request for the lease of the island to the Joseon government through the Japanese government. However, Nakai submitted a petition to incorporate Dokdo, instead of a lease request, to the Japanese government in September of 1904, having been influenced by officials of the Japanese Ministry of Foreign Affairs and the Japanese Navy Department.

The Japanese Ministry of Home Affairs attempted to reject his petition based upon the opinion that "the gains would be extremely small while the situation would become grave if the acquisition of a barren islet (Dokdo) suspected of being Korean territory [...] would amplify the suspicions of various foreign countries that Japan had an ambition to annex Korea." However, the Japanese Ministry of Foreign Affairs proceeded to incorporate the island with the rationale that hostile warships would be better monitored if watch towers were constructed, and wireless or submarine cables were installed there.

Japan's incorporation of Dokdo in 1905 is void by international law. Japan argues that it incorporated the island based on the rationale of "occupation of terra nullius." However, Korea had established its sovereignty over Dokdo in ancient times, and reaffirmed this under the modern law by issuing Imperial Ordinance No. 41 (See Material 5, 5-1) on October 25, 1900.

Japan discussed and notified it incorporation of Dokdo to Western countries, including the United States. However, Korea did not receive any query or notification regarding the unilateral incorporation. In March of 1906 the Governor of Uldo (Ulleungdo) learned of the incorporation from Japanese officials of Shimane Prefecture visiting Ulleungdo. The next day, the Governor of Uldo reported this to the central government in Seoul and to the governor of Gangwon Province. On receiving this report, the Minister of Interior and the State Council Minister stated that it was groundless for Japan to claim sovereignty over Dokdo, and ordered an investigation of the facts relating to what Japan had done. (See Material 6) The Korean government, having been deprived of its diplomatic rights following the protectorate treaty in November 1905, was not able to take any diplomatic action against such a situation. However, Korean newspapers, including the Daehan Daily Newspaper (Daehan maeil sinbo) (May 1, 1906) (See Material 7,7-1) and The Hwangseong Newspaper (Hwangseong sinmun) (May 9, 1906), published articles protesting against the Japanese act.

Material 4.	
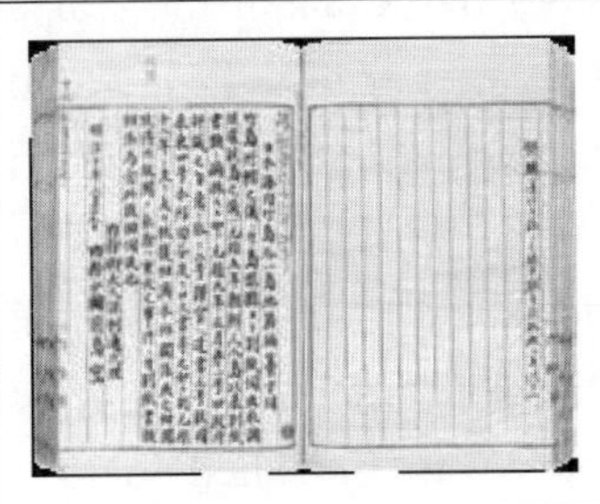 	This is an order given by the Dajōkan, the highest administrative body of Japan at the time, to the Japanese Ministry of Home Affairs, confirming that Ulleungdo and Dokdo were islands outside of Japan's territory. As a result of consultations with the government of Joseon (regarding the Ulleungdo Dispute), the Dajōkan concluded that Ulleungdo and Dokdo did not belong to Japan, and ordered the Japanese Ministry of Home Affairs as follows: "Regarding Takeshima [Ulleungdo] and one other island [Dokdo] about which an inquiry was submitted, bear in mind that our country [Japan] has nothing to do with them."

Material 5.	
	Korea renamed Ulleungdo as Uldo, and raised the highest administrative position in Ulleungdo to County Magistrate of Uldo. The County Magistrate gained authority over the whole of Ulleungdo, Jukdo, and Seokdo. Korean Imperial Ordinance No. 41 was issued in Korean Gazette No. 1716 on October 27, 1900.

Material 5-1.	
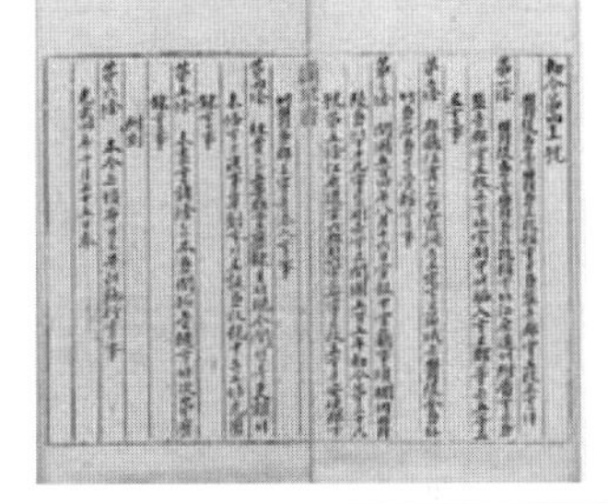	The Gazette Containing Imperial Ordinance No. 41

Material 6.	
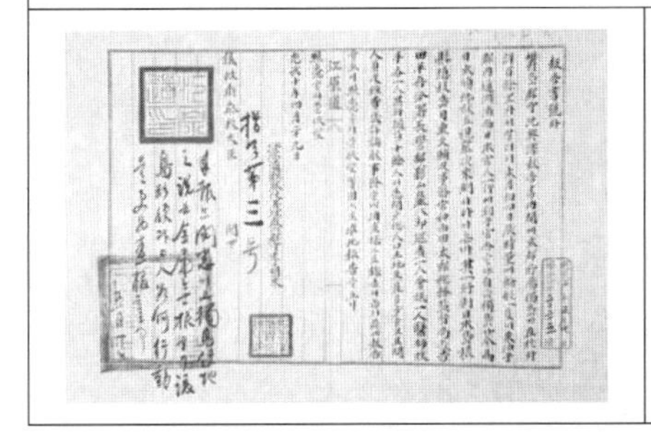	The Report of Yi Myeong-nae, Chuncheon County Magistrate and acting Governor of Gangwon Province (April 29, 1906), and Order No. 3 of Bak Je-sun, the State Council Minister (May 20, 1906)

In 1906, the Chuncheon County Magistrate and acting Governor of Gangwon Province Yi Myeong-nae informed State Council Minister Bak Je-sun of Japan's incorporation of Dokdo, which belonged to Korea, immediately after the actions of the Japanese were reported by the Uldo (Ulleungdo) Governor Sim Heung-taek (Material 6). In response to this, Bak stated that Japan's claims to Dokdo were unfounded and through Order No. 3 commanded that a close eye be kept on the situation on Dokdo and the movements of the Japanese there.

Material 7.	
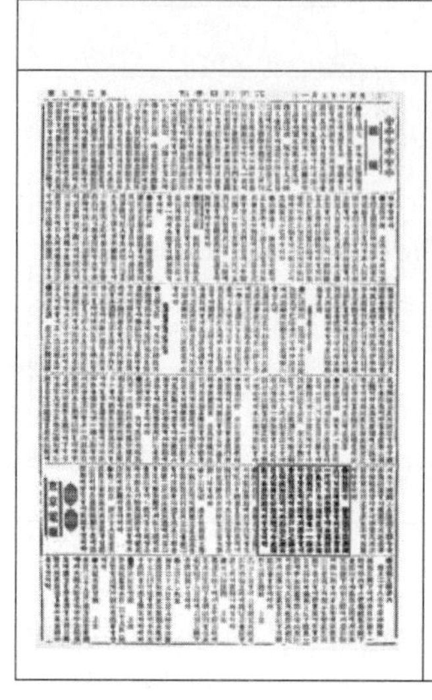	Daehan Daily Newspaper (Daehan maeil sinbo)

Material 7-1.	
	The Uldo governor Sim Heung-taek reported that some Japanese officials had come to Ulleungdo and claimed Dokdo as Japanese territory, surveyed the island, and then counted the number of households. In response to the report from Sim Hueng-taek, the Korean government stated, 'Their claiming Dokdo as Japanese territory does not make sense at all. We find the Japanese claim shocking.'

3. Japan's Claims: that while drafting the San Francisco Peace Treaty the United States suggested that Dokdo was under the jurisdiction of Japan.

While drafting the San Francisco Peace Treaty, the United States rejected the Republic of Korea's request to include Dokdo as one of the areas Japan must renounce by sending a diplomatic letter called the "Rusk Note." Consequently, Dokdo was not included as an area that Japan should relinquish under the San Francisco Peace Treaty, which was signed in September, 1951.[25]

3-1. Korea's Response

It is not true because the San Francisco Peace Treaty succeeded the Cairo Declaration and the Potsdam Declaration. The truth is as follows: the General Headquarters of the Allied Powers had treated Dokdo as being separate from Japan until the San Francisco Peace Treaty took effect after World War II. The General Headquarters applied SCAPIN - 677 (January 29, 1946), which provides that Dokdo, along with Ulleungdo, belongs to the area that is excluded from Japan's governmental or administrative authority (See Material 8, 8-1).

※ SCAPIN - 677: Governmental and Administrative Separation of Certain Outlying Areas from Japan

"3. For the purpose of this directive, Japan is defined to include the four main islands of Japan (Hokkaido, Honshu, Kyushu, and Shikoku) and the approximately 1,000 smaller adjacent islands, … excluding (a) Utsuryo (Ulleung) Island, Liancourt Rocks [that is, Dokdo] …."

The Allied Powers' decision to exclude Dokdo from Japan's territory was part of postwar measures to implement the results from the Cairo Declaration (1943) and the Potsdam Declaration (1945), which obligated Japan to renounce territories it had taken by "violence and greed."

Thus, Dokdo was rightly included as an area Japan should relinquish because it was Korea's territory, which Japan usurped through violence and greed during the Russo-Japanese War.

These measures taken by the Allied Powers were succeeded in the San Francisco Peace Treaty signed in September of 1951. Even though Dokdo was not explicitly mentioned in the treaty, it is only natural to see Dokdo as having been included in the Korean territory that Japan should relinquish. Even islands larger than Dokdo were not all referred to in the treaty, because it was impossible to mention all of the islands belong to the Republic of Korea. Also the “Rusk Note,” upon which Japan bases its claim for sovereignty over Dokdo, has no legal effect in determining the holder of sovereignty over the island, as this note only reflected the opinion of the United States, not the opinion of the Allied Powers as a whole.

Dokdo was reclaimed as an island annexed to the Korean Peninsula as the Allied Powers won the war in August, 1945 and the Government of the Republic of Korea was established on August 15, 1948, in accordance with a United Nations resolution. The San Francisco Peace Treaty merely confirmed these facts.

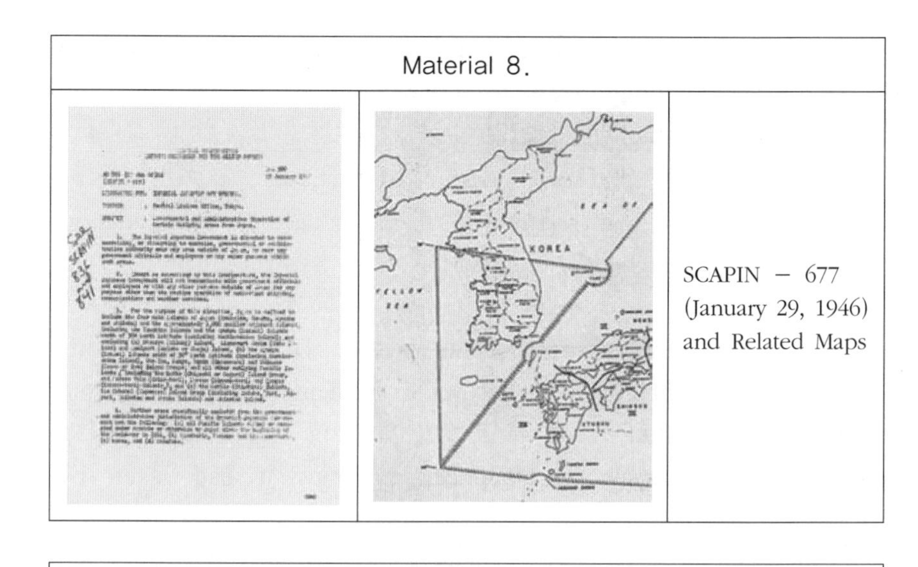

Material 8.		
		SCAPIN – 677 (January 29, 1946) and Related Maps

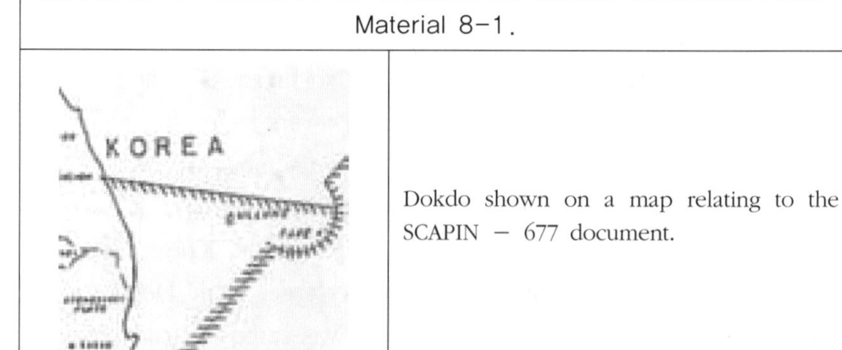

Material 8-1.	
	Dokdo shown on a map relating to the SCAPIN – 677 document.

4. Japan's Claims: that the Republic of Korea is illegally occupying Dokdo without any basis in international law.[26] Thus no measure taken by the Republic of Korea during the illegal occupation with regard to Dokdo has any legal justification.[27] Japan strongly protests against and request withdrawal of the measures taken by the Republic of Korea.[28]

4-1. Korea's Response

It is not true because the Republic of Korea is exercising its legitimate sovereignty over Dokdo. The Truth is as follows: Japan annexed Dokdo through the Shimane Prefectural Notice in 1905, and the Japanese Government-General of Korea began to illegally rule Korea from 1910. However, as the Allied Powers won World War II, Korea regained its territorial sovereignty over Dokdo. Immediately after its establishment in August of 1948, the Republic of Korea gave Dokdo an address (1, Dodong, Nam-myeon, Ulleung-gun, North Gyeongsang Province), and began exercising its sovereignty over the island, and neither the Allied Powers nor Japan raised any objection to this.

Now the island has its own residents (See Material 9). South Korean police officers and public officials are protecting the island and operating various installations such as a lighthouse and a radiation detector all year round (See Material 9-1). Currently, ferries based in Ulleungdo sail between Ulleungdo and Dokdo. Every year 100,000 tourists from home and abroad visit Dokdo.

The Republic of Korea government designated the island as "Natural Monument No. 336: Dokdo Breeding Ground for Seabirds" in 1982 and as an "Environmentally Protected Area" in 1999. As elaborated so far, the Republic of Korea government exercises firm territorial sovereignty over Dokdo based upon legal grounds.

<table>
<tr><td colspan="2">Material 9.</td></tr>
<tr><td></td><td>Resident housing on Dokdo</td></tr>
<tr><td colspan="2">Material 9-1.</td></tr>
<tr><td></td><td>Lighthouse(1954) and radiation detector installed on Dokdo.</td></tr>
</table>

6. THE TRUTH OF THE DOKDO UNDER INTERNATIONAL LAW

The so-called "Dokdo" Islets or "Takeshima" issue is a historical one caused by Japan's past invasion of the Korean peninsula, and not a territorial controversy between the Republic of Korea and Japan. Japan's history of aggression originates the Dokdo issue. With Japan's defeat in its war of aggression in 1945, Korea was liberated from colonial rule.

In January 1699, Korean territorial sovereignty over Ullung Island and Dokdo Islets was perfected with the Japanese diplomatic Note Verbale (the affirmative response to the Korean stance to

Ullung island and Dokdo Islets) of the Japanese Tsushima Chief, Taira Yoshi Makodo (宗義眞), representing the Shogun government of Japan. Korea's territorial sovereignty was accepted by the Shogun government in light of general international law following several years of diplomatic negotiations. Since then, the subsequent Japanese governments have respected Korean territorial sovereignty over Dokdo Islets for more than 300 years before the Japanese government of 1905 illegally annexed the Dokdo Islets to Japan during the Russo-Japanese War (1904-1905), breaching the principle of Estoppel according to general international law. Japan has never had a legitimate territorial sovereignty over the Dokdo Islets but only through occupation by "violence" and "greed" as stated in the Cairo Declaration (December 1, 1943).

After WWII, the Directive of SCAPIN 677 (Supreme Commander for the Allied Powers Index Number) dated January 29, 1946 explicitly excluded the 'Dokdo Islets' (Liancourt Rocks or Take island) together with 'Korea' from Japanese sovereignty in accordance with the Potsdam Declaration(8). The Japanese government at the time complied with the Directive of SCAPIN 677 (January 29, 1946) which explicitly stated the exclusion of Dokdo Islets from Japan's sovereignty. This led to the issuance of the Japanese Prime Ministerial Ordinance No. 24 (June 6, 1951) which stated that the Dokdo Islets were non-Japanese islands. In addition to the exclusion of Dokdo islets, 'Korea' was also excluded from Japanese sovereignty based on the Directive of SCAPIN 677 and the Korean people established the Republic of Korea on the land ('Korea') excluded from Japanese sovereignty on August 15, 1948, which was about three years prior to the conclusion of the Peace Treaty on September 8, 1951 in accordance with the provisions of the Potsdam Declaration(8) with the Dokdo Islets as being a part of Korea.[29]

The Dokdo Islets (Takeshima) fell in the purview of "all other territories which she (Japan) has taken by violence and greed" as stated in the Cairo Declaration (December 1, 1943). Anyone who might claim that the 'exclusion of Dokdo Islets' by the Directive of SCAPIN 677 (January 29, 1946) was a temporary one who could not reasonably interpolate how the Republic of Korea was established on the Korean peninsula on August 15, 1948, more than three years prior to the conclusion of the Peace Treaty in San Francisco. The Article 2(a) of the Peace Treaty forced Japan to renounce 'Ullung Island,' the main island of the Dokdo Islets which can be seen with unaided eyes from Ullung Island, but not from the Okishima island in Japan. The Dokdo Islets as the subordinate Islets to Ullung Island were renounced by Japan when Ullung Island itself was renounced. As Judge Max Huber indicated in his award of the Palmas island Case in 1928, "the fate of the main island involve the rest" (the subordinate Islets).[30]

The Japanese government requested the ratification of the Peace Treaty of San Francisco on October 6, 1951 to the Japanese Diet, attaching the "Reference Map for the Japanese Territorial Boundary" (日本領域參考圖). On this "Reference Map," Liancourt Rocks (Dokdo Islets or Takeshima) were drawn outside of the Japanese Territorial Boundary Line but within the Korean boundary belonging to Ullung, the main island. "The attached Map, ... may be said to assume the character of primary or original evidence"[31] The Peace Treaty was duly ratified by the Japanese Diet (Lower and Upper) on October 26, 1951 and November 18 of the same year, respectively. The Japanese Diet's ratification of the Peace Treaty indicated the fact that Japan officially recognized the Korean territorial sovereignty over Dokdo Islets in compliance with the special international law (Article 2(a), Peace Treaty).

Furthermore, because korea was not a party to the San Francisco Peace Treaty, it could not be bound to a provision, which is contrary to Korea's interest in restoring its full sovereignty over all its territory taken by Japan according to Article 34[32] and 35[33] of

Vienna Convention of the Law of Treaties (23.5.1969). Therefore it is worth reviewing Article 2 of the San Francisco Peace Treaty and international legal principle on the sovereignty of Dokdo from the perspective of a non-party to the treaty.

In summary, the main arguments for Korea include the continuity of Korea's historical title[34] to Dokdo up until 1905 and the illegal taking of Dokdo by Japan in 1905 and its return to Korea after the end of World War II.[35]

7. EXIT STRATEGY FOR HISTORY EDUCATION IN EAST ASIA

Most of the Japanese history textbooks used by middle and high school students approved by Tokyo since 2012 include a considerable number of distorted descriptions of how things happened, with even some notable omissions. For instance, these books state that the Dokdo islets are "Japan's sovereign territory," and add that "Korea is occupying them illegally." They also omit the forceful mobilization of Korean girls and women as sex slaves before and during World War II.

What should be done for History Education in East Asia?

The first letter concerning the kidnapped Korean fishermen ('Ahn Yong Bok') from Tsushima's chief (of the diplomatic agency of the Japanese Shogun government), Taila Yoshitsuku'(宗義倫), dated in September 1693 arrived at the Korean local government office in Busan along with the two repatriated Korean fishermen in November 1693. In the letter there was the phrase "Japanese territory Takeshima" which referred to the 'Ullung Island' in Korea. This phrase in the letter was never accepted by the Korean government. It ignited prolonged diplomatic negotiations on the territorial controversy over 'Ullung Island and its subordinate Dokdo Islets (Liancourt Rocks, Take island)' in the 17th century. The Korean government's response to the Japanese letter was sent in February 1694. Numerous exchanges of diplomatic messages on the issue were made until the Korean government's justification for its territorial sovereignty over both the Islands 'Ullung and its subordinate Dokdo Islets' with 'Dongguk Yoji Senglam' which included an evidentiary map was presented to Japan (Korean Government Published Geography and its map titled as "Paldo Chongdo" (八道總圖), General Map of 8 Provinces of Korea, published by Government in 1531) in March 1698. On this map, the two islands were drawn as belonging to the Gangwon Province of Korea. In January 1699, the Korean government received Japan's response to the justification message, admitting Korea's territorial sovereignty over the 'Ullung Island and its subordinate Dokdo Islets' (Liancourt Rocks, Take island). This closed the territorial controversy. With this letter from Japan, the Korean territorial sovereignty over both the 'Ullung Island and Dokdo Islets was perfected in accordance with general international law in the year 1699.

Since 1699, subsequent Japanese governments had respected Korean territorial sovereignty over the 'Ullung Island and its subordinate Dokdo Islets' (Takeshima) for more than 300 years until the Japanese government of 1905 made a clandestine decision to illegally annex Korean Dokdo Islets to Japanese territory, breaching the principle of estoppel in general international law during the Russo-Japanese War (1904-1905). The invasion of Dokdo by Japan happened during the Russio-Japanese War. Japan thus came to illegally occupy Korean Dokdo Islets (Liancourt Rocks) with "violence and greed" without legitimate territorial sovereignty in 1905 until the time she surrendered in WWII to the Allied Powers in 1945. Therefore, it must be noted that even though Japan occupied Dokdo Islets for a certain period of time by military force, she has never had any legitimate territorial sovereignty over the Dokdo Islets based on general international law from 1905 to the end of WW II in 1945. Therefore, the so-called 'Dokdo Issue' of today is not a territorial issue, but a historical one.[36]

For example, the Korean clause in Cairo Declaration (December 1, 1943) reads as follows:

> "...Japan will also be expelled from all other territories which she has taken by violence and greed. The aforesaid Three Great Powers, mindful of the enslavement of the people of Korea, are determined that in due course Korea shall become free and independent."

It is impossible for the Japanese government to lay any claim to the Korean Dokdo Islets without violating the provisions of Article 2(a) and Article 19(d)[37] of the Peace Treaty, Potsdam Declaration(8) and SCAPIN 677 (January 29, 1946), as well as the UNGA Res. 2625 (October 24, 1970) which provided that "the territory of a State shall not be the object of acquisition by another State resulting from threat or use of force," in light of the provision of Article 2, Chapter of the United Nations. Furthermore, "Dokdo Islets are the very symbol of the independence of the Republic of Korea. Without anticipating furious resistance and revenge to come from all the Korean race, can any foreign State dare to extend her greedy hand out again to take the Islets away from the Korean bosom?"[38] The Japanese government is required to respect the Korean territorial sovereignty over Dokdo Islets to promote peaceful coexistence and prosperity for both the peoples of the Republic of Korea and Japan, and to a grater extent for peace in East Asia.

Therefore, the Dokdo is the first Korean territorial victim of Japanese aggression and a symbol of its sovereignty. There is no dispute to carry to the ICJ because the islets, a part of Ulleung County in North Gyeongsang Province, are inherently Korean territory. Japan's history of aggression is the origin of the Dokdo issue. Japan's continued attempts to claim Dokdo are tantamount to denying Japan's imperialist history and invasion of the Korean Peninsula.

Teaching a distorted view of Dokdo's history to school pupils who are yet immature in historical perception and making judgments can lead to a repeated history of aggression, which could jeopardize peace in East Asia. Japan must withdraw its policy of writing distorted history textbooks from the legacy of imperialist colonialism and war. The best prospect of accomplishing it shall be through the renewal and reinforcement of the civic initiatives associated the 100th anniversary statements[39] and the systematic balanced thinking history education in East Asia.[40]

> The Korean Government's Basic Position on Dokdo is as follows:
> • Dokdo is an integral part of Korean territory, historically, geographically and under international law.
> • No territorial dispute exists regarding Dokdo, and therefore Dokdo is not a matter to be dealt with through diplomatic negotiations or judicial settlement.
> • The government of the Republic of Korea exercises Korea's irrefutable territorial sovereignty over Dokdo.
> • The government will deal firmly and resolutely with any provocation and will continue to defend Korea's territorial integrity over Dokdo.[41]

In conclusion, in order to solve distortion of history in history textbooks including all unresolved issues in East Asia during Japan's illegal colonial rule, Korea need to overcome the unreasonable 1965 Regime and limitations of the San Francisco Peace Treaty.[42]

Notes

1. Song Byeong-ki (translation), Historical Verification of Korea's Sovereignty over Ulleungdo and Dokdo, National Assembly Library (2010), pp. 22-24.
2. For detailed process of distorted textbooks in Japan, Seong Keun, Hong, "Research on the Actual Conditions and Policy Making regarding Territorial Claims over Dokdo in Japanese Textbooks," interdisciplinary Studies on the Sovereignty over Dokdo, Korea: Northeast Asian Foundation (2009), pp. 95-143.
3. Why Dokdo is Korean Territory?, http://dokdo.mofa.go.kr/eng/dokdo/reason.jsp.
4. Jon M. Van Dyke, "Addressing and Resolving the Dokdo Matter," Dokdo, Historical Appraisal and International Justice, Martinus Nijhoff Publishers, pp. 29-30.
5. http://dokdo.mofa.go.kr/eng/include/print.jsp.
6. Alan J. Day (ed.), Border and Territorial Disputes, 2nd edition, Longman, 1987, p. 338.
7. March 19, 2016, The Korea Herald.
8. "Takeshima, Senkakus cited in all new social studies textbooks," The Japanese Times, April 6, 2015.
9. "Seoul issues protest against Tokyo's textbook authorization," March 18, 2016, The Korea Times.
10. Dokdo multiple Question: Which country occupied the Takeshima illegally among following countries?: Russia, North Korea, south Korea, China (See Material 1).
11. "Korea condemns Japan for claiming sovereignty over Dokdo in textbook guidelines," March 30, 2018, The Korea Times.
12. *Ibid.*
13. "S. Korea strongly denounces Japan's claim to Education guidelines," March 11, 2017, The Korea Times.
14. *See supra* note 10.
15. Hong-Ju Nah, Article 2(a), Peace treaty with Japan (September 8, 1951), San Francisco, and Dokdo Islets (Liancourt Rocks, Take Island), Korean Branch of ILA, Korean Yearbook of International Law, Vol. 2 (2014), pp. 97-98.
16. Jiriji of Goryeosa.
17. Sinjeung Dongguk Yeoji Seungnam.
18. *See supra* note 1, p. 23-24.
19. The Japanese Ministry of Foreign Affairs, Definitive clarifications as to why Takeshima is Japan's territory! 10 points to understand the Takeshima Dispute, Q & A, Point 2.
20. NORTHEAST ASIAN HISTORY FOUNDATION, TEN TRUTHS ABOUT DOKDO Not Known in Japan, http://www.nahf.or.kr/data/board_100/dokdo_Truth/English.pdf.
21. *Ibid.*

22. *Ibid.*
23. The Japanese Ministry of Foreign Affairs, Definitive clarifications as to why Takeshima is japan's territory! 10 points to understand the Takeshima Dispute, Q & A, Point 6.
24. Japan claimed this families exercised title to the islets in the 17th century (when they were known in Japan as Matsushima) and that subsequently they were consistently regarded as part of Japanese territory, Alan J. Day (ed.), Border and Territorial Disputes, (2nd. Edition, Longman, 1987), pp. 337-338.
25. The Japanese Ministry of Foreign Affairs, Definitive clarifications as to why Takeshima is japan's territory! 10 points to understand the Takeshima Dispute, Q & A, Point 7.
26. The Ministry of Foreign Affairs of Japan, Takeshima Seeking Solution based on Law, http://www.mofa.go.jp/
27. https://www.mofa.go.jp/region/asia-paci/takeshima/index.html
28. The Japanese Ministry of Foreign Affairs, Definitive clarifications as to why Takeshima is japan's territory! 10 points to understand the Takeshima Dispute, Q & A, Point 9.
29. *See supra* note 14, pp. 121-122.
30. Max Huber, Arbitral Award Respecting Sovereignty Over the Island of Palmas (or Miangas), April 4, 1928, (the American Journal of International Law) p. 894.
31. Durward v. Sandifer, Evidence Before the Tribunals, (Charottesville : University of Virginia Press, 1975), pp. 229-30.
32. Vienna Convention of the Law of Treaties (May 23, 1969), Article 34 (General rule regarding third States): "A treaty does not create either obligations or rights for a third State without its consent."
33. Vienna Convention of the Law of Treaties (May 23, 1969), Article 35 (Treaties providing for obligations for third States): "An obligation arises for a third State from a provision of treaty if the parties to the treaty intend the provision to be the means of establishing the obligations and the third State expressly accepts that obligation in writing."
34. Xuechan Ma, "Historic Title over Land Maritime Territory," Journal of Territorial and Maritime Studies, Vol. 4, No. 1, Winter/Spring 2017, pp. 32-35.
35. Jang-Hie Lee, "Dokdo Island Dispute and International Law," Koresn Art & Culture Vol. 19, No. 3, Koreans, June 22, 2005.
36. *See supra* note 1, pp. 95-96.
37. Article 19(d), Peace Treaty: "Japan recognizes the validity of all acts and omissions done during the period of occupation under or in consequence of directives of the Occupation Authorities or authorized by the Japanese law at that time, and will take no action subjecting Allied nationals the civil or criminal liability arising out of such acts of omissions."
38. Excerpt from the Statement on October 28, 1954 made by Korean Ex-Foreign Minister Byun, Young Tae, refuting Japanese governmen's proposal to refer Dokdo issue to ICJ.

39. Joint Statement by Japanese and Korean Intellectuals on the 100th Anniversary of the Annexation of Korea (May/August 2010). English Text. Gavan McCormack, "Overcoming the 1965 Japan-Republic of Korea Normalization System and Peace in East Asia," 2014 Tokyo International Conference of NGOs on History and Peace (June 20-22, 2014), Proceedings, pp. 165-170.
40. Seong Keun, Hong, "Necessity of Systematic Education about Dokdo," Kyung hyangshinmun. March 21, 2016.
41. http://dokdo.mofa.go.kr/eng/include/print.jsp.
42. Jang-Hie Lee, "Limitations of the San Francisco Peace Treaty and Peace in East Asiafrom the Perspective of Colonial State Responsibility," International Conference, Beyond the San Francisco System: Seeking a Peace Regime in East Asia, Proceedings of Papers (Organizers: The Center for Korean Research. North East East Peace Center/ October 28, 2016, Colombia University).

KYIL

The Interpretation of Human Rights Treaties in the Korean Courts with Reference to the Issue of Conscientious Objection to Military Service*

LEE Whie-Jin
Visiting Professor, Dongguk University, Seoul, Korea

Key Words

Human Rights Treaties, Conscientious Objection to Military Service, International Covenant on Civil and Political Rights (ICCPR), Self-Executing, *Jus Cogens*

1. THE ISSUE OF CONSCIENTIOUS OBJECTION TO MILITARY SERVICE

1-1. The Rulings of Korean Courts

Articles 19 and 20(1) of the Constitution of Korea respectively provide for freedom of conscience and freedom of religion. Whether refusing the obligation of military service on account of religious belief is in the realm of freedom of religion and conscience is at issue.

A host of cases on which decisions have been taken by the courts invoking human rights treaties are concerned with conscientious

* The article in part derives from the author's doctoral thesis.

objection to military service. The Constitutional Court and the Supreme Court, denying the direct effect of human rights treaties, have ruled that punishing conscientious objectors to military service would not contravene the right to freedom of conscience in the Constitution.

In a decision of 2011,[1] the Constitutional Court by a majority of 7:2 held that taking into account Korea's real circumstances such as "its specific security situation where South and North Korea have been confronted against each other, the possible reduction of military manpower in case of the introduction of alternative service, and the difficulty of examining whether military objector is attributable to genuine conscience, the introduction of alternative service would impede social unity and cause serious damage to national capabilities, if public opinion is critical of conscientious objection." It looks difficult to realize conscientious objection to military service, while not infringing the principle of minimum encroachment legally. Whether it violates the International Covenant on Civil and Political Rights (ICCPR) and the principle of respect for international law, the Constitutional Court stated:[2] "In respect of the ICCPR, it is difficult to recognize the right of conscientious objection in the covenant itself or for the covenant to have legally binding force concerning conscientious objection. There are no human rights treaties recognizing the right of conscientious objection explicitly. Even though some European states guarantee the right of conscientious objection, it is not considered that customary international law on the guarantee of the right of conscientious objection throughout the world is formed. Therefore, the right of conscientious objection cannot be accepted in Korea as the generally recognized international norm, and accordingly the punishment of conscientious objectors pursuant to the applicable provision of the law would not violate Article 6(1) of the Constitution which proclaims the principle of respect for international law."

The minority opinion of the Constitutional Court decision,

without judging explicitly upon Article 6(1) or the principle of respect for international law, articulated the recommendation of the Human Rights Committee (hereinafter "the Committee") made to every state of the world on numerous occasions to recognize the right of conscientious objection and enforce alternative service of no disciplinary nature, while citing examples of foreign states enforcing conscientious objection.

The Constitutional Court on June 28, 2018 changed its position and found that Article 5(1) of the Military Service Act which does not allow alternative service to conscientious military service objectors would not conform to the Constitution.[3] The Court has refrained from making decisions on the possible breach of human rights treaties, even after referring to relevant provisions of the ICCPR, and resolutions, recommendations and decisions of international organizations, for reasons that it has judged that non-inclusion of alternative service in the Military Service Act has violated the Constitution. Two Justices, Mr. Ahn Changho and Mr. Cho Yongho, in their dissenting opinion, expressed that treaties and generally recognized customary international law would take effect in Korea in accordance with Article 6(1) of the Constitution. Nevertheless, their findings were that since Article 18 and other provisions of the ICCPR have not explicitly recognized the right of conscientious objection as a fundamental human right, and the opinions of the Committee and the UN Commission on Human Rights have no binding force etc., the right of conscientious objection could not be recognized under the ICCPR. So was the case with the customary international law in their dissenting opinion.

In the decision of 2007,[4] the Supreme Court dismissed the lawsuit, for reasons that the right to exemption from the obligation of military service cannot be derived from the provisions of the ICCPR itself, since Article 18 of the ICCPR provides for the same content as the scope of protection of basic human rights guaranteed in the interpretation of the Constitution in Article 19 on the freedom of conscience and Article 20 on the freedom of religion. With regard to the application of the ICCPR, the Supreme Court held that "not only Article 18 of the ICCPR, but any other provisions of the covenant have not stated the right of conscientious objection to military service as one of basic human rights, and in fact though there was argument to include conscientious objection in Article 18 of the ICCPR in the process of drafting, general opinions of negotiating states seemed to be negative. ... Article 8(3)(c)(ii) of the Covenant on the Prohibition of Forced Labor provides for 'any service of a military character and, in countries where conscientious objection is recognized, any national service required by law of conscientious objectors' as one of those which are excluded from the scope of forced labor prohibited in the covenant."

Following the above decision of the Constitutional Court in 2018, which ordered the amendment to the Military Service Act to allow alternative military service to the conscientious objectors, the Supreme Court decided[5] on November 1, 2018 that conscientious military service objectors shall not be punished criminally, considering that the conscientious objection to military service is applicable to justifiable reason for refusal of military service in the Military Service Act.

1-2. The Opinion of International Organizations

In the interpretation of the ICCPR on conscientious objection, the ICCPR Committee and the European Court of Human Rights turn toward positive position from the negative one they have taken before. In considering an individual communication, the ICCPR Committee reached a conclusion that Article 18 of the ICCPR does not guarantee conscientious objection in consideration of Article 8(3)(c)(ii) of the covenant.[6] The European Commission of Human Rights, in numerous decisions, held that Article 9 of the European Convention on Human

Rights (ECHR), merely protecting the freedom of thought, conscience, and religion in the general sense, is not interpreted to confer the right to demand exemption from the obligation of military service upon conscientious objectors.[7]

The main reason for not recognizing conscientious objection is that Article 8(3)(ii) of the ICCPR and Article 4(3)(b) of the ECHR provide that "in countries where conscientious objection is recognized, any national service required by law of conscientious objectors" is excluded from the scope of forced labor prohibited in the covenant. The phrase 'where conscientious objection is recognized' in the relevant provision presupposes that the state party can determine for itself whether conscientious objection could be recognized or not.

From the above opinion, the position has changed in the 1990s, shifting toward recognizing the conscientious objection. The Committee, in its general comment no. 22 in 1993,[8] adopted the position that "the Covenant does not explicitly refer to a right to conscientious objection, but the Committee believes that such a right can be derived from Article 18, inasmuch as the obligation to use lethal force may seriously conflict with the freedom of conscience and the right to manifest one's religion or belief." Such position of the Committee opened the possibility of recognizing conscientious objection, but not definitively recognizing the right to conscientious objection.

Following this decision, the Committee has intensified its position and point of argument. In an individual communication case adopted on November 3, 2006,[9] the Committee held that "Article 8 of the Covenant itself neither recognizes nor excludes a right of conscientious objection. Thus, the present claim is to be assessed solely in the light of Article 18 of the Covenant, the understanding of which evolves like that of any other guarantee of the Covenant over time in view of its text and purpose," judging that the Korean government's measure is unjustifiable. Thereafter, the Committee made public its views of accepting five individual communications[10] concerning conscientious objection. In its decision of 2011, the Committee held that "military service inheres in the right to freedom of thought, conscience and religion. It entitles any individual to an exemption from compulsory military service if this cannot be reconciled with that individual's religion or beliefs. The right must not be impaired by coercion,"[11] strengthening its point of argument. In the decision of 2014, the Committee referred to the violations of the prohibition of arbitrary detention in Article 9(1) of the ICCPR, in addition to the freedom of conscience and religion in Article 18(1) of the covenant.

Thus, internationally the decisions of the Committee and sentence of the European Court of Human Rights that recognized the right of conscientious objection have further evolved into provisions of the Charter of Fundamental Rights of the European Union[12] which explicitly recognizes the right of conscientious objection.

2. THE LEGAL STATUS OF HUMAN RIGHTS TREATIES IN KOREA

2-1. Overview

It is a general majority opinion that like other treaties the human rights treaties have identical effect to municipal law under Article 6(1) of the Constitution. Most scholars assert that the treaties which require the consent of the National Assembly[13] are treated as identical to municipal law in the legal status, and those treaties outside the range of National Assembly's consent are equivalent to the presidential decree.[14] Some opinion says that *jus cogens* in general international law has the effect superior to the law.[15] *Jus cogens*, as accepted and approved by the international community as international norm, is non-derogable and can be modified only by the later-in-time international norm of identical nature.[16] To take some examples, the prohibition of act of aggression, elimination of slavery, genocide, piracy, and prohibition of torture are mentioned. Municipal laws in breach of these principles are null and void.

As in the general majority view, in case of conflict between treaty and law, the issue will be dealt with in the same manner as in case of conflict among laws. The issue will be settled by means of *lex specialis* principle or *lex posterior* principle. The status of special law is not to be decided in a uniform manner, and depending upon the circumstance a treaty may be accorded the special law status, thus prevailing against municipal law.[17] It coincides with the reality of rising importance of human rights.

In light of the universality and customary nature of human rights as fundamental rights entrenched in the Constitution, the argument is very persuasively put forth that human rights should be accorded effect superior to law at minimum. It is argued that as the contents of the Universal Declaration of Human Rights (UDHR) have been embodied in the human rights covenants and these human rights have been applicable as customary international law, the human rights should be observed domestically. In particular, it is claimed that the international bill of human rights like the UDHR, the ICCPR and the International Covenant on Economic, Social and Cultural Rights (ICESCR) should be accorded constitutional law status.[18]

According to the theory that human rights treaties have constitutional value, human rights treaties can become a judicial norm for adjudication on constitutionality of law and constitutionality appeal can be raised about the act that infringes the value of international human rights law.[19] On the other hand, another opinion argues that despite recognizing the constitutional value of international human rights law they are not accorded judicial norm status, only to be used as complementary reference for interpretation of the Constitution.

Another theory is that human rights treaties, though subordinate to the Constitution, have normative value superior to law. It asserts that human rights treaties, being made in the form of multilateral treaty for the protection of universal human rights of an individual, should be treated differently from other general treaties which usually take the form of exchange of mutual duties and rights among states.[20]

The persuasiveness of the above argument affording different legal status on the domestic plane depending upon the contents of human rights treaties stands to reason. In reality, though, it is hard to distinguish between treaties with the nature of the bill of human rights and other treaties. If the contents of human rights treaties happen to be identical to those of the Constitution, with the status of treaties being identical to the Constitution as a result, actually the provisions of treaties have domestic application for effect. In conclusion, in Korean legal system, human rights treaties, in the strict sense, have domestic effect identical to law.[21]

2-2. Government's Opinion

The Korean government's reports to the human rights treaty committee express its position on the treaty. The government's initial report on the ICCPR was submitted to the committee in 1992, in which it was remarked that the ICCPR has status superior to municipal law except the Constitution and if municipal law breaches the ICCPR, it is deemed unconstitutional.[22] The Korean government's position shows a slight different aspect in the report submitted to the Convention against Torture (CAT) committee in 1996. The report observed that even though the CAT has direct domestic effect without domestic legislative procedure, the principle of *lex specialis* or *lex posterior* applies, in case of conflict with municipal law.[23] It is unclear whether the report implies that the CAT has different legal nature than the ICCPR, or the CAT is referred to as a treaty in general having identical status to law.

The second government report that was submitted in 1996 expresses the status of the ICCPR superior to law. The report remarked:[24] "In the event that a law enacted prior to the Covenant's ratification conflicts with its provisions, the Covenant has greater authority. No law enacted in the Republic of Korea may encroach on the rights provided in the Covenant; any such law would be viewed as unconstitutional." The Korean government's view is that according the same highest normative effect as the Constitution upon the ICCPR, law in breach of the ICCPR would be deemed unconstitutional. It seems that the contents set out in the ICCPR are given the legal status identical to the Constitution's basic rights.

2-3. Courts' Judgment

In an appellate decision[25] in 1999 on a state compensation claim made by Sohn Jonggyu, the Supreme Court ruled that Article 2(3) of the ICCPR[26] which obliges the state party to undertake to ensure that any person whose rights or freedoms as herein recognized are violated shall have an effective remedy, is deemed as creating no special rights for an individual to claim remedial measures inclusive of compensation from the state party under the ICCPR, denying the direct application of the provision of the ICCPR. With this decision alone, it is not considered that judgment on the self-execution or otherwise of the ICCPR in whole was made. Article 2(2) of the ICCPR[27] which provides that a state party undertakes to take the necessary steps to adopt laws and other measures appears to exhibit its non-self-executing effect. The judgment on the non-self-executing effect of the ICCPR as shown in the court decision is distinct from the opinion expressed in the government report submitted to the ICCPR Committee. From a standpoint of separation of power among the state branches, the judiciary which is vested with final interpretive power on law and treaty prevails against the interpretation of government on the ICCPR.

Meanwhile, the highest courts in Korea consider trade treaties as having the status identical to law, recognizing their direct applicability. The Constitutional Court, in the case[28] concerning the adjudication on the constitutionality of Article 9(3) of the International Monetary Fund (IMF) Agreement etc., ruled that the IMF Agreement is considered as the object of adjudication on the constitutionality of law, seeing it as norm that could be directly applied to domestically in its nature. In a decision[29] imposing aggravated punishment in the World Trade Organization (WTO) Agreement, the Constitutional Court recognized its direct applicability. The Supreme Court took the same position in the decision[30] on the GATT and the WTO Agreement. Though different in nature, the Constitutional Court, in the Korea-Japan Fisheries Agreement case, dismissed the case, seeing the Agreement as having the same legal effect as law domestically and not violating the basic rights of petitioners.[31]

As seen above, Korea's highest courts, without putting forth or articulating the ground, have been reluctant to recognize domestic effect of human rights treaties, but active in recognizing the domestic effect of WTO and trade-related treaties.[32] Depending upon the character of treaties, it has been argued with stronger support that in the case concerning human rights or trade which are directly related to the rights and interests of an individual the individual has to be competent to bring actions against state on the basis of the provisions of treaties.[33]

3. CONCLUDING REMARK

Despite the domestic effect of treaties provided for in the Constitution, doubt is raised whether it is justified to make a distinction between self-executing and non-self-executing treaties.

Since Article 6(1) of the Korean Constitution explicitly provides that treaties concluded and promulgated by this Constitution and generally accepted international law have the same effect as municipal law, it has been argued that it is unjustifiable to raise the question whether treaties could be self-executing or not.[34] The reason is that the Constitution establishes an explicit provision for the effect of treaties identical to municipal law[35] and no special procedure or conditions have been required for treaties to have domestic effect.[36]

Relative to municipal law which is applied as judicial norm once legislated by the National Assembly and entered into force, the argument is that dealing with treaties differently from municipal law despite the provisions of the Constitution for the domestic effect of treaties would be illogical, unnecessary, and discriminatory treatment. In short, it is not worth distinguishing among treaties around the factor of self-execution.

Concerning the issue of conscientious objection to the military service, which has been filed the most frequently with the Committee by Korean complainants, the Supreme Court and Constitutional Court disregarded the recommendation and views of the Committee to recognize the right of conscientious objection. Positively, some minority opinion of the Court showed different perspectives, recognizing the self-executing effect of treaties under the Constitution. Even this opinion refused to recognize the right of conscientious objection in the ICCPR.

Under the circumstance, following the decision of the Constitutional Court in 2018, which has evaded the decision on the domestic effect of human rights treaties, conscientious objectors are not to be punished, being required to perform alternative service. In consequence, the issue of conscientious objection to military service has been settled without directly touching upon the provisions of the ICCPR.

Notes

1. Constitutional Court August 30, 2011, decision 2008Hunga22.
2. More concretely, as to the issue of the application of the ICCPR and formation of customary international law, the Constitutional Court held: "not only Article 18 of the ICCPR, but any other provisions of the covenant have not stated the right of conscientious objection to military service as one of basic human rights, and in fact though there was argument to include conscientious objection in Article 18 of the ICCPR in the process of drafting, general opinions of negotiating states were negative, and the interpretation of international organizations has only recommendatory effect in each state, with no legally binding force. The issue of recognizing conscientious objection of military service and introducing alternative service, as the field in which policy choice should be respected in light of disparate and diverse factors in respective states such as history and security environment, the structure of social strata, and political, cultural, religious, or philosophical value of a state ... ."
3. Constitutional Court June 28, 2018, decision 2011Hunba379 full bench. The Constitutional Court ruled: "Categories of military service, which have not included alternative service program for conscientious objectors, infringe on objectors' freedom of conscience by violating principle of excessive restriction."
4. Supreme Court December 27, 2007, decision 2007Do7941.
5. Supreme Court November 1, 2018, decision 2016Do10912 full bench.
6. L.T.K. v. Finland, Communication no. 185/1984, UN doc. CCPR/C25/D/185/1984, July 9, 1985. The complainant was initially not recognized as conscientious objector, and on appeal was ordered to perform unarmed military service, which he refused, He was subsequently sentenced to nine months' imprisonment for refusing military service.
7. N. v. Sweden, no. 10410/83, Commission decision of October 11, 1984, DR 40, p. 203; Autio v. Finland, no. 17086/90, Commission decision of December 6, 1991, DR 72, p. 246, etc.
8. Human Rights Committee, General Comment No. 22 (1993) CCPR/C/21/Rev.1/Add.4.
9. Human Rights Committee, Communication, January 23, 2007, CCPR/C/88/D/1321-1322/2004. The Human Rights Committee made a decision in Yoon Yeobeom and Choi Myungjin Communication case of 2006 that Korea violated Article 18 of the ICCPR.
10. March 23, 2010, Oh Taeyang *et al.* case (Communication 1953~1603/2007); March 24, 2011, Chung Mingyu etc. case (Communication 1642~1741/2007); October 25, 2012, Kim Jongnam *et al.* case (Communication 1786/2008); December 8, 2014, Kim Younggwan *et al.* case (Communication 2179/2012) etc.
11. Human Rights Committee, April 5, 2011, Communication. CCPR/C/101/D/1642-1741/2007.

12. Article 10(2) of the Charter provides as follows: "The right to conscientious objection is recognized, in accordance with the national laws governing the exercise of the right."
13. Article 60(1) of the Constitution enumerates the type of treaties which require the consent of the National Assembly: "The National Assembly shall have the right to consent to the conclusion and ratification of treaties pertaining to mutual assistance or mutual security; treaties concerning important international organizations; treaties of friendship, trade and navigation; treaties pertaining to any restriction in sovereignty; peace treaties; treaties which will burden the State or people with an important financial obligation; or treaties related to legislative matters."
14. Kim Daesun, *International Law* (Seoul: Samyoung-sa, 2010), p. 264; Chung Insup, *New International Law* (Seoul: Parkyoung-sa, 2018), pp. 123-124; Park Chanwoon, *Human Rights Law* (Seoul: Hanwool Academy, 2008), p. 282.
15. Kim Daesun, *ibid.*
16. The Vienna Convention on the Law of Treaties provides in Article 53: "A treaty is void, if at the time of its conclusion, it conflicts with a preemptory norm of general international law. For the purposes of the present Convention, a peremptory norm of general international law is a norm accepted and recognized by the international community of States as a whole as a norm from which no derogation is permitted and which can be modified only by a subsequent norm of general international law having the same character."
17. Park Chanwoon, *ibid.*; Lee Hanki, *New International Law* (Seoul: Parkyoung-sa, 1992), pp. 155-156.
18. Han Heewon, *International Human Rights Law* (Seoul: Samyoung-sa, 2012), pp. 347-349. Prof. Han argues that without making reference to the hierarchical order within the international human rights themselves, the discussion on the relationship between international human rights and municipal law in the academic circle has been dealt with on the same plane as the relationship between international law and municipal law in general. He continues to assert that the UDHR, the ICCPR and the ICESCR are superior or at least identical to the constitution and the other 5 human rights treaties and treaties that get approval of parliament are identical to law in their effect.
19. Lee Myungwoong, "Domestic Legal Effect of International Human Rights Law - Relations with Constitution and Legal Source in Constitutional Trial Proceedings," Symposium of National Human Rights Commission on 「Issues and Alternatives in Domestic Implementation of International Human Rights Law」, October 27, 2004, pp. 54-55, quoted from Woo Gitack, "Domestic Implementation of International Human Rights Law," Kyunghee Law Journal, vol. 51, no. 2, 2016, p. 246.
20. Chun Haksun, "International Human Rights law and Constitutional Court," American Constitutional Research Journal, vol. 19, no. 1, February 2008, pp. 181-183.
21. Cho Hongsuk, "Domestic Legal Guarantee of International Human Rights Law in Korea," Constitution Research Journal, vol. 4, no. 2, Korean Society of Constitution, 1998, pp. 84-85.

22. UN GAOR, Human Rights Committee, 45th Session, 1154, p. 3, para. 8, Doc. CCPR/C/SR 1154(July 20, 1992), The report observes as follows:
"Under Article 6(1) of the Constitution, the Covenant had the same effect as domestic law. The delegate could not accept the claim that the guarantees contained in the Covenant might be overturned by subsequent domestic legislation, since such a suspicion underestimated the Republic of Korea's commitment to human rights and the increasing public awareness of the rights enshrined in the Covenant. ... Moreover, since the principal rights enshrined in the Covenant were also embodied in the Constitution, any conflicting domestic legislation would be deemed unconstitutional."
23. Initial Report of States Parties due in 1996: Republic of Korea (May 30, 1996), U.N. Doc. CAT/C/32/Add. 1. para. 20. The report observes as follows: "Therefore, when conflicts between domestic laws and the Convention arise, *lex posterior* rule and the principle of the precedence of special law shall be applied."
24. Second periodic report of States Parties due in 1996: Republic of Korea. 20/08/98 CCPR/C/114/Add.1. para. 9.
25. Supreme Court, March 26, 1999, decision 96Da55877.
26. As Article 2(3)(a) of the ICCPR states that any person whose rights or freedoms as herein recognized are violated shall have an effective remedy, notwithstanding that the violation has been committed by persons acting in an official capacity, the Supreme Court was of the opinion that due to lack of concreteness this provision is difficult to be interpreted as enshrining the contents creating the right of state compensation claim by an individual.
27. Article 2(2) of the ICCPR provides as follows: "Where not already provided for by existing legislative or other measures, each State Party to the present Covenant undertakes to take the necessary steps, in accordance with its constitutional processes and with the provisions of the present Covenant, to adopt such laws or other measures as may be necessary to give effect to the rights recognized in the present Covenant."
28. Constitutional Court September 27, 2001 2000Hunba20; Chung Insup, *supra* note 14, p. 119.
29. Constitutional Court November 26, 1998 97Hunba65; *ibid.*, pp. 118-119.
30. Supreme Court September 9, 2005 decision 2004Chu10. The Supreme Court held that as the GATT 1994, which is a supplementary agreement to the Marrakesh Agreement on the Establishment of WTO, and the Agreement on the Government Procurement (AGP) have the same effect as domestic laws and regulations in accordance with Article 6(1) of the Constitution, the ordinance of local autonomous government, if in breach of the GATT and the AGP, loses its effect.
31. Constitutional Court March 21, 2001 99Hunma139; Chung Insup, *supra* note 14, p. 129.
32. Kim Yonghoon, "Treaties in the Constitutional Court," European Constitutional Research, vol. 10, December 2011, pp.138-139.
33. Paik Jinhyun, "Domestic Effect of Treaty- comparative analysis of theory,

practice, policy and implication for Korea," Korean Journal of International Law, vol. 45, no. 1, June 2000, p. 104.

34. Han Heewon, *supra* note 18, p.351.

35. Jordan Paust, "Self-Executing Treaties," 82 AJIL, pp. 760, 782; Kim Daesun, *supra* note 14, p. 230; Oh Seungjin, "Domestic Application of International Human Rights Treaties and the Issues," Korean Journal of International Law, vol. 56, no. 2, June 2011, p. 121; Lee Hanki, *supra* note 17, p. 154. Prof. Lee H. is of the view that Article 6(1) of the Constitution is interpreted to express explicitly the acceptance of international law as part of municipal law of Korea. He also mentions that the interpretation is relevant that treaties concluded in accordance with the Constitution will have domestic effect by promulgation only, as is the general trend in most democratic states following World War II.

36. Andrew Clapham, *Brierly's Law of Nations* (Oxford University Press, 2014), pp. 96-97. Prof. Clapham states that without further legislative measures, a number of states allow international law to take effect in domestic legal order. It was summarized by Virginia Leary in her comparative study as follows: 'In general, treaty provisions are considered by national courts and administrators as self-executing when they lend themselves to judicial or administrative application without further legislative implementation.' Virginia Leary, *International Labor Law and Conventions: The Effectiveness of Automatic Incorporation of Treaties in National Legal Systems* (The Hague: Nijhoff, 1982), p. 39.

The National Assembly's Role in Denuclearizing North Korea and Resuming South-North Korean Economic Cooperation: Legislative Consent to the Conclusion of the South-North Korean Agreement

CHUNG Min-Jung
Legislative Research Officer, National Assembly Research Service, Seoul, Korea

Key Words

National Assembly-approved South-North Korean agreements, Non-approved South-North Korean agreements, Development of Inter-Korean Relations Act, Panmunjom Declaration on Peace, Prosperity and Reunification on the Korean Peninsula

1. INTRODUCTION

Moon Jae-in, President of the Republic of Korea (hereinafter referred to as "South Korea") and Kim Jong-Un, Chairman of the State Affairs Commission of the Democratic People's Republic of Korea (hereinafter referred to as "North Korea") held the Inter-Korean Summit Meeting at the "Peace House" at Panmunjom on 27 April 2018, despite international tensions regarding North Korea's consistent nuclear tests. The two leaders solemnly promised before 80 million Koreans and the whole world that there will be no more war and that a new era of peace has begun on the Korean peninsula in the *Panmunjom Declaration on Peace, Prosperity and Reunification on the Korean Peninsula* (hereinafter referred to as "*Panmunjom Declaration*").[1]

Inter-Korean relations are international anomalies in that South Korea has two largely interchangeable commitment devices by which the President can conclude and ratify the vast majority of the agreements with North Korea. One instrument is the National Assembly-approved South-North Korean agreement. In place of National Assembly-approved South-North Korean agreements, commitments can be made in the form of a non-approved South-North Korean agreement, which requires only the deliberation of the State Council before the President's ratification and promulgation by the President after his ratification (Art. 22 of Development of Inter-Korean Relations Act).

Many legislators are skeptical of the utility of having two policy instruments to conclude South-North Korean agreements, with most of the critique directed at the National Assembly-approved South-North Korean agreements due to their supposed inflexibility and costliness. Commentators wonder why the President tried to use the slow and cumbersome consent procedure of the *Panmunjom Declaration* if the policy objectives could be fulfilled more easily by using a non-approved South-North Korean agreement, which is not similarly constrained.

Some commentators suggest that a president's use of the National Assembly-approved South-North Korean agreement signals a particularly high level of commitment, while others suggest that the greater stability resulting from the National Assembly's consent helps to ensure long-term compliance. What all these accounts have in common is an assumption that National Assembly-approved South-North Korean agreements, although more politically costly than non-approved South-North Korean agreements, confer certain benefits on the parties, justifying their continuing existence as a valuable inter-Korean relations policy tools. There are two reasons why the executive uses the National Assembly-approved South-North Korean agreements, namely, comity towards the National Assembly and the powerful political message that is sent to the world through the consent process.

Currently, the debate surrounding the ongoing relevance of National Assembly-approved South-North Korean agreements in a context in which non-approved South-North Korean agreements are so readily available and widely used remains unsettled. This manuscript seeks to shed light on the question of whether National Assembly-approved South-North Korean agreements are qualitatively different from non-approved South-North Korean agreements.

The rest of the manuscript proceeds as follows: Section 2 lays out the history of South-North Korean agreements. Section 3 provides the legal foundation of the different commitment devices and reviews the theories regarding how National Assembly-approved South-North Korean agreements may or may not differ from non-approved South-North Korean agreements with regard to their durability, while Section 4 discusses their implications. The final section concludes.

2. HISTORY OF SOUTH-NORTH KOREAN AGREEMENTS

South Korea and North Korea occasionally held inter-Korean dialogues through high-level military talks and have concluded several inter-Korean agreements.

Before the 2000 Inter-Korean summit, there were several meaningful South-North Korean agreements, such as the *4 July Joint Communiqué of 1972, the Agreement on Reconciliation, Nonaggression, and Exchanges and Cooperation* (South-North Basic Agreement), and the *Joint Declaration of Denuclearization of the Korean Peninsula* in 1991. However, those events and agreements occurred irregularly and intermittently.[2]

With the exception of the *4 July Joint Communiqué of 1972*, which addressed unification issues, these two antithetical nations remained bitterly opposed until 1990 when great initial strides were taken towards normalization. The 1990s ushered in momentous changes in North Korea's habitual relations with the Soviet Union (and later Russia) and China, resulting in the North Korea's acceptance of a more conciliatory policy towards its traditional opponents, such as South Korea and Japan. By the fall of 1991, prime ministerial talks, which had begun a year earlier, began making rapid progress towards rapprochement, culminating with the signing in December of two major agreements: *the Agreement on Reconciliation, Nonaggression and Exchanges and Cooperation and the Joint Declaration on the Denuclearization of the Korean Peninsula.*[3]

Additionally, the two Koreas had four inter-Korean agreements aimed solely at the Kaesung Industrial Complex (hereinafter referred to as "KIC") project. The four agreements on investment guarantees, the avoidance of double taxation, the resolution of commercial disputes, and the settlement of clearance were signed in December 2000 after the ministerial conference in August 2000 and went into effect in August 2003. These agreements were initially signed by administrative officials and received approval and consent from the National Assembly to take effect.

However, the quality and quantity of these four KIC-related South-North Korean agreements were still insufficient.[4] Thus, both Koreas need to make comprehensive new South-North Korean agreements for the KIC project. In particular, to prevent future shutdowns of the KIC, the two Koreas should conclude a South-North Korean agreement securing continuity and guaranteeing commitment.

3. DEVELOPMENT OF INTER-KOREAN RELATIONS ACT

South Korea has two different mechanisms for concluding South-North Korean agreements. The first option is the National Assembly-approved South-North Korean agreement. The National Assembly has the right to consent to the conclusion and ratification of South-North Korean agreements, which place heavy financial burdens on the state or nationals, or South-North Korean agreements concerning legislative matters under Article 21, paragraph (3) of the Development of Inter-Korean Relations Act. The second option is the non-approved South-North Korean agreement approach.

From an inter-Korean relations viewpoint, it is clear that the National Assembly-approved South-North Korean agreement and the non-approved South-North Korean agreement are perfect substitutes. The Development of Inter-Korean Relations Act stipulates that "South-North Korean agreements shall be only applicable to inter-Korean relations." (Art. 23, para. 1) Since both the National Assembly-approved South-North Korean agreement and the non-approved South-North Korean agreement are South-North Korean agreements, there is no legal difference between these commitment devices from the perspective of the Development of Inter-Korean Relations Act. The question of which procedure should be used is a political judgment that is made in the first instance by the President; the decision is subject to the possibility that the National Assembly might refuse to approve an agreement.

The President's choice between the two instruments can be explained by the "evasion hypothesis."[5] If an agreement is easy to push through the National Assembly, according to this argument, the President will rely on the National Assembly-approved South-North Korean agreement. If, however, securing a majority proves difficult, the President, according to this argument, can simply switch to a non-approved South-North Korean agreement without any significant consequences. The view that a National Assembly-approved South-North Korean agreement and a non-approved South-North Korean agreement can be considered legal substitutes naturally raises the question of why the President persistently insisted on the former form to regulate the Panmunjom Declaration, even though securing a majority of support in the National Assembly proved difficult.

Domestically, on the other hand, the prevailing view is that the non-approved South-North Korean agreement cannot be used as an alternative to the National Assembly-approved South-North Korean agreement method in every instance. The Development of Inter-Korean Relations Act provides that "[t]he President may suspend all or part of effects of each South-North Korean agreement for a fixed specific period, when significant changes occur in inter-Korean relations or when it is deemed necessary for national security, maintenance of order or public welfare" (Art. 23, para. 2). However, "[t]he President shall obtain approval from the National Assembly, when he/she intends to suspend the effect of each South-North Korean agreement, the conclusion or ratification of which has been ratified by the National Assembly" (Art. 23, para. 3).

The provisions reveal that the difference between the instruments is pronounced. Additionally, the provisions show that promises made in the form of National Assembly-approved South-North Korean agreements are qualitatively different from those made as part of a non-approved South-North Korean agreement. Against the backdrop of this provision, it seems premature to call for the abandonment of the National Assembly-approved South-North Korean agreement instrument, which may still serve important North Korean policy functions that cannot similarly be fulfilled by a non-approved South-North Korean agreement.

The choice to use the National Assembly-approved South-North Korean agreement, although more politically costly, may confer certain benefits on inter-Korean relations, which ultimately may lead to a more robust commitment towards stability and peace on the Korean peninsula. In interactions in which the benefits outweigh the costs, a National Assembly-approved South-North Korean agreement would be the preferable instrument, whereas a non-approved South-North Korean agreement would be preferred in other situations.

4. IMPLICATIONS

South Korea and North Korea have not yet established amicable economic or diplomatic relations. As a result, the Korean Peninsula cannot be completely at peace because it still faces elements of war today.[6] The Korean Peninsula is instead in a state of peace that possesses certain elements of war.[7] More specifically, most of the South-North Korean relations are still governed by the laws of peace, and the laws of neutrality are not activated between the antagonists and third parties because a state of peace continues to prevail. Nevertheless, actual fighting would be governed by *jus in bello*.[8]

South Korea and North Korea intended to end the war, and modern armistice agreements are held to terminate war under international law. Consequently, absent special circumstances, *jus in bello* should not apply, and belligerent rights should not be recognized because of the legal effects of an armistice agreement. However, *jus in bello* can apply when there are actual hostilities between the two Koreas.

According to observers, broader strategic considerations were the primary driver behind the President's submission of the consent bill of the Panmunjom Declaration. If a given agreement between South Korea and North Korea is concluded as a National Assembly-approved South-North Korean agreement, does this lead to a different outcome than if the agreement is concluded as a non-approved South-North Korean agreement? If the answer is yes, then this suggests that a National Assembly-approved South-North Korean agreement is qualitatively different from a non-approved South-North Korean agreement. If the answer is no, then National Assembly-approved South-North Korean agreements and non-approved South-North Korean agreements are substantively similar, and their use might be motivated solely by circumstances that are irrelevant to the substantive characteristics of the agreement.

The South Korean President determines North Korean policy, and he serves for one term of five years[9] and is therefore much less controlled by popular opinion once elected.[10] Maybe President Moon thought that the use of a National Assembly-approved South-North Korean agreement was associated with different outcome than a non-approved South-North Korean agreement.

The use of the National Assembly-approved South-North Korean agreement instrument can best be explained through a historical lens. In 2002, President Roh Moo-hyun was elected to replace President Kim Dae-jung. While President Roh continued the Sunshine Policy that was employed by his predecessor, Roh's policy was actually termed the "Peace and Prosperity Policy."[11] President Roh promised to maintain the Sunshine policy while seeking permanent peace on the peninsula and encouraging common prosperity in Asia.[12] President Roh's Peace and Prosperity Policy involved a three-point approach: resolve North Korea's nuclear crisis in the short term, bring lasting peace to the peninsula in the mid-term, and build a Northeast Asian economic hub in the long term.[13] However, the Roh Administration was tasked with dealing with yet another North Korean crisis as North Korea began removing all international monitoring equipment from its nuclear reactor, and tensions were high considering that it was possible that North Korea would soon be a target of America in its war against terrorism.[14]

In July of 2007, nevertheless, the two Koreas happily arranged a summit between Kim Jung-il and President Roh for late August.[15] The summit was agreed to despite protests from the conservative party that Roh, as a lame duck president, would not be able to make a lasting deal with Kim Jong-il.[16] The summit was postponed until October due to severe floods in North Korea; however, on October 2, President Roh flew to North Korea for a summit with leader Kim Jong-il.[17] Kim Jong-il met President Roh upon his arrival in

Pyongyang, though the reception was slightly chilly, and the two leaders eventually negotiated and signed an eight-point agreement.[18] The agreement was substantial and focused on creating a permanent peace between the two Koreas, and it contained the statement that the two Koreas shall uphold and endeavor to actively realize the past South-North Korean Declaration. Most South Koreans found the summit useful. However, the summit ultimately did not help to keep the ruling party in charge after the 2007 elections.[19] The subsequent Presidents ran in opposition to the Sunshine Policy.

It seemed likely that President Moon instinctively sensed not only the legal differences but also the political implications of withdrawing from a National Assembly-approved South-North Korean agreement *vis-à-vis* a non-approved South-North Korean agreement. Generally, promises made in the form of a National Assembly-approved South-North Korean agreement are significantly more durable than those made as non-approved South-North Korean agreements. The finding that National Assembly-approved South-North Korean agreements outlast non-approved South-North Korean agreements could be interpreted as indicating that National Assembly-approved South-North Korean agreements are harder to terminate by future administrations both as a matter of law and as a matter of political reality.

We currently lack a comprehensive theory of the political costs of terminating a National Assembly-approved South-North Korean agreement. The writings of some commentators imply that part of the political cost differential between withdrawing from a National Assembly-approved South-North Korean agreement and withdrawing from a non-approved South-North Korean agreement may be found in reputational sanctions. That is, the use of a National Assembly-approved South-North Korean agreement represents the complete pledge of a nation's reputational capital, and the President who tried to use it risked that reputational capital in the diplomatic world.

However, in order for this mechanism to explain why National Assembly-approved South-North Korean agreements are not terminated at the same rate as non-approved South-North Korean agreements, one would have to assume that South Korea has a single reputation as a nation that is independent of the administration currently in power. Otherwise, it would be difficult to understand why future administrations feel bound to promises their predecessors made with North Korea.

5. CONCLUSION

President Moon submitted the consent bill for the Panmunjom Declaration, which had been signed between President Moon Jae-in of South Korea and North Korea's leader Kim Jong-un in June 2018. Generally, treaties follow the consent procedure set forth in Article 60, paragraph 1 of the Constitution of the Republic of Korea in order for a treaty to be ratified and to become binding international law. However, some politicians have argued that National Assembly-approved South-North Korean agreements are irrelevant in South Korea because South-North Korean agreements are not treaties between two autonomous states,[20] and their role can be fulfilled by their close but less politically costly cousin, the non-approved South-North Korean agreement.

To confirm the interpretation, the Development of Inter-Korean Relations Act stipulates that "South-North Korean agreements shall be only applicable to inter-Korean relations" (Art. 23, para. 1). Similarly, inter-Korean relations were formally defined as "special relations established in the course of pursuing unification" rather than "relations between nations" (Art. 3, para. 1).

This manuscript showed that National Assembly-approved South-North Korean agreements are more durable than non-approved South-

North Korean agreements, supporting the President's view that there are qualitative differences between the two instruments. Abandoning National Assembly-approved South-North Korean agreements may therefore lead to unintended consequences by decreasing the tools that the executive has available to design optimal South-North Korean agreements.

References

1. Books

Jae-Cheon Lim, *Kim Jong Il's Leadership of North Korea* (Abingdon: Routledge, 2009).
Lisa L. Martin, *Democratic Commitments: Legislatures and International Cooperation* (Princeton: Princeton University Press, 2000).
Yoram Dinstein, *War, Aggression and Self-defence* (UK: Cambridge University Press, 2005).

2. Articles

Adam de Bear, "From Sunshine to Storm Clouds: An Examination of South Korea's Policy on North Korea," 23 *Mich. St. Int'l. L. Rev.* 823 (2015).
Aidan Foster-Carter, "North Korea-South Korea Relations: Summit Success?," 3 *Comp. Connections: Q. E-Journal One. Asian Bilateral Rel.* 1 (2007).
Angela Semee Kim, "An End to the Korean War: The Legal Character of the 2018 Summit Declarations and Implications of an Official Korean Peace Treaty," *Asian J. Int'l L.* (published online: Jan. 11, 2019).
Jeehye You, "Legislative Reform of the Kaesong Industrial Complex in North Korea," 29 *UCLA Pac. Basin L. J.* 36 (2011).
Julian Nyarko, "Giving the Treaty a Purpose: Comparing the Durability of Treaties and Executive Agreements," 113 *Am. J. Int'l L.* 54 (2019).
Seunghyun Sally Nam, "War on the Korean Peninsula? Application of *Jus in Bello* in the Cheonan and Yeonpyeong Island Attacks," 8 *E. Asia L. Rev.* 43 (2013).

3. Articles in Collections

James M. Minnich, "Resolving the North Korean Nuclear Crisis: Challenges and Opportunities in Readjusting the U.S. - ROK Alliance," *in A Turning Point: Democratic Consolidation in the ROK and Strategic Readjustment in the US-ROK Alliance* (Alexandre Y. Mansourouv Honolulu: Asia-Pacific Centre for Security Studies, 2005).

4. Articles in Newspaper

Chung-in Moon, "A Real Path to Peace on the Korean Peninsula: The Progress and Promise of the Moon-Kim Summit," *Foreign Affairs*, April 30, 2018.

5. Working Papers and Reports

Choong Nam Kim, *The Roh Moo Hyun Government's Policy Toward North Korea*, E.-W. Ctr., Working Paper No. 11, 2005.

6. Internet Sources

Ministry of Unification, *Panmunjom Declaration on Peace, Prosperity and Reunification on the Korean Peninsula*, Press Release, April 30, 2018 *available at* https://www.unikorea.go.kr/eng_unikorea/news/releases/?boardId=bbs_0000000000000034&mode=view&cntId=54179 [Accessed on May 9, 2019].

Declaration on the Advancement of South-North Korean Relations, Peace and Prosperity, Pyongyang, October 4, 2007, *available at* https://peacemaker.un.org/sites/peacemaker.un.org/files/KP%20KR_071004_Declaration%20on%20Advancement%20of%20South-North%20Korean%20Relations.pdf [accessed on May 10, 2019].

Notes

1. For the full text, see Ministry of Unification, *Panmunjum Declaration on Peace, Prosperity and Reunification on the Korean Peninsula*, Press Release, April 30, 2018 *available at* https://www.unikorea.go.kr/eng_unikorea/news/releases/?boardId=bbs_0000000000000034&mode=view&cntId=54179 [Accessed on May 9, 2019].
2. Jae-Cheon Lim, *Kim Jong Il's Leadership of North Korea* 119 (2009).
3. James M. Minnich, "Resolving the North Korean Nuclear Crisis: Challenges and Opportunities in Readjusting the U.S. - ROK Alliance," in Alexandre Y. Mansourouv (ed.), *A Turning Point: Democratic Consolidation in the ROK and Strategic Readjustment in the US-ROK Alliance*, 2005, p. 281.
4. Jeehye You, "Legislative Reform of the Kaesong Industrial Complex in North Korea," 29 *UCLA Pac. Basin L. J.* 36, 70-71 (2011).
5. *See* Lisa L. Martin, *Democratic Commitments: Legislatures and International Cooperation* 53 (2000).
6. Seunghyun Sally Nam, "War on the Korean Peninsula? Application of *Jus in Bello* in the Cheonan and Yeonpyeong Island Attacks," 8 *E. Asia L. Rev.* 43, 69-70 (2013).
7. Yoram Dinstein, *War, Aggression and Self-defence*, 4th (ed.), 2005, p. 16.
8. *Ibid.*
9. *The Constitution of the Republic of Korea*, Art. 70. Please note, however, that the single five year term has only been a part of the South Korean constitution since 1987; Presidents Rhee and Park Chung-hee were in power for 12 and 20 years, respectively.
10. Adam de Bear, "From Sunshine to Storm Clouds: An Examination of South Korea's Policy on North Korea," 23 *Mich. St. Int'l. L. Rev.* 823, 827 (2015).
11. Choong Nam Kim, *The Roh Moo Hyun Government's Policy Toward North Korea* 12 (E.-W. Ctr., Working Paper No. 11, 2005).
12. *Ibid.*, pp. 12-13.
13. *Ibid.*, p. 14.
14. *Ibid.*, p. 13.
15. Aidan Foster-Carter, "North Korea-South Korea Relations: Summit Success?," 3 *Comp. Connections: Q. E-Journal One. Asian Bilateral Rel.* 1, 1-2 (2007).
16. *Ibid.*, p. 2.
17. *Ibid.*, pp. 4-5.
18. *Ibid.*, pp. 5-6. *See Declaration on the Advancement of South-North Korean Relations, Peace and Prosperity*, Pyongyang, October 4, 2007, *available at* https://peacemaker.un.org/sites/peacemaker.un.org/files/KP%20KR_071004_Declaration%20on%20Advancement%20of%20South-North%20Korean%20Relations.pdf [accessed on May 10, 2019].
19. Foster-Carter, *supra* note 15, p. 9.
20. *See* Angela Semee Kim, "An End to the Korean War: The Legal Character of the 2018 Summit Declarations and Implications of an Official Korean Peace Treaty," *Asian J. Int'l L.* (published online: Jan. 11, 2019).

Adoption of Judicial Insolvency Network Guidelines by Seoul Bankruptcy Court and Follow-ups

KIM Young-Seok
Judge, Seoul Bankruptcy Court, Seoul, Korea

Key Words

Cross-border Insolvency, Cooperation, JIN Guidelines, Judicial Network Insolvency, Seoul Bankruptcy Court

1. ADOPTION OF JIN GUIDELINES

It has been 8 months since Seoul Bankruptcy Court (hereinafter "SBCourt") adopted the "Guidelines for Communication and Cooperation between Courts in Cross-Border Insolvency Matters (hereinafter "JIN Guidelines")"[1] which was established by the Judicial Insolvency Network (hereinafter "JIN")[2] in October, 2016.

The above JIN Guidelines is a kind of Model Code[3] for inter-court cooperation procedures designed to efficiently handle Cross-Border Insolvency cases with specific provisions in terms of communication process and method such as telephone, video conference calls, and other electronic means.

SBCourt started discussing about the adoption of JIN Guidelines through an internal seminar which was held on November 15, 2017,[4] and sent a delegation[5] to the Supreme Court of Singapore which has taken the leading role in JIN to observe and review the practice of JIN Guidelines on May 16, 2018.[6] The SBCourt finally adopted JIN Guidelines after consulting with relevant institutions including Seoul Bar Association, by revising 『Procedural Guideline No. 504 (Cooperation between Courts in Cross-Border Insolvency Matters)』 (hereinafter "Guideline No. 504")[7] on July 1, 2018.

Although SBCourt has cooperated with a few foreign courts including the U.S. Bankruptcy Court for the District of New Jersey, U.S. Bankruptcy Court for the Eastern District of Virginia and Federal Court of Australia with respect to cases of Hanjin Shipping Co. and others,[8] it seems that SBCourt has taken a step forward by sharing rules of cooperation with other distinguished foreign courts around the world especially famous for their insolvency practices.

2. A FEW ISSUES DISCUSSED IN THE ADOPTION PROCESS

In the course of JIN Guidelines adoption, the possibility of conflicts with Korean national law such as Debtor Rehabilitation and Bankruptcy Act (hereinafter "DRBA"), a Korean national Insolvency Law, and Act on International Judicial Mutual Assistance in Civil Matters (hereinafter "IJMA") was discussed as follows.

2-1. Conflicts with DRBA

Article 641 of DRBA is one and only codified rules stipulating Cooperation in Cross-Border Insolvency Matters, which states in full as follows:[9]

> Article 641 (Cooperation)
>
> (1) **The court** shall cooperate with **any foreign court** and **the representative of foreign insolvency procedures** with

respect to the matters falling under each of the following subparagraphs in order to ensure the smooth and fair execution of domestic insolvency procedures, foreign insolvency procedures or between multiple foreign insolvency procedures that are proceeding over the same debtor and other debtors related with the former:

1. The exchange of opinions;
2. The management and supervision of the debtor's business and properties;
3. The coordination of the progression of multiple procedures;
4. Other necessary matters.

(2) **The court** may exchange information and opinions directly with **any foreign court** or **the representative of foreign insolvency procedures** in order for the cooperation referred to in the provisions of paragraph (1).

(3) **Any administrator and any trustee** in insolvency who are in charge of domestic insolvency procedures may exchange information and opinions with **any foreign court** or **the representative of foreign insolvency procedures** under the court's supervision.

(4) **Any administrator and any trustee** in insolvency in charge of domestic insolvency procedures may reach an agreement with **any foreign court** or **the representative of foreign insolvency procedures** on the coordination of insolvency procedures after obtaining permission therefor from the court.

As shown in the text, there are largely four kinds of cooperation under the Article 641: ① Cooperation between Courts, ② Cooperation with Court and foreign representative, ③ Cooperation between domestic representative and foreign court, ④ Cooperation between domestic representative and foreign representative. Therefore, the JIN Guidelines applying only to the Cooperation between Courts (①) is not against

DRBA's entire system and rather helps the cooperation practice to be implemented according to more predictable and stable process.

Furthermore, the full text of JIN Guidelines explains the purpose, nature of the co-operative norms and specific methods clarifying that JIN Guidelines are not absolute binding norms and can be applied in a flexible manner considering special circumstances for each individual issue.[10] Also, Guidelines No. 504 of SBCourt which based on the Article 641 was already drafted and finalized by reference to the full text of the JIN Guidelines, and any actual or legal struggles has not been found in implementing cooperation with foreign courts.

2-2. Conflicts with IJMA

If the subject of cooperation overlaps with that of IJMA, which requires cooperation only through Minister of Foreign Affairs, Ambassador or Consul of the Republic of Korea in the foreign country and other institutions other than court, direct communication between courts might look somewhat inconsistent with IJMA.

However, the term "judicial cooperation" under IJMA means any cooperation on service of documents or examination of evidence in a trial (Article 2(1), IJMA)[11], meaning that the subject of IJMA is different from that of DRBA (Article 641(1) as follows.

	IJMA, Article 2(1)	DRBA, Article 641(1)
Subject of Cooperation	–Service of documents –Examination of evidence	–Exchange of opinions –Management and supervision of the debtor's business and properties –Coordination of the progression of multiple procedures –Other necessary matters

In other words, it is unlikely that JIN Guidelines allowing each court to communicate directly with each other and exchange opinions is in conflict with IJMA. Yet, it should also be noted that cooperation between courts should not be carried out directly with regard to the service and investigation of evidence in each country's insolvency proceedings. In particular, due to the differences regarding who takes the duty to serve in judicial proceedings between an interested party and a court, more caution is needed for Civil Law county like the Republic of Korea when discussing the issue with Common Law countries.

2-3. Conflicts with Treaty

In line with the same reasoning discussed above, JIN Guidelines is not expected to have a clash with treaties below that the Republic of Korea has signed with a foreign country on Judicial Assistance in Civil and Commercial matters.

#	Name of treaty	Contracting State	Effective date
1	Treaty on Judicial Assistance in Civil and Commercial Matters between the Republic of Korea and Australia	Australia	Jan. 16, 2000
2	Treaty between the Republic of Korea and the People's Republic of China on Judicial Assistance in Civil and Commercial Matters	People's Republic of China	Apr. 27, 2005
3	Treaty on Judicial Assistance in Civil and Commercial Matters between the Republic of Korea and Mongolia	Mongolia	May. 8, 2010
4	Treaty on Judicial Assistance in Civil and Commercial Matters between the Republic of Korea and the Republic of Uzbekistan	Republic of Uzbekistan	Aug. 11, 2013
5	Treaty on Judicial Assistance in Civil and Commercial Matters between the Republic of Korea and the Kingdom of Thailand	Kingdom of Thailand	Apr. 16, 2015

Because the purpose of all the treaties above, generally, is to provide mutual judicial cooperation concerning the service of documents, the investigation of evidence and the exchange of legal information between the Contracting States, the cooperation based on JIN Guidelines is compatible with that under the treaties.

Interestingly enough, in addition to the aforementioned elements, the treaty signed with the People's Republic of China includes the "recognition and enforcement of arbitral awards" as the subject of judicial cooperation,[12] which is assumed to have been included in the scope by China's suggestion after experiencing importance of reciprocity in the phase of recognition and enforcement of foreign judgments. However, the clause does not seem to be of great benefit because Korea does not demand the reciprocity as one of the requirements for foreign arbitral awards, and both Korea and China are members of the Convention on the Recognition and Enforcement of Foreign Arbitral Awards (New York Convention).[13]

3. NEWLY REVISED GUIDELINE NO. 504

After the above review, SBCourt finally decided to adopt JIN Guidelines as a way to add new Article 7, which states that all or part of JIN Guidelines can be followed as for specific methods not stipulated by the pre-existing Articles in individual cases, to Guideline No. 504.

Procedural Guidelines No. 504
(Cooperation between courts in Cross-Border matters)[14]

Article 1 (Purpose)
Article 2 (Cooperation with Foreign courts)
Article 3 (Two-way communication)

Article 4 (Cooperation of administrators)
Article 5 (Concluding of procedural agreements)
Article 6 (Participation)
Article 7 (Others)
With regard to anything relating to the cooperation between courts not specified in Procedural Guideline No. 504, SBCourt may order to apply the 『Guidelines for Communication and Cooperation between Courts in Cross-Border Insolvency Matters』 established by Judicial Insolvency Network (JIN) to individual cases, in whole or in part, following an application by the parties or on its own motion.

The language of Article 7 was drafted referring to Rule 9029-2 (Guidelines for Communication and Cooperation Between Courts in Cross-Border Insolvency Matters), a local rule of U.S. Bankruptcy Court for the District of Delaware which also adopted JIN Guidelines, which allowed the application of some or all of the Guidelines flexibly on a case-by-case basis so that the Guidelines is anticipated to be properly balanced with pre- existing Korean Cooperation practices.

4. JIN 2nd CONFERENCE IN 2018

JIN held a second conference in September 2018 in New York and continued to check the current issues and discuss about some specific matters.[15] In particular, participation of judges from U.S. Bankruptcy Court for the District of Southern Texas and Southern Florida other than Southern District of New York and Delaware showed that the interest of the courts in cooperation in Cross-Border insolvency is increasing.[16]

Notably, JIN's judges decided to conduct practical study on

some issues so that the cooperation between courts can actually help with the handling cases in the conference. Four topics that has been decided at the conference and continues to be studied are ① A set of core principles on recognition of foreign insolvency proceedings, ② Modalities for court-to-court communication), ③ Interaction between insolvency law and admiralty law,[17] and ④ Alternative dispute resolution for insolvency disputes, in particular mediation and arbitration.

Meanwhile, following suggestions were made by the Supreme Court of Singapore at the conference: the JIN secretariat, which actually consists of Assistant Registrar of the Supreme Court of Singapore, was finally established. In addition to the establishment of Secretariat, JIN's official "Internet homepage"[18] was also launched. In particular, the above website received much attention for demonstrating the interface supporting multilateral meetings (chatting, voice, etc.) between JIN members during the conference. Remarkably, the homepage links to each member's homepage including that of SBCourt, through which Guidelines No. 504 can be accessed. The website above will also include resources folder, which can share key issues, such as treatment of maritime-lien in insolvency proceeding[19] currently discussed in each court.

5. FUTURE PROSPECTS

In a modern society where individuals and businesses have property in many countries, recognition and relief relating to a foreign proceeding has become an inevitable concept to prevent unnecessary parallel insolvency procedures and to seek efficiency. Thus, major insolvency courts around the world seem to be paying attention to the Cross-Border Insolvency, especially for the cooperation between the courts.[20]

It is understandable that stakeholders, including foreign corporations or individuals who are familiar with the Common Law will have a vague fear of the insolvency laws of the Civil Law countries and be concerned about whether they will be treated fairly there.

At this time, the adoption of JIN Guidelines by SBCourt can be a signal to the world that insolvency system in Korea is not much different from that of Common Law Countries. Although there is a procedural difference, such matters can be discussed through cooperation between courts to ensure that foreign creditors are not treated unfairly and given enough opportunities to participate in the Korean insolvency proceeding.

Hope SBCourt, the court adopted JIN Guidelines for the first time in the Civil Law country, will be acknowledged as one of the best attractive insolvency jurisdictions by many stakeholders worldwide.

Notes

1. JIN Guidelines consists of 14 guidelines as well as 6 introductions and 1 Annex (Joint Hearing) stipulating specific procedures and method of cooperation and fundamental Principles. For the details Young-Seok KIM, *Cooperation between Courts, Korean Practice*, Korean Year book of International Law (KYIL) Vol. 5, 2018. 12, at 201-203.
2. JIN is a network of insolvency judges from across the world, which serves as a platform for sustained and continuous engagement for the furtherance of Judicial thought leadership, Best practices, and Communication Cooperation.
3. Accordingly, JIN Guidelines is not binding in itself, meaning that incorporation by establishing or revising local rules or procedural guidelines in each court is needed to make JIN Guidelines effective.
4. The internal seminar was the 1st session on "Study on Cross-Border Insolvency Practice," which has been one of the study teams composed of Judges in SBCourt.
5. Kyung-Chun LEE who was then the Chief Judge of SBCourt, a presiding judge Jin-Woong LEE and a judge Young-Seok KIM visited the Supreme Court of Singapore as the delegation of SBCourt.
6. On the same day, SBCourt also concluded the 『Memorandum of Understanding between the Supreme Court of Singapore and the Seoul Bankruptcy Court』 with Supreme Court of Singapore.
7. SBCourt established Procedural Guidelines based on the SBCourt's local rule No. 34 in order to set reasonable standard for practice. The Procedural Guidelines consists of about 60 part from the General Rules through Corporate Rehabilitation, Individual Rehabilitation and Bankruptcy to Cross-Border Insolvency. Guideline No. 504 is one of four parts stipulating Cross-Border Insolvency.
8. For the details, please refer to, Young-Seok KIM, *supra* note 1, at 198-200.
9. Emphasis added by the author.
10. Introduction E of the JIN Guidelines.
11. IJMA Article 2 (Definition): For the purpose of this Act, the definition of terms shall be as follow:
    1. The term "judicial cooperation" means any cooperation made by a court, other public office, etc. for carrying out in a foreign country domestic formality on service of documents or examination of evidence in a trial, or for carrying out in Korea the foreign formalities thereon;
12. The Article 3 (Scope of judicial assistance) of this treaty is as follows.
    The judicial assistance in civil and commercial matters to be provided under this treaty shall include:
    (a) service of judicial documents;
    (b) taking of evidence;
    (c) recognition and enforcement of arbitral awards; and
    (d) provision of legal information or judicial records.

13. Korea accessed the New York Convention on Feb. 8, 1973 and China accessed the Convention on Jan. 22, 1987.
14. For the Article 1 through 6, please refer to Young-Seok KIM, *supra* note 1, at 192-195.
15. The author representing SBCourt attended the Conference as an observer with about sixteen other distinguished judges from U.S. Bankruptcy Court (SDNY, DE, SDFL, SDTX), Federal Court of Australia, Court of Appeal of England & Wales, Supreme Court of Singapore, High Court of Hong Kong, Tokyo District Court, etc.
16. The Tokyo District Court has not yet adopted JIN Guides, but it was worth noting that the court dispatched two judges to participate as an Observer.
17. In Korea, the handling of maritime-lien in insolvency proceedings had become a hot issue recently. Where shipping companies are concerned, it is highly likely that cross-border insolvency issues will be raised because (i) ships, which are major assets of shipping companies, are easily movable; (ii) maritime liens, which is a type of lien put on a ship or another maritime property, are universalized; and (iii) governing laws concerning shipping contracts, bills of lading, marine insurance contracts, marine fuel oil supply contracts, etc., are designated as foreign laws in many cases. For the details, please refer to Young-Seok KIM, *Study on the Cross-Border Insolvency of Shipping Companies*, Supreme Court Law Journal Vol. 8, 2018. 6.
18. See the official homepage (http://www.jin-global.org/index.html).
19. Steven Chong, Justice of Supreme Court of Singapore, also noted at the presentation during the conference on Maritime Insolvency Law during that a series of conflicts with maritime laws have become more frequent and controversial in insolvency proceedings. For maritime-related cases in Korean insolvency proceedings, please refer to Young-Seok KIM, *Cross-Border Insolvency in Korea*, Korean Yearbook of International Law (KYIL) Vol. 4, 2016, at 111-112.
20. For more Korean practice in terms of conflicts between a maritime lien and an insolvency proceeding, please refer to Young-Seok KIM, *Study on the Cross-Border Insolvency of Shipping Companies - Focusing on Maritime issues*, Supreme Court Law Journal, Vol. 8, Supreme Court of Korea, 2018.

How Did We Get Here: The Chronology of THADD Deployment

OH Sun-Young
Associate Professor, Soongsil University, Seoul, Korea

The story of the deployment in the Republic of Korea (hereinafter, "Korea") of the Terminal High Altitude Area Defense (hereinafter, "THAAD") goes back to the year 2014. On June 3, 2014, the United States Forces Korea (USFK) first mentioned that the U.S. was considering deploying the THAAD in Korea to counter North Korea's ballistic threats, but no advancement in the talks had been actually made until 2016.[1]

On February 4, 2015, China expressed their sincere concerns over the possible deployment of the THAAD in Korea, and the Korean government emphasized that no decision was made on whether to allow the U.S. to deploy the THAAD in Korea by adding that as of March 11, 2015 there had not even been a request to consult from the U.S. regarding the deployment of the THAAD.

Due to continual push of nuclear and intercontinental ballistic missile tests from North Korea in early 2016, Korea President Park announced on January 13, 2016 that Korea would consider and review the issue of whether to deploy U.S. THAAD system from the perspective of national security and interests. And thus, Korea and the United States' military officials announced that they had agreed to begin negotiations for the "earliest possible" deployment in Korea of the THAAD anti-missile system on February 7, 2016.

Following the announcement of Korea and U.S. military officials, China resolutely and firmly opposed the deployment of the THAAD system on the Korean Peninsula by expressing that no harm shall be done to China's strategic security interests. Despite China's strong opposition, Korea and the United States, as part of the measures to upgrade the Korea-U.S. alliance's missile defense posture against North Korea's threats, officially started working-group-level talks on March 4, 2016 about the deployment of a THAAD, but no decision was officially made. During the 2016 Hangzhou summit, President Xi Jinping of China expressed firm opposition to the deployment of a THAAD battery in Korea, but Korean Defense Minister Han mentioned during the Asia Security Summit on June 4, held in Singapore, that Korea would deploy the THAAD system in response to North Korea's threats.[2]

After months of subsequent discussion between South Korea and the U.S., they formally announced that the THAAD would be deployed in Korea on July 8, and Korea announced on July 13, 2016 that Seongju in Kyoungsangbukdo province would be the location of the THAAD deployment. This was a bold decision for the South Korean government as well, given its long hesitation to approve THAAD in part because of strong domestic resistance.

The Korea's Ministry of National Defense signed a formal land swap deal with LOTTE group for the THAAD deployment sites on February 28, 2017. After China's strong protests, there were notices sent on March 1 over the internet during Korea's visitation schedule that all schedules relating to the Korean corporation LOTTE would be canceled. Indeed, JSBC International Tour Service Co. Ltd, a state-owned corporation, gave notice that all schedules relating to the Korean corporation LOTTE would be canceled (only the major measures China took in relation to THAAD are listed). The website of China's Ministry of Culture and Tourism gave public notice on its website (March 3) entitled "On Travel to Korea (赴韩国旅游提示)," advising travelers to choose their destinations cautiously in relation to the prohibition of Chinese tourism to Jeju Island.

Because of President Park's political scandal in Korea, it was unclear when the THAAD system would be deployed. In the meantime, two launchers out of the six that would make up the THAAD battery arrived in Korea on March 6, 2017. Both South Korea and the U.S. finally completed a land provision process on April 20 for THAAD deployment, and the USFK began installing the equipment for the THAAD at the former golf course in Seongju on April 28, 2017.

This prompted China to issue a series of strong retaliatory measures. All work relating to Korean travel packages was suspended (from March 15); all work relating to individual travel to Korea was suspended; all products related to LOTTE were delisted; and cruises were prohibited from anchoring at Korean ports. There were a complete cessation from March 15 of group tour visa applicants to Korea, the major tour companies in China ceased Korea-related work, and the Chinese state-run tour companies even stopped all work on preconditions for Korean travel such as simply reserving flights and tickets, and agent work for individual visas.

The first two THAAD launchers were declared operational in Korea in early May, 2017, days before the president election. President Moon, shortly after his election, postponed the permanent deployment of THADD and ordered a close scrutiny of the entry of four THAAD missile launchers into Korea on May 30. After North Korea fired another intercontinental ballistic missile on July 29, 2017, President Moon ordered the resumption of consultations with the U.S. over the provisional deployment of the four remaining THAAD launchers.[3]

Due to the continued domestic opposition in Korea, the Korean Ministry of Environment conducted a small-scale environment impact assessment, citing the importance of establishing procedural legitimacy, on the THAAD system partially operational at a site in Seongju. On September 4, 2017, Korea announced the four THAAD launchers would be temporarily deployed on September 7, 2017. Four months later, Korea launched a full environmental assessment of the THAAD by order of President Park, which was going to take 10 to 15 months, and thus, the deployment of all six launchers of the THAAD was postponed until this assessment of the site was finalized. The extensive environmental review, which was required for the full deployment of the THAAD system, has been delayed as the USFK postponed the submission of the management plan on the site.

China maintained its harsh sanctions on Korea, but soon after Korea and China agreed on October 31, 2017 to work swiftly to improve their relations and restore exchange and cooperation in all areas to a normal track. This was followed on November 11, 2017 by the ASEAN summit meeting between President Moon of Korea and President Xi of China. Eventually President Moon visited Beijing in December 2017 and on the surface, Korea and China relations seemed to be on the mend.

Since the series of inter-Korean summits between South and North on April 27, and the historical meeting of President Trump of the U.S. and North Korean leader Kim in Singapore in June 2018, some Koreans argued that there was less need for the THAAD system. In fact, clashes took place between protesters and riot police on April 23, 2018 in the city of Seongju over the construction equipment entering the THAAD site.

The USFK submitted to Korea a detailed management plan for THAAD site in February 2019, paving the way for a long-overdue environmental assessment of the site.

Tensions raised by THAAD at the domestic and international levels are still unsettled, and the conflict has only been postponed, not resolved. It is highly likely that support for THAAD deployment will remain unchanged unless denuclearization in North Korea is confirmed.

Notes

1. *Chronology of events leading to THAAD deployment*, YONHAPNEWS AGENCY, https://en.yna.co.kr/view/AEN20170906009800315 (last visited July 29, 2019).
2. *Xi Tells South Korea that China Opposes THAAD Anti-missile Defense: Xinhua*, REUTERS https://www.reuters.com/article/us-g20-china-southkorea-idUSKCN11B04A, (last visited July 25, 2019).
3. *President Moon's THAAD flip-flopping continues with call for additional launchers*, HANKYOREH, http://english.hani.co.kr/arti/english_edition/e_national/805423.html (last visited July 30, 2019).

KYIL

International Law-Related Resolutions of the 20th National Assembly with a Focus on Territorial Sovereignty and International Environmental Law

CHUNG Min-Jung
Legislative Research Officer, National Assembly Research Service, Seoul, Korea

A resolution adopted by the National Assembly (hereafter referred to as "legislative resolution") of the Republic of Korea (hereafter referred to as "Korea") is an expression of legislative will. Legislative resolutions do not comply with the procedural formalities that would be necessary to give them legal status, yet they nonetheless influence the behavior of domestic and foreign administrations and of the public. Legislative resolutions affect behavior by informing the public and domestic and foreign political institutions about the intentions and foreign policy preferences of the National Assembly; they are informative about the National Assembly's view of international affairs that is relevant to the decision making of various political agents as well as the public, and thus, they are influential in directing foreign policy initiatives. The National Assembly uses the rhetoric of international law as the practical art of persuasive discourse because international law is considered to have a shared logic and a common understanding.

Periodically, proposals surface to pay more attention to legislative resolutions as mechanisms for influencing foreign policy. A total of 8 legislative resolutions were adopted at the plenary assembly after the deliberations of various standing or select committees in the third quarter of the 20th Session (June 1, 2018~April 26, 2019).[1] There were two legislative resolutions related to foreign relations: one is the legislative resolution against Japan, primarily under the auspices of the Foreign Affairs and Reunification Committee (standing committe e)[2]; the other is a legislative resolution that was brought against the People's Republic of China (hereafter referred to as "China") under the purview of the Committee for the Management of Small Particulate Dusts (special committee).[3]

This paper presents these selected legislative resolutions related to territorial sovereignty and international environmental law. The legislative resolutions introduced here are primarily geared towards urging the country that the National Assembly complained against to implement specific measures regarding the issue, encouraging the Korean government to use active diplomacy to their end and promoting alliance with the international community for their purpose.

1. LEGISLATIVE RESOLUTION ON RECTIFYING THE APPROVAL OF JAPANESE TEXTBOOKS CONTAINING FABRICATIONS ABOUT DOKDO ISLAND

The Japanese Ministry of Education, Culture, Sports, Science, and Technology reviewed and approved elementary school social-studies textbooks on March 26, 2019, after holding the "Meeting for Review of Books to be Used as Textbooks." These books contained content regarding Dokdo Island.

Korea is in a dispute with Japan over the legal title to the island of Dokdo (Takeshima in Japanese). Dokdo is a rock island located in the East Sea/Sea of Japan between Korea and Japan. It consists of two main volcanic islets with approximately thirty-two small rocks circling them. While Korea currently effectively possesses the island,

Japan has been claiming it since 1952. The issue of sovereignty over these barren islets emerged as a major source of contention between Korea and Japan on January 18, 1952, when the Korean government included the area around Dokdo within the Syngman Lee Line Zone (a Korean version of the Truman line) for the sovereignty and protection of Korea. Contesting the legitimacy of the Zone itself, the Japanese government challenged Korea's territorial and maritime jurisdiction over the islets on the grounds that it had historically been part of Japan's territory. The controversy was rekindled in March and April 2019, when the Japanese Education Ministry, on March 26, 2019, approved 10 elementary social-studies textbooks that asserted that "Dokdo is inherently Japanese territory."

The fabrications contained in the textbooks were made worse by statements such as "Korea unilaterally took possession of Dokdo Island" and "(Dokdo Island) should be submitted to the UN Security Council or the International Court of Justice." The review and approval of the social-studies textbooks containing territorial claims over Dokdo Island are a clear act of provocation that infringes upon Korea's territorial sovereignty, which could have serious adverse effects on the future relationship between the two nations. As expected, the textbooks provoked a virulent reaction from the National Assembly of Korea. It criticized the textbook approval, claiming that Japan had tried to justify a colonial past. From the perspective of the National Assembly, this was the tip of an iceberg concealing the broader problem of an erroneous view of history that would in reality affect all Japanese textbooks to a varying degree. Japan has been showing some troubling signs of returning to its nationalistic past through history textbooks that have whitewashed Japan's atrocities. The movement away from pacifism by removing war renunciation language from history textbooks would likely aggravate tensions in an already volatile region, because Japan would send a message to the international community that it did not desire subsequent generations to be fully aware of the extent of their nation's past culpability.

Accordingly, the 367th Session of the National Assembly (provisional session) adopted a resolution on April 5, 2019, in which Japan must realize that its act of reviewing and approving textbooks containing fabrications is an act that threatens peace not only with Korea but also with other Asian nations that have suffered from Japan's imperialism and that the Japanese government must immediately revoke its approval of the relevant textbooks. The legislative resolution proposed that the Japanese government correct the information in the textbooks that showed biased content regarding the territorial issue of Dokdo.

In addition, the National Assembly urged the Japanese government to adhere to the so-called Neighboring Country Clause (kinrin shokoju jōkō), stipulating the need to show understanding and seek international harmony when dealing with Asia's modern and contemporary history in the textbook authorization system. Additionally, it urged the Korean government to take a firm and consistent stance against Japan's territorial claims over Dokdo Island and its movements to distort history and to make various efforts to ensure that Korea's history and its development are recounted accurately in the textbooks of other countries.

2. LEGISLATIVE RESOLUTION URGING KOREA'S GOVERNMENT TO FIND SOLUTIONS TO THE LONG-RANGE TRANSPORT OF SMALL PARTICULATE DUST FROM CHINA

As China's industrialization has rapidly advanced, trans-boundary pollution has swept eastward across the Yellow Sea into Korea. Although Korea and China contribute to the air pollution problems of each other to some degree, Korea is more vulnerable to the long-range transport of small particulate dust from China. However, Korea's government has neither strongly advocated for nor resorted to immediate and effective responses to prevent the trans-boundary atmospheric pollution confronting its population; this has not matched the magnitude of the health and environmental problems confronting the region due to China's energy consumption path.

On December 7, 2018, the National Assembly adopted a legislative resolution urging its government to manifest a clear intent to cope with the problem in the diplomatic sphere. However, it also carefully refrained from characterizing small particulate dust from China as a "dispute." Rather, it approached the issue first and foremost as an occasion for inter-ministerial and scientific cooperation. In other words, it urged its government to make best efforts to provide funding and technical assistance to various regional and sub-regional agencies dedicated to measuring and mitigating trans-boundary air pollution.

Until now, this non-confrontational approach has not been called into question. Because of the priority allocated to strategic considerations in trade, energy security, and industrial policy, Korea and China have almost uniformly opted for policy autonomy in environmental matters. Perhaps in the next legislative resolution, the National Assembly may suggest some international environmental law principles and bilaterally accepted concepts that can underpin a bilateral environmental governance mechanism for regional air quality control.

Notes

1. The National Assembly of the Republic of Korea, *Bill Information, available at* http://likms.assembly.go.kr/bill/stat/statFinishBillSearch.do [Accessed on April 29, 2019].
2. *Legislative resolution for the Correction of Approval of Japanese Textbooks Containing Fabrications about Dokdo Island*, Submitted by Foreign Affairs and Reunification Committee Chairman, 2019564, (2019.4.4.) [adopted as submitted].
3. *Legislative Resolution Urging the South Korea's government to Find Solutions to the Long-range Transport of Small Particulate Dusts from China*, Submitted by Small Particulate Dusts Management Committee Chairman, 2013808, (2018.5.28.) [adopted as submitted].

Recent WTO Disputes and Related Issues Involving Korea*

KANG Sung-Jin
Advisor, Kim & Chang, Seoul, Korea; PhD, Korea University; LLM, University of Michigan

1. INTRODUCTION

For the last few years, Korea has been an active user of the WTO dispute settlement system. This paper provides brief summaries of the recent WTO cases involving Korea, as well as Korea's participation in the WTO reform process.

2. RECENT WTO CASES INVOLVING KOREA

2-1. Korea as a Complainant

2-1-1. *United States — Anti-Dumping and Countervailing Measures on Large Residential Washers from Korea (WT/DS464/R, WT/DS464/AB/R)*

This dispute was about Definitive anti-dumping and countervailing duties applied by the US Department of Commerce ("USDOC") on imports of large residential washers from Korea. In 2013, the USDOC

* The views expressed in this paper is strictly personal, and does not reflect any views or opinion of the office. All mistakes belong to the author.

imposed antidumping duties of 9.29% (Samsung Electronics), 13.02% (LG Electronics) and countervailing duties of 1.95% against Samsung. Korea requested consultation to the U.S. on August 29, 2013.

Before the Panel and Appellate Body (AB), Korea argued that the price comparison methodology by the USDOC was inconsistent with the WTO Anti-Dumping Agreement as well as the Agreement on Subsidies and Countervailing Measures. The Panel and AB found that 1) the U.S. acted inconsistently with Article 2.4.2 of the ADA by failing to explain why it cannot take into account both the weighted average-to-weighted average ("W-W") and the transaction-to-transaction methodologies ("T-T") before having recourse to the weighted average-to-transaction ("W-T") methodology; 2) the exclusion of non-pattern transactions in establishing dumping margins under the W-T methodology was consistent with the Article 2.4 of the ADA; 3) the U.S. acted inconsistently with Articles 2.4.2, 2.4, and 9.3 and GATT Article VI: 2 when it applied "zeroing" in the W-T methodology; 4) Korea provided certain subsidies to certain enterprises located in a designated region within the Korean territory, and therefore, Korea had failed to establish that the USDOC's determination of regional specificity was inconsistent with Article 2.2 of the ASCM; 5) USDOC's attribution of Korea's subsidies to Samsung was incorrect, which resulted in countervailing duties in excess of the subsidization margin, in violation of Article 19.4 of the ASCM and GATT Article VI: 3.

The DSB adopted the Panel and AB reports on September 26, 2016, and the U.S. stated its intention to implement the DSB's recommendations. However, Korea argued that the U.S. failed to implement the DSB's recommendation and brought the case for an arbitration to authorize suspension of concession under Article 22.6 of the DSU. On February 8, 2019, an arbitral tribunal granted Korea to impose retaliatory measures amounting to US$74.40 million (Antidumping duty) and US$10.41 million (Countervailing duty) annually, adjusted by inflation.[1]

2-1-2. *United States — Anti-Dumping Measures on Certain Oil Country Tubular Goods from Korea (WT/DS488/R)*

Korea challenged the USDOC's final anti-dumping duties on imports of oil country tubular goods (OCTG) from Korea on September 10, 2014, and its remand determination on February 22, 2016, following the US Court of International Trade's remand orders. In its Panel report dated November 14, 2017, the Panel found that the remand determination in 2016 was outside its terms of reference, and focused on the USDOC's original determination in 2014.

The Panel rejected most of Korea's claims regarding the U.S. laws on normal value calculation, construction of export prices, cost calculation, etc. However, the Panel found that "the USDOC failed to determine constructive value (CV) profit using the respondents' actual data pertaining to home market sales, finding that the USDOC had no basis for not using data pertaining to those sales as a basis for determining CV profit."

The Panel also found that the USDOC defined "the same general category of products" more narrowly than "the like product," by excluding some OCTG products which would otherwise have been "like products."

The Panel also held that USDOC acted inconsistently with Article 2.2.2(iii) by failing to calculate and apply a profit cap. The Panel also held that the profit determined by the USDOC was not a "reasonable amount" within the meaning of Article 2.2 of the Anti-Dumping Agreement, as it was calculated without profit cap.

The implementation of this case is still pending, as Korea and the U.S. agreed to set the reasonable period of time to July 12, 2019.

2-2. Korea as a Respondent

2-2-1. *Korea — Import Bans, and Testing and Certification Requirements for Radionuclides (WT/DS495/R, WT/DS495/ AB/R)*

After a huge accident at the Fukushima Daiichi nuclear power plant which caused massive scale of radioactive contamination, the Korean government imposed (a) import bans on certain food products from 8 Japanese Prefectures in the Northeast Honshu Island; and (b) additional testing and certification requirements regarding the presence of certain radionuclides as a result of the public awareness of the issue.

On May 21, 2015, Japan requested consultations with Korea alleging that Korea's measures were inconsistent with its obligations under the WTO's Agreement on Sanitary and Phytosaniary Measures (SPS Agreement). The Panel report was circulated to Members on February 22, 2018.

In the Panel Report, the Panel found that Korea's additional testing requirements and blanket import bans to 28 fishery products from 8 Japanese prefectures were maintained in a manner inconsistent with Article 5.6 of the SPS Agreement, because they were more trade-restrictive than required.

In addition, the Panel found that the additional testing requirements and blanket import bans were inconsistent with Article 2.3, first sentence of the SPS Agreement and, as a consequence, with Article 2.3, second sentence, when Korea adopted them. The Panel also found that Korea's failure to publish all measures and Korea's SPS Enquiry Point's failure to respond at all to Japan's follow-up query in conjunction with its earlier failure, were sufficient to establish that Korea acted inconsistently with the obligation in Annex B(3) and as a consequence Article 7 of the SPS Agreement.

However, the Appellate Body reversed key parts of the Panel's findings: Article 5.6 and 2.3 of the SPS Agreement, while upholding other arguments presented before it.

1) **Article 5.6 of the SPS Agreement**: Korea argued that Korea's appropriate level of protection (ALOP) had both quantitative and qualitative elements, and the Panel disregarded this. Appellate Body found that the Panel's analysis of the alternative measure proposed by Japan effectively focused only on the quantitative element of Korea's ALOP. The Appellate Body concluded that, having identified all elements of Korea's ALOP, the Panel erred by not accounting for all of these elements in its assessment under Article 5.6, and therefore reversed the Panel's finding.[2]

2) **Article 2.3 of the SPS Agreement**: Korea argued that the Panel erroneously treated the risk present in products as the only relevant "condition" under Article 2.3, to the exclusion of conditions in the territories of different Members. The Appellate Body found that the Panel erred in its interpretation of Article 2.3 by considering that relevant "conditions" under this provision may be exclusively limited to "the risk present in products." The Appellate Body considered that the analysis under Article 2.3 would entail consideration of all relevant conditions in different Members, and thus the AB reversed the Panel findings under Article 2.3.[3]

This case gained high media attention as Japan challenged only Korea's measures to prohibit imports of the seafoods from the 8 Northeastern Prefectures of Japan. At the same time, this is the first case where the AB reversed key findings of the Panel in an SPS-related case. In this regard, this case set an important precedent in the WTO dispute settlement system.

2-2-2. *Korea — Anti-Dumping Duties on Pneumatic Valves from Japan (WT/DS504/R)*

Korea Trade Commission (KTC) imposed anti-dumping duties on Pneumatic valves from Japan on January 20, 2015. Japan challenged the KTC's dumping calculation as well as causation analysis before the WTO Panel, and the WTO Panel issued report on April 12, 2018.

While the Panel rejected most of Japan's arguments, the Panel upheld one particular argument regarding causation. There was consistent "overselling" of the Japanese imports, which undermined the KTC's price effects analysis. Japan argued that it undermined the KTC's findings of causation between dumped price and the domestic injury.[4]

In upholding Japan's argument, the Panel found that: (1) there was not sufficient evidence on the record to demonstrate whether and how the Office of Trade Investigation (OTI) conducted the necessary simulations and analysis about this issue, and how it reached the relevant conclusions; and (2) customer statements, even combined with the large number of price comparisons in the evidence, did not adequately explain the KTC's price suppression and depression findings, in light of the consistent average price overselling by the dumped imports. As a result, Japan won the key issue of the case. However, the case is currently pending before the AB, and we will have to see how it will end.

3. WTO REFORM AND KOREA

On October 25, 2018, delegations of 13 governments including Korea issued a joint communique for the reform of the WTO.[5] In this Joint Communique, the delegations emphasized "the urgent need to unblock the appointment of Appellate Body members" and called for discussions to address the concerns on the future of the WTO dispute settlement system. Since then, the EU, the US, and other governments submitted the proposal for reform. Right now, Korea supports 1) the EU's proposal on November 27, 2018; and 2) communique at the G20 Summit on the WTO reform, while it has not submitted its own WTO reform proposal. However, Korea may need to prepare its own reform proposal to actively engage in the discussion on the reform of the WTO dispute settlement system, especially the dispute settlement system, as Korea has been one of the major beneficiaries of the system.

Notes

1. Decision by Arbitrator, *United States — Anti-Dumping and Countervailing Measures on Large Residential Washers from Korea* (22.6), WT/DS464/ARB.
2. AB Report, *Korea — Import Bans, and Testing and Certification Requirements for Radionuclides*, WT/DS495/R, WT/DS495/AB/R, paras. 5.18. - 5.39.
3. *Ibid.*, paras. 5.53 - 5.93.
4. Panel Report, *Korea — Anti-Dumping Duties on Pneumatic Valves from Japan*, WT/DS504/R, paras. 7.297 - 7.322.
5. Joint Communiqué of the Ottawa Ministerial on WTO Reform, https://www.canada.ca/en/global-affairs/news/2018/10/joint-communique-of-the-ottawa-ministerial-on-wto-reform.html (Visited on April 24, 2019).

Judicial Decisions in Public International Law (2018)*

LEE Keun-Gwan
Professor, School of Law, Seoul National University, Seoul, Korea

Supreme Court Judgment No. 2013DA61381 Rendered on October 30, 2018

(A 4-member chamber of the Supreme Court rendered a judgment on 24 May 2012 (No. 2009DA68620), remanding the case to the Seoul High Court. The latter court rendered a judgment on 10 July 2013 (No. 2012NA44947). The defendant, Nippon Steel Corporation(in Japanese, *Shin Nittetsu Sumikin*), appealed again from the latter judgment to the Supreme Court. In October 2018, the full chamber of the Supreme Court rendered this judgment).

Main Issue

Whether claims held by the Korean individuals forced into labor during the 2nd World War were covered and extinguished by the 1965 Claims Settlement Agreement

* The cases presented in this section are selected and translated from "Korean Judicial Decisions Related to Public International Law" edited by Professor Chung In-Seop (School of Law, Seoul National University) as carried in *Seoul International Law Journal*, volume 25 no. 2. The editor of this section sincerely acknowledges Prof. Chung's great efforts at systematically documenting Korean judicial practice in public international law.

Facts

In the period extending from 1941 to 1945, the plaintiffs, Korean nationals, were forced into labor in various steelworks run by the defendant. The working conditions were extremely severe and the wages were not properly paid. The plaintiffs returned to Korea after the defeat of Japan in 1945. Even after the conclusion of the 1965 Claims Settlement Agreement between Korea and Japan,[1] no satisfactory compensation was provided to them. In 1997, some of the plaintiffs instituted lawsuits against the defendant in Japan. However, their claims were finally rejected by the Japanese Supreme Court in 2003. In 2005, the plaintiffs instituted lawsuits against the defendant before a Korean court. The Korean courts of first and second instance declined to accept the plaintiffs' arguments in 2008 and 2009 respectively. On appeal to the Supreme Court, a 4-member chamber of the Court revoked the original judgment and remanded the case to the Seoul High Court in May 2012. In July 2013, the latter court rendered a judgment in accordance with the 2012 judgment of the Supreme Court. The defendant then re-appealed to the Supreme Court. After a 5-year delay, the full chamber of the Supreme Court handed down this 'historic' judgement in October 2018.

Judgment

Majority Opinion

"In the light of the actual facts of this case and the following circumstances ascertainable from the evidence admitted in court, it cannot be accepted that the claims for damages put forth by the plaintiff against the defendant were included within the subject-matter of the [1965] Claims Settlement Agreement. The reasons are as follows.

(1) It is necessary to make clear in advance that the plaintiffs'

claim for damages in this case concern the claim for solatium, put forth by the victims of forced mobilization, against the Japanese companies involved in the mobilization (hereinafter, "claim for *solatium* for forced mobilization"). Such forced mobilization was directly connected with Japan's illegal colonial domination over the Korean peninsula and its waging of war of aggression, entailing the concerned company's liability for the illegal acts of an inhumane character. The plaintiffs are requesting in this case *vis-à-vis* the defendant, not the payment of unpaid wages or personal compensation, but the payment of *solatium* for forced mobilization.

[The Court goes on to establish: (i) the defendant, that is, the former Nippon Steel, actively cooperated with the Japanese Government in the policy of forcefully mobilizing labor force for the purpose of prosecuting wars of aggression such as the Sino-Japanese War (1937-1945) and the Pacific War (1941-1945); (ii) "against the background of Japan's illegal and brutal domination over the Korean peninsula and the Korean people, the plaintiffs, poorly informed of what kind of labor they would engage in under what circumstances, were mobilized by means of systematic deceit"; (iii) the defendants were forced into labor under very harsh circumstances, for instance, "under the atrocious system of war-time total mobilization put in place by the Japanese Government, it was difficult to leave the company premises. Due to the constant surveillance, it was impossible to escape from the labor sites and, if caught in the attempt to escape, severe corporal punishment was meted out"; (iv) "such acts committed by the former Nippon Steel against the plaintiffs constituted illegal acts of an inhumane nature that were directly connected with the illegal colonial domination over Korea and the prosecution of wars of aggression by the Japanese Government. It is empirically clear that the plaintiffs should have suffered emotional distress because of the illegal acts."]

(2) Considering the negotiating process of the Claims Settlement

Agreement and the relevant circumstances, in particular, the following ones, it appears that the Claims Settlement Agreement was not an agreement to settle the question of compensation for the wrongs arising from Japan's illegal colonial rule. It was concluded for the purposes of settling, on the basis of Article 4 of the San Francisco Peace Treaty, the claims and debts of a financial or civil character subsisting between Korea and Japan.

① … Article 4(a) of the San Francisco Treaty, which was concluded between the 48 Allied Powers (including the United States of America) and Japan, provides that "the disposition of the claims and debts of a financial character between the authorities presently administering the areas released from the Japanese rule (including the Republic of Korea) and the nationals, on the one hand, and Japan and its nationals, on the other, shall be the subject of special arrangements between such authorities and Japan."[2]

② The first round of negotiations between Korea and Japan (from 15 February 1951 until 25 April 1951) was held soon after the conclusion of the San Francisco Peace Treaty. During the negotiations, the Korean side put forth the list of 'Eight Items' which concerned basically the claims and debts of a financial or civil character subsisting between Korea and Japan. Among the eight items, paragraph 5 mentioned "settlement of the unpaid wages, compensation and other claims held by the Koreans forced into labor." However, within the document setting out the eight items there was nothing premised on the illegality of Japanese colonial domination. From this it follows that the above-mentioned paragraph 5 did not take the illegality of Japanese colonial domination as its premise. Therefore, it is difficult to interpret "settlement of the unpaid wages, compensation and other claims held by the Koreans forced into labor" as including the claim for solatium for forced mobilization.

③ According to the 'White Paper on the Korea-Japan Negotiations' published by the Korean Government on 20 March 1965, Article 4 of the San Francisco Peace Treaty constituted the basis for the negotiations for the claims settlement between Korea and Japan. The document went on to explain as follows. "The claims against Japan as provided for in Article 4 [of the San Francisco Peace Treaty] is different from the claims for reparations held by the victorious powers [as provided for in Article 14 of the Treaty]. Because Korea was not a party to the San Francisco Peace Treaty, its claim for reparations for 'damage and suffering' as enjoyed by the victorious powers was not recognized. Such claims for reparations cannot be included in the questions of claims between Korea and Japan."

④ The illegality of Japanese colonial domination was not mentioned anywhere in the text of the Claims Settlement Agreement or its Annexes.[3] Article 2(1) of the Agreement provides that "the problems concerning the claims … including those stipulated in Article IV(a) of the San Francisco Treaty have been settled completely and finally."[4] Based on this provision, one could argue that the claims other than those included in Article 4(a) of the Treaty were capable of being the subject-matter of the Agreement. However, considering the fact that the illegality of Japanese colonial domination was not mentioned at all, it is difficult to regard the claims going beyond those included in Article 4(a), that is, the claims directly connected with the illegality of colonial domination, as having been covered by the Agreement. Paragraph 2(g) of the First Agreed Minutes to the Claims Settlement Agreement also stops at just providing that the claims falling under the purview of the Eight Items should be included in 'those to be settled completely and finally.'

⑤ The 2005 Civil Society-Government Joint Committee put forth the official opinion that "the Claims Settlement Agreement was basically intended to settle the claims and debts of a financial or civil character subsisting between Korea and Japan on the basis of Article 4 of the San Francisco Peace Treaty, not to resolve the question of reparations for the Japanese colonial domination."

(3) Furthermore, it is not clear whether there exists a relationship of contractual consideration or legal *quid pro quo* between the monies provided by Japan to Korea for economic cooperation under Article 1 of the Agreement, on the one hand, and the settlement of claims as provided for in Article 2, on the other hand.

It is true that Article 1 of the Agreement provides for the supply of grants in the amount of 300 million US dollars and of loans in the amount of 200 million US dollars. However, there is no indication whatsoever for what purpose the grants and loans were provided. … The preamble of the Agreement mentions the 'settlement of questions of property and claims,' but there is no provision within the Agreement that is specifically connected with the provision of 500 million US dollars (300 million US dollars in grants, 200 million US dollars in loans). … At the time [of conclusion of the Agreement], Japan's position was that the monies to be supplied under Article 1 of the Agreement were basically intended for economic cooperation and that there existed no legal relationship of contractual consideration or legal *quid pro quo* between Article 1 and 2 of the Agreement.

(4) The 2005 Civil Society-Government Joint Committee opined that the Korean Government had been placed under a 'moral obligation' to use substantial part of the grants supplied by Japan for the purpose of providing remedies for the victims of forced mobilization. It also concluded that the compensation scheme implemented according to the 1975 Act on Compensation for the Claims against Japan Held by Civilians had been insufficient from 'moral perspective.' Both the 2007 Act and the 2010 Act on the Support for the Victims [of Forced Mobilization] make clear that the monies provided under the Acts for consolation of or support for the victims are of 'a humanitarian character.' [This means that the Korean Government did not provide these monies in discharge of its legal duties that might

have been brought into existence by the receipt of grants in accordance with Article 1 of the Agreement. Therefore, according to the Court, the question of compensating the individual Korean victims remains unresolved at the 'legal dimension.' *Ed.*] As a result, the two Governments could not reach consensus on the legal characterization of Imperial Japan's rule over the Korean peninsula. Under the circumstances, it is difficult to conclude that the claims for *solatium* for forced mobilization was included within the subject-matter of the Claims Settlement Agreement.

(5) The evidence additionally submitted by the defendant [to the Busan High Court to which the case was remanded by the Supreme Court in May 2012] does not affect the above conclusion that the claims for *solatium* for forced mobilization was not included within the subject-matter of the Claims Settlement Agreement.

According to this [additional] evidence, it comes to light that on 10 May 1961 in one of the preparatory meetings for the 5th round of negotiations, the Korean side adverted to 'compensation for the mental and physical suffering inflicted on the nationals of another State who were forcefully mobilized into labor.' It is also ascertained that on 15 December 1961 in one of the preparatory meetings for the 6th round of negotiations, the Korean side asked for the amount of 1.22 billion US dollars as compensation for the Eight Items, out of which amount 364 million US dollars (approximately 30 % of the total amount) was allotted for the compensation of damage and suffering for the forced mobilization (the amount of 364 million was calculated based on the following: 200 US dollars to be paid to each survivor, 1,650 dollars for each deceased, 2,000 dollars for each disabled).

However, such statements, being no more than mere remarks made in the middle of negotiations, did not represent the official position of Korea or Japan. It needs to be noted that they were not put forth in a consistent manner during the negotiations extending for

13 years. There is much basis for interpreting that 'compensation for the mental and physical suffering inflicted on the nationals of another State who were forcefully mobilized into labor' was raised merely for the purpose of securing a favorable position in the negotiations. Indeed, the 5th round of negotiations was not brought to a successful conclusion due to Japan's intransigence. Furthermore, despite the fact that the amount of 1.22 billion dollars was put forward, the finally agreed amount was no more than 300 million dollars (counting only grants). It would beggar belief to conclude that, even when the settlement was reached with the receipt of an amount which far undershoots the amount asked for, the claims for *solatium* for forced mobilization was included within the subject-matter of the Claims Settlement Agreement.

The judgment by the original court to which the case was remand that the claims for *solatium* for forced mobilization was not included within the subject-matter of the Claims Settlement Agreement is correct. In that judgment, no reversible error can be found concerning the interpretation of the subject-matter of and the legal consequences arising from the Claims Settlement Agreement and other matters, as was asserted in the grounds for appeal to the Supreme Court.

In the meanwhile, the defendant claims in the relevant part of its grounds for appeal to the Supreme Court, proceeding from the premise that the claim for *solatium* for the forced mobilization was included in the subject-matter of the Claims Settlement Agreement, that not only the right of diplomatic protection held by States, but also the individual claims themselves were waived and extinguished through the conclusion of the Claims Settlement Agreement. However, this claim is based on the hypothetical consideration engaged in by the court below to which the case was remanded, not deserving of any further examination."

Joint Separate Opinion by Justices Kim So-Young, Lee Dong-won and Noh Jeong-hee

"A. We concur in the conclusion reached by the majority that the plaintiffs are entitled to exercise their claims *vis-à-vis* the defendant despite the Claims Settlement Agreement. However, we do not share the reasoning offered by the majority.

The majority hold that "the claims for compensation put forth by the plaintiffs *vis-à-vis* the defendant cannot be regarded as having been included in the subject-matter of the Claims Settlement Agreement." However, a correct interpretation of the Agreement would be to regard the claims for compensation held by the plaintiffs as having been included in the subject-matter of the Agreement. The caveat is that the individual claims of the plaintiffs as such cannot be considered to have been extinguished by the Agreement. What was renounced by the conclusion of the Agreement was the right of diplomatic protection held by the Republic of Korea only. Therefore, the plaintiffs are still entitled to exercise their rights by instituting lawsuits in Korea against the defendant.

The reasons for such a conclusion are as follows.

A. We do not differ from the majority in respect of what method should be employed to interpret the given treaty. When one looks at the facts of the case on the basis of the evidence lawfully considered and adopted by the original court [the Supreme Court which handed down the judgment on 24 May 2012], complemented by the evidence submitted to the lower court seized of the case after remand [the Seoul High Court which rendered the judgment on 10 July 2013] … it would be correct to hold that, differently from the majority, the claims for compensation held by the plaintiffs *vis-à-vis* the defendant was included in the subject-matter of the Claims Settlement Agreement.

[The three justices go on to discuss "the detailed process leading to the conclusion of the Claims Settlement Agreement as ascertained by the adopted evidence."]

…

At the 13th meeting of the General Claims Subcommittee of the Preliminary Talks for the 5th round of Korea-Japan Negotiations which was held on 10 May 1961, the Korean side submitted its request to the Japanese side for 'compensation for the individuals who suffered as a consequence of forced mobilization'. This question was part of Item 5 (Request for satisfaction of claims including those relating to the banknotes of the Bank of Japan held by the Korean legal and natural persons, the unpaid wages and compensation of Koreans subjected to forced mobilization) of the 'Eight Items.' The Korean side clarified that it was putting forth 'claims for compensation for all those subjected to forced mobilization including the survivors, the injured, the dead, the missing, and the military personnel and the civilians attached to the military.' The Korean side further explained that the compensation was "for the mental and physical sufferings inflicted upon those [Koreans] who were forcibly mobilized as foreigners." Being confronted with this request, the Japanese side inquired the Korean counterpart of whether the Korean side was asking for compensation for the Korean individuals and whether the Korean Government was willing to conduct detailed investigations into the Korean victims. In response to this inquiry, the Korean side made clear that it was "demanding the compensation as a country [and that] individual compensations would be handled domestically."

…

At the 7th meeting of the Subcommittee on General Claims of the Preliminary Talks for the 6th round of Korea-Japan Negotiations which was held on 15 December 1961, the Korean side demanded the total amount of 1.22 billion US dollars for the satisfaction of claims enumerated in the 'Eight Items.' In so doing, it set the compensation for the damage caused by forced mobilization at 364 million US dollars (calculated based on 200 dollars per survivor,

1,650 dollars per war dead, 2,000 dollars for an injured individual).

...

The preamble to the Claims Settlement Agreement prefaces that "Japan and the Republic of Korea, desiring to settle problems regarding the property of both countries and their peoples and the claims between both countries and between their peoples, and desiring to promote economic cooperation between the two countries, have agreed as follows." Article 2(1) of the Agreement provides that "The High Contracting Parties confirm that the problems concerning property, rights, and interests of the two High Contracting Parties and their peoples (including juridical persons) and the claims between the High Contracting Parties and between their peoples, including those stipulated in Article IV(a) of the Peace Treaty with Japan signed at the city of San Francisco on September 8, 1951, have been settled completely and finally."

The Agreed Minutes (I) to the Claims Settlement Agreement which was concluded on the same day as the Agreement provides concerning Article 2 of the Agreement that "the problems concerning [property, rights, and interests] and the claims which are regarded as having been settled completely and finally in Article 2(1) shall include all the claims falling under the purview of 'Outlines of Korea's Claims *vis-à-vis* Japan' (the so-called 'Eight Items'), and consequently it is confirmed that no claim whatsoever shall be raised concerning the Outlines of Korea's Claims." Paragraph 5 of the 'Eight Items' includes 'request for satisfaction of claims including the unpaid wages and compensation of Koreans subjected to forced mobilization.'

According to such wording of the Claims Settlement Agreement, it is evident that not only the claims of Korea and Japan against each other as a State, but also the claims of one party's nationals against the other party and its nationals were included in the subject-matter of the Agreement. The Agreed Minutes (I) to the

Claims Settlement Agreement makes clear that the claims arising from the forced mobilization were included in the subject-matter of the Claims Settlement Agreement.

…

Furthermore, the Republic of Korea promulgated and implemented the Act on Funds Secured by Claims Settlement and the Act on Registration of Claims to provide for the basic guidelines on how to disburse the funds secured by the Claims Settlement Agreement. In accordance with these Acts, the claims held by those Koreans who had been forced into labor by Japan and died before 15 August 1945 were included in the civilian claims to be settled under the Claims Settlement Agreement. The registration and settlement of the claims of those deceased [by paying 300,000 *won* per each deceased] was completed with the implementation of the Acts. This appears to be premised on the understanding that the claims for compensation held by those forced into labor were included in the subject-matter of the Claims Settlement Agreement.

[The three justices adduce some other practices corroborating the conclusion.]

In the light of the foregoing, that is, taking into account comprehensively the wording of the Claims Settlement Agreement and the Agreed Minutes to the Agreement, the circumstances surrounding the conclusion of the Agreement and the presumed intent of the parties, the measures taken subsequently to the conclusion of the Agreement and other relevant circumstances, it would be correct to hold that the claims of the victims of forced mobilization were included in the subject-matter of the Claims Settlement Agreement.

The lower court seized of the case after remand held, differently from the above conclusion, that it was difficult to regard the claims of the plaintiffs against the defendant as having been included in the subject-matter of the Claims Settlement Agreement. To that extent, the court was wrong in, among others, misunderstanding the law on treaty interpretation.

B. However, despite such mistake, the hypothetical judgment rendered by the lower court seized of the case after remand that "it would not be correct to conclude that the individual claims of the plaintiffs would be extinguished *ipso facto* with the conclusion of the Claims Settlement Agreement; the legal consequence of the Agreement is no more than the waiver of the right of diplomatic protection held by Korea as a State, meaning merely that Korea could not invoke its right of diplomatic protection even if the claims in question were to be extinguished by the measures taken by Japan through its domestic means" would be acceptable for the following reasons.

(1) There is no sufficient and clear ground in the Claims Settlement Agreement that supports the conclusion that there was consensus between the two Governments on the extinction of individual claims. …

(2) … Japan promulgated an Act on Measures on Property Rights immediately after the conclusion of the Claims Settlement Agreement to extinguish the rights of Korean nationals *vis-à-vis* Japan and its nationals within the territory of Japan. This measure can be understood only upon the premise that the Claims Settlement Agreement alone cannot extinguish the claims held by individual Korean nationals. As we saw above, it is the clear position of Japan that the conclusion of the Claims Settlement Agreement had the consequence of, not the extinction of claims held by individuals, but merely the waiver of States' right of diplomatic protection. The other party to the Agreement, that is, Korea, appears to have been well aware of this position. Therefore, it would be reasonable to consider that the genuine will of both parties converged on the view that only the right of diplomatic protection was waived.

…

(3) In connection with the effect and interpretation of lump-sum agreements, the judgment rendered by the International Court of

Justice on 3 February 2012 in the case of *Jurisdictional Immunities of the State* (Germany v. Italy: Greece intervening) is being discussed from international law perspective. However, to say nothing of many other points at issue, the circumstances surrounding the conclusion of the Treaty on the Settlement of Certain Property-Related, Economic and Financial Questions and the Agreement on Compensation for Italian Nationals Subjected to National-Socialist Measures of Persecution (both of which were concluded between Italy and West Germany on 2 June 1961), and their content and wording are not similar to those of the Claims Settlement Agreement. It would not be appropriate to compare the Claims Settlement Agreement with those treaties between Italy and West Germany in simple terms.

C. In conclusion, we cannot concur in the position of the majority that the claims held by the plaintiffs *vis-à-vis* the defendant are not included in the subject-matter of the Claims Settlement Agreement. However, the conclusion reached by the lower court seized of the case after remand that the plaintiffs are entitled to exercise their claims against the defendant despite the conclusion of the Claims Settlement Agreement is correct."

<u>Joint Dissenting Opinion of Justices Kwon Soon-il and Cho Jae-youn</u>

We concur in the Separate Opinion of Justices Kim So-young, Lee Dong-won and Noh Jeong-hee to the effect that the proper interpretation of the Claims Settlement Agreement is that the claims of the plaintiffs are included in the subject-matter of the Claims Settlement Agreement.

However, we find it difficult to agree to their conclusion that merely the waiver of the right of diplomatic protection held by Korea as a State resulted from the Claims Settlement Agreement and that, as a result, the plaintiffs are entitled to exercise their rights by instituting lawsuits in Korea against the defendant. The reasons are as follows.

...

(3) The preamble to the Claims Settlement Agreement prefaces that "Japan and the Republic of Korea, desiring to settle problems regarding the property of both countries and their peoples and the claims between both countries and between their peoples, and desiring to promote economic cooperation between the two countries, have agreed as follows." Article 2(1) of the Agreement provides that "The High Contracting Parties confirm that the problems concerning property, rights, and interests of the two High Contracting Parties and their peoples (including juridical persons) and the claims between the High Contracting Parties and between their peoples, including those stipulated in Article IV(a) of the Peace Treaty … have been settled completely and finally." Article 2(3) provides that " … no claims shall be made with respect … to all the claims of either High Contracting Party and its people ... ." Furthermore, the Agreed Minutes (I) to the Claims Settlement Agreement provides concerning Article 2 of the Agreement that "the problems concerning property, rights, and interests and the claims which are regarded as having been settled completely and finally in Article 2(1) shall include all the claims falling under the purview of 'Outlines of Korea's Claims *vis-à-vis* Japan' (the so-called 'Eight Items'), and consequently it is confirmed that no claim shall be raised concerning the Outlines of Korea's Claims." The Outlines of Claims against Japan ('Eight Items') includes 'request for satisfaction of claims including the unpaid wages and compensation of Koreans subjected to forced mobilization.'

If one interprets Article 2 of the Claims Settlement Agreement in accordance with the ordinary meaning to be given to its terms in the light of the terms of Article 2 of the Claims Settlement Agreement, the Agreed Minutes (I) to the Claims Settlement Agreement and other relevant documents, and the context and the object and purpose of the Claims Settlement Agreement, it is evident that "those which have been settled completely and finally" refer to the problems concerning all the claims of Korea and Korean nationals against Japan and Japanese nationals, and all the claims of Japan and Japanese nationals against Korea and Korean nationals. Since Article 2(3) provides that "no claims shall be made," the phrase "have been settled completely and finally" should be interpreted to mean that not only both parties but also their nationals could not exercise their claims any more. …

It is in conformity with the ordinary meaning of the terms to interpret the terms "have been settled completely and finally" as provided for in Article 2(1) to mean that the problems concerning the claims have been settled completely and finally not only between the contracting States but also between their nationals. It cannot be interpreted to mean an agreement merely between the contracting States not to exercise the right of diplomatic protection against each other.

…

(4) Since the conclusion of the Claims Settlement Agreement, Japan has taken the position that the conclusion of the Agreement resulted in merely the waiver of the right of diplomatic protection, not in the extinction of claims held by individuals. This is ascribable to the fact that the Japanese Government has taken the position that "Japan waived its right of diplomatic protection concerning the claims held by Japanese nationals" in order to avoid its own duty of compensation for its own people. However, as will be shown below, the Republic of Korea from the very beginning demanded compensation for the victims of forced mobilization by putting forth the Outlines of Claims against Japan ('Eight Items') and took the position that the distribution of monies to be provided by Japan was purely a matter of [Korean] domestic law, which position it persisted in maintaining until the conclusion of the Claims Settlement Agreement.

The following can be ascertained from the factual circumstances we have considered above and the records. ① The Korean side put forward the 'Eight Items' to the Japanese side on 15 February 1952 during the 1st round of Korea-Japan Talks. At the 13th meeting of the General Claims Subcommittee of the Preliminary Talks for the 5th round of Korea-Japan Negotiations which was held on 10 May 1961, the Korean side submitted its request to the Japanese side for 'compensation for the individuals who suffered as a consequence of forced mobilization.' When the Japanese side inquired the Korean counterpart of whether the Korean side was asking for compensation for the Korean individuals, the Korean side clarified its position that it was "demanding the compensation as a country [and that] individual compensations would be handled domestically." ② At the 7th meeting of the Subcommittee on General Claims of the Preliminary Talks for the 6th round of Korea-Japan Negotiations which was held on 15 December 1961, the Korean side demanded the total amount of 1.22 billion US dollars for the satisfaction of claims enumerated in the 'Eight Items.' In so doing, it set the compensation for the damage caused by forced mobilization at 364 million US dollars ③ On 5 July 1965, that is, immediately after the conclusion of the Claims Settlement Agreement, he Korean Government published "*Daehan Minguk gwa Ilbonguk ganui Joyak mit Hyeopjeong Haeseol*" [The Treaty and Agreements between Korea and Japan Explained]. In the publication, it is recorded that "As regards the content of our property and claims to be extinguished ['*somyeol*'] through the provisions on the settlement of problems of property and claims, all those which we demanded from Japan by putting forward the 'Eight Items' at the beginning [of the negotiations] will be extinguished. Therefore, … the claims for unpaid wages and compensation … the claims held by Korean nationals *vis-à-vis* the Japanese Government and Japanese nationals will be all extinguished completely and finally." ④ In August 1965, the then Minister of the Board of Economic Planning stated that the grant in the amount of 300 million US dollars as provided for in Article 1 of the Claims Settlement

Agreement in effect had the character of compensation for the Korean victims. ⑤ After the conclusion of the Claims Settlement Agreement, the Korean Government paid out compensation for the victims of forced mobilization by adopting the laws such as the Act on the Fund Secured by the Claims Settlement, the Act on the Registration of Claims against the Japanese Side, the Acts on Provision of Support for the Victims (2007 and 2010 respectively). The total amount of *wirogeum* [consolation money] paid out until September 2016 based on the decisions rendered by the Commission for the Verification and Support for the Victims of Forced Mobilization under Japanese Colonialism in Korea (the decisions rendered by the predecessor of this commission, that is, the Commission for the Support of Victims Forcibly Mobilized during or in connection with the Pacific War, are also included) is as follows: 360.1 billion KR won as consolation money for the dead and the disappeared, 102.2 billion won as consolation money for the injured, 52.2 billion won for the unpaid wages, 800,000 won per person for medical support, the total amount coming to approximately 550 billion won.

Taking into these facts comprehensively, it is ascertainable that at the time of conclusion of the Claims Settlement Agreement Korea took the position that with the conclusion of the Agreement the claims of individual victims would be extinguished or at least limitations would be placed on the exercise of them. Therefore, it would not be correct to hold that the genuine intention of both parties converged on the waiver of the right of diplomatic protection only.

(5) On the other hand, the so-called 'lump-sum agreements' through which sovereign States, after conducting diplomatic negotiations, reach an across-the-board resolution of problems concerning property or interests of their respective nationals in cases such as post-war compensation, was a generally recognized form of treaties under customary international law which served as a means for the prevention or settlement of international disputes.

Lump-sum agreements are an avenue used by States to bring about an across-the-board settlement to the pending problems including claims held by individuals. Therefore, these agreements are premised on the extinction of claims held by the nationals of a State in exchange for the compensation received from the other State. This remains unaffected whether the funds thus received were not used for the satisfaction of claims held by the nationals of the receiving State. (In this regard, one is referred to the case of *Jurisdictional Immunities of the State*, Germany v. Italy: Greece intervening, commonly known as *Ferrini* case)

As regards the Claims Settlement Agreement, Korea received from Japan a lump sum concerning the Outlines of Claims against Japan ('Eight Items') which included the claims for compensation held by the victims of forced mobilization. Korea transferred [part of] the funds thus received [from Japan] directly to the individual victims; it also adopted the 'indirect' mode of compensation by using the funds for the development of national economy such as the reconstruction of infrastructure. In the light of such circumstances, the Claims Settlement Agreement, as a treaty intended to settle, in an across-the-board manner, the questions of compensation for the Korean Government and its nationals, can be regarded as falling under the category of lump-sum agreement which enjoyed wide international acceptance when the Claims Settlement Agreement was concluded. In the light of this fact as well, it is difficult to interpret that the Agreement was intended for the waiver of the right of diplomatic protection only, leaving untouched the question of claims held by individual victims.

C. It would be correct to interpret the phrases "have been settled completely and finally" and "no claims shall be made" as stipulated in Article 2 of the Claims Settlement Agreement as meaning that "Korean nationals are restricted from exercising their rights *vis-à-vis* Japan or Japanese nationals by means of lawsuits," if not going so far as to interpret those phrases as meaning the complete extinction of individual claims.

…

It is true that there still is a controversy over how to historically evaluate the decision by the Korean Government to go ahead with the conclusion of the Claims Settlement Agreement while the Japanese Government declined to recognize the illegality of its colonial domination in the negotiating process. However, if the Claims Settlement Agreement should not be regarded as null and void for the violation of the [Korean] Constitution or international law, it should be observed in accordance with its terms and contents, whether one likes it or not. The State should no longer procrastinate in providing just compensation for those [Korean] nationals who sustained a damage because they were prevented from making their individual claims due to the conclusion of the Claims Settlement Agreement. The obligation owed by the Korean Government to these individual victims is of a legal, not merely of a humanitarian or charitable nature. The Korean Government is under an obligation to provide just compensation irrespective of whether lawsuits are instituted; if lawsuits are instituted against itself, the Korean Government should not invoke the defence of extinctive prescription.

D. In conclusion, the claims held by Korean nationals against Japan or its nationals were, with the conclusion of the Claims Settlement Agreement, placed under such restriction that they could not be raised in the form of lawsuits, although the claims were not extinguished or waived as the direct effect of the Agreement. Therefore, it would be correct to interpret that the plaintiffs are restricted from making their claims *vis-à-vis* Japanese nationals as the defendants in Korean courts. The original court diverged from the reasoning offered in this opinion, misinterpreting the scope of application and the effect of the Claims Settlement Agreement. The view presented in the judgment ordering remand [judgement of 24

May 2012] on which the original court placed reliance should be amended to the extent of its incompatibility with the interpretation put forth in this opinion.

For these reasons, we dissent from the majority opinion."

[Justices Kim Jae-hyung and Kim Seon-soo attached a joint complementary opinion the translation of which is omitted here.]

Supreme Court Judgment No. 2016DO10912
Rendered on November 1, 2018

Main Issue

Whether refusal to perform military service for conscientious reasons falls under the category of 'legitimate reasons' [for exemption from military service] as provided for in Article 88(1) of the Act on Military Service

Facts

The accused in this case was a member of Jehovah's Witnesses. He refused to enlist in the Korean armed forces by reason of his religious conscience. He was prosecuted under Article 88(1) of the Act on Military Service and was sentenced to a one and half years' imprisonment in the courts of first and second instance. He appealed to the Supreme Court, arguing that the refusal to enlist by reason of religious conscience falls within the purview of 'legitimate reasons' of the Act because such refusal is in conformity with Article 19 of the Korean Constitution and freedom of conscience as provided for in the International Covenant on Civil and Political Rights (hereinafter, "ICCPR"). Until the rendition of this judgment, the Supreme Court and the Constitutional Court persisted in the view that 'conscientious objection' did not fall within the purview of 'legitimate reasons' as stipulated in Article 88(1) of the Act on Military Service.[5]

Judgment

Majority Opinion

"Criminal sanctions should not be imposed on those who, for the reason of conscience formed in one's innermost self, refuse to discharge the duty of military service which involves military training and use of [lethal] weapons. To impose the duty of military service on the conscientious objectors in a uniform manner and subject them to criminal sanctions in case of non-discharge of the duty is not reasonable in the light of the [Korean] Constitution that guarantees basic rights including freedom of conscience. It also violates the spirit of liberal democracy which sets great store by the tolerance and inclusion of minorities. Therefore, if one refuses, genuinely heeding the call of one's conscience, to discharge the duty of military service, this can be regarded as falling under one of the 'legitimate reasons' [for non-discharge of the duty]."

Joint Dissenting Opinion of Kim So-young, Cho Hee-de, Park Sang-ok and Lee Ki-taik

"(2) Consideration of the present state of international norms

(a) The accused claims, proceeding from the premise that Article 18 of the ICCPR has the same effect as domestic law, that the so-called 'right of conscientious objection' is derived from this provision.

(b) However, neither Article 18 of the ICCPR nor any other provision of the Covenant unambiguously stipulates it as one of the basic human rights by recognizing the right to refuse the duty of military service in accordance with one's own conscience. In the light of the terms of the Covenant such as Article 8, the ICCPR does not require the contracting party to recognize the right of conscientious objection without fail. Non-provision of an alternative service system cannot be simplistically regarded as being violative of the ICCPR. The criminal punishment of conscientious objectors in accordance with the relevant provision of the Act being discussed in this case [Article 81(1) of the Act on Military Service] without providing for the exemption of military service or the opportunities for alternative service does not constitute a violation of Article 18(1). (among others, Supreme Court judgment 2007DO7941; Constitutional Court decision 2008HEONGA22). Furthermore, even if the Human Rights Committee [established under the ICCPR] offered a recommendation, one would not be obligated to ascribe any legally binding force to it. (among other, Supreme Court judgment rendered 11 December 2014, 2014DO7972).

Furthermore, in considering whether to impose criminal sanctions on the conscientious objectors in a given State, it would not be appropriate, merely placing reliance on the superficial fact that a substantial number of states have abolished the military service or provide for alternative service, to compare in simple and abstract terms Korea and other countries. This is so in the light of the overwhelming significance and importance to be attributed to the national task of state security and territorial defence. *A contrario*, it is evident that, in deciding this question, the policy choice of each State, based on the widely differing and diverse factors such as the history and security environment, the system of social stratification, political, cultural, religious or philosophical values of each nation, should be more respected.

The relevant records show that the main reason why the Human Rights Committee, in dealing with the communications submitted by those other than the accused in this case, gave its views in which the Committee accepted the claims of those petitioners was that the petitioners should be granted the right of conscientious objection founded on their religious conviction in accordance with Article 18 of the ICCPR.

However, in the light of the reasons we have considered above, it is difficult for the views of the Human Rights Committee to enjoy the normatively binding force within the Korean domestic law. Furthermore, one of the core rationales of the Committee is the so-called 'right of conscientious objection' which the Constitutional Court as well as the Supreme Court have consistently declined to recognize, thus lacking compatibility with the domestic normative system. Therefore, one cannot regard the view of the Committee as evidence of change in the state of international norms which should be seriously taken into consideration.

(c) The same applies to the other grounds similarly invoked by the accused in his application for appeal to the Supreme Court such as the resolutions for member states adopted by the Human Rights Committee and the Human Rights Council, the results of reports by the Office of High Commissioner for Human Rights concerning Korea, the content of the Charter of Fundamental Rights of the European Union adopted by the European Parliament, the judgment rendered by the European Court of Human Rights in cases filed before the Court against member states [of the European Convention on Human Rights] because all of them diverge from the normative reality obtaining in Korea."

Joint Complementary Opinion by Justices Kwon Soon-il, Kim Jae-hyung, Cho Jae-youn and Min You-sook

"...

Interpretations offered by [the human rights bodies such as] the Human Rights Committee on [the international human rights treaties under which they are established such as] the ICPR should be respected. However, the interpretations cannot be said to be the terms [of the treaties] themselves, thus lacking in the legally binding force. The position of the European Union and the European Court of Human Rights cannot be regarded as rules of international law which are generally accepted or customary international law (among others, Supreme Court, judgment rendered on 27 December 2007, 2007DO7941; Constitutional Court, decision rendered n 26 July 2018, 2011HEONMA306). However, the above-mentioned change in the international attitude [towards the issue of conscientious objection] provides an important point of reference in deciding whether conscientious objection can be regarded as one of the 'legitimate reasons' under Article 88(1) of the Act on Military Service. It is because freedom of conscience is a universal question of humanity."

Joint Complementary Opinion by Justices Park Jung-hwa, Kim Seon-soo and Noh Jung-hee

"…

The dissenting opinion and the views of the Supreme Court and the Constitutional Court are not correct because it ignores the view of international society which accepts that the right of conscientious objection is derived from Article 18 of the ICCPR since the Human Rights Committee adopted in 1993 General Comment 22 [in which the Committee overturned its previous view that the question of whether to recognize the right of conscientious objection was a matter falling under the domestic jurisdiction of contracting parties. *Ed.*]. Not only the Human Rights Committee, but also the UN Commission on Human Rights functioning under the auspices of the UN Economic and Social Council (and the Human Rights Council which succeeded to the Commission in March 2006) and the European Court of Human Rights have consistently recognized that Article 18 of the ICCPR includes the right of conscientious objection, thus turning this interpretation into an international standard. If one insists on the narrow interpretation of the ICCPR which is a universal treaty on human rights, arguing that the ICCPR recognizes only 'those rights which are provided for in clear terms', then one ends up backing away from the meaningful performance of international duties provided for in the Covenant.

…

Even if one accepts the interpretation that the right of conscientious objection is not derived from Article 18 of the ICCPR itself, the General Comment of the Human Rights Committee, the recommendations offered after reviewing the reports submitted by the Korean Government, the views adopted by the Human Rights Committee in the cases of individual communication submitted by Korean nationals and the recommendations by the UN Human Rights Council should constitute, in the light of the constitutional principle of respect for international law, persuasive rationales for the interpretation of 'legitimate reasons' of Article 88(1) of the Act on Military Service.

…

The main rationales of the dissenting opinion are the particularity of Korea's historical, religious and cultural context and the particularity of severe reality in respect of national security. However, international covenants on human rights are norm-creating treaties of an objective character in that they create general norms similarly applicable to all the contracting parties. Such norms should be applied irrespective of how other parties implement them; excessive weight should not be given to the particular situation of a given State. In international covenants of human rights, the principle of reciprocity is not applied as in other traditional treaties. As Article 27 of the Vienna Convention on the Law of Treaties provides that "A party may not invoke the provisions of its internal law as justification for its failure to perform a treaty," Korea cannot justify its failure to perform duties arising from international by invoking the situation surrounding its domestic law. To respect the decisions or recommendations of international human rights bodies to the maximum extent possible and interpret the [domestic] law in a way compatible with the decisions or recommendations, thereby aiming to extricate itself from the violation of international law, would amount to acting in accordance with the constitutional principle of respect for international law. Given that human rights are universal rights evolving with the passage of time, it would be a disregard of the duty to respect international law if Korea, which is regarded by international society as an economically successful state, engages in the interpretation that negates the duty to observe the ICCPR, invoking the particular situation Korea is confronted with."

Notes

1. The full title of the Agreement is the Agreement between the Republic of Korea and Japan concerning the Settlement of Problems in Regard to Property and Claims and Economic Cooperation.
2. This is a condensed quotation of the original provision which reads "the disposition of property of Japan and of its nationals in the areas referred to in Article 2, and their claims, including debts, against the authorities presently administering such areas and the residents (including juridical persons) thereof, and the disposition in Japan of property of such authorities and residents, and of claims, including debts, of such authorities and residents against Japan and its nationals, shall be the subject of special arrangements between Japan and such authorities." The translation is from the wikisource which is not necessarily correct. <https://en.wikisource.org/wiki/Agreement_Between_Japan_and_the_Republic_of_Korea_Concerning_the_Settlement_of_Problems_in_Regard_to_Property_and_Claims_and_Economic_Cooperation>.
3. In connection with the Claims Settlement Agreement, no document entitled 'Annex' was adopted. The Court seems to have in mind the 2 protocols which constituted "an integral part of the Agreement," 4 exchanges of notes and 2 agreed minutes that were signed in the context of conclusion of the Agreement.
4. Article 2(1) of the 1965 Claims Settlement Agreement provides that "The High Contracting Parties confirm that the problems concerning property, rights, and interests of the two High Contracting Parties and their peoples (including juridical persons) and the claims between the High Contracting Parties and between their peoples, including those stipulated in Article IV(a) of the Peace Treaty with Japan signed at the city of San Francisco on September 8, 1951, have been settled completely and finally."
5. For a similar case, see Korean Yearbook of International Law 2014 (Seoul Central District Court Judgment No. 2013GAHAB565833, Rendered June 11, 2014).

Judicial Decisions in Private International Law (2018)

JANG Ji-Yong
Research Fellow (Judge), Judicial Policy Research Institute, Seoul, Korea

1. GOVERNING LAW

1-1. Clause Paramount - Designation of Governing law

Supreme Court Decision 2014Da41469 Decided March 29, 2018 [Indemnification]

Main Issues

Whether a "Clause Paramount" is a partial designation of a governing law (affirmative in principle)

Facts

[1] According to the preamble of the Bill of Lading (B/L), the governing law of the maritime transport agreement is the law of the United Kingdom. The latter part of the instant B/L expressly provides that the scope of liability of the carrier (Defendant in the instant case) shall be governed by the U.S. Carriage of Goods by Sea Act (hereinafter "U.S. Statute").

[2] (a) A corporation ("Party A") and a foreign entity ("Party B") entered into a sales agreement; (b) an accident occurred involving cargo becoming loose or unfastened during inbound shipments and subsequently caused product defects; (c) Plaintiff, an insurance company, provided coverage for damages to Party A based on a maritime cargo insurance policy; and (d) thereafter, Plaintiff sought compensation for tort-related damages against Defendant, a foreign entity, which transported the cargo upon receipt of the B/L from Party A.

Summary of Decision

[1] The principle of party autonomy serves as the basis for permitting the designation of governing laws in international contracts. Whether a "Clause Paramount," a clause preferentially incorporating the law of a specific country that legislated an international convention on a carrier's liability limitation despite the stipulation of a general governing law clause under a B/L, constitutes partial designation of a governing law or inclusion under relevant international conventions or foreign statutes is a matter of interpretation of a party's declaration of intent. Albeit a governing law clause is already incorporated into a B/L, a provision on complying with the law of a specific country that adopted an international convention on the limitation of a carrier's liability is stipulated thereunder and the application requirements of the law is met, the parties' intent would be preferentially applying the law of that country in governing a carrier's liability limitation, barring special circumstances.

[2] U.K. law is deemed the general and overall law governing the instant B/L. In such a case where the law of a specific country is applied to the limitation on a carrier's liability despite there being a general governing law clause, applying the U.S. Statute to the limitation on a carrier's liability should be deemed as a party's

intent. The Defendant's liability is limited to USD 500 per ton according to the U.S. Statute, which is the applicable law on the limitation of liability (of the Defendant).

1-2. Governing Law of Legal Persons

Supreme Court Decision 2017Da246739 Decided August 1, 2018

Main Issues

Governing Law of Legal Persons

Facts

The Plaintiff is a legal person established under the law of the State of California, USA, and the Defendants are the members of the farming legal persons.

Summary of Decision

There is a foreign factor in this case, so the governing law should be designated in accordance with the Act on Private International Law.

Article 16 of the Act on Private International Law, which constitutes "the legal persons or other organizations shall be governed by the applicable law of the establishment" designates the governing law of the establishment as the governing law of the legal persons in principle. As there is no regulation that restricts the application of the Article, it would cover the whole range of legal issues, e.g. the establishment and dissolution of the legal persons, organization and internal relationship, rights and obligations of the organs and the members, and the legal capacity of legal persons. Therefore, whether a member of the legal person is reliable to a creditor of the legal person or if yes, the scope of the reliability shall be subject to the governing law of the establishment.

Since the instant legal person is established by the law of the Republic of Korea, in a case the Defendants, members of the legal person is claimed to be liable with the creditor of the legal person, the governing law shall be the law of the Republic of Korea, the law of the establishment of the legal person.

Reference Provisions

Article 16 of the Act of Private International Law

Legal persons and other organizations shall be governed by the applicable law of the establishment thereof: in case legal persons or other organizations established in foreign countries have their principal business offices located in the Republic of Korea or transact their principal business in the Republic of Korea, such legal persons and other organizations shall be governed by the law of the Republic of Korea.

1-3. Trademark

Supreme Court en banc Decision 2015Hu1454 Decided June 21, 2018 Denial Adjudication (Trademark)

Main Issues

Whether a lawsuit seeking the registration, nullification, revocation, etc. of a trademark falls under the jurisdiction of a court in the country where the trademark has been registered or the country where its registration has been applied (affirmative), and the governing law relating thereto (held: the law of the country where the trademark has been registered or the country where its registration has been applied)

Facts

Party A, who operates AMERICAN UNIVERSITY located in Washington D.C. (U.S.A.), applied for the registration of the pending service mark "AMERICAN UNIVERSITY" with "university education, teaching, etc." as its designated services, but the Korean Intellectual Property Office (KIPO) denied registration on the ground that it falls under Article 6(1) Subparags. 4 and 7 of the former Trademark Act.

Summary of Decision

[1] A trademark right is acquired according to the law of the country where the trademark has been registered. As such, a lawsuit seeking the registration, nullification, revocation, etc. of a trademark generally falls under the jurisdiction of a court situated in the country where the trademark has been registered or the country where its registration has been applied (*see, e.g.*, Supreme Court Decision 2009Da19093, Apr. 28, 2011). Moreover, the governing law relating thereto ought to be deemed as the law of the country where the trademark has been registered or the country where its registration has been applied. Accordingly, notwithstanding that the Plaintiff is an American corporation, insofar as the Plaintiff applied for registration of the instant service mark in the Republic of Korea so as to use the same therein, the Trademark Act of Korea shall be the governing law relating to the legality of such application for registration.

[2] (a) in light of the instant university's history, its number of students and facilities, the reputation of the university domestically and internationally, the number of times "AMERICAN UNIVERSITY" has been searched on portal sites, etc.; (b) the pending service mark can be deemed to be widely known among general consumers, such as students preparing to study in the United States, as the name of

Party A's university relating to its designated services including university education; (c) accordingly, the combination of a conspicuous geographical name "AMERICAN" and a descriptive mark "UNIVERSITY" resulted in the creation of a novel concept and the development of a new distinctive character; and (d) thus, the pending service mark in its entirety does not fall under Article 6 Subparags. 4 (connspicuous geographical name) or 7 (unrecognizable) of the former Trademark Act and can be registered.

Reference Provisions

Article 6 of the former Trademark Act (Requirements for Trademark Registration)

(1) Trademark registration may be obtained, excluding the following trademarks:

4. A trademark consisting solely of a conspicuous geographical name, the abbreviation thereof, or a map;
7. In addition to trademarks under subparagraphs 1 through 6, a trademark which is unrecognizable for consumers to identify which goods related to whose business it indicates.

(2) Even if a trademark falls under any of paragraph (1)3 through 6, where such trademark is recognizable to consumers as a trademark indicating the source of goods of a specific person as a result of using the trademark before filing an application for trademark registration, trademark registration may be granted limited to the goods on which such trademark is used.

2. RECOGNITION AND ENFORCEMENT OF ARBITRAL AWARDS

2-1. Supreme Court Decision 2017Da225084 Decided July 26, 2018 [Decision on Enforcement]

Main Issues

[1] Governing law for determining the establishment of an arbitral agreement and its validity under Article V(1)(a) of the Convention on the Recognition and Enforcement of Foreign Arbitral Awards (hereinafter "New York Convention")

[2] Meaning of Article V(1)(e) of the New York Convention: Whether the Article 5(1)(e) can preclude filing of claims for enforcement decision in enforcing country on the ground that an affirmative decision was rendered in the country where arbitrary award was given (negative)

Facts

The Plaintiff filed three lawsuits against the Defendant, seeking compensation for damages incurred by the Defendant's failure to implement the instant contract. The Plaintiff (a) filed a request with the International Chamber of Commerce International Court of Arbitration (hereinafter "International Court of Arbitration"); (b) sought the enforcement judgments of the arbitration awards before a U.S. court; and (c) sought the enforcement of the arbitral awards and the parts of the U.S. court judgments before a Korean court. The Plaintiff obtained an arbitral award from the International Court of Arbitration and a judgment from a U.S. court. The instant case is concerned with seeking an enforcement decision on the arbitral award in question and the parts of the U.S. court judgment (which is part of money judgment ordering the Defendant to make payment to the Plaintiff and is distinct from the part where the U.S. court approved of recognition and enforcement of the arbitral award given by the International Court of Arbitration) before a Korean court.

Summary of Decision

[1] The gravamen of the instant case pertains to whether or not an arbitral agreement in writing was included in the instant contract. According to the latter part of Article V(1)(a) of the New York Convention, one of the grounds for refusing recognition and enforcement of arbitral awards is when the pertinent arbitral agreement is not valid under the law to which the parties have subjected it or, failing any indication thereon, under the law of the country where the award was made. According to the provision supra, the governing law for determining the establishment of an arbitral agreement and its validity would primarily be the law to which the parties have subjected the said agreement, and where there exists no indication thereon, the law of the country where the award was made (*see, e.g.*, Supreme Court Decision 2012Da84004, Mar. 24, 2016).

(a) Article 12 of the standard terms and conditions in the instant case, which have been incorporated into the elements of the instant contract, stipulated that California law would be the governing law of the instant contract; and (b) Article 13 stipulates that all disputes arising from the instant case shall be conclusively settled by arbitration in Los Molinos, California, U.S., pursuant to the arbitral rules set by the International Chamber of Commerce. As such, it appears that the Plaintiff and the Defendant selected California law as the governing law of the arbitral agreement.

[2] The New York Convention removed the need for double enforcement judgment or double exequatur by stipulating that an

arbitral award has to become binding on the parties (Article V(1)(e)), instead of requiring proof of finality of the award. It means that the party applying for recognition and enforcement of foreign arbitral awards may obtain a decision of enforcement in a country where the said party seeks the enforcement, instead of applying for separate procedures, such as enforcement decision or declaration of enforceability. The purport of this pertinent provision may not be construed as having prohibited filing of claims for enforcement judgment in the country where the enforcement is sought on the ground that the country where the arbitrary award was given rendered an affirmative judgment.

The Plaintiff is not precluded from seeking an enforcement judgment on the instant arbitral award in the Republic of Korea, where the enforcement is sought, based on the mere fact that an affirmative judgment is rendered from a court in the U.S., the country where an arbitral award is made. Furthermore, insofar as the Plaintiff is seeking an enforcement judgment only with regard to the remaining part of the instant U.S. court judgment after excluding the part on recognition of the instant arbitral award, the issue of double exequatur cannot be brought up on the remaining part *supra.*

2-2. Supreme Court Decision 2016Da18753 Decided November 29, 2018 [Decision on Enforcement]

Main Issues

[1] In a case where grounds for a demurrer arose upon the recognition of a foreign arbitral award, whether enforcement of the arbitral award may be denied through the application of Article V(2)(b) of the New York Convention (affirmative)

[2] Meaning of "believing the granting of representation right

based on one's expression of intent and act" pursuant to Article 3:61(2) of the Dutch Civil Code; Whether a counterparty is warranted protection in cases where the existence of representation right in appearance was created by oneself or arose from a situation within the scope that is to be endured by oneself (affirmative); If there is doubt as to the existence of representation right given that it unclear whether a person undertaking a representative act has such right, whether a counterparty has the duty to investigate the representation right (affirmative); If the external situation that one created is obvious to the extent that it is reasonable to believe the existence of representation right, whether a counterparty has the duty to investigate the representation right (negative)

[3] Legislative purport of Article V(2)(b) of the New York Convention; Method of deciding whether recognition or enforcement of an arbitral award would be contrary to the public policy of the relevant country.

[4] Meaning of arbitrability, which is the subject of dispute under Article V(2)(a) of the Convention on the Recognition and Enforcement of Foreign Arbitral Awards

Whether arbitrability of a dispute itself may be denied solely on the basis that a specific means of relief regarding the dispute at issue falls under the exclusive territorial jurisdiction of a court of the enforcing country (negative)

Facts

(a) The Defendant (licensee) concluded with the Plaintiff (licensor, foreign company) a license agreement on the Plaintiff's patent and trademark, as well as various information in the Republic of Korea (hereinafter "License Agreement"). According to Article 15 of the License Agreement, "In cases where license-related disputes arise, Hague (the Netherlands) shall be the place of arbitral award and the dispute shall be resolved via arbitration in English pursuant to the Arbitration Rules of the Netherlands Arbitration Institute (hereinafter 'NAI')." (b) On grounds that the Defendant violated the License Agreement when applying for a patent, the Plaintiff invoked an arbitration seeking the restitution of all rights and interests pertaining to the applied patent; and (c) an arbitral award was made ordering the Defendant to transfer the entire rights and interests related to the patent to the Plaintiff, and, upon nonperformance of the same, ordering the Defendant's indirect compulsory performance of compensatory payment.

Summary of Decision

[1] A judgment of execution, which grants executability of a foreign arbitral award so that it may proceed as compulsory enforcement under the laws of the Republic of Korea, determines the existence or absence of executory power based on the time of the closing of pleadings. In a case where the emergence of grounds for a demurrer under the Civil Execution Act, i.e., extinguishment of a claim following an arbitral award, leads to the revelation during pleadings in a judgment of execution that permitting compulsory enforcement based on a written arbitral award contradicts the fundamental principle of laws of Korea, a court may refuse the enforcement of such arbitral award by deeming the same as going against the public order under Article V(2)(b) on the Convention on the Recognition and Enforcement of Foreign Arbitral Awards.

According to Paragraph 7 of the written arbitral award of this case, the Defendant is obligated to (a) transfer to the Plaintiff all rights and interests regarding the India Patent within thirty (30) days following the notice of the instant arbitral award, and (b) submit all necessary documents prepared and signed to effectuate the foregoing patent rights and interests pursuant to India's patent law and the requirements under the applicable Indian law within three (3) days from the date of the Plaintiff's first request. Paragraph 9 of the written arbitral award prescribes that the Defendant shall be subject to indirect compulsory payment of damages upon the nonperformance of the obligation in Paragraph 7, *supra.* Therefore, in the case where the indirect compulsory payment of damages (Paragraph 9) extinguishes upon the Defendant's performance of the obligations under Paragraph 7 (i.e., transfer of the India Patent and submission of the necessary documents) of the written arbitral award, the enforcement of arbitral award can be denied due to the emergence of grounds for a demurrer with respect to Paragraph 9 of the instant written arbitral award.

[2] Following the arbitral award, an agent representing the Plaintiff underwent negotiations with the Defendant on drafting the deed of assignment for the transfer of the India Patent during which dispute arose between the Plaintiff's agent and the Defendant on the validity of the prepared deed of assignment.

Inasmuch as there exists a foreign element, the governing law ought to be prescribed according to the Korean Act on Private International Law. Article 18(1) of the Act provides, "The relationship between a principal and his/her agent shall be governed by the applicable law of the legal relations between the parties." Article 18(2) stipulates, "Whether or not a principal shall assume a duty for a third party resulting from the act of his/her agent shall be governed by the law of a country where a business office of the agent is located [...]" and Article 18(5) provides, "The provision of paragraph (2) shall apply *mutatis mutandis* in the case of the relationship between an agent without the agency right and a third party."

The Plaintiff is a Dutch company and the Plaintiff's agent is a Dutch law firm. The relationship between the Plaintiff and the Plaintiff's agent, as well as whether the Plaintiff assumes a duty for the Defendant upon the agent's act, shall be determined by Dutch law

As regards apparent representation, Article 3:61(2) of the Dutch

Civil Code provides that, in cases where a person without the right of representation took legal action in one's name and a counterparty believed that the right of representation was granted based on one's expression of intent and act and the same was reasonably believable in such a situation, the effectiveness of said legal act is vested to oneself.

As above, believing the granting of representation right based on one's expression of intent and act refers to cases where one creates a situation in which the right of representation exists, in appearance, to a person who undertook a representative act, or where one has to endure the risks of being responsible for making a counterparty of a legal act believe in the fact or circumstance that there exists the right of representation from a transactional standpoint standpoint [*see, e.g.*, HR 19 februari 2010, NJ 2010, 115 (*ING Bank/Bera Holding*)]. Therefore, a counterparty is warranted protection in both cases where the existence of representation right was created by oneself or arose from a situation within the scope of risk that is to be endured by oneself.

As regards an attorney representing a party, the right of representation may be inferred with respect to acts in litigation proceedings but not so for other acts. A counterparty of a legal act should believe that there exists the right of representation based on rationale. In view of various circumstances, where the existence of representation right is doubtful given that it is unclear whether a person undertaking a representative act has such right, a counterparty has the duty to investigate the representation right (onderzoeksplicht). However, if the external situation that one created is obvious to the extent that it is reasonable to believe the existence of representation right, a counterparty does not have such duty [see Danny Busch, Laura J. Macgregor (eds.), *The Unauthorised Agent: Perspectives from European and Comparative Law*, 2009, pp. 152-153].

The Defendant appears to have reasonably believed that the effectiveness of the agreement with the agent on drafting the

Assignment Deed of the India Patent can be vested to the Plaintiff, and such reasonable belief can be said to have been based on the Plaintiff's commission or omission of expression of intent or action. Inasmuch as the Dutch Code does not provide for a time limit on objection to the right of apparent representation, the Plaintiff's prolonged silence does not necessarily mean the confirmation of the act of apparent representation; yet, examining the foregoing circumstances, the Defendant's reasonable belief related to the representation right of the Plaintiff's agent is recognizable. In addition, even though the agreement on preparing the Assignment Deed of the India Patent is not an enforcement of the instant arbitral award, it is a partial performance of the award in the continuing arbitral proceedings. In light of the circumstance that the Plaintiff's agent represented the Plaintiff not only in the pertinent arbitral proceeding but also in the arbitral proceeding leading up to the second arbitral award as well as during the performance of obligation subsequent to the arbitral award, the Defendant's obligation to investigate the representation right can be seen as having substantially weakened. Ultimately, the legal action that the Plaintiff's agent took with the Defendant regarding the Assignment Deed of the India Patent is effectuated upon the Plaintiff.

[3] Article V(2)(b) of the Convention on the Recognition and Enforcement of Arbitral Awards provides that the court of an enforcing country may refuse the recognition or enforcement of an arbitral award in cases where the court finds that such recognition or enforcement would be contrary to the public policy of the country where recognition or enforcement is sought. The underlying purpose is to protect the enforcing country's fundamental moral conviction and social order from hurting by the recognition or enforcement of an arbitral award. Therefore, the foregoing provision ought to be construed by factoring in not only domestic circumstances but also the perspective of ensuring the stability of international transaction order. The fact that a foreign law applied to a foreign arbitral award

contravenes the compulsory enforcement rule under the Korean positive law does not necessarily become grounds for non-recognition. Rather, in the event that an arbitral award is acknowledged, the recognition and enforcement of a foreign arbitral award may be denied if the consequence arising from the acknowledgment of the same is contrary to Korea's good morals and other social order.

The Court determined that: (a) where a judgment becomes final and conclusive regarding an obligation of expression of intent, such as transfer of patent right, indirect compulsory performance is impermissible with respect to patent right transfer according to the principle of the subsidiarity of indirect compulsory performance, inasmuch as the method of compulsory enforcement is stipulated in Article 263(1) of the Korean Civil Execution Act; (b) however, albeit an arbitral award ordering indirect compulsory performance of an obligation to express intent is recognized, unlike the Civil Execution Act, indirect compulsory performance is merely inducing voluntary expression of intent through an indirect means of applying psychological pressure; (c) as such, the level of restricting the freedom of decision-making is relatively low, so readily concluding the infringement of the constitutional personality right solely based on such indirect compulsory performance is difficult; and (d) in light of the above, the lower court is justifiable to have deemed that the portion of the arbitral award ordering indirect compulsory performance did not go against public order and good morals to the extent of denying enforcement.

[4] According to Article V(2)(a) of the Convention on the Recognition and Enforcement of Foreign Arbitral Awards, the recognition or enforcement of an arbitral award can be denied in cases where the subject matter of dispute is insolvable via arbitration based on the law of the relevant country. Here, arbitrability refers to whether the subject of dispute may be resolved, given the nature of the dispute, via an agreement between the parties via arbitration pursuant to the principle of private autonomy. The arbitrability of a

dispute may vary among countries, but the same should not be limited based on a complex standard that is difficult to be regarded as a global universal norm. In particular, the arbitrability of a dispute itself cannot be denied solely on the basis that a specific means of relief regarding said dispute falls under the exclusive territorial jurisdiction of a court of the enforcing country.

2-3. Supreme Court Decision 2016Da49931 Decided December 13, 2018 [Decision on Enforcement]

Main Issues

[1] Whether the degree of infringement of a party's procedural right via an arbitral proceeding ought to be apparent to the extent that it is intolerable to constitute grounds for recognition and enforcement of an arbitral award under Article V(1)(d) of the Convention on the Recognition and Enforcement of Foreign Arbitral Awards (affirmative)

[2] In a case where grounds for a demurrer arose upon the recognition of a foreign arbitral award, whether enforcement of the arbitral award may be denied through the application of Article V(2)(b) of the New York Convention (affirmative)

[3] Whether enforcement of a foreign arbitral award may be denied solely on the basis that the foreign arbitral award is unlawful as it contradicts the substantive rights relationship or that an executory claimant based thereto was aware of such circumstance (negative)

Whether enforcement of an arbitral award may be denied on the grounds that the same constitutes abuse of rights or contravenes public order and good morals (affirmative)

Standard for determining the constitution of rights abuse, etc. in the event that the substance of a foreign arbitral award contradicts the substantive rights relationship

In a case where enforcement of a foreign arbitral award is apparently unlawful as there exist grounds for a retrial under the Civil Procedure Act and having a counterparty accept its enforcement violates justice to the extent that is deemed socially intolerable, whether such case may be considered as grounds for a demurrer (affirmative)

Facts

According to the arbitration clause in this case, the pertinent dispute is the subject of arbitration and both the Plaintiff and the Defendant are the parties thereto. However, the foregoing arbitral provision does not provide for (i) the Plaintiff's right to designate an arbitrator unlike the Defendant and (ii) the Plaintiff and the Defendant, pursuant to Article 10(c) of the instant arbitration clause, to "resolve matters via arbitration according to the Arbitration Rules of the International Chamber of Commerce (ICC) when the parties are unable to resolve matters based on other clauses."

The Plaintiff and the Defendant, as the parties of arbitration, are entitled to appoint an arbitrator pursuant to Article 8(4) of the ICC Arbitration Rules. In the instant arbitral request form, the Plaintiff exercised such right and appointed Nonparty 1 as the arbitrator for the petitioner's side whereas the Defendant reserved the right of objection and appointed Nonparty 1 as the arbitrator for the respondent's side. The International Court of Arbitration (ICA) of the ICC, in place of the Plaintiff, chose Nonparty 1, who was appointed by the Plaintiff, as the arbitrator, and confirmed Nonparty 2, who was appointed by the Defendant, as the arbitrator. The ICA instructed the two arbitrators, who were appointed by the parties, to agree on and select a presiding arbitrator within thirty (30) days pursuant to the instant arbitration clause; subsequently, the ICA chose Nonparty

3, who was jointly selected by the two appointed arbitrators, as the presiding arbitrator.

In the instant arbitral award, among the costs incurred by the Defendant with respect to the sale of the pertinent land according to the instant agreement, the Defendant is obligated to pay the Plaintiff the amount equivalent to 50% of the portion shouldered by the Defendant. The amount includes KRW 11,861,411,345, which is 50% of the total amount of taxes (KRW 23,722,822,690), including corporate tax, imposed with respect to the sale of the pertinent land, and accounts for one-third of the total arbitral award-based amount.

Summary of Decision

[1] In light of the characteristics of the arbitration system, the composition of an arbitral tribunal is the most pivotal and inherent element in arbitral agreements and procedures. That said, any breach of matters agreed between the parties with respect to the composition of an arbitral tribunal shakes the foundation of the tribunal's authority (*see, e.g.*, Supreme Court Decision 2017Da240991, 241000, Apr. 10, 2018). Article V(1)(d) of the Convention on the Recognition and Enforcement of Foreign Arbitral Awards provides that the recognition or enforcement of an arbitral award can be denied when either the composition of an arbitral tribunal or arbitral proceeding, which serves as the basis for an arbitral award, does not coincide with a party's arbitral agreement or violates a discretionary provision. However, the mere fact that a party's agreement or discretionary provision had been infringed is insufficient to constitute grounds for the denial of recognition and enforcement of an arbitral award as stipulated in the foregoing provision. Rather, the degree of infringement of a party's procedural right via the relevant arbitral proceeding ought to be apparent to the extent that it is intolerable (*see, e.g.*, Supreme Court Decision 2017Da238837, Dec. 22, 2017).

The arbitral tribunal in this case was comprised according to the ICC's Arbitration Rules when comprehensively taking account of the following: (i) although the ICA did not directly choose a presiding arbitrator, it set the method of selecting a presiding arbitrator by respecting the wishes of the arbitration parties; and (ii) the ICA is granted final authority with respect to the decision on arbitrator selection pursuant to Article 7(4) of the ICC Arbitration Rules.

[2] A foreign arbitral award has *res judicata*, the same effect as a final and conclusive judgment, and the compulsory enforcement procedure by law of the Republic of Korea may proceed once the existence of the claim right is affirmed and the enforceability is granted through judgment of enforcement. A judgment of enforcement, which grants executability of a foreign arbitral award to proceed compulsory enforcement under the laws of the Republic of Korea, determines the existence of executory power at the closing of pleadings. In a case where the emergence of grounds for a demurrer under the Civil Execution Act leads to the revelation during pleadings in a judgment of execution that permitting compulsory enforcement based on a written arbitral award contradicts the fundamental principle of Korean law, a court may refuse the enforcement of such arbitral award by deeming the same as going against the public order under Article V(2)(b) of the New York Convention (*see, e.g.*, Supreme Court Decision 2001Da20134, Apr. 11, 2003).

[3] The mere fact that a foreign arbitral award is unlawful as it contravenes the substantive rights relationship or that a claimant who had been granted executability via an arbitral award was aware of such fact is insufficient to deny enforcement upon the arbitral award (*see, e.g.*, Supreme Court Decision 2004Da8814, Dec. 23, 2005). However, even a right granted upon a foreign arbitral award with the same effect as a final and conclusive judgment ought to be exercised in line with the good faith principle, and the same should not be permissible if constituting abuse of rights or contravening public

order and good morals. Whether the substance of a foreign arbitral award contradicted the substantive rights relationship to the extent of constituting rights abuse, etc. ought to be examined by fully considering the following, i.e., nature and content of the right in question, developments leading up to the recognition of an arbitral award and ex post rendition of a judgment of execution, and impact on a party upon permission of execution. In particular, where enforcement of a foreign arbitral award is apparently unlawful as there exist grounds for a retrial under the Civil Procedure Act and having a counterparty accept its enforcement violates justice to the extent that is deemed socially intolerable, seeking enforcement of an arbitral award may be deemed as grounds for a demur since it either constitutes abuse of rights or transgression of public order and good morals.

Articles 451(1)8 of the Civil Procedure Act provides "when an administrative disposition on which the final and conclusive judgment was based has been altered by a different judgment or administrative disposition" as one of the grounds for retrial. If an administrative disposition, which served as the basis for an arbitral award that has the same effect as a final and conclusive judgment, was revised by a different judgment or administrative disposition following the establishment of the arbitral award in question, it ought to be examined whether recognizing the validity of said arbitral award as is and permitting the compulsory enforcement procedure to be conducted based on that written arbitral award contravenes the fundamental principle of Korean law.

The right established in the instant arbitral award pertains to the settlement of costs that incurred during the process of selling the relevant land according to the agreement in this case. Of the foregoing incurred costs, upon the substantial reduction in the corporate tax amount equivalent to one-third of the arbitral award-based amount, the substance of the arbitral award was consequentially in discord with the substantive rights-relationship. Moreover, when factoring in the special nature of an arbitral award in which a lawsuit for retrial cannot be initiated, it is desirable to allow the Defendant to argue such circumstances in a trial for enforcement judgment with respect to the instant arbitral award. Furthermore, in fully viewing the circumstances, such as how the Defendant will be affected upon enforcement of the arbitral award that is at variance with the substantive rights-relationship despite the fact that the Plaintiff's Korean branch had been shut down, inasmuch as (i) permitting the compulsory enforcement based on the instant arbitral award is evidently unlawful, and (ii) having the Defendant accept such enforcement apparently violates justice and, therefore, constitutes an abuse of right or a contravention of public order and good morals, there is sufficient room to deem that there exists grounds for a demurrer. Rather than having the Defendant proceed through filing a motion against the Plaintiff to once again argue the request for arbitration, etc. after the enforcement judgment becomes final and conclusive, such interpretation not only accords with the judicial economy but also tenable in light of Korea's legal system according to which a judgment of enforcement ought to be rendered in the form of a judgment after the oral pleading.

3. HAGUE CHILD ABDUCTION CONVENTION

Supreme Court Order 2017Seu630 Dated April 17, 2018 [Petition for Return of a Child (The Hague Convention 1980 on the Civil Aspects of International Child Abduction)]

Main Issues

In a case where a person whose right of custody has been breached as a result of a wrongful removal or retention of a child to or in the Republic of Korea requests to the court for the child's return, whether "a grave risk," prescribed as the grounds for exception to return under Article 12(4)3 of the Act on the Implementation of the Hague Child Abduction Convention, includes the following: (i) where a child may be exposed to psychological harm due to frequent violence committed by one parent against the other parent; and (ii) where a child's return to the State of the habitual residence may place the child in severe suffering by depriving him/her of appropriate protection or care (affirmative); and in such cases, factors to be taken account of by the court receiving application for the return of a child

Facts

The Applicant (husband) and Respondent (wife) was married in 2006 in Japan. Following the marriage, they remained in Japan and had two children: a girl born in 2007 and a boy born in 2009. Following an argument, the Respondent left Japan for Korea with children in 2016, without the Applicant's consent. Since then, the Respondent has lived with the children in her sister's house in Seoul and the children started to attend the Korean School. The Applicant filed a claim under the Hague Convention of 25 October 1980 on the Civil Aspects of International Child Abduction.

Summary of Order

According to the Convention on the Civil Aspects of International Child Abduction (hereafter "Convention") and the Act on the Implementation of the Hague Child Abduction Convention (hereafter "Act"), a person whose right to custody under the Convention has been breached as a result of a wrongful removal or retention of a child to or in the Republic of Korea may file with the court a petition seeking the return of the child (Article 12(1) of the Act), and in such case, the court is obliged to act expeditiously with the welfare of the child as its top priority (Article 3 of the Act).

In the meantime, the court may dismiss the petition seeking the return of a child even where the right of custody has been breached as a result of a wrongful removal of a child, provided that "there is a grave risk that the return of the child would expose the child to physical or psychological harm or otherwise place the child in an intolerable situation" (Article 12(4) of the Act).

The grounds for exception to return under Article 12(4)3 of the Act are placed in order to prevent harm, which may arise from violation of the specific and individual welfare of a child, as a result of prompt return of the child. Thus, the construction of the said provision should place priority on the rights and interests of a child before the right to custody of either parent or the promptness of the procedure.

Therefore, a "grave risk" includes not only cases where there is a concern for harmful effects on a child's mind and body because of the petitioner's direct violence or abuse against the child, but also cases where the child is at risk of psychological harm due to frequent violence committed against the other parent, and cases where the child may suffer severely by deprivation of appropriate protection or care upon his/her return to the State of habitual residence.

Along with the aforementioned circumstances, the court receiving the petition for the return of a child must examine comprehensively the entirety of circumstances, including the degree of the harm and whether there are concerns of a recurrence of the harm, the specifics of the environment in which the child is brought up both before and after his/her return, and the psychological and physical impact of the return on the child, and then render judgment on the child's best interests and on whether the return rather poses a grave violation of the welfare of the child after taking into account factors such as the custody right of the petitioner and his/her counterpart.

Rendered in accordance with the aforementioned legal principle and evidence duly adopted, the lower court was justifiable to have dismissed the petition by the petitioner. The lower court rendered its judgment in view of the circumstances that (i) the petitioner had verbally and physically abused the counterparty multiple times, which caused the psychological suffering of the child 1 who witnessed such abuse, and that (ii) in a case where only the principals or only child 2 is returned to Japan, there are concerns that such separation is likely to cause psychological suffering on the principals in the instant case. Hence, the lower court did not err and affect the conclusion of the judgment by misapprehending the legal principle regarding "a grave risk" or by exceeding the bounds of the principle of logic and experience.

Territorial Sea and Contiguous Zone Act

[Enforcement on June 14, 2018.]
[Act No. 15429, Partial Amendment on Mar. 13, 2018]

The Editorial Board
ILA Korean Branch

1. Reasons for the Amendment [Partial Amendment]

◇ Reasons and Key Amendment Points

Under the current law, the foreign ships that engage in any activity deemed prejudicial to the peace, public order, or the security of the Republic of Korea, including any threat against its sovereignty and any exercise or practice with weapons; or disobedience to any order issued to stop their passage to guarantee the security of the country, are subject to imprisonment for not more than five years or a fine not exceeding 200 million won. In addition, imprisonment for not more than two years or a fine not exceeding 10 million won are imposed on the foreign ships that refuse to obey or hinder any order including stopping issued in the case that they are suspected of engaging in any of the above-specified activities. However, in recent security crises, it has been suggested that foreign ships engaging in activities prejudicial to the peace, public order, or the security of the Republic of Korea be punished in a stricter manner. Therefore, the amendment intends to increase the maximum fine imposed on the foreign ships that are involved in any of the above-stated activities or disobey the order of stopping issued to guarantee the security of the country from 200 million won to 300 million won. Furthermore, the maximum fine imposed on the foreign ships when they refuse to obey or hinder any of such orders or measures, including stopping, shall be increased from 10 million won to 100 million won, thereby more strictly punishing such activities that could harm the security of the country.

<Provided by the Ministry of Government Legislation>

2. Amendment

The Partial Amendment to the Territorial Sea and Contiguous Zone Act, which was passed by the National Assembly, is promulgated as here set forth.

President Moon Jae-in (seal)

March 13, 2018

Prime Minister Lee Nak-yeon

Cabinet Member and Minister of Foreign Affairs Kang Kyung-hwa

⊙Act No. 15429

The Partial Amendment to the Territorial Sea and Contiguous Zone Act

The Territorial Sea and Contiguous Zone Act is partially amended as follows.

In the first paragraph of Article 8, “200 million won” is replaced by “300 million won” and in the second paragraph of the same article, “10 million won” is replaced by “100 million won.”

3. Addenda

This Act shall enter into force after three months of its promulgation.

4. Full Text[1]

TERRITORIAL SEA AND CONTIGUOUS ZONE ACT
[Enforcement Date June 14, 2018.]
[Act No. 15429, March 13, 2018, Partial Amendment]

Article 1 (Breadth of Territorial Sea) The territorial sea of the Republic of Korea shall be the zone not extending beyond 12 nautical miles measured from the baseline: Provided, That in cases of specified areas, the breadth of the territorial sea may be otherwise determined within the breadth of 12 nautical miles, as prescribed by Presidential Decree.

[This Article Wholly Amended by Act No. 10524, April 4, 2011]

Article 2 (Baseline) (1) The ordinary baseline for measuring the breadth of the territorial sea shall be the low-water line along the coasts as marked on large-scale charts officially recognized by the Republic of Korea.

(2) In cases of the area of the sea where special geographical circumstances exist, straight lines joining points as prescribed by Presidential Decree may be employed.

[This Article Wholly Amended by Act No. 10524, April 4, 2011]

Article 3 (Internal Waters) Waters on the landward side of the baseline for measuring the breadth of the territorial sea shall be the internal waters.

[This Article Wholly Amended by Act No. 10524, April 4, 2011]

---

1) This English translation is not official translation.

Article 3-2 (Breadth of Contiguous Zone) The contiguous zone of the Republic of Korea shall be the zone, excluding the territorial sea of the Republic of Korea, not extending beyond 24 nautical miles outwards measured from the baselines: Provided, That in specified areas, the breath of the contiguous zone may be otherwise determined within 24 nautical miles from the baseline, as prescribed by Presidential Decree.

[This Article Wholly Amended by Act No. 10524, April 4, 2011]

Article 4 (Delimitation between States with Adjacent or Opposite Coasts) The delimitation of the territorial sea and contiguous zone between the Republic of Korea and states with adjacent or opposite coasts shall, unless otherwise agreed between the states concerned, be the median line joining every point of which is equidistant from the nearest points on the baselines from which the breadth of the territorial sea of each of the two states is measured.

[This Article Wholly Amended by Act No. 10524, April 4, 2011]

Article 5 (Passage of Foreign Vessels) (1) Foreign ships may enjoy the right of innocent passage through the territorial sea of the Republic of Korea so long as it is not prejudicial to peace, public order, or security of the Republic of Korea. When a foreign warship or government ship operated for non-commercial purposes intends to pass through the territorial sea, it shall give prior notice to the authorities concerned as prescribed by Presidential Decree.

(2) Passage of a foreign ship shall be considered to be prejudicial to peace, public order, or security of the Republic of Korea, if the ship engages in any of the following activities in the territorial sea: Provided, That this shall not apply to cases where the activities prescribed in subparagraphs 2 through 5, 11, and 13 have been permitted, approved, or given consent by the authorities concerned:

1. Any threat or use of force against the sovereignty, territorial integrity, or independence of the Republic of Korea, or in any other manner in violation of the principles of international law embodied in the Charter of the United Nations;
2. Any exercise or practice with weapons;
3. The launching, landing, or taking on board of any aircraft;
4. The launching, landing, or taking on board of any military device;
5. Underwater navigation;
6. The collection of information prejudicial to the security of the Republic of Korea;
7. The propaganda or instigation prejudicial to the security of the Republic of Korea;
8. The loading or unloading of any commodity, currency, or person which violates the statutes of the Republic of Korea concerning customs, finances, immigration, or health and hygiene;
9. The discharge of pollutants exceeding the standards prescribed by Presidential Decree;
10. Any fishing activities;
11. Conduct of research or survey activities;
12. Any act of interfering with any communications system, or any other facilities or installations of the Republic of Korea;
13. Any other activity prescribed by Presidential Decree not having a direct bearing on passage.

(3) The innocent passage of foreign ships may be temporarily suspended in specified areas of the territorial sea as prescribed by Presidential Decree if such suspension is essential for security of the Republic of Korea.

[This Article Wholly Amended by Act No. 10524, April 4, 2011]

Article 6 (Stopping of Vessels, etc.) If a foreign ship (excluding foreign warships and government ships operated for non-commercial purposes; hereinafter the same shall apply) is deemed to have violated Article 5, the authorities concerned may stop, search, or seize the ship, or issue other necessary orders or take other necessary measures.

[This Article Wholly Amended by Act No. 10524, April 4, 2011]

Article 6-2 (Power of Competent Authorities in Contiguous Zones) In the contiguous zone of the Republic of Korea, the competent authorities may exercise their official authority within the extent required for the following purposes, as prescribed by the statutes:

1. Preventing infringement of the statutes of the Republic of Korea concerning customs, finances, immigration, or health and hygiene within the territory or territorial sea of the Republic of Korea;
2. Punishing violations of the statutes of the Republic of Korea concerning customs, finances, immigration, or health and hygiene within the territory or territorial sea of the Republic of Korea.

[This Article Wholly Amended by Act No. 10524, April 4, 2011]

Article 7 (Relationship with Treaties, etc.) Matters which are not provided for in this Act with regard to the territorial sea and contiguous zone of the Republic of Korea shall be governed by treaties concluded and promulgated in accordance with the Constitution of the Republic of Korea or by generally accepted international laws.

[This Article Newly Inserted by Act No. 14607, March 21, 2017]

Article 8 (Penalty Provisions) (1) Crew or other passengers on board of a foreign ship who have violated Article 5 (2) or (3) shall be punished by imprisonment for not more than five years or a fine not exceeding 300 million won, and when necessary in consideration of the circumstances, the relevant ship, its equipment, its catches, or other articles in violation may be confiscated. <Amended by Act No. 15429, March 13, 2018>

(2) Crew or other passengers on board of a foreign ship who have

disobeyed, hindered, or evaded any order issued or measure taken in accordance with Article 6 shall be punished by imprisonment for not more than two years or a fine not exceeding 100 million won. <Amended by Act No. 15429, March 13, 2018>

(3) In cases of paragraph (1) or (2), imprisonment and fines may be imposed concurrently.

(4) In applying this Article, if the act referred to in this Article concurrently constitutes a crime under other Acts other than this Act, it shall be punished by the severest punishment among the penalty provisions of each Act.

[This Article Wholly Amended by Act No. 10524, April 4, 2011]

Article 9 (Special Cases concerning Warships, etc.) If a foreign warship or government ship operated for non-commercial purposes or its crew or passengers on board violate this Act or other relevant statutes, such ship may be required to remedy the violation or to leave the territorial sea.

[This Article Wholly Amended by Act No. 10524, April 4, 2011]

ADDENDA <Act No. 4986, Dec. 6, 1995>

This Act shall enter into force on the date as prescribed by the Presidential Decree within the limit of one year from the date of its promulgation.

ADDENDA <Act No. 10524, Apr. 4, 2011>

This Act shall enter into force on the date of its promulgation.

ADDENDA <Act No. 14607, Mar. 21, 2017>

This Act shall enter into force on the date of its promulgation.

ADDENDA <Act No. 15429, Mar. 13, 2018>

This Act shall enter into force three months after the date of its promulgation.

Adjustment of International Taxes Act

[Enforcement on Jan. 1, 2019]
[Act No. 16099, Partial Amendment on Dec. 31, 2018]

The Editorial Board
ILA Korean Branch

1. Reasons for the Amendment [Partial Amendment]

◇ Reasons for the Amendment

The purpose of this amendment is to establish clear legal grounds for tax adjustment based on arm's length prices in accordance with the substance of international transactions to prevent tax avoidance through such transactions with specially concerned foreign parties. It also intends to expand those required, by the request of the head of the competent tax office, to provide information on the source of the unreported amount in their overseas financial accounts from residents to corporations, in order to prevent offshore tax evasion. As such, the amendment aims to complement some of the limitations of the current law revealed in the course of its enforcement.

◇ Key Points

A. The enhancement of the effectiveness of tax adjustment based on arm's length prices [the insertion of Article 5 (2) and (3)]

In the case that any international transaction between a resident and a specially concerned foreign party lacks commercial rationality compared with any transaction performed in the similar conditions between independent business operators with no special relationships and thus becomes significantly difficult to compute arm's length prices, the transaction can be denied or restructured into a new one in order to compute arm's length prices.

B. The mandated notification of the contents of mutual agreement [Article 27 (2)]

In order to ensure the transparency of the mutual agreement procedure carried out in relation to the application/interpretation of a tax treaty or unfair taxation between the contracting parties, the Minister of Economy and Finance shall notify the contents of the agreement reached upon the closing of the mutual agreement procedure regarding the application/interpretation of the tax treaty.

C. The deletion of the article on the precedence of tax treaties over the domestic law for income classification [the deletion of the existing Article 28]

The existing article stipulates that any tax treaty takes precedence over the domestic law for the classification of the domestic source income of nonresidents or foreign corporations; however, as this article can be misinterpreted that income classification under tax treaties determines that under the domestic law, the article has been deleted.

D. The transfer of articles on punishment to the Punishment of Tax Evaders Act [the deletion of the existing Article 31 (2) and (3), and Article 34 (2)]

Articles on the punishment of the offenses regarding the exchange of tax and financial information and overseas financial account reporting obligation shall be transferred to the Punishment of Tax Evaders Act to stipulate the punishment of any violation of tax laws in an integrated way in the act.

E. The supplementation of the overseas financial account reporting system [Article 34 (5), Article 34-3 (1)]

1) The criterion for determining those exempt from the obligation to report information on their overseas financial accounts has been relaxed from a residence period in Korea of 183 days or less within the two years before the end of the relevant year subject to reporting to a residence period in Korea of 183 days or less within a year before the end of the above-stated year.

2) Corporations have been included among those required to provide information on the source of the money in their overseas financial accounts by the request of the head of the competent tax office due to the violation of their reporting obligation.

<Provided by the Ministry of Government Legislation>

2. Amendment

The Partial Amendment to the Adjustment of International Taxes Act, which was passed by the National Assembly, is promulgated as here set forth.

President Moon Jae-in (seal)

December 18, 2018

Prime Minister Lee Nak-yeon

Cabinet Member and Minister of Economy and Finance Hong Nam-gi

⊙Act No. 16099

The Partial Amendment to the Adjustment of International Taxes

Act

The Adjustment of International Taxes Act is partially amended as follows.

In Article 2 (1) 5 of this Act, "interpretation" shall be replaced by "application/interpretation."

Article 5 Paragraph 2 shall be renumbered as Paragraph 4, with the insertion of new Paragraphs 2 and 3 in the same article as follows. In Paragraph 4 (the former Paragraph 2) of the same article, "Paragraph 1" shall be changed to "provisions of Paragraphs 1 to 3."

② When applying Paragraph 1, the taxing authority shall clearly identify the substance of the relevant international transaction taking into account the commercial or financial relationship between the resident and the specially concerned foreign party and the important transaction conditions in the relevant international transaction. In addition, the authority shall judge whether it is a commercially reasonable transaction compared with a transaction performed in the similar conditions between independent business operators that have no special relationship.

③ If, based on the judgment under Paragraph 2, the taxing authority finds that any international transaction between a resident and a specially concerned foreign party is not commercially reasonable and thus that it is significantly difficult to compute arm's length prices based on the relevant international transaction, the authority may consider it invalid or restructure it into a new one to apply Paragraph 1 to the transaction.

In Article 21 (4), "Article 4-2 (1) and (2) of the Inheritance Tax and Gift Tax Act" shall be changed to "Article 4-2 (1) and (3) of the Inheritance Tax and Gift Tax Act."

In the latter part of Article 27 (2), “may publicly notify the contents of the agreement reached” shall be replaced by “shall publicly notify the contents of the agreement reached upon the closing of the agreement procedure in accordance with Article 22 (1) 1.”

Article 28 shall be deleted.

In Article 29 (1) 1 and 2, “Article 156 (1) 3 of the Income Tax Act or Article 98 (1) 3 of the Corporate Tax Act” shall be changed to “Article 156 (1) 1, 2, and 6 of the Income Tax Act or Article 98 (1) 1, 2, and 6 of the Corporate Tax Act,” respectively.

Article 31-2 and Article 31-3 shall be deleted.

In Article 34 (5) 1, “two years” shall be replaced by “one year.”

Article 34-2 shall be deleted.

In Article 34-3 (1), “a resident required to report information on his/her overseas financial account” shall be replaced by “a person required to report information on his/her overseas financial account” and “amount unreported” by “amount not reported by the reporting deadline or the under-reported amount (hereafter referred to as “amount unreported”).”

Paragraph 4 shall be newly inserted in Article 35 as follows.

④ In the case that any non-fulfillment of this obligation is punished in accordance with Article 16 (1) of the Punishment of Tax Evaders Act, an administrative fine pursuant to Paragraph 1 shall not be imposed on it.

3. Addenda

Article 1 (Enforcement Date) This Act shall enter into force on January 1, 2019.

Article 2 (General Applicability) This Act shall begin to apply from the taxable year that begins after this Act enters into force.

Article 3 (Applicability concerning the Enforcement of Mutual Agreements) The amended provisions provided in the latter part of Article 27 (2) apply upon the closing of any mutual agreement procedure after this Act enters into force.

Article 4 (Transitional Measures concerning Punishment) Notwithstanding the amended provisions of Article 31 (2) and (3) and Article 34 (2), the previous provisions shall apply to the offenses that have occurred before this Act enters into force.

Article 5 (Transitional Measures concerning the Obligation to Report Overseas Financial Accounts) Notwithstanding the amended provisions of Article 34 (5) 1 and Article 34-3 (1), in the case of the reporting of any overseas financial accounts obtained prior to the enforcement of this Act in accordance with Article 34 (1) or Article 37, the transitional measures shall be carried out pursuant to the previous provisions.

4. Full Text[1)]

ADJUSTMENT OF INTERNATIONAL TAXES ACT
[Enforcement Date 1 Jan. 2019.]
[Act No. 16099, 31 Dec. 2018., Partial Amendment]

1) This English translation is not official translation.

CHAPTER I GENERAL PROVISIONS

Article 1 (Purpose)

The purpose of this Act is to prevent double taxation and tax avoidance and to facilitate cooperation in tax affairs among countries by establishing rules to coordinate taxation on international transactions and to promote international cooperation in tax administration.

[This Article Wholly Amended by Act No. 9914, Jan. 1, 2010]

Article 2 (Definitions) (1) The terms used in this Act are defined as follows: <Amended by Act No. 10410, Dec. 27, 2010; Act No. 11126, Dec. 31, 2011; Act No. 11606, Jan. 1, 2013>

1. The term "international transaction" means a transaction in which either or both of the parties are nonresidents or foreign corporations (excluding a domestic place of business of a nonresident or foreign corporation), including trading or leasing tangible or intangible property; providing services; lending or borrowing money; and all other transactions involving profits or losses and property of the parties;
2. The term "tax treaty" means any type of international agreement governed by international law, such as a treaty, convention, pact or note, which the Republic of Korea enters into with another State with respect to taxes on income, capital, and property or cooperation in tax administration;
3. The term "Contracting State" means any country that enters into a tax treaty with the Republic of Korea;
4. The term "competent authority" means the Minister of Strategy and Finance or his/her delegate in the case of the Republic of Korea; and a person who is designated as the competent authority in the tax treaty in the case of the other Contracting State;
5. The term "mutual agreement procedure" means the procedure

by which application/interpretation of a tax treaty, unreasonable taxation, or adjustment of taxable income are resolved through consultations between the competent authority of the Republic of Korea and that of the other Contracting State; <Amended by Act No. 16099, Dec. 31, 2018>

6. The term "domestic place of business" means a domestic place of business of a nonresident, as provided in Article 120 of the Income Tax Act, or a domestic place of business of a foreign corporation, as provided in Article 94 of the Corporate Tax Act;
7. The term "tax authority" means the head of the tax office having jurisdiction over the place of tax payment or the commissioner of the regional tax office;
8. The term "special relationship" means any relationship described below, and the specific criteria therefor shall be prescribed by Presidential Decree:
   (a) A relationship in which either party to a transaction owns directly or indirectly at least 50 percent of the voting stocks (including the equity shares; hereinafter the same shall apply) of the other party;
   (b) A relationship between both parties to a transaction where a third party owns directly or indirectly at least 50 percent of their respective voting stocks;
   (c) A relationship in which the parties to a transaction have a common interest through an investment in capital, trade in goods or services, grant of a loan, etc. and either party to the transaction has the power to substantially determine the business policy of the other party;
   (d) A relationship between both parties to a transaction where the parties have a common interest through an investment in capital, trade in goods or services, grant of a loan, etc. and a third party has the power to substantially determine the business policies of both parties;

9. The term "foreign related party" means any nonresident or foreign corporation (excluding a domestic place of business of a nonresident or foreign corporation) in a special relationship with a resident, domestic corporation or domestic place of business;
10. The term "arm's length price" means a price that is applied or deemed to be applied in an ordinary transaction between a resident, domestic corporation or domestic place of business and a person other than a foreign related party;
11. The term "foreign controlling stockholder" means any of the following persons who substantially controls either a domestic corporation or a domestic place of business of a foreign corporation, and the specific criteria therefor shall be prescribed by Presidential Decree:
   (a) In the case of a domestic corporation, a foreign stockholder or investor (hereinafter referred to as "foreign stockholder") or a foreign corporation financed by such foreign stockholder;
   (b) In the case of a domestic place of business of a foreign corporation, the head office or a branch of the foreign corporation, a foreign stockholder of the foreign corporation, or a foreign corporation financed by the foreign corporation or the foreign stockholder;
12. The term "limited tax rate" means the maximum tax rate at which a resident or corporation of the other Contracting State may be taxed under a tax treaty.

(2) Any other term used in this Act and not defined in paragraph (1), unless otherwise specifically provided in this Act, has the meaning defined under Article 2 (1) of the Restriction of Special Taxation Act and the Acts provided in Article 3 (1) 1 through 12, 18, and 19 of the same Act.

[This Article Wholly Amended by Act No. 9914, Jan. 1, 2010]

Article 2-2 (Substance over Form Principle concerning International Transactions) (1) In an international transaction, tax treaties shall apply to the person in whom the taxable income, earnings, property, act, or transaction is actually vested, if a nominal person in the transaction is different from the person in whom the income, earnings, property, act, or transaction is actually vested.

(2) In an international transaction, tax treaties shall apply to the computation of tax base according to the substance of a transaction, regardless of the name or form of the taxable income, earnings, property, act, or transaction.

(3) In an international transaction, if deemed that both parties have conducted such transaction either indirectly through a third party or via at least two acts or transactions to benefit wrongfully from tax treaties and this Act, the tax treaties and this Act shall apply according to the economic substance of the transaction, assuming that such transaction has been conducted directly by both parties or such acts or transactions are a single continuous act or transaction.

[This Article Wholly Amended by Act No. 9914, Jan. 1, 2010]

Article 3 (Relationship to Other Acts) (1) This Act shall take precedence over other Acts providing for national taxes and local taxes.

(2) Article 41 of the Income Tax Act and Article 52 of the Corporate Tax Act shall not apply to any international transactions: Provided, That the same shall not apply to the donation, etc. of assets prescribed by Presidential Decree.

[This Article Wholly Amended by Act No. 9914, Jan. 1, 2010]

CHAPTER II ADJUSTMENT OF TAXATION ON TRANSACTIONS WITH FOREIGN RELATED PARTIES

Article 4 (Tax Adjustment by Arm' s Length Price) (1) Where the price of an international transaction in which either party to the transaction is a foreign related party is lower or higher than the arm's length price, the tax authority may determine or rectify the tax base and tax amount of a resident (including a domestic corporation and a domestic place of business; hereafter the same shall apply in this Chapter) based on the arm's length price: Provided, That where the same method of computing the arm's length price among the methods prescribed in Article 5 applies to computation of the arm's length price for at least two taxable years, and the tax base and tax amount for some of such taxable years are determined or rectified based on the arm's length price so computed, the tax base and tax amount for the remaining taxable years shall also be determined or rectified based on the same arm's length price. <Amended by Act No. 10410, Dec. 27, 2010; Act No. 11126, Dec. 31, 2011>

(2) Paragraph (1) shall not apply where a taxpayer obviously proves that he/she is not in any of the special relationships provided in Article 2 (1) 8 (c) and (d).

[This Article Wholly Amended by Act No. 9914, Jan. 1, 2010]

Article 5 (Methods of Computing Arm's Length Prices) (1) The arm's length price in relation to an international transaction shall be determined by any of the following methods, being the most appropriate method, in consideration of the terms and conditions of transaction, such as the characteristics and functions of goods or services and the economic environment, which are applied or deemed to be applied in an ordinary transaction with a person other than a foreign related party: Provided, That the method provided in subparagraph 6 shall apply only where the arm's length price cannot be determined by any of the methods provided for in subparagraphs 1 through 5: <Amended by Act No. 10410, Dec. 27, 2010; Act No. 11126, Dec. 31, 2011; Act No. 15221, Dec. 19, 2017>

1. Comparable uncontrolled price method: A method that, in an

international transaction between a resident and a foreign related party, regards as the arm's length price, a trade price between independent unrelated parties in comparable transactions;

2. Resale price method: Where a resident and a foreign related party trade in an asset and the purchaser of the asset, being a party to such transaction, subsequently resells it to an unrelated party, a method that regards as the arm's length price, the amount computed by deducting the amount considered as the normal profit of the purchaser from the resale price;
3. Cost plus method: A method that, in an international transaction between a resident and a foreign related party, regards as the arm's length price, the price computed by adding the amount considered as the normal profit of the seller of an asset or the provider of services to the cost incurred in the course of producing and selling the asset or of providing the services;
4. Profit split method: A method that, in an international transaction between a resident and a foreign related party, allocates a net trading profit created by both parties to the transaction according to each such party's relative contribution, which is measured with a reasonable allocation standard, and regards the trade price computed from such allocated profit as the arm's length price;
5. Transactional net margin method: A method that, in an international transaction between a resident and a foreign related party, regards as the arm's length price, a trade price calculated on the basis of an ordinary transactional net margin realized in comparable transactions between a resident and a unrelated party;
6. Other methods recognized as appropriate by Presidential Decree.

(2) When applying paragraph (1), the taxing authority shall clearly identify the substance of the relevant international transaction taking into account the commercial or financial relationship between the resident and the specially concerned

foreign party and the important transaction conditions in the relevant international transaction. In addition, the authority shall judge whether it is a commercially reasonable transaction compared with a transaction performed in the similar conditions between independent business operators that have no special relationship. <Newly Inserted by Act No. 16099, Dec. 31, 2018>

(3) If, based on the judgment under paragraph (2), the taxing authority finds that any international transaction between a resident and a specially concerned foreign party is not commercially resonable and thus that it is significantly difficult to compute arm's length prices based on the relevant international transaction, the authority may consider it invalid or restructure it into a new one to apply paragraph (1) to the transaction. <Newly Inserted by Act No. 16099, Dec. 31, 2018>

(4) Further details concerning the methods of computing arm's length prices provided in provisions of paragraph (1) to (3) shall be prescribed by Presidential Decree. <Amended by Act No. 16099, Dec. 31, 2018>

[This Article Wholly Amended by Act No. 9914, Jan. 1, 2010]

Article 6 (Advance Pricing Agreements) (1) Where a resident intends to apply a method of computing an arm's length price for a specific period of taxable years, he/she may file an application for an advance pricing agreement with the Commissioner of the National Tax Service by not later than the day before the commencement of the first taxable year in the specific period of taxable years to which he/she intends to apply the method of computing an arm's length price, as prescribed by Presidential Decree. <Amended by Act No. 15221, Dec. 19, 2017>

(2) Upon receipt of a resident's application for an advance pricing agreement pursuant to paragraph (1), the Commissioner

of the National Tax Service may accept such application if agreed with the competent authority of the other Contracting State by mutual agreement, as prescribed by Presidential Decree: Provided, That he/she may make an advance pricing agreement without undergoing the mutual agreement procedure (hereafter in this Article referred to as "unilateral advance pricing agreement") in cases prescribed by Presidential Decree.

(3) Upon receipt of a resident's application for the retroactive application of a method of computing an arm's length price to a taxable year before the period subject to the application for an advance pricing agreement, the Commissioner of the National Tax Service may approve the method to apply retroactively to a maximum of five years immediately preceding the period subject to the application for such agreement: Provided, That where an application for the retroactive application of a method of computing an arm's length price is filed as regards a unilateral advance pricing agreement, he/she may approve the method to apply retroactively to a maximum of three years immediately preceding the period subject to the application for such agreement. <Amended by Act No. 10410, Dec. 27, 2010>

(4) Where a method of computing an arm's length price is agreed upon pursuant to paragraphs (2) and (3), the Commissioner of the National Tax Service and the resident shall use the agreed method: Provided, That the same shall not apply in cases prescribed by Presidential Decree.

(5) Where a method of computing an arm's length price is agreed upon pursuant to paragraphs (2) and (3), the resident shall submit a report containing the arm's length price computed by the method and the process of computation to the Commissioner of the National Tax Service, as prescribed by Presidential Decree. [This Article Wholly Amended by Act No. 9914, Jan. 1, 2010]

Article 6-2 (Tax Adjustment by Arm' s Length Cost Sharing)

(1) Where a resident enters into an agreement with a foreign related party on the sharing of the cost, expenses, risks (hereafter in this Article referred to as "cost") to jointly develop or secure intangible property (hereafter referred to as "joint development" in this Article) and performs such joint development in accordance with the agreement, the tax authority may adjust the cost share of the resident based on the arm's length cost share to determine or rectify the tax base and tax amount of the resident, if the cost share of the resident is less or more than the arm's length cost share. <Amended by Act No. 11126, Dec. 31, 2011>

(2) Where a resident has determined shares of respective participants through reasonably allotting the cost for intangible property jointly developed with a foreign related party, but the benefits expected from the jointly-developed intangible property (hereafter in this Article referred to as "expected benefits") are subsequently changed by not less than the rate prescribed by Presidential Decree, the tax authority may determine or rectify the tax base and tax amount of the resident by adjusting the original shares of the participants based on the expected benefits as changed. <Amended by Act No. 11126, Dec. 31, 2011>

(3) For the purposes of paragraphs (1) and (2), the scope of intangible property, the determination of arm's length cost shares and expected benefits, the computation of the changed shares of participants, and other necessary matters, shall be prescribed by Presidential Decree.

[This Article Wholly Amended by Act No. 9914, Jan. 1, 2010]

Article 6-3 (Pre-Adjustment of Arm' s Length Transfer Prices for National Taxes and Customs Duties) (1) A resident who applies for an advance pricing agreement on national tax under Article 6 (1) (limited to cases subject to a unilateral advance pricing agreement pursuant to the proviso to Article 6 (2)) may simultaneously file an application for prior examination of the method of determining the dutiable value under Article 37 (1) 3 of the Customs Act (hereafter in this Article referred to as "prior examination of dutiable value") with the Commissioner of the National Tax Service for pre-adjustment of the arm's length price for national tax and the dutiable value (hereafter in this Article referred to as "pre-adjustment"). <Amended by Act No. 15221, Dec. 19, 2017>

(2) Upon receipt of an application under paragraph (1), the Commissioner of the National Tax Service shall notify the Commissioner of the Korea Customs Service that he/she has received such application, along with an application for prior examination of dutiable value, and shall consult with the Commissioner of the Korea Customs Service about the method of computing an arm's length price, the method of determining a dutiable value, and the range of price to be pre-adjusted, as prescribed by Presidential Decree. <Amended by Act No. 15221, Dec. 19, 2017>

(3) The Commissioner of the National Tax Service shall make a pre-adjustment based on the results of consultation under paragraph (2). <Amended by Act No. 15221, Dec. 19, 2017>

(4) The Commissioner of the National Tax Service shall notify the applicant for pre-adjustment and the Minister of Strategy and Finance of the results of processing the application under paragraph (1). <Amended by Act No. 15221, Dec. 19, 2017>

(5) The method and procedure for applying for pre-adjustment under paragraphs (1) through (4), and other necessary matters, shall be prescribed by Presidential Decree.

[This Article Newly Inserted by Act No. 12849, Dec. 23, 2014]

Article 7 (Transaction Involving Third Party)

Even when a resident engages in an international transaction with a person who is not a foreign related party, Articles 4, 5, and 6-2 shall apply to the international transaction, assuming that such transaction is conducted with a foreign related party, if the transaction satisfies all of the following criteria: <Amended by Act No. 11126, Dec. 31, 2011>

1. The resident and the foreign related party have made prior arrangements (including where a substantial agreement is deemed to have been reached in advance based on evidence of transaction; hereinafter the same shall apply) for the relevant transaction;
2. The resident and the foreign related party have imposed conditions of the transaction between themselves.

[This Article Wholly Amended by Act No. 9914, Jan. 1, 2010]

Article 8 (Recognition of Setoff Transactions) (1) Where an international transaction price differs from the arm's length price, if a resident has entered into an agreement in advance with the same foreign related party to offset the difference through another international transaction conducted during the same taxable year and proves the fact and details of such transaction, the tax authority shall apply Articles 4 and 5, treating all the international transactions so offset as a single international transaction. <Amended by Act No. 11126, Dec. 31, 2011>

(2) Where any of the offset transactions proved in accordance with paragraph (1) becomes subject to withholding tax as provided in Articles 98, 98-2, and 98-3 of the Corporate Tax Act and Articles 156 and 156-2 of the Income Tax Act, withholding tax-related provisions shall apply, assuming that there is no offset transaction.

[This Article Wholly Amended by Act No. 9914, Jan. 1, 2010]

Article 9 (Secondary Income Adjustment and Tax Adjustment after Income Adjustment) (1) Where it is not verified that the amount to be included in gains has been returned by a foreign related party to a domestic corporation as prescribed by

Presidential Decree for the purposes of Article 4 or 6-2, such amount shall be adjusted as a dividend to or an investment in the foreign related party as prescribed by Presidential Decree, notwithstanding Article 67 of the Corporate Tax Act. <Amended by Act No. 11126, Dec. 31, 2011; Act No. 11606, Jan. 1, 2013>

(2) For the purposes of paragraph (1), the method of income adjustment and other necessary matters shall be prescribed by Presidential Decree.

[This Article Wholly Amended by Act No. 9914, Jan. 1, 2010]

Article 10 (Special Provisions on Income Computation) (1) Where any other Contracting State adjusts a transaction price between a resident and a foreign related party at the arm's length price and the mutual agreement procedure thereon are completed, the tax authority may adjust and calculate the amount of income and the assessed amount of tax of the resident for each taxable year pursuant to the relevant agreement. <Amended by Act No. 11126, Dec. 31, 2011>

(2) Methods of applying for adjustments of the amount of income and the assessed amount of tax and methods of adjustment under paragraph (1), and other necessary matters, shall be prescribed by Presidential Decree.

[This Article Wholly Amended by Act No. 9914, Jan. 1, 2010]

Article 10-2 (Rectification Claim for Adjustment of Arm's Length Transfer Prices for National Taxes and Customs Duties) (1) Where a taxpayer has submitted a return on his/her corporate tax base or income tax base to the tax authority in connection with the import transaction of goods from a foreign related party and, subsequently, any difference occurs between the dutiable value and the transaction price used for computing the tax base and tax amount of the corporate tax or income tax returned due to a rectification made by the head of a customs office under Article 38-3 (4) of the Customs Act, the taxpayer may file a claim for rectifying the tax base and tax amount of the corporate tax or income tax with the tax authority within three months from the date he/she becomes aware of the rectification (where he/she receives notice of such rectification, from the date of receipt), as prescribed by Presidential Decree. <Amended by Act No. 15221, Dec. 19, 2017>

(2) Upon receipt of a claim for rectification under paragraph (1), the tax authority may rectify the tax amount if he/she deems that, in connection with the relevant transaction, the method of, and grounds for, computation of the transaction price of the imported goods used for calculating the tax base and tax amount of the corporate tax or income tax conform to Article 5. <Newly Inserted by Act No. 12849, Dec. 23, 2014>

(3) The tax authority shall rectify the tax base or tax amount or notify the claimant of the purport that no ground exist to make a rectification within two months from the date of receipt of a claim for rectification under paragraph (1). <Amended by Act No. 12849, Dec. 23, 2014>

[This Article Newly Inserted by Act No. 11126, Dec. 31, 2011]

Article 10-3 (Adjustment of Taxation on International Trade Price)

(1) A taxpayer may request the Minister of Strategy and Finance to adjust the arm's length price for national tax and the dutiable value within 30 days from the date of receipt of notice given under Article 10-2 (3) (or upon expiration of 2 months if he/she receive no notice within 2 months). In such cases, the Minister of Strategy and Finance may recommend the tax authority or the head of the customs office to adjust taxes on the transaction price, and shall request a plan for fulfilling the recommendation for adjustment (in the case of nonfulfillment, including the grounds therefor) from the tax authority or the head of the customs office and notify the taxpayer thereof within 90 days from the date of receipt of the request for adjustment.

<Amended by Act No. 14384, Dec. 20, 2016>

(2) Making requests for adjustment and the methods of adjustment under paragraph (1), and other necessary matters, shall be prescribed by Presidential Decree.

(3) The period from the date of a request for adjustment to the date of receipt of notice provided in paragraph (1) shall be excluded from the period for filing requests or applications provided in Articles 61, 66, and 68 of the Framework Act on National Taxes and Articles 121, 131, and 132 of the Customs Act.

[This Article Newly Inserted by Act No. 11126, Dec. 31, 2011]

Article 11 (Obligation to Submit Data on International Transactions)

(1) A taxpayer that conducts international transactions with a foreign related party shall submit a statement of international transactions in the form prescribed by Ordinance of the Ministry of Strategy and Finance (hereinafter referred to as "statement of international transactions") to the head of the tax office having jurisdiction over the place for tax payment by the deadline for filing a tax return set under Articles 70, 70-2, 71, 73, and 74 of the Income Tax Act or Articles 60 (1) and 76-17 (1) of the Corporate Tax Act. <Amended by Act No. 15221, Dec. 19, 2017>

(2) A taxpayer, if he/she meets the requirements prescribed by Presidential Decree in the volume of international transactions with a foreign related party and the turnover therefrom, shall submit a consolidated business report, individual business reports, and reports by country prescribed by Presidential Decree regarding his/her business activities, the details of transactions, etc. (hereinafter referred to as "consolidated report on international transaction information") to the head of the tax office having jurisdiction over the place for tax payment within 12 months from the last day of the month in which the end date of the business year under Article 6 of the Corporate Tax Act falls.

<Newly Inserted by Act No. 15221, Dec. 19, 2017>

(3) Where a taxpayer is unable to submit a statement of international transactions or a consolidated report on international transaction information by the deadline referred to in paragraph (1) or (2) in extenuating circumstances prescribed by Presidential Decree and files an application to extend such deadline, the head of the tax office having jurisdiction over the place for tax payment may extend the deadline for submission by up to 1 year. <Newly Inserted by Act No. 13553, Dec. 15, 2015; Act No. 14384, Dec. 20, 2016; Act No. 15221, Dec. 19, 2017>

(4) For the purposes of Articles 4, 5, and 6-2, the tax authority may request a taxpayer to submit related data, such as the method of computing transaction prices, as prescribed by Presidential Decree.

(5) A person in receipt of a request to submit data under paragraph (4) shall submit the relevant data within 60 days of receipt of the request: Provided, That where the person files an application to extend the deadline for submission for good cause prescribed by Presidential Decree, the tax authority may extend the deadline by up to 60 days on one occasion only. <Amended by Act No. 13553, Dec. 15, 2015; Act No. 15221, Dec. 19, 2017>

(6) Where a person in receipt of a request to submit data under paragraph (4) fails to submit data by the deadline without good cause prescribed by Presidential Decree and submits the data at the time of applying for appeal, or of the mutual agreement procedure, the tax authority and related agencies need not use such data for assessing taxes. <Amended by Act No. 13553, Dec. 15, 2015; Act No. 15221, Dec. 19, 2017>

(7) The detailed scope of information to be contained in the statements of international transactions or consolidated reports on international transaction information, the methods and procedures for submitting the same, and other necessary matters, shall be

prescribed by Presidential Decree. <Amended by Act No. 14384, Dec. 20, 2016; Act No. 15221, Dec. 19, 2017>

[This Article Wholly Amended by Act No. 9914, Jan. 1, 2010]

Article 11-2 (Provision of Information on International Transactions)

(1) The tax authority may request information or data prescribed by Presidential Decree from the head of the customs office where necessary to assess and collect taxes in relation of an international transaction and adjust the arm's length price for national tax and the dutiable value.

(2) The head of the customs office in receipt of a request under paragraph (1) shall comply therewith except in extenuating circumstances.

[This Article Newly Inserted by Act No. 11126, Dec. 31, 2011]

Article 12 (Sanctions against Non-Compliance with Obligation to Submit Data) (1) Any of the following persons who fails to submit data by the deadline without good cause prescribed by Presidential Decree or submits false data shall be subject to an administrative fine not exceeding 100 million won: <Amended by Act No. 10410, Dec. 27, 2010; Act No. 12849, Dec. 23, 2014; Act No. 13553, Dec. 15, 2015; Act No. 15221, Dec. 19, 2017>

1. A person obligated to submit a statement of international transactions or a consolidated report on international transaction information;
2. A person in receipt of a request to submit data under Article 11 (4).

(2) An administrative fine provided in paragraph (1) shall be assessed and collected by the tax authority, as prescribed by Presidential Decree.

[This Article Wholly Amended by Act No. 9914, Jan. 1, 2010]

Article 13 (Special Provisions on Application of Penalty Tax)

(1) For the purposes of Articles 4 through 6, 6-2, and 7 through 9, the tax authority shall not assess a penalty tax for under-

reporting provided in Article 47-3 of the Framework Act on National Taxes if any of the following is applicable: <Amended by Act No. 15221, Dec. 19, 2017>

1. Where it is confirmed by the mutual agreement procedure that a taxpayer has not made any mistake with regard to the difference between the trade price reported and the arm's length price (referring to where the Commissioner of the National Tax Service determines that the taxpayer has not made any mistake, if an advance pricing agreement was made without undergoing the mutual agreement procedure as provided in the proviso to Article 6 (2));
2. Where a taxpayer keeps and provides data verifying the method of computing an arm's length price applied in filing his/her income tax or corporate tax return or submits individual business reports pursuant to Article 11 (2) within the deadline and is acknowledged as having selected and applied the method of computing an arm's length price based on reasonable determination.

(2) Whether the taxpayer has made a mistake or whether the determination is reasonable as provided in the subparagraphs of paragraph (1) shall be determined based on the standards prescribed by Presidential Decree.

[This Article Wholly Amended by Act No. 9914, Jan. 1, 2010]

CHAPTER III ADJUSTMENT OF TAX ON INTEREST PAID TO FOREIGN CONTROLLING STOCKHOLDERS, ETC.

Article 14 (Exclusion of Interest Deemed Dividend from Deductible Expenses) (1) Where a domestic corporation (including a domestic place of business of a foreign corporation; hereafter in this Chapter the same shall apply) borrows funds from a foreign controlling stockholder (including funds borrowed from a related party of a foreign controlling stockholder prescribed by Presidential Decree, including relatives) or from a third party under a payment guarantee (including security provided to guarantee payments) by a foreign controlling stockholder, and such borrowings exceed twice the amount invested by the foreign controlling stockholder, the interest and discount fees paid in relation to the excess amount shall be excluded from deductible expenses of the domestic corporation and shall be deemed to have been disposed of as a dividend of or an outflow from the domestic corporation pursuant to Article 67 of the Corporate Tax Act, as prescribed by Presidential Decree. In such cases, the scope of borrowings and the methods of computing the amount deemed excluded from deductible expenses and the amount of investment shall be prescribed by Presidential Decree. <Amended by Act No. 11606, Jan. 1, 2013; Act No. 12849, Dec. 23, 2014>

(2) The multiplier of the borrowings against the amount of investment by a foreign controlling stockholder provided in paragraph (1) may be separately prescribed by Presidential Decree for each type of business. <Amended by Act No. 11606, Jan. 1, 2013>

(3) Where a domestic corporation attests that the amount and conditions of borrowings are identical or similar to the amount and conditions of ordinary borrowings between the persons who are not in a special relationship, as prescribed by Presidential Decree, paragraphs (1) and (2) shall not apply to the interest and discount fees paid in relation to such borrowings.

(4) Where a domestic corporation subject to paragraph (1) has withheld income tax or corporate tax on the interest and discount fees it has paid to a foreign controlling stockholder in each business year, it shall offset such withheld tax amount against the income tax or corporate tax assessed on the dividend

provided in paragraph (1).

(5) For the purposes of paragraphs (1) through (4), if there exist different interest or discount fees whereto separate interest rates apply, the interest or discount fees shall be excluded from deductible expenses in order of those subject to a higher interest rate. <Newly Inserted by Act No. 15221, Dec. 19, 2017>

[This Article Wholly Amended by Act No. 9914, Jan. 1, 2010]

Article 15 (Borrowing Transactions through Third Party)

Where funds borrowed by a domestic corporation from a person who is not a foreign controlling stockholder satisfy all of the following criteria, Article 14 shall apply to the funds, assuming that such funds are borrowed directly from a foreign controlling stockholder: Provided, That Article 14 shall apply even when only the criteria provided in subparagraph 2 is satisfied if the domestic corporation has borrowed funds from a foreign related party other than a foreign controlling stockholder: <Amended by Act No. 11126, Dec. 31, 2011>

1. The domestic corporation and the foreign controlling stockholder have made prior arrangements;
2. The domestic corporation and the foreign controlling stockholder have imposed conditions of borrowings between themselves.

[This Article Wholly Amended by Act No. 9914, Jan. 1, 2010]

Article 15-2 (Exclusion of Interest Expense Exceeding Income from Deductible Expenses) (1) If the net interest expense in subparagraph 1 on funds borrowed by a domestic corporation from its foreign related parties exceeds 30/100 of the adjusted gross income in subparagraph 2, the excess amount shall be excluded from deductible expenses and deemed disposed of as other outflow from the domestic corporation pursuant to Article 67 of the Corporate Tax Act:

1. Net interest expense: Interest and discount fees paid to foreign related parties less the amount of interest income received

from the foreign related parties;

2. Adjusted gross income: The amount of income before subtracting both the depreciation cost and the net interest expense referred to in subparagraph 1.

(2) Paragraph (1) shall not apply to any domestic corporation prescribed by Presidential Decree that engages in financial business or other similar business.

(3) For the purpose of paragraph (1), if there exist different interest or discount fees whereto separate interest rates apply, the interest or discount fees shall be excluded from deductible expenses in order of those subject to a higher interest rate.

(4) The method of computing the net interest expenses and adjusted gross income pursuant to paragraph (1) and other necessary matters shall be prescribed by Presidential Decree.

[This Article Newly Inserted by Act No. 15221, Dec. 19, 2017] <<Enforcement Date: Jan. 1, 2019>>

Article 15-3 (Exclusion of Interest Expenses Incurred in Hybrid Financial Instrument Transactions from Deductible Expenses)

(1) The interest and discount fees paid by a domestic corporation in relation to transactions in financial instruments (referring to financial instruments prescribed by the Presidential Decree that have the nature of both capital and liabilities; hereafter in this Article the same shall apply) with a foreign related party, which are not included in the income of the counter-party to such transactions nor taxable in the country where the counter-party is located within the period of time prescribed by Presidential Decree (hereafter in this Article referred to as "reasonable period of time"), shall be excluded from deductible expenses of the domestic corporation, as prescribed by Presidential Decree, in calculating the amount of income for the pertinent business year, and deemed disposed of as other outflow from the domestic corporation pursuant to Article 67 of the Corporate Tax Act.

(2) If the amount that a domestic corporation has excluded from deductible expenses in accordance with paragraph (1) is included in the income of the counter-party to transaction or taxable in the country where the counter-party is located within a reasonable period of time, it may be included in deductible expenses, as prescribed by Presidential Decree, in calculating the amount of income for the business year in which the end date of the reasonable period of time falls.
(3) If an amount equivalent to interest paid by a domestic corporation in relation to financial instrument transactions is included in deductible expenses in calculating the amount of income for the pertinent taxable year on the assumption that it does not fall under paragraph (1), but thereafter the amount is found to fall under paragraph (1), it shall be included in gains, as prescribed by Presidential Decree, in calculating the amount of income for the business year in which the end date of the reasonable period of time falls and shall be deemed disposed of as other outflow from the domestic corporation pursuant to Article 67 of the Corporate Tax Act. In such cases, the domestic corporation shall additionally pay an amount equivalent to interest calculated pursuant to Presidential Decree, plus the corporate tax for the business year in which the end date of the reasonable period of time falls.
(4) The scope of financial instrument transactions pursuant to paragraph (1), the scope of non-taxable amounts, and other necessary matters, shall be prescribed by Presidential Decree.
[This Article Newly Inserted by Act No. 15221, Dec. 19, 2017]

Article 16 (Order of Applying Exclusion of Paid Interest from Deductible Expenses) (1) Where both Articles 14 and 15-2 can be applicable, only one of them shall be applied if the amount calculated according thereto to be excluded from deductible expenses is relatively larger. In such cases, if the

amounts calculated according to both Articles are the same, Article 14 shall apply.
(2) Article 14 or 15-2 shall take precedence over Articles 4 and 15-3 of this Act and Article 28 of the Corporate Tax Act.
(3) Article 15-3 shall take precedence over Article 4 of this Act and Article 28 of the Corporate Tax Act.
[This Article Wholly Amended by Act No. 15221, Dec. 19, 2017]
<<Enforcement Date of the amended provisions of Article 16 (applicable only in relation to Article 15-2: Jan. 1, 2019>>

CHAPTER IV ACCUMULATIVE TAXATION OF RETAINED EARNINGS OF SPECIFIC FOREIGN CORPORATIONS

Article 17 (Specific Foreign Corporations' Retained Earnings Deemed Dividends) (1) Where a Korean national has invested in a foreign corporation, the head office or principal office of which is located in a country or region in which the tax burden does not exceed 15/100 of the income actually earned by the corporation, the amount attributable to the Korean national out of the corporation's retained earnings distributable as at the end of each business year shall be deemed a dividend paid to the Korean national if the corporation (hereinafter referred to as "specific foreign corporation") is in a special relationship (in determining whether it is in the relationship provided in Article 2 (1) 8 (a), stocks held directly or indirectly by a related party of the Korean national prescribed by Presidential Decree, including relatives, shall be included) with the Korean national. <Amended by Act No. 11606, Jan. 1, 2013; Act No. 12849, Dec. 23, 2014>
(2) The scope of Korean nationals eligible under paragraph (1) shall be those who directly or indirectly hold at least 10 percent of the total outstanding stocks or the total equity investment of a

specific foreign corporation as at the end of each business year. In such cases, outstanding stocks or equity investment held directly by persons prescribed by Presidential Decree among related persons, as defined in subparagraph 20 of Article 2 of the Framework Act on National Taxes, shall be included for the purposes of determining 10 percent of the total outstanding stocks or the total equity investment. <Amended by Act No. 11126, Dec. 31, 2011; Act No. 11606, Jan. 1, 2013>

(3) Paragraph (1) shall not apply where the income actually earned by a specific foreign corporation as at the end of each business year does not exceed the amount specified by Presidential Decree.

(4) For the purposes of paragraphs (1) and (2), the scope of the income actually earned, non-taxable income and its scope, methods of computing distributable retained earnings and the amount deemed a dividend, the method of computing the stock-holding ratio, and other necessary matters, shall be prescribed by Presidential Decree. <Amended by Act No. 11606, Jan. 1, 2013>

[This Article Wholly Amended by Act No. 9914, Jan. 1, 2010]

Article 18 (Scope of Application) (1) Article 17 shall not apply where a specific foreign corporation owns a permanent establishment required for business activities, such as an office, a store, or a factory, in a country or region provided in Article 17 (1) and engages in business activities mainly in such a country or region by managing, controlling, or operating the business for itself: Provided, That the same shall not apply to the following specific foreign corporations: <Amended by Act No. 11126, Dec. 31, 2011; Act No. 11606, Jan. 1, 2013>

1. A specific foreign corporation that engages in wholesale trade; financial and insurance activities; real estate activities and real estate lease; professional, scientific and technical services (excluding architectural, engineering and related services); or

business facilities management and business support services and that satisfies the criteria prescribed by Presidential Decree;

2. A corporation, the primary business of which is to hold stocks or bonds; to provide intellectual property rights; to lease ships, aircraft or equipment; or to invest in investment trusts or funds.

(2) Where a foreign corporation has its place of actual business control in a country or region provided in Article 17 (1), the tax authority may apply Article 17 to the corporation, assuming that the place of actual business control is its head office or principal office provided in Article 17 (1).

(3) For the purposes of paragraph (1) 1, the classification of businesses by type shall be governed by the Korean Standard Industrial Classification publicly notified by the Commissioner of the Statistics Korea under Article 22 of the Statistics Act.

(4) Article 17 shall not apply where a specific foreign corporation that engages in wholesale trade referred to in paragraph (1) 1 sells goods to a person not in a special relationship who is in the same country or the same area prescribed by Ordinance of the Ministry of Strategy and Finance (hereinafter referred to as "same country, etc.") and satisfies the criterion prescribed by Presidential Decree. <Amended by Act No. 11606, Jan. 1, 2013>

(5) Where the income that a specific foreign corporation not subject to Article 17 pursuant to the main sentence of paragraph (1) and paragraph (4) earns by engaging in the following activities satisfies the criterion prescribed by Presidential Decree, such income shall be deemed distributable retained earnings subject to Article 17, as prescribed by Presidential Decree: <Newly Inserted by Act No. 12164, Jan. 1, 2014>

1. Holding stocks or bonds;

2. Providing intellectual property rights;
3. Leasing ships, aircraft, or equipment;
4. Investing in investment trusts or funds.

[This Article Wholly Amended by Act No. 9914, Jan. 1, 2010]

Article 18-2 (Special Provisions on Overseas Holding Companies' Retained Earnings Deemed Dividends)

Article 17 shall not apply where a specific foreign corporation (hereafter in this Article referred to as "overseas holding company") the primary business of which is to hold stocks and which holds stocks issued by any of its affiliates (referring to a foreign corporation the stocks of which are held by the specific foreign corporation and which satisfies the criteria prescribed by Presidential Decree; hereafter the same shall apply in this Article) meets all of the following conditions, regardless of whether the corporation engages in business activities at a permanent establishment, such as an office, a store, or a factory: <Amended by Act No. 11126, Dec. 31, 2011; Act No. 11606, Jan. 1, 2013>

1. The overseas holding company has held stocks issued by any of its affiliates for at least six consecutive months as of the date of record for dividends by that affiliate;
2. The rate of the total amount of interest income, dividend income, and other income prescribed by Presidential Decree that the overseas holding company has received from any of its affiliated companies having its head office or principal office in the same country, etc. among the affiliates referred to in subparagraph 1 to the income (excluding the income generated by actually engaging in any business other than those provided in the subparagraphs of Article 18 (1) at a permanent establishment, such as an office, a store, or a factory, and the income generated by disposing of stocks of the affiliate) of that overseas holding company shall be equal

to or exceed the rate prescribed by Presidential Decree.

[This Article Wholly Amended by Act No. 9914, Jan. 1, 2010]

Article 19 (Timing of Treating Dividends as Taxable Gains) (1) The amount deemed a dividend as provided in Article 17 (1) (hereafter in this Article referred to as "deemed dividend") shall be included in a Korean national's gains or dividend income (hereafter in this Chapter referred to as "gains") for the taxable year in which the sixtieth day after the end of the pertinent business year of the specific foreign corporation falls. <Amended by Act No. 11606, Jan. 1, 2013>

(2) Where a specific foreign corporation has paid taxes to a foreign country when actually distributing a dividend to a Korean national, a deemed dividend for the taxable year, which is included in gains in accordance with paragraph (1), shall be treated as foreign source income, while the taxes paid to the foreign country as at the time of the actual distribution shall be deemed paid to the foreign country in the taxable year during which the amount is included in gains in accordance with paragraph (1), and Article 57 (1) and (2) of the Corporate Tax Act and Article 57 (1) and (2) of the Income Tax Act shall apply thereto. <Amended by Act No. 11606, Jan. 1, 2013>

(3) For the purposes of Article 57 (4) of the Corporate Tax Act, a deemed dividend included in gains in accordance with paragraph (1) shall be deemed a dividend earned during the taxable year in which it is included in gains. <Amended by Act No. 11126, Dec. 31, 2011; Act No. 11606, Jan. 1, 2013>

(4) Any person who wishes to quality for paragraph (2) may file a request for rectification with the head of the tax office having jurisdiction over the place of tax payment, as prescribed by Presidential Decree, within one year following the expiration of the deadline for filing the income tax or corporate tax return of the taxable year in which he/she has actually received a dividend.

[This Article Wholly Amended by Act No. 9914, Jan. 1, 2010]

Article 20 (Exclusion of Actually Dividends from Taxable Gains)

(1) Where a specific foreign corporation actually distributes its retained earnings as dividends (including dividends or distributions provided in Article 16 of the Corporate Tax Act) subsequent to the inclusion of the retained earnings in the gains of a Korean national under Article 17 (1), the distributed amount shall be deemed the gross income carried forward referred to in subparagraph 2 of Article 18 of the Corporate Tax Act or deemed not to fall within the dividend income provided in Article 17 (1) of the Income Tax Act. <Amended by Act No. 10410, Dec. 27, 2010>

(2) Where the retained earnings of a specific foreign corporation are included in the gains of a Korean national under Article 17 (1) and the Korean national transfers stocks of the specific foreign corporation, the amount provided in subparagraph 1, less the amount provided in subparagraph 2 (if the amount so calculated is less than zero, it shall be deemed zero) shall be deemed the gross income carried forward referred to in paragraph (1) or deemed not to fall within the income generated from the transfer of stocks, as provided in subparagraph 3 of Article 118-2 of the Income Tax Act. In such cases, if the amount deemed the gross income carried forward or deemed not to fall within the income generated from the transfer of stocks exceeds the capital gains on transfer of such stocks, the excess amount shall be deemed nil: <Amended by Act No. 10410, Dec. 27, 2010; Act No. 11606, Jan. 1, 2013>

1. The amount equivalent to the aggregate of the amounts treated as the dividends on the transferred stocks;
2. The amount of actually distributed dividends on the transferred stocks.

(3) The books of account and evidentiary documents necessary for calculating the gross income carried forward pursuant to

paragraphs (1) and (2) shall be preserved until the expiration of the statutory deadline for filing a return for the taxable year in which the date of dividend payment or transfer falls, notwithstanding Article 85-3 (2) of the Framework Act on National Taxes. <Amended by Act No. 10410, Dec. 27, 2010>

[This Article Wholly Amended by Act No. 9914, Jan. 1, 2010]

Article 20-2 (Submission of Data on Specific Foreign Corporations)

Each Korean national subject to Article 17, 18, 18-2, 19, or 20 shall submit the following documents to the head of the tax office having jurisdiction over the place for tax payment by the deadline for filing a tax return set under Articles 70 (1) and 70-2 (2) of the Income Tax Act, or Articles 60 (1) and 76-17 (1) of the Corporate Tax Act, as prescribed by Presidential Decree: <Amended by Act No. 13553, Dec. 15, 2015>

1. Financial statements of a specific foreign corporation;
2. A corporate tax return of a specific foreign corporation and supporting documents;
3. A detailed statement on calculation of retained earnings of a specific foreign corporation;
4. Other documents prescribed by Presidential Decree.

[This Article Newly Inserted by Act No. 12164, Jan. 1, 2014]

CHAPTER V SPECIAL PROVISIONS ON ASSESSMENT OF GIFT TAX ON OVERSEAS DONATION

Article 21 (Special Provisions on Assessment of Gift Tax on Overseas Donation) (1) Where a resident donates (excluding a donation that takes effect upon the death of a donor) his/her overseas property to a nonresident, the donor is liable to pay gift tax pursuant to this Act: Provided, That such donor shall be exempt from gift tax when the donee is not in a special relationship, as defined in subparagraph 20 of Article 2 of the

Framework Act on National Taxes, with the donor, and gift tax (including taxes substantially similar thereto) is assessed (including exemption) on the property pursuant to statutes of the relevant foreign country. <Amended by Act No. 11606, Jan. 1, 2013; Act No. 12849, Dec. 23, 2014; Act No. 13553, Dec. 15, 2015; Act No. 14384, Dec. 20, 2016>

(2) For the purposes of the main sentence of paragraph (1), the value of donated property shall be based on its market price reflecting the situations as at the time of such donation in the foreign country wherein the donated property is located, but the matters concerning the computation of such market price shall be prescribed by Presidential Decree: Provided, That where it is impracticable to compute a market price, the market price shall be computed by the methods specified by Presidential Decree, taking account of the type, scale, and circumstances of the transaction of the relevant property. <Amended by Act No. 12849, Dec. 23, 2014>

(3) For the purposes of the main sentence of paragraph (1) and paragraph (2), where gift tax has been paid pursuant to statutes of the relevant foreign country, the amount equivalent to the gift tax paid shall be deducted from the amount of gift tax computed, as prescribed by Presidential Decree. <Newly Inserted by Act No. 12849, Dec. 23, 2014>

(4) Articles 4-2 (1) and (3), 47, 53, 56 through 58, 68, 69 (2), 70 through 72, and 76 of the Inheritance Tax and Gift Tax Act shall apply mutatis mutandis the assessment of gift tax under paragraph (1). <Amended by Act No. 11126, Dec. 31, 2011; Act No. 12849, Dec. 23, 2014; Act No. 13553, Dec. 15, 2015; Act No. 16099, Dec. 31, 2018>

(5) The resident referred to in paragraph (1) includes a non-profit corporation that has its head office or principal office in the Republic of Korea, and the nonresident referred to in

paragraph (1) includes a non-profit corporation that has no head office or principal office in the Republic of Korea. <Newly Inserted by Act No. 11606, Jan. 1, 2013; Act No. 12849, Dec. 23, 2014>

[This Article Wholly Amended by Act No. 9914, Jan. 1, 2010]

CHAPTER VI MUTUAL AGREEMENT PROCEDURES

Article 22 (Conditions for Commencing Mutual Agreement Procedure) (1) Any national, resident, or domestic corporation of the Republic of Korea, any nonresident or foreign corporation may apply for commencing the mutual agreement procedure to any of the following persons, as prescribed by Presidential Decree: <Amended by Act No. 14384, Dec. 20, 2016>

1. The Minister of Strategy and Finance where it is necessary to consult with the other Contracting State on the application and interpretation of the tax treaty;
2. The Commissioner of the National Tax Service where any tax has been or is likely to be assessed by the tax authority of the other Contracting State, not in compliance with the provisions of the tax treaty;
3. The Commissioner of the National Tax Service where a tax adjustment is required under the tax treaty between the Republic of Korea and the other Contracting State.

(2) Upon receipt of an application for commencing the mutual agreement procedure under paragraph (1), the Minister of Strategy and Finance or the Commissioner of the National Tax Service shall request the competent authority of the other Contracting State to commence the mutual agreement procedure and notify the applicant of the fact of such request, except in the following circumstances:

1. Where the final ruling has been made by a domestic or foreign

court;

2. Where the application has been filed by a person ineligible under the tax treaty;
3. Where it is recognized that the taxpayer intends to utilize the mutual agreement procedure for tax avoidance;
4. Where the application has been filed three years after the applicant became aware of the tax assessed.

(3) Upon receipt of an application under paragraph (1), the Commissioner of the National Tax Service shall report thereon to the Minister of Strategy and Finance, and the Minister of Strategy and Finance may give an instruction as to the mutual agreement procedure, if necessary.

(4) In the circumstances provided in paragraph (1) 1, the Minister of Strategy and Finance may ex officio request the competent authority of the other Contracting State to commence the mutual agreement procedure.

(5) In the circumstances provided in paragraph (1) 2 or 3, the Commissioner of the National Tax Service may ex officio request the competent authority of the other Contracting State to commence the mutual agreement procedure. Paragraph (3) shall apply mutatis mutandis to such cases.

[This Article Wholly Amended by Act No. 9914, Jan. 1, 2010]

Article 23 (Commencing and Closing Dates of Mutual Agreement Procedure) (1) The commencement date of the mutual agreement procedure shall be either of the following dates:

1. Where the competent authority of the other Contracting State makes a request to commence the mutual agreement procedure, the date of notifying the competent authority of the other Contracting State of its intent to accept the request;
2. Where a request to commence the mutual agreement procedure is forwarded to the competent authority of the other Contracting State, the date of receiving an intent to accept the request from

the competent authority of the other Contracting State.

(2) The closing date of the mutual agreement procedure shall be the date on which the competent authority of the Republic of Korea enters into a written agreement with the other Contracting State: Provided, That where no mutual agreement is reached, the closing date of the mutual agreement procedure shall be the date on which five years elapse from the date following the commencement date.

(3) Where the competent authority of the Republic of Korea agrees with the other Contracting State to continue the mutual agreement procedure, the mutual agreement procedure shall not be closed, notwithstanding the proviso to paragraph (2). In such cases, the closing date of the mutual agreement procedure shall not exceed eight years, beginning on the date following the commencement date.

(4) In any of the following cases, a date classified accordingly shall be the closing date of the mutual agreement procedure: <Amended by Act No. 14384, Dec. 20, 2016>

1. Where the final ruling is made by a court in the course of the mutual agreement procedure: The date the final ruling is made;
2. Where the applicant withdraws his/her application for commencing the mutual agreement procedure in the course of the mutual agreement procedure: The date the application is withdrawn.

[This Article Wholly Amended by Act No. 9914, Jan. 1, 2010]

Article 24 (Special Provisions on Period for Applying for Appeal, Deferment of Collection, etc.) (1) Where the mutual agreement procedure has commenced, the period from the commencement date to the closing date of the mutual agreement procedure shall be excluded from the period for making requests provided in Articles 56 (3), 61, and 68 of the Framework Act on National Taxes and Article 91 of the Framework Act on Local Taxes and in the period for making decisions provided in Articles 65 and

81 of the Framework Act on National Taxes and Article 96 of the Framework Act on Local Taxes. <Amended by Act No. 10219, Mar. 31, 2010; Act No. 14474, Dec. 27, 2016>

(2) Where the mutual agreement procedure has commenced before a notice of the amount of tax payable is given, the head of the tax office having jurisdiction over the place for tax payment or the head of the local government may either defer a notice of the amount of tax until the end of the mutual agreement procedure or notify an installment payment of the assessed amount of tax. In such cases, the head of the tax office having jurisdiction over the place of tax payment or the head of the local government shall notify the amount of tax payable within 30 days from the date following the closing date of the mutual agreement procedure.

(3) Where the mutual agreement procedure has commenced after the notice of tax payment or a demand notice was served on the taxpayer, the head of the tax office having jurisdiction over the place for tax payment or the head of the local government may either defer the collection of tax or defer the seizure of property due to disposition for arrears or the sale of seized property from the commencement date to the closing date of the mutual agreement procedure. In such cases, the head of the tax office having jurisdiction over the place for tax payment or the head of the local government shall set a new payment deadline and collect the deferred tax amount, within 30 days from the date following the closing date of the mutual agreement procedure.

(4) Paragraphs (2) and (3) shall apply only where the other Contracting State allows the deferment of tax collection and of disposition for arrears, in the course of the mutual agreement procedure.

(5) Where the head of the tax office having jurisdiction over the place for tax payment or the head of the local government

allows the deferment of tax collection or of disposition for arrears under paragraph (3), he/she shall additionally collect the amount equivalent to the interest for the relevant period as calculated pursuant to Presidential Decree.

(6) Any person who wishes to qualify for paragraphs (2) and (3) shall file an application for the special provisions on the deferment of tax collection or of disposition for arrears with the head of the tax office having jurisdiction over the place for tax payment or the head of the local government, as prescribed by Presidential Decree.

(7) Where any of the deferred notice, notice of installment payment, deferment of tax collection, and deferment of disposition for arrears (hereafter in this paragraph referred to as "deferred notice") is applied to the amount of income tax or corporate tax under paragraph (2) or (3), the deferred notice shall also be applied, as it stands, to the amount of local tax to be added to the amount of income tax or corporate tax without undergoing any separate procedure provided in this Article. In such cases, the Commissioner of the National Tax Service shall notify the head of the local government of the fact of deferred notice, as prescribed by Presidential Decree.

[This Article Wholly Amended by Act No. 9914, Jan. 1, 2010]

Article 25 (Special Provisions on Statute of Limitations for Tax Assessment) (1) Where the mutual agreement procedure agreed upon with the other Contracting State commences, no national taxes shall be assessed upon the expiration of the one-year period beginning on the date following the closing date of the mutual agreement procedure and of the period provided in Article 26-2 (1) of the Framework Act on National Taxes, whichever comes later.

(2) Where the mutual agreement procedure agreed upon with the other Contracting State commences, no local taxes shall be

assessed upon the expiration of the one-year period beginning on the date following the closing date of the mutual agreement procedure and of the period provided in Article 38 (1) of the Framework Act on Local Taxes, whichever comes later. <Amended by Act No. 10219, Mar. 31, 2010>

[This Article Wholly Amended by Act No. 9914, Jan. 1, 2010]

Article 26 (Taxpayer's Obligation to Cooperate) (1) The Minister of Strategy and Finance or the Commissioner of the National Tax Service may request a taxpayer who has applied for commencement of the mutual agreement procedure to submit documents necessary for proceeding with the mutual agreement procedure.

(2) The Minister of Strategy and Finance or the Commissioner of the National Tax Service may terminate ex officio the mutual agreement procedure if the taxpayer fails to comply conscientiously with a request to submit documents under paragraph (1). In such cases, the closing date of the mutual agreement procedure shall be the date the applicant is notified of the termination of such procedure.

[This Article Wholly Amended by Act No. 9914, Jan. 1, 2010]

Article 27 (Enforcement of Terms and Conditions Mutually Agreed Upon) (1) The Commissioner of the National Tax Service shall report the terms and conditions mutually agreed upon to the Minister of Strategy and Finance upon closing of the mutual agreement procedure.

(2) Upon closing of the mutual agreement procedure, the Minister of Strategy and Finance or the Commissioner of the National Tax Service shall notify the tax authority, the head of a local government, the Director of the Tax Tribunal, other relevant agencies, and the applicant for the commencement of the mutual agreement procedure of the terms and conditions mutually agreed upon within 15 days from the date following the closing date of the mutual agreement procedure. In such

cases, the Minister of Strategy and Finance shall publicly notify the contents of the agreement reached upon the closing of the agreement procedure in accordance with Article 22 (1) 1. <Amended by Act No. 11126, Dec. 31, 2011; Act No. 16099, Dec. 31, 2018>

(3) The tax authority or the head of a local government shall assess taxes, determine to make a rectification, or take other necessary action under the tax laws pursuant to the terms and conditions mutually agreed upon.

(4) Where a final ruling has been made by a court after conclusion of the mutual agreement procedure, and the contents of such final ruling are contrary to any of the terms and conditions mutually agreed upon, the said mutual agreement shall be deemed nonexistent from the beginning.

[This Article Wholly Amended by Act No. 9914, Jan. 1, 2010]

Article 27-2 (Extended Application, etc. of Terms and Conditions Mutually Agreed Upon) (1) Where a person who applied for commencement of the mutual agreement procedure, after the mutual agreement has been concluded, files an application for applying the terms and conditions mutually agreed upon to transactions between the applicant and a related party who resides in any country, other than the country bound by the mutual agreement, within three years from the date the notice of conclusion of the mutual agreement is delivered, as prescribed by Presidential Decree, the tax authority or the head of the relevant local government may apply the terms and conditions mutually agreed upon to the transactions with the related party who resides in any country, other than the country bound by the mutual agreement, if all of the following requirements are met: <Amended by Act No. 11126, Dec. 31, 2011>

1. The transactions are of the same type as that upon which the terms and conditions were mutually agreed;

2. Taxes have been assessed in the same manner as stipulated in the terms and conditions mutually agreed upon;
3. Other requirements prescribed by Presidential Decree are met.

(2) Article 27 shall apply mutatis mutandis to the extended application of the terms and conditions mutually agreed upon in accordance with paragraph (1) to a related party who resides in any country, other than the country bound by the mutual agreement. <Amended by Act No. 11126, Dec. 31, 2011>

[This Article Wholly Amended by Act No. 9914, Jan. 1, 2010]

CHAPTER VII INTERNATIONAL COOPERATION IN TAX AFFAIRS

Article 28 (Preferential Application of Income Classification under Tax Treaty)

Deleted. <By Act No. 16099, Dec. 31, 2018>

Article 29 (Special Provisions on Application of Tax Rates to Interest, Dividends, and Royalties) (1) The lower of the limited tax rate provided by a tax treaty or any of the following tax rates shall apply to interest, dividends, or royalties on intellectual property, etc. (where any income generated from the rental of industrial, commercial, or scientific machinery, facilities, equipment, etc. provided in subparagraph 4 of Article 119 of the Income Tax Act and subparagraph 4 of Article 93 of the Corporate Tax Act is classified as a royalty on intellectual property under the tax treaty, including such royalty) that constitute a domestic source income of a nonresident or foreign corporation under the tax treaty: Provided, That for the purposes of Article 156-4 (1) of the Income Tax Act or Article 98-5 (1) of the Corporate Tax Act, taxes shall be withheld in accordance with Article 156-4 (1) of the Income Tax Act or Article 98-5 (1) of the Corporate Tax Act. In such cases, the lower of the limited tax rate provided by the tax treaty or any of the following tax rates shall apply where the tax base and tax amount are rectified pursuant to Article 156-4 (3) of the Income Tax Act or Article 98-5 (3) of the Corporate Tax Act: <Amended by Act No. 9924, Jan. 1, 2010; Act No. 10221, Mar. 31, 2010; Act No. 11606, Jan. 1, 2013; Act No. 12153, Jan. 1, 2014>

1. Where no local income tax is included in taxes subject to the tax treaty, the tax rate provided in Article 156 (1) 1, 2, and 6 of the Income Tax Act or Article 98 (1) 1, 2, and 6 of the Corporate Tax Act; <Amended by Act No. 16099, Dec. 31, 2018>
2. Where local income tax is included in taxes subject to the tax treaty, the tax rate computed by adding ten percent of the income tax withheld under Article 103-18 (1) of the Local Tax Act or ten percent of the corporate tax withheld under Article 103-52 (1) of the same Act to the tax rate provided in Article 156 (1) 1, 2 and 6 of the Income Tax Act or Article 98 (1) 1, 2 and 6 of the Corporate Tax Act. <Amended by Act No. 16099, Dec. 31, 2018>

(2) Where the other Contracting State requests a resident or domestic corporation to furnish a resident certificate in relation to the application of the limited tax rate, the tax authority may issue such certificate, as prescribed by Presidential Decree.

[This Article Wholly Amended by Act No. 9914, Jan. 1, 2010]

Article 30 (Entrustment of Tax Collection) (1) The head of a tax office having jurisdiction over the place for tax payment or the head of a local government may request that the Commissioner of the National Tax Service request the other Contracting State to take measures necessary to collect taxes where it is deemed inevitable that the other Contracting State collects the taxes payable as it is impracticable to collect such taxes in the Republic of Korea.

(2) Upon receipt of a request under paragraph (1), the Commissioner

of the National Tax Service may entrust the competent authority of the other Contracting State with the collection of the relevant taxes, as prescribed by Presidential Decree.

(3) Where the competent authority of the other Contracting State request the collection of taxes payable to the other Contracting State in the Republic of Korea under the tax treaty, the Minister of Strategy and Finance or the Commissioner of the National Tax Service may have the head of the tax office having jurisdiction over the place for tax payment collect such taxes in the same manner as national taxes are collected, as prescribed by Presidential Decree.

[This Article Wholly Amended by Act No. 9914, Jan. 1, 2010]

Article 31 (Exchange of Tax and Financial Information) (1) The competent authority may obtain tax information required for the assessment and collection of taxes, review of tax appeals, and criminal prosecution as well as tax information generalized by international practices to the extent not in contravention of other Acts, and exchange such information with the other Contracting State. <Amended by Act No. 10410, Dec. 27, 2010>

(2) Where the competent authority of the other Contracting State demands financial information (referring to information or data relating to the details of financial transactions defined in subparagraph 3 of Article 2 of the Act on Real Name Financial Transactions and Confidentiality; hereafter in this Article the same shall apply) on residents, domestic corporations, nonresidents, or foreign corporations under the tax treaty, the competent authority may request a specific branch (or the head of a finance company, etc. where a general inquiry about financial property is made under Article 83 (1) of the Inheritance Tax and Gift Tax Act or where the information requested by the competent authority of the other Contracting State is about a group that is unable to specify the personal information of a title holder

related to the specific financial transaction) of a finance company, etc. (referring to a finance company, etc. defined in subparagraph 1 of Article 2 of the Act on Real Name Financial Transactions and Confidentiality; hereinafter the same shall apply) to provide any of the following financial information, notwithstanding Article 4 of the Act on Real Name Financial Transactions and Confidentiality, and no employee of the finance company, etc. shall reject such request: <Amended by Act No. 10410, Dec. 27, 2010; Act No. 10854, Jul. 14, 2011; Act No. 11606, Jan. 1, 2013; Act No. 12164, Jan. 1, 2014>

1. Financial information that constitutes data for tax assessment that shall be submitted under tax-related Acts;
2. Financial information necessary to verify property acquired by inheritance or donation;
3. Financial information necessary for the competent authority of the other Contracting State to verify data sufficient to prove a suspicion of tax avoidance;
4. Financial information necessary to inquiry about the property of a delinquent taxpayer of the other Contracting State;
5. Financial information required by the competent authority of the other Contracting State due to any of the causes provided in the subparagraphs of Article 14 (1) of the National Tax Collection Act.

(3) The competent authority may request the head of a finance company, etc. to provide financial information, such as details of financial transactions of residents, domestic corporations, nonresidents, and foreign corporations, necessary for the assessment, collection, and management of taxes by the other Contracting State where necessary for regularly exchanging financial information with the other Contracting State on the principle of reciprocity under the tax treaty, notwithstanding Article 4 of the Act on Real Name Financial Transactions and

Confidentiality. In such cases, an employee of the finance company, etc. shall provide such financial information, as prescribed by Presidential Decree. <Newly Inserted by Act No. 11606, Jan. 1, 2013; Act No. 12164, Jan. 1, 2014>

(4) Although the competent authority makes no request under paragraph (3), a finance company, etc. may verify and maintain beforehand personal information, including the taxpayer numbers (referring to a unique number assigned to each taxpayer by an individual country for identification purposes) of the counter-parties to financial transactions (including the counter-parties to financial transactions of countries other than the other Contracting State under the tax treaty) of the finance company, etc. to the minimum extent necessary for supporting the exchange of financial information among the Contracting States. <Newly Inserted by Act No. 13553, Dec. 15, 2015>

(5) None of the following persons shall unreasonably interfere with or delay the acquisition, exchange, or provision of any tax or financial information referred to in paragraphs (1) through (4): <Amended by Act No. 13553, Dec. 15, 2015>

1. A person related to the tax or financial information referred to in paragraphs (1) through (3);
2. A counter-party to financial transactions referred to in paragraph (4).

(6) Each employee of a finance company, etc. shall refuse to provide financial information upon receipt of a request, in violation of paragraph (2) or (3). <Amended by Act No. 10410, Dec. 27, 2010; Act No. 10854, Jul. 14, 2011; Act No. 11606, Jan. 1, 2013; Act No. 13553, Dec. 15, 2015>

(7) No person who has become aware of financial information under paragraphs (2) through (4) shall provide or divulge such information to any third person, other than the competent authority of the other Contracting State, or misappropriate such

information, and no person shall request any person that has become aware of financial information to provide such financial information. <Amended by Act No. 10410, Dec. 27, 2010; Act No. 11606, Jan. 1, 2013; Act No. 13553, Dec. 15, 2015>

(8) No person who has obtained financial information provided or divulged in violation of paragraph (2), (3), or (7) shall provide or divulge such financial information to any third person if he/she becomes aware of the violation. <Amended by Act No. 10410, Dec. 27, 2010; Act No. 11606, Jan. 1, 2013; Act No. 13553, Dec. 15, 2015>

(9) Notwithstanding paragraph (2), the competent authority may restrict the provision of financial information to the other Contracting State on the principle of reciprocity. <Amended by Act No. 10410, Dec. 27, 2010; Act No. 11606, Jan. 1, 2013; Act No. 13553, Dec. 15, 2015>

(10) The head of a finance company, etc. who intends to provide financial information under paragraph (3), or to verify financial information under paragraph (4), may request the counter-party to a financial transaction to submit data necessary to verify its personal information, etc. <Newly Inserted by Act No. 12164, Jan. 1, 2014; Act No. 13553, Dec. 15, 2015>

(11) Detailed matters concerning the exchange of tax information under paragraph (1), exchange of financial information under paragraphs (2) and (3), and verification of personal information, etc. under paragraph (10) shall be prescribed by Presidential Decree. <Amended by Act No. 10410, Dec. 27, 2010; Act No. 11606, Jan. 1, 2013; Act No. 12164, Jan. 1, 2014; Act No. 13553, Dec. 15, 2015>

[This Article Wholly Amended by Act No. 9914, Jan. 1, 2010]

Article 31-2 Deleted. <Amended by Act No. 16099, Dec. 31, 2018>

Article 31-3 Deleted. <Amended by Act No. 16099, Dec. 31, 2018>

Article 31-4 (Administrative Fines) (1) Where a finance company, etc. in receipt of a request to provide financial information under Article 31 (2) or (3) fails to provide it without good cause, or provides false financial information, it shall be subject to an administrative fine not exceeding 30 million won. <Amended by Act No. 12164, Jan. 1, 2014>

(2) The administrative fine provided in paragraph (1) shall be imposed and collected by the tax authority, as prescribed by Presidential Decree. <Amended by Act No. 13553, Dec. 15, 2015>

[This Article Newly Inserted by Act No. 11126, Dec. 31, 2011]

Article 32 (Cooperation in Tax Audit) (1) Where it is deemed necessary to conduct a tax audit on a transaction with a person to whom the tax treaty applies, the competent authority may conduct a tax audit on the transaction along with the other Contracting State; dispatch tax officials to the other Contracting State to directly conduct a tax audit; or to participate in a tax audit by the other Contracting State. <Amended by Act No. 11126, Dec. 31, 2011>

(2) Where the other Contracting State requests cooperation in a tax audit under the relevant tax treaty, the competent authority may accept such request. <Amended by Act No. 11126, Dec. 31, 2011>

[This Article Wholly Amended by Act No. 9914, Jan. 1, 2010]

Article 33 (Enforcement of Tax Treaties)

Matters necessary for the enforcement of tax treaties shall be prescribed by Presidential Decree.

[This Article Wholly Amended by Act No. 9914, Jan. 1, 2010]

CHAPTER VIII REPORTING ON OVERSEAS FINANCIAL ACCOUNTS

Article 34 (Reporting on Overseas Financial Accounts) (1) A resident or domestic corporation holding an overseas financial account at an overseas finance company, the balance of which (or the aggregate balance of all accounts, if the resident or domestic corporation holds more than one account) as at the last day of any month of the relevant year exceeds the amount prescribed by Presidential Decree (hereafter in this Chapter referred to as "person required to report"), shall report the following information (hereafter in this Chapter referred to as "information on overseas financial account") to the head of the tax office having jurisdiction over the place for tax payment from June 1 to 30 of the following year: <Amended by Act No. 11606, Jan. 1, 2013>

1. Information on the identity of the account holder, such as the name and address;
2. Information on the account held, such as the account number, the name of the finance company, and the largest balance of the account as at the last day of each month;
3. Information on persons related to the overseas financial account referred to in paragraph (4).

(2) "Overseas finance company" in paragraph (1) means a finance company prescribed by Presidential Decree, which is located overseas (including a domestic corporation's places of business in foreign countries, but excluding a foreign corporation's places of business in the Republic of Korea) and engages in the business of finance, insurance, pension, or finance and insurance-related service business, or other similar business. <Amended by Act No. 11606, Jan. 1, 2013>

(3) "Overseas financial account" in paragraph (1) means any of the following accounts opened for financial transactions (including financial transactions defined in subparagraph 3 of Article 2 of the Act on Real Name Financial Transactions and Confidentiality and similar transactions) with an overseas finance company: <Amended by Act No. 11606, Jan. 1, 2013>

1. An account opened in connection with banking services pursuant to Article 27 of the Banking Act;
2. An account opened for trading securities defined in Article 4 of the Financial Investment Services and Capital Markets Act and similar overseas securities;
3. An account opened for trading derivatives defined in Article 5 of the Financial Investment Services and Capital Markets Act and similar overseas derivatives;
4. An account, other than those prescribed in subparagraphs 1 through 3, which is opened with an overseas finance company for other financial transactions.

(4) Persons related to an overseas financial account as provided in paragraph (1) (referring to the nominal holder and the actual holder of an overseas financial account if the nominal holder and the actual holder are different, and each of the nominal holders of an overseas financial account if it is a joint checking account) shall be deemed to hold the relevant account, respectively.

(5) A person required to report shall be exempt from the obligation to report if the person is: <Amended by Act No. 10854, Jul. 14, 2011; Act No. 11126, Dec. 31, 2011; Act No. 11606, Jan. 1, 2013; Act No. 13553, Dec. 15, 2015; Act No. 16099, Dec. 31, 2018>

1. A foreign resident referred to in the proviso to Article 3 (1) of the Income Tax Act, or a Korean national residing abroad as defined in subparagraph 1 of Article 2 of the Act on the Immigration and Legal Status of Overseas Koreans, who has his/her residence in the Republic of Korea for a total period not exceeding 183 days within the one year period before the end of the relevant year subject to reporting (in such cases, a total period having a residence in the Republic of Korea shall be computed in the manner prescribed by Presidential Decree);
2. The State, a local government, or a public institution provided

in the Act on the Management of Public Institutions;
3. A finance company, etc.;
4. A person who meets the requirements prescribed by Presidential Decree, including where the information on his/her overseas financial account is verifiable through a report by another nominal holder of the overseas financial account among those related to the overseas financial account provided in paragraph (4);
5. An institution prescribed by Presidential Decree, which is subject to management and supervision by the State under other statutes.

(6) Matters necessary for reporting overseas financial accounts, such as standards for determining persons required to report, methods for computing the balance of the account held, and methods of reporting, shall be prescribed by Presidential Decree. [This Article Newly Inserted by Act No. 10410, Dec. 27, 2010]

Article 34-2 Deleted. <By Act No. 16099, Dec. 31, 2018>

Article 34-3 (Explanation about Source of Amount Unreported in Relation to Overseas Financial Accounts) (1) Where a person required to report information on his/her overseas financial account under Article 34 (1) fails to do so by the reporting deadline or under-reports the relevant amount, the head of the tax office having jurisdiction over the place for tax payment may request him/her to explain the source of the amount not reported by the reporting deadline or the under-eported amount (hereafter referred to as "amount unreported"). <Amended by Act No. 16099, Dec. 31, 2018>

(2) Upon receipt of a request for explanation pursuant to paragraph (1), person required to report shall give an explanation in a manner prescribed by Presidential Decree within 90 days after receipt of the notice (hereafter in this paragraph referred to as "period for explanation"): Provided, That where the person

required to report requests an extension of the period for explanation in any extenuating circumstances prescribed by Presidential Decree, such as collecting and preparing data require considerable time, the head of the tax office having jurisdiction over the place for tax payment may extend the period by up to 60 days on only one occasion.

(3) Paragraphs (1) and (2) shall not apply where a person required to report files a revised report or after-deadline report under Article 37 (excluding where he/she files such a report, knowing beforehand the intent of the tax authority to impose an administrative fine).

[This Article Newly Inserted by Act No. 12164, Jan. 1, 2014]

Article 35 (Administrative Fines for Non-Fulfillment, etc. of Obligation to Report Overseas Financial Accounts) (1) Where a person required to report under Article 34 (1) fails to report his/her overseas financial account by the reporting deadline or under-reports the relevant amount, an administrative fine not exceeding 20 percent of the amount calculated as follows shall be imposed: <Amended by Act No. 12849, Dec. 23, 2014>

1. Where the person fails to report: The amount not reported;
2. Where the person under-reports: The difference between the amount actually reported and the amount that should have been reported.

(2) Where a person required to report fails to explain the source of the amount unreported or submits a false explanation in violation of Article 34-3 (2), the person shall be subject to an administrative fine equivalent to 20 percent of the amount that has not been explained or has been falsely explained: Provided, That no administrative fine shall be imposed where there exists good cause prescribed by Presidential Decree, such as a natural disaster. <Newly Inserted by Act No. 12164, Jan. 1, 2014; Act No. 12849, Dec. 23, 2014>

(3) Administrative fines provided in paragraphs (1) and (2) shall be imposed and collected by the tax authority, as prescribed by Presidential Decree. <Amended by Act No. 11126, Dec. 31, 2011; Act No. 12164, Jan. 1, 2014>

(4) In the case that any non-fulfillment of this obligation is punished in accordance with Article 16 (1) of the Punishment of Tax Evaders Act, an administrative fine pursuant to paragraph (1) shall not be imposed on it. <Newly inserted by Act No. 16099, Dec. 31, 2018>

[This Article Newly Inserted by Act No. 10410, Dec. 27, 2010]

Article 36 (Confidentiality of Information on Overseas Financial Accounts) (1) No tax official shall offer or divulge any information on overseas financial accounts to any third person or misappropriate it: Provided, That he/she may provide information on overseas financial accounts within the limits of the purposes in any of the circumstances provided in the subparagraphs of Article 81-13 (1) of the Framework Act on National Taxes.

(2) No person who has become aware of any information on overseas financial accounts under paragraph (1) shall provide or divulge it to any third person or misappropriate it.

[This Article Newly Inserted by Act No. 10410, Dec. 27, 2010]

Article 37 (Revised and After-Deadline Reports of Overseas Financial Accounts) (1) A person who has reported information on his/her overseas financial account by the reporting deadline prescribed in Article 34 (1) but has under-reported the amount thereof, may file a revised report on the information on his/her overseas financial account before the tax authority imposes an administrative fine pursuant to Article 35 (1). <Amended by Act No. 12164, Jan. 1, 2014>

(2) A person who has failed to report information on his/her overseas financial account by the reporting deadline prescribed in Article 34 (1) may report information on his/her overseas financial

account before the tax authority imposes an administrative fine pursuant to Article 35 (1). <Amended by Act No. 12164, Jan. 1, 2014>

(3) Methods of filing revised or after-deadline reports on overseas financial accounts pursuant to paragraphs (1) and (2), and other necessary matters, shall be prescribed by Presidential Decree.

[This Article Newly Inserted by Act No. 11126, Dec. 31, 2011]

Article 38 (Special Provisions on Voluntary Reporting) (1) Notwithstanding the Framework Act on National Taxes and any other tax law, the Minister of Strategy and Finance may set a specific period on only one occasion and permit a Korean national who has failed to report the income generated from international transactions and overseas, and the overseas property (including property acquired through inheritance or donation) subject to reporting under tax law, by the statutory reporting deadline, or who has under-reported the amount thereof (excluding persons prescribed by Presidential Decree, such as those undergoing a tax audit or investigation), to report the relevant income and property and to pay the amount of tax payable under tax law, as prescribed by Presidential Decree (hereafter in this Article referred to as "voluntary reporting system"), at the request of the Commissioner of the National Tax Service.

(2) A person who has filed a voluntary report pursuant to paragraph (1) may be granted a reduction of, or an exemption from a penalty tax (excluding penalty tax for unconscientious payment provided in Article 47-4 of the Framework Act on National Taxes) or an administrative fine to be imposed under the Framework Act on National Taxes, tax law, or the Foreign Exchange Transactions Act regarding the reported income and property, as prescribed by Presidential Decree, and may be excepted from a list of delinquent taxpayers subject to publication.

(3) The Minister of Strategy and Finance and the heads of the relevant central administrative agencies may render administrative and financial support to operate the voluntary reporting system efficiently.
(4) Notwithstanding Article 81-13 of the Framework Act on National Taxes, the Commissioner of the National Tax Service may provide the heads of the relevant central administrative agencies with the information related to the reporting referred to in paragraph (1), as prescribed by Presidential Decree.
(5) Matters necessary for implementing the voluntary reporting system, including procedures and methods therefor, shall be prescribed by Presidential Decree.
[This Article Newly Inserted by Act No. 12849, Dec. 23, 2014]
[This Article is valid until December 31, 2016 under Article 2 of the Addenda to this Act, Act No. 12849 (Dec. 23, 2014)]

ADDENDA <Act No. 5193, Dec. 30, 1996>

Article 1 (Enforcement Date)

This Act shall enter into force on January 1, 1997.
Articles 2 through 15 Omitted.

ADDENDA <Act No. 5581, Dec. 28, 1998>

Article 1 (Enforcement Date)

This Act shall enter into force on January 1, 1999. (Proviso Omitted.)
Articles 2 through 15 Omitted.

ADDENDA <Act No. 5584, Dec. 28, 1998>

Article 1 (Enforcement Date)

This Act shall enter into force on January 1, 1999. (Proviso Omitted.)
Articles 2 through 19 Omitted.

ADDENDA <Act No. 6299, Dec. 29, 2000>

Article 1 (Enforcement Date)

This Act shall enter into force on September 1, 2001.

Articles 2 and 3 Omitted.

ADDENDA <Act No. 6304, Dec. 29, 2000>

Article 1 (Enforcement Date)

This Act shall enter into force on January 1, 2001.

Article 2 (Applicability concerning Advance Pricing Agreements)

The amended provisions of Article 6 shall begin to apply from the first application for advance pricing agreement filed on or after the date this Act enters into force.

Article 3 (Applicability concerning Obligation to Submit Data on International Transactions)

The amended provisions of the proviso to Article 11 (1) shall begin to apply from the first taxable year on which a tax return is filed on or after the date this Act enters into force.

Article 4 (Applicability concerning Computation of Gains from Transfer of Stocks, etc. by Specific Foreign Corporations)

The amended provisions of Article 20 (2) shall begin to apply from the first transfer of stocks, etc. made on or after the date this Act enters into force.

Article 5 (Applicability concerning Special Provisions on Assessment of Gift Tax on Overseas Donation)

The amended provisions of Article 21 (1) shall begin to apply from the first donation made on or after the date this Act enters into force.

Article 6 (Applicability concerning Special Provisions on Application of Appeal Period Following Mutual Agreement Procedure)

The amended provisions of Article 24 (1) and (7) shall begin to apply from the first application for commencement of the mutual agreement procedure, which is filed on or after the date this Act enters into force.

ADDENDA <Act No. 6779, Dec. 18, 2002>

Article 1 (Enforcement Date)

This Act shall enter into force on January 1, 2003.

Article 2 (Applicability concerning Scope, etc. of Special Relationship)

The amended provisions of Articles 2 (1) 8 (d) and 4 (2) shall begin to apply from the first transaction made on or after the date this Act enters into force.

Article 3 (Applicability concerning Scope of Foreign Controlling Stockholders)

The amended provisions of Article 2 (1) 11 shall begin to apply from the first funds borrowed from a foreign controlling stockholder on or after the date this Act enters into force.

Article 4 (Applicability concerning Relationship with Other Acts)

The amended provisions of Article 3 (2) shall begin to apply from the first transaction made on or after the date this Act enters into force.

Article 5 (Applicability concerning Transaction Involving Third Party)

The amended provisions of Article 7 shall begin to apply from the first transaction made on or after the date this Act enters into force.

Article 6 (Applicability concerning Exclusion, etc. of Interest Deemed Dividends from Deductible Expenses)

The amended provisions of Articles 14 (1) and 16 shall begin to apply from the first funds borrowed on or after the date this Act enters into force.

Article 7 (Applicability concerning Applicable Scope of Tax Haven)

The amended provisions of Article 18 (1) 1 shall begin to apply from the first taxable year that begins on or after the date this Act enters into force.

Article 8 (Applicability concerning Closing Date of Mutual Agreement Procedure)

The amended provisions of Article 23 (3) shall begin to apply from the first-arriving close date of the mutual agreement procedure on or after the date this Act enters into force: Provided, That the amended provisions shall also apply where the competent authorities agree to continue the mutual agreement procedure even though the closing date of the mutual agreement procedure has arrived prior to this Act entering into force.

Article 9 (Applicability concerning Exchange of Tax and Financial Information)

The amended provisions of Articles 31 and 31-2 shall begin to apply from the first request for exchange of information made on or after the date this Act enters into force.

ADDENDA <Act No. 7956, May 24, 2006>

Article 1 (Enforcement Date)

This Act shall enter into force on the date of its promulgation: Provided, That the amended provisions of Article 29 (1) shall enter into force on July 1, 2006.

Article 2 (General Applicability)

This Act shall apply as of the taxable year in which this Act enters into force.

Article 3 (Applicability concerning Scope of Special Relationship)

The amended provisions of Article 2 (1) 8 (c) and (d) shall begin to apply from the first transaction made on or after the date this Act enters into force.

Article 4 (Applicability concerning Advance Pricing Agreements)

The amended provisions of Article 6 (3) shall begin to apply from the first application filed on or after the date this Act enters into force.

Article 5 (Applicability concerning Tax Adjustment by Arm' s Length Cost Sharing)

The amended provisions of Article 6-2 shall begin to apply from the first agreement on cost sharing made on or after the date this Act enters into force.

Article 6 (Applicability concerning Recognition of Setoff Transactions)

The amended provisions of Article 8 (2) shall begin to apply from the first transaction made on or after the date this Act enters into force.

Article 7 (Applicability concerning Secondary Income Adjustment and Tax Adjustment after Income Adjustment)

The amended provisions of Article 9 shall begin to apply from the first income adjustment or tax adjustment made on or after the date this Act enters into force.

Article 8 (Applicability concerning Conditions for Commencing Mutual Agreement Procedure)

The amended provisions of Article 22 (1) shall begin to apply from the first application filed on or after the date this Act enters into force.

Article 9 (Applicability concerning Extended Application of Terms and Conditions Mutually Agreed Upon)

The amended provisions of Article 27-2 shall begin to apply from the first application filed on or after the date this Act enters into force.

Article 10 (Applicability concerning Special Rule for Application of Tax Rates to Interest, Dividends and Royalties)

The amended provisions of Article 29 (1) shall begin to apply from the first tax withheld on or after the date this Act enters into force.

ADDENDA <Act No. 8139, Dec. 30, 2006>

Article 1 (Enforcement Date)

This Act shall enter into force on January 1, 2007. (Proviso Omitted.)

Articles 2 through 15 Omitted.

Article 16 (Transitional Measures Following Amendment of Other Acts)

A penalty that has been assessed or to be assessed pursuant to the provisions of any of the following tax laws, before this Act enters into force, shall be governed by the former provisions of such tax laws, notwithstanding the amended provisions of the following tax laws pursuant to Article 15 (1) through (7) of the Addenda:

1. The Adjustment of International Taxes Act: Article 13 of the Adjustment of International Taxes Act;
2. The Act on Special Rural Development Tax: Article 11 of the Act on Special Rural Development Tax;
3. The Inheritance Tax and Gift Tax Act: Article 78 (1) and (2) of the Inheritance Tax and Gift Tax Act;
4. The Stamp Tax Act: Article 8-2 of the Stamp Tax Act;
5. The Liquor Tax Act: Article 27 of the Liquor Tax Act;
6. The Securities Transaction Tax Act: Article 14 of the Securities Transaction Tax Act;
7. The Special Consumption Tax Act: Article 13 and Article 24 (1) 1 of the Special Consumption Tax Act.

ADDENDA <Act No. 8387, Apr. 27, 2007>

Article 1 (Enforcement Date)

This Act shall enter into force six months after the date of its promulgation.

Articles 2 through 9 Omitted.

ADDENDA <Act No. 8852, Feb. 29, 2008>

Article 1 (Enforcement Date)

This Act shall enter into force on the date of its promulgation: Provided, That … <Omitted> … any amendment of the Acts made under Article 6 of this Addenda, which were promulgated before this Act comes into force, but the enforcement date of which has yet to arrive, shall enter into force on the date the corresponding Act takes effect.

Articles 2 through 7 Omitted.

ADDENDA <Act No. 8860, Feb. 29, 2008>

Article 1 (Enforcement Date)

This Act shall enter into force on the date of its promulgation.

Articles 2 through 6 Omitted.

ADDENDA <Act No. 9266, Dec. 26, 2008>

(1) (Enforcement Date) This Act shall enter into force on the date of its promulgation.

(2) (General Applicability) This Act shall begin to apply from the first taxable year that starts after the date this Act enters into force.

(3) (Applicability concerning Special Provisions on Application of Penalty Taxes) The amended provisions of Article 13 shall begin to apply from the first rectification of a tax base or tax amount made on or after the date this Act enters into force.

(4) (Applicability concerning Request for Rectification of Tax Amounts Paid to Foreign Countries) The amended provisions of Article 19 (4) shall begin to apply from the first request for rectification of a tax base or tax amount filed on or after the date this Act enters into force.

ADDENDA <Act No. 9914, Jan. 1, 2010>

Article 1 (Enforcement Date)

This Act shall enter into force on the date of its promulgation.

Article 2 (Applicability)

This Act shall begin to apply from the first taxable year that starts after the date this Act enters into force.

ADDENDA <Act No. 9924, Jan. 1, 2010>

Article 1 (Enforcement Date)

This Act shall enter into force on January 1, 2010.

Articles 2 through 7 Omitted.

ADDENDA <Act No. 10219, Mar. 31, 2010>

Article 1 (Enforcement Date)

This Act shall enter into force on January 1, 2011.

Articles 2 through 12 Omitted.

ADDENDA <Act No. 10221, Mar. 31, 2010>

Article 1 (Enforcement Date)

This Act shall enter into force on January 1, 2011.

Articles 2 through 8 Omitted.

ADDENDA <Act No. 10410, Dec 27, 2010>

Article 1 (Enforcement Date)

This Act shall enter into force on the date of its promulgation.

Article 2 (General Applicability)

This Act shall begin to apply from the first taxable year that starts after the date this Act enters into force.

Article 3 (Applicability concerning Tax Adjustment by Arm' s Length Price)

The amended provisions of the proviso to Article 4 (1) shall begin to apply from the first determination or rectification of a tax base or tax amount made on or after the date this Act enters into force.

Article 4 (Applicability concerning Methods of Computing Arm's Length Prices)

The amended provisions of Article 5 (1) shall begin to apply from the first taxable year on which a tax return is filed on or after the date this Act enters into force.

Article 5 (Applicability concerning Advance Pricing Agreements)

The amended provisions of Article 6 (3) shall begin to apply from the first advance pricing agreement made on or after the date this Act enters into force.

Article 6 (Applicability concerning Sanctions against Non-Compliance with Obligation to Submit Data)

The amended provisions of Article 12 (1) shall begin to apply from the first request to submit documents made on or after the date this Act enters into force.

Article 7 (Applicability concerning Exclusion of Actually Distributed Dividends, etc. from Taxable Gains)

The amended provisions of Article 20 shall begin to apply from the first distribution of dividends or the first transfer of stocks made on or after the date this Act enters into force.

Article 8 (Applicability concerning Exchange of Tax and Financial Information)

The amended provisions of Articles 31 and 31-2 shall begin to apply from the first tax or financial information exchanged on or after the date this Act enters into force.

Article 9 (Applicability concerning Reporting on Overseas Financial Accounts and Administrative Fines)

The amended provisions of Articles 34 and 35 shall begin apply from the overseas financial accounts held in 2010 and thereafter: Provided, That for the purposes of the amended provisions of Article 35, an administrative fine not exceed five percent of an amount calculated as provided in each of the subparagraphs thereof an overseas shall be imposed in relation to the financial accounts held in 2010.

ADDENDA <Act No. 10854, Jul. 14, 2011>

Article 1 (Enforcement Date)

This Act shall enter into force on the date of its promulgation. (Proviso Omitted.)

Articles 2 and 3 Omitted.

ADDENDA <Act No. 11126, Dec. 31, 2011>

Article 1 (Enforcement Date)

This Act shall enter into force on the date of its promulgation: Provided, That the amended provisions of Articles 10-2 and 10-3 shall enter into force on July 1, 2012.

Article 2 (General Applicability)

This Act shall begin to apply from the first taxable year that begins on or after this Act enters into force.

Article 3 (Applicability concerning Rectification Claim for Adjustment of Arm's Length Transfer Prices for National Taxes and Customs Duties)

The amended provisions of Article 10-2 shall begin to apply from the first rectification of customs duties made on or after the date the amended provisions of Article 10-2 enter into force as provided in the proviso to Article 1 of the Addenda.

Article 4 (Applicability concerning Provision of Information on International Transactions)

The amended provisions of Article 11-2 shall begin to apply from the first request to provide information filed on or after the date this Act enters into force.

Article 5 (Applicability concerning Scope, etc. of Application of Accumulative Taxation of Retained Earnings of Specific

Foreign Corporations)

The amended provisions of Articles 18 (1) and 18-2 shall begin to apply from the business year in which the date this Act enters into force falls.

Article 6 (Applicability concerning Public Notification of Terms and Conditions Mutually Agreed Upon)

The amended provisions of Article 27 (2) shall begin to apply from the first mutual agreement reached on or after the date this Act enters into force.

Article 7 (Applicability concerning Administrative Fines)

The amended provisions of Article 31-3 shall begin to apply from the first request for financial information filed on or after the date this Act enters into force.

Article 8 (Applicability concerning Exemption from Obligation to Report Overseas Financial Accounts)

The amended provisions of Article 34 (5) shall begin to apply from the overseas financial account held in 2011 and thereafter.

Article 9 (Applicability concerning Revised and After-Deadline Reports of Overseas Financial Accounts)

The amended provisions of Article 37 shall begin to apply from the overseas financial account held in 2010 and thereafter.

ADDENDA <Act No. 11606, Jan. 1, 2013>

Article 1 (Enforcement Date)

This Act shall enter into force on January 1, 2013.

Article 2 (General Applicability)

This Act shall begin to apply from the taxable year that begins on after this Act enters into force.

Article 3 (Applicability concerning Obligation to Submit Data on International Transactions)

The amended provisions of Article 11 (1) shall begin to apply from the taxable year in which the date this Act enters into force falls.

Article 4 (Applicability concerning Scope of Application of Specific Foreign Corporations' Retained Earnings Deemed Dividends)

The amended provisions of Article 18 (1) 1 shall begin to apply from the taxable year in which the date this Act enters into force falls.

Article 5 (Applicability concerning Special Provisions on Assessment of Gift Tax on Overseas Donation)

The amended provisions of Article 21 (1) and (4) shall begin to apply from donations made after this Act enters into force.

Article 6 (Applicability concerning Special Provisions on Application of Tax Rates to Interest, Dividends, and Royalties)

The amended provisions of Article 29 (1) shall begin to apply from the income paid after this Act enters into force.

Article 7 (Applicability concerning Exchange of Financial Information with Foreign Countries)

The amended provisions of Article 31 (3) through (9) shall begin to apply from the exchange of financial information with the other Contracting State made after this Act enters into force.

Article 8 (Applicability concerning Reporting on Overseas Financial Accounts)

The amended provisions of Article 34 (1) and (3) shall begin to apply from the overseas financial account held as of 2013 that shall be reported in 2014.

Article 9 (Applicability concerning Penalty Provisions for Non-Fulfillment of Obligation to Report Overseas Financial Accounts)

The amended provisions of Article 34-2 shall apply begin to apply from the overseas financial account held as of 2013 that shall be reported in 2014.

ADDENDA <Act No. 12153, Jan. 1, 2014>

Article 1 (Enforcement Date)

This Act shall enter into force on January 1, 2014. (Proviso Omitted.)

Articles 2 through 19 Omitted.

ADDENDA <Act No. 12164, Jan. 1, 2014>

Article 1 (Enforcement Date)

This Act shall enter into force on January 1, 2014: Provided, That the amended provisions of Article 18 (5) shall enter into force on January 1, 2015.

Article 2 (General Applicability)

This Act shall begin to apply from the taxable year that begins on after this Act enters into force.

Article 3 (Applicability concerning Exchange of Financial Information with Foreign Countries)

The amended provisions of Articles 31 (2) and (3) and 31-3 (1) shall begin to apply from the exchange of financial information with the other Contracting State made after this Act enters into force.

Article 4 (Applicability concerning Request for Submission of Data Made by Finance Companies, etc. to Counter-Parties to Financial Transactions)

The amended provisions of Article 31 (9) and (10) shall apply where the head of a finance company, etc. requests the counterparty to a financial transaction to submit data necessary to verify its personal information, etc. on or after the date this Act enters into force.

Article 5 (Applicability concerning Explanation about Source of Amount Unreported)

The amended provisions of Articles 34-3 and 35 (2) and (3) shall begin to apply from the overseas financial account held as of 2014 that shall be reported in 2015 pursuant to Article 34.

ADDENDA <Act No. 12849, Dec. 23, 2014>

Article 1 (Enforcement Date)

This Act shall enter into force on January 1, 2015.

Article 2 (Period of Validity)

@Article 38 shall remain in effect until December 31, 2016.

Article 3 (General Applicability)

This Act shall begin to apply from the taxable year that begins on or after this Act enters into force.

Article 4 (Applicability concerning Sanctions against Non-Compliance with Obligation to Submit Data)

The amended provisions of Article 12 (1) shall begin to apply from the obligation to submit a statement of international transactions that arises in relation to a taxable year that begins on or after this Act enters into force.

Article 5 (Applicability concerning Special Provisions on Assessment of Gift Tax on Overseas Donation)

The amended provisions of Article 21 (1) shall begin to apply from donations made after this Act enters into force.

Article 6 (Applicability concerning Penalty Provisions and Administrative Fines for Non-Fulfillment, etc. of Obligation to Report Overseas Financial Accounts)

The amended provisions of Articles 34-2 (1) and 35 (1) and (2) shall begin to apply from the overseas financial accounts held in the year, in which the enforcement date of this Act falls, that shall be reported.

ADDENDA <Act No. 13553, Dec. 15, 2015>

Article 1 (Enforcement Date)

This Act shall enter into force on January 1, 2016.

Article 2 (General Applicability)

This Act shall begin to apply from the taxable year that begins after this Act enters into force.

Article 3 (Applicability concerning Submission of Consolidated Reports on International Transaction Information)

The amended provisions of Articles 11 (1), (2), and (6) and 12 (1) shall begin to apply from the obligation to submit a consolidated report on international transaction information that arises in relation to a taxable year that begins after this Act enters into force.

Article 4 (Applicability concerning Submission of Data on Specific Foreign Corporations)

The amended provisions of Article 20-2 shall begin to apply from the submission of the documents referred to in the subparagraphs of the same Article in relation to the taxable year immediately preceding the taxable year in which the deadline for filing a tax return by a corporation subject to consolidated tax return falls after this Act enters into force.

Article 5 (Applicability concerning Verification, etc. of Personal Information of Counter-Parties to Financial Transactions by Finance Companies, etc.)

The amended provisions of Article 31 (4), (5), and (10) shall also apply to the counter-party to a financial transaction of a finance company, etc. existing as at the time this Act enters into force.

Article 6 (Transitional Measures concerning Reporting on Overseas Financial Accounts)

An overseas financial account held before this Act enters into force, reported in the year in which the enforcement date of this Act falls, shall be subject to the former provisions, notwithstanding the amended provisions of Article 34 (5) 1.

ADDENDA <Act No. 14384, Dec. 20, 2016>

Article 1 (Enforcement Date)

This Act shall enter into force on January 1, 2017.

Article 2 (Applicability concerning Submission of Consolidated Reports on International Transaction Information)

The amended provisions of Article 11 (1) and (2) shall begin to apply from a consolidated report on international transaction information submitted after this Act enters into force.

Article 3 (Applicability concerning Special Provisions on Assessment of Gift Tax on Overseas Donation)

The amended provisions of Article 21 (1) shall begin to apply from a case in where a resident donates his/her overseas property to a nonresident after this Act enters into force.

Article 4 (Applicability concerning Closing Date of Mutual Agreement Procedure)

The amended provisions of Article 23 (4) 2 shall also apply where an applicant for the mutual agreement procedure, which is ongoing as at the time this Act enters into force, withdraws his/her application after this Act enters into force.

ADDENDA <Act No. 14474, Dec. 27, 2016>

Article 1 (Enforcement Date)

This Act shall enter into force three months after the date of its promulgation.

Articles 2 through 14 Omitted.

ADDENDA <Act No. 15221, Dec. 19, 2017>

Article 1 (Enforcement Date)

This Act shall enter into force on January 1, 2018: Provided, That the amended provisions of Article 6-3 shall enter into force on July 1, 2018, and the amended provisions of Articles 15-2 and 16 (applicable only in relation to Article 15-2) on January 1, 2019.

Article 2 (General Applicability)

This Act shall apply from the taxable year that begins after this Act enters into force.

Article 3 (Applicability concerning Advance Pricing Agreements)

The amended provisions of Article 6 (1) shall apply to an application for an advance pricing agreement for a specific period of taxable years that begins on or after January 1, 2019 when a method of computing an arm's length price will apply.

Article 4 (Applicability concerning Pre-Adjustment of Arm's Length Transfer Prices for National Taxes and Customs Duties)

The amended provisions of Article 6-3 shall apply to applications for pre-adjustment filed on or after July 1, 2018.

Article 5 (Applicability concerning Rectification Claim for Adjustment of Arm' s Length Transfer Prices for National Taxes and Customs Duties)

(1) The amended provisions of Article 10-2 (1) shall apply to a claim for rectification filed after this Act enters into force.

(2) Notwithstanding paragraph (1), the previous provisions shall apply with respect to a claim for which the deadline has expired pursuant to the previous provisions of Article 10-2 (1) before this Act enters into force.

ADDENDA <Act No. 16099, Dec. 31, 2018>

Article 1 (Enforcement Date)

This Act shall enter into force on January 1, 2019.

Article 2 (General Applicability)

This Act shall begin to apply from the taxable year that begins after this Act enters into force.

Article 3 (Applicability concerning the Enforcement of Mutual Agreements)

The amended provisions provided in the latter part of Article 27 (2) apply upon the closing of any mutual agreement procedure after this Act enters into force.

Article 4 (Transitional Measures concerning Punishment)

Notwithstanding the amended provisions of Article 31 (2) and

(3) and Article 34 (2), the previous provisions shall apply to the offenses that have occurred before this Act enters into force.

Article 5 (Transitional Measures concerning the Obligation to Report Overseas Financial Accounts)

Notwithstanding the amended provisions of Article 34 (5) 1 and Article 34-3 (1), in the case of the reporting of any overseas financial accounts obtained prior to the enforcement of this Act in accordance with Article 34 (1) or Article 37, the transitional measures shall be carried out pursuant to the previous provisions.

Act on Combating Bribery of Foreign Public Officials in International Business Transactions

[Enforcement on Dec. 18, 2018]
[Act No. 15972, Partial Amendment on Dec. 18, 2018]

The Editorial Board
ILA Korean Branch

1. Reasons for the Amendment [Partial Amendment]

◇ Reasons and Key Amendment Points

The Criminal Law prescribes that each of the following acts—promising, giving, or expressing the intent to give a bribe to a directly related party; giving money or valuables to a third party for the purpose of bribing; and accepting the money or other articles fully aware of the intent—is subject to punishment.

Under the current law, however, only those who have promised, given, or expressed their intent to give a bribe to a directly related party are punished, while those who have given a bribe to a third party remain unpunished, which creates a loophole in the penal system.

In addition, the OECD Anti-Bribery Convention (the Convention on Combating Bribery of Foreign Public Officials in International Business Transactions), which served as a momentum for Korea to enact this law, has continued to recommend that the same law should apply to the cases in which a bribe to a foreign public official is given to a third party. Therefore, without provisions prescribing the punishment of such offenses, there is a concern that the credibility of Korea will be reduced due to the rise in the corruption index.

Therefore, this amendment intends to provide legal grounds for the punishment of those who have bribed a third party as well as those who have received it knowing the intent of it.

<Provided by the Ministry of Government Legislation>

2. Amendment

The Partial Amendment to the Act on Combating Bribery of Foreign Public Officials in International Business Transactions, which was passed by the National Assembly, is promulgated as here set forth.

President Moon Jae-in (seal)

December 18, 2018

Prime Minister Lee Nak-yeon

Cabinet Member and Minister of Justice Park Sang-ki

⊙Act No. 15972

The Partial Amendment to the Act on Combating Bribery of Foreign Public Officials in International Business Transactions

The Act on Combating Bribery of Foreign Public Officials in International Business Transactions is partially amended as follows.

Article 3 Paragraphs 2 and 3 shall be renumbered as Paragraphs 3 and 4, respectively, with the insertion of a new Paragraph 2 in the same article as follows. In both the part excluding each subparagraph of Paragraph 3 (the former Paragraph 2) and Paragraph 4 (the former

Paragraph 3), "Paragraph 1" shall be changed to "Paragraph 1 or Paragraph 2."

② Those who have given a bribe to a third party so that it serves the purposes specified in Paragraph 1 and those who receive such a bribe knowing the intent shall be subject to the punishment provided in Paragraph 1.

3. Addenda

This Act shall enter into force on the date of its promulgation.

4. Full Text[1)]

ACT ON COMBATING BRIBERY OF FOREIGN PUBLIC OFFICIALS IN INTERNATIONAL BUSINESS TRANSACTIONS

[Enforcement Date Dec. 18, 2018.]

[Act No. 15972, Dec. 18, 2018, Partial Amendment]

Article 1 (Purpose)

The purpose of this Act is to contribute to establishing sound order in international business transactions by punishing offenses of bribing foreign public officials in conducting international business transactions and to provide for matters necessary therefor to perform the Convention on Combating Bribery of Foreign Public Officials in International Business Transactions. [This Article Wholly Amended by Act No. 10178, Mar. 24, 2010]

Article 2 (Scope of Foreign Public Officials)

The term "foreign public official" in this Act means any of the following persons:

---

1) This English translation is not official translation.

1. Any person holding legislative, administrative, or judicial office in a foreign government (including governments in all levels from central level to a local level; hereinafter the same shall apply), whether appointed or elected;
2. Any person exercising a public function for a foreign country and falling under any of the following persons:
   (a) Any person conducting public affairs delegated by a foreign government;
   (b) Any person holding office in a public organization or public agency established by any Act and subordinate statutes to conduct specific public affairs;
   (c) Any executive officer or employee of an enterprise in which a foreign government has invested in excess of 50 percent of its paid-in capital or over which a foreign government has de facto control as regards all aspects of its management, such as decision-making on important business operations and the appointment and removal of executive officers: Provided, That excluded herefrom is any enterprise engaging in a business in competition at arm's length with general private business entities without any privilege conferred thereon, such as discriminative subsidies;
3. Any person acting for a public international organization.

[This Article Wholly Amended by Act No. 10178, Mar. 24, 2010]

Article 3 (Criminal Liability of Persons Offering Bribery, etc.)

(1) Any person who has promised, given, or expressed his/her intent to give a bribe to a foreign public official in relation to any international business transaction with intent to obtain any improper advantage for such transaction shall be punished by imprisonment with labor for not more than five years or by a fine not exceeding twenty million won. In such cases, if the pecuniary advantage obtained by such offense exceeds ten million

won, the offender shall be punished by imprisonment with labor for not more than five years or by a fine not exceeding an amount equivalent to double the pecuniary advantage.

(2) Those who have given a bribe to a third party so that it serves the purposes specified in paragraph (1) and those who receive such a bribe knowing the intent shall be subject to punishment provided in paragraph (1). <Newly Inserted by Act No. 15972, Dec. 18, 2018>

(3) Of cases under paragraph (1) or paragraph (2), any case falling under any of the following subparagraphs shall be excluded therefrom: <Amended by Act No. 15972, Dec. 18, 2018>

1. Where such payment is permitted or demanded pursuant to any applicable Act and subordinate statutes of the country to which a foreign public official belongs;
2. Deleted. <by Act No. 12775, Oct. 15, 2014>

(4) Where any person who has committed an offense under paragraph (1) or paragraph (2) is punished by imprisonment with labor, a fine provided for in paragraph (1) or paragraph (2) shall be imposed concurrently. <Amended by Act No. 15972, Dec. 18, 2018>

[This Article Wholly Amended by Act No. 10178, Mar. 24, 2010]

Article 4 (Joint Penalty Provisions)

If the representative of a corporation, or an agent or employee of, or any other person employed, by a corporation commits an offense under Article 3 (1) in connection with the business affairs of the corporation, not only shall such offender be punished, but also the corporation shall be punished by a fine not exceeding one billion won. In such cases, if the pecuniary advantage obtained by such offense exceeds 500 million won, the corporation shall be punished by a fine not exceeding an amount equivalent to double the pecuniary advantage: Provided, That this shall not apply where such corporation has not been negligent in giving due attention and supervision concerning the relevant duties to prevent such offence.

[This Article Wholly Amended by Act No. 10178, Mar. 24, 2010]

Article 5 (Confiscation)

Any bribe given in the course of committing an offense and owned by the offender (including a corporation subject to the punishment under Article 4) or knowingly acquired by any person other than the offender shall be confiscated.

[This Article Wholly Amended by Act No. 10178, Mar. 24, 2010]

ADDENDA <Act No. 10178, Mar. 24, 2010>

This Act shall enter into force on the date of its promulgation.

ADDENDA <Act No. 12775, Oct. 15, 2014>

Article 1 (Enforcement Date)

This Act shall enter into force on the date of its promulgation.

Article 2 (Applicability)

This amended provisions of this Act shall begin applying to the first offence under Article 3 (1) committed after this Act enters into force.

ADDENDA <Act No. 15972, Dec. 18, 2018>

This Act shall enter into force on the date of its promulgation.

Treaties/Agreements Concluded by the Republic of Korea[1]

The Editorial Board
ILA Korean Branch

1. BILATERAL AGREEMENTS

1-1. MILITARY/SECURITY

Agreement between the Government of the Republic of Korea and the Government of the Republic of Indonesia on Cooperation in the Field of Defense

[Adopted October 12, 2013, Entered into force September 7, 2018][2]

Agreement between the Government of the Republic of Korea and the Government of the Kingdom of Saudi Arabia on the protection of classified Military Information

[Adopted September 7, 2017, Entered into force July 19, 2018]

---

1) Treaties are found at the homepage of Ministry of Foreign Affairs, Republic of Korea, http://www.mofa.go.kr/
2) Entered into force the Republic of Korea

1-2. COOPERATION FUND

Framework Arrangement between the Government of the Republic of Korea and the Government of Mongolia concerning Loans from the Economic Development Cooperation Fund for the years 2017 through 2019

[Adopted January 16, 2018, Entered into force April 19, 2018]

Framework arrangement between the Government of the Republic of Korea and the Government of the People's Republic of Bangladesh concerning Loans from the Economic Development Cooperation Fund for the years 2017 through 2020

[Adopted January 29, 2018, Entered into force January 29, 2018]

Arrangement between the Government of the Republic of Korea and the Government of the Republic of Cote D' Ivoire concerning a Loan from the Economic Development Cooperation Fund for the National Radiotherapy and Oncology Center Project

[Adopted February 8, 2018, Entered into force February 8, 2018]

Framework Arrangement between the Government of the Republic of Korea and the Government of the Republic of the Philippines concerning Loans from the Economic Development Cooperation Fund for the years 2017 through 2022

[Adopted May 4, 2018, Entered into force May 4, 2018]

Arrangement between the Government of the Republic of Korea and the Government of the Arab Republic of Egypt concerning a Loan from the Economic Development Cooperation Fund for the Supply of (32)Trains for Greater Cairo Metro Line 3 – Phases 3&4 (Group G5)

[Adopted August 26, 2018, Entered into force November 22, 2018]

1-3. MUTUAL WAIVER OF VISA REQUIREMENTS FOR HOLDERS OF DIPLOMATIC AND OFFICIAL PASSPORTS

Agreement between the Government of the Republic of Korea and the Government of the Republic of Vanuatu on the Mutual Waiver of Visa Requirements for Holders of Diplomatic and Official Passports

[Adopted December 5, 2017, Entered into force February 21, 2018]

1-4. EXEMPTION FROM VISA REQUIREMENTS FOR HOLDERS OF DIPLOMATIC PASSPORTS

Agreement between the Government of the Republic of Korea and the Government of the United Republic Tanzania on the Mutual Exemption from Visa Requirements for Holders of Diplomatic and Official/Service Passports

[Adopted July 22, 2018, Entered into force October 5, 2018]

1-5. MUTUAL RECOGNITION AND EXCHANGE OF DRIVER'S LICENSES

Agreement between the Government of the Republic of Korea and the Government of the Republic of Mozambique on the Mutual Recognition and Exchange of Driver's Licenses

[Adopted April 30, 2018, Entered into force December 1, 2018]

Agreement between the Government of the Republic of Korea and the Government of the Republic of Colombia on the Mutual Recognition and/or Exchange of Driver's Licenses

[Adopted August 01, 2018, Entered into force October 31, 2018]

1-6. INFORMATION RELATING TO TAX MATTERS

Agreement between the Government of the Republic of Korea and the Government of the Republic of Costa Rica for the Exchange of Information relating to Tax Matters

[Adopted October 12, 2016, Entered into force november 13, 2018]

1-7. TAX

Protocol amending the Convention between the Government of the Republic of Korea and the Government of the Federative Republic of Brazil for the Avoidance of Double Taxation and the Prevention of Fiscal Evasion with respect to Taxes on Income

[Adopted April 24, 2015, Entered into force January 10, 2018]

1-8. PROMOTION AND PROTECTION OF INVESTMENTS

Agreement between the Government of the Republic of Korea and the Government of the Republic of Cameroon for the Promotion and Protection of Investments

[Adopted December 24, 2013, Entered into force April 13, 2018]

Agreement between the Government of the Republic of Korea and the Government of the Republic of the Union of Myanmar for the Promotion and Protection of Investments

[Adopted June 5, 2014, Entered into force October 31, 2018]

1-9. CRIMINAL MATTERS

Treaty between the Republic of Korea and the Islamic Republic of Iran on Mutual Assistance in Criminal Matters

[Adopted May 2, 2016, Entered into force February 9, 2018]

1-10. EXTRADITION

Treaty on Extradition between the Republic of Korea and the Islamic Republic of Iran

[Adopted May 2, 2016, Entered into force March 8, 2018]

1-11. FREE TRADE AREA

Agreement on Trade in Services under the Framework Agreement establishing a Free Trade Area between the Republic of Korea and the Republic of Turkey

[Adopted February 26, 2015, Entered into force August 1, 2018]

Agreement on Investment under the Framework Agreement establishing a Free Trade Area between the Republic of Korea and the Republic of Turkey

[Adopted February 26, 2015, Entered into force August 1, 2018]

Exchange of Notes for the Adjustment of the Annex D of the Agreement on Trade in Services under the Framework Agreement Establishing a Free Trade Area between the Republic of Korea and the Republic of Turkey

[Adopted February 1, 2018, Entered into force August 1, 2018]

1-12. AIR/MARITIME TRANSPORT

Agreement of Maritime Transport between the Government of the Republic of Korea and the Government of the Islamic Republic of Iran

[Adopted May 2, 2016, Entered into force January 4, 2018]

Exchange of Notes for the Amendment to the Agreement between the Government of the Republic of Korea and the Government of the Republic of Panama for Air Services between and beyond their Respective Territories

[Adopted March 29, 2017, Entered into force January 12, 2018]

Exchange of Notes for the Amendment to the Air Transport Agreement between the Government of the Republic of Korea and the Government of the Kingdom of the Netherlands

[Adopted September 14, 2017, Entered into force August 19, 2018]

1-13. GRANTS AID

Framework Agreement for Grant Aid between the Government of the Republic of Korea and the Government of the Democratic Republic of Congo

[Adopted December 29, 2014, Entered into force June 7, 2018]

Exchange of Notes between the Government of the Republic of Korea and the Government of the Arab Republic of Egypt regarding a Grant for contribute in Implementing a Project on 'Project for Establishment of Egyptian-Korean Technological College in Beni Suef'

[Adopted October 14, 2017, Entered into force July 16, 2018]

1-14. OTHERS

Agreement between the Government of the Republic of Korea and the Government of the Kingdom of Spain concerning a Youth Mobility Programme

[Adopted December 18, 2017, Entered into force October 24, 2018]

Agreement between the Government of the Republic of Korea and the Government of the Republic of Poland on a Working Holiday Programme

[Adopted January 24, 2018, Entered into force June 1, 2018]

Agreement between the Government of the Republic of Korea and the International Committee of the Red Cross

[Adopted February 26, 2018, Entered into force September 28, 2018]

2. MULTILATERAL AGREEMENTS

2-1. TRADE

Second Amendment to the Asia-Pacific Trade Agreement

[Adopted January 18, 2018, Entered into force July 1, 2018]

2-2. EDUCATION

Asia-Pacific Regional Convention on the Recognition of Qualifications in Higher Education

[Adopted November 26, 2011, Entered into force February 1, 2018]

2-3. ENVIRONMENT

Amendments to Annexes A and C to the Stockholm Convention on Persistent Organic Pollutants

[Adopted May 15, 2015, Entered into force October 17, 2018]

Agreement on the Establishment of the Asian Forest Cooperation

[Adopted September 22, 2015, Entered into force April 27, 2018]

2-4. FOOD

Food Assistance Convention

[Adopted April 25, 2012, Entered into force January 31, 2018]

2-5. POST

Ninth Additional Protocol to the Constitution of the Universal Postal Union

[Adopted October 6, 2016, Entered into force January 1, 2018]

First Additional Protocol to the General Regulations of the Universal Postal Union

[Adopted October 6, 2016, Entered into force January 1, 2018]

Universal Postal Convention and Final Protocol to the Universal Postal Convention

[Adopted October 6, 2016, Entered into force January 1, 2018]

Postal Payment Services Agreement and Final Protocol to the Postal Payment Services

[Adopted October 6, 2016, Entered into force January 1, 2018]

2-6. EUROPEAN UNION

Protocol to the Framework Agreement between the Republic of Korea, on the one part, and the European Union and its Member States, on the other part, to take Account of the Accession of the Republic of Croatia to the European Union

[Adopted June 21, 2017, Entered into force August 1, 2018]

INDEX

AUTHOR GUIDELINES AND STYLE SHEET

I. SUBMISSION

Manuscripts should be submitted in Microsoft Word and electronically send to ilakoreanbranch@gmail.com

II. GENERAL TERMS AND PEER-REVIEW SYSTEM OF PUBLICATION

All manuscripts are subject to initial evaluation by the KYIL Editorial Board and subsequently sent out to independent reviewers for a peer review. The Editorial Board accepts manuscripts on a rolling basis and will consider requests for an expedited review in appropriate cases.

III. FORMATING

1. ABSTRACT

Please include an abstract (no more than 150 words) at the beginning of an article

2. TEXT

Main Text: Times New Roman, font size 12, 1.5 spacing
Endnotes: Times New Roman, font size 12, single spacing

3. CITING REFERENCE

The KYIL requires endnotes with subsequent numbering; the initial endnote should be indicated with '*,' if it is necessary to provide explanatory information about the manuscript.

Please include a reference list for all works the are cited at the end of the manuscript.

IV. NOTES

1. BOOKS

P. Malanczuk, *Akehurst's Modern Introduction to International Law*, 7th ed. (New York: Eoutledge, 1997), p. 1.

2. ARTICLES

Chao Wang, *China's Preferential Trade Remedy Approaches: A New Haven School Perspective*, Vol.21 No.1, Asia Pacific Law Review, (2013), p. 103.

3. ARTICLES IN COLLECTIONS

J. Paulsson & Z. Douglas, *Indirect Expropriation in Investment Treaty Arbitrations, in* Arbitration Foreign Investment Disputes 148 (N. Horn & S. Kroll eds., Kluwer Law International, 2004).

4. ARTICLES IN NEWSPAPER

YI Whan-Woo, *Korea, New Zealand embrace free trade pact*, Korea Times, November 14, 2014.

5. UNPUBLISHED MATERIALS

PARK Jung-Won, *Minority Rights Constraints on a State's Power to Regulate Citizenship under International Law*, Ph.D thesis (2006), on file with author.

6. WORKING PAPERS AND REPORTS

OECD, *'Indirect Expropriation' and the 'Right to Regulate' in International Investment Law*, OECD Working Paper, 2014/09.

7. INTERNET SOURCES

C. Schreuer, The Concept of Expropriation under the ETC and Other Investment Protection Treaties (2005), http://www.univie,ac,at/intlaw/pdf/csunpuyblpaper_3pdf. [Accessed on September 22, 2015]

V. GUIDELINE FOR AUTHORS

1. ARTICLE

Manuscripts must be in the form of a regular paper including endnotes and references. The length for an articles should not exceed 10,000 words in English excluding notes and references.

2. SPECIAL REPORT

Manuscripts for special Report must be in the form of a descriptive report which covers the International law issues related to Korea in the past 5 years. Special Report must include author's comments with less than 10 endnotes and 5 references. The length for an special report should be no more the 5,000 words.

3. RECENT DEVELOPMENT

Manuscripts must cover the trends in international law related to Korea in the preceding year. Recent Development must be in the form of a short report, including less than 5 endnotes. The length for Recent Development should be no more than 2,000 words.